Professional Perspectives on Fixed Income Portfolio Management

Volume 2

Frank J. Fabozzi, Ph.D., CFA
Editor

Published by Frank J. Fabozzi Associates

ISBN: 1-883249-99-6

Printed in the United States of America

Table of Contents

Contributing Authors

Jonathan Carmel	Lehman Brothers
Chris P. Dialynas	Pacific Investment Management Company
Michael Dorigan	Andrew Kalotay Associates
Lev Dynkin	Lehman Brothers
Frank J. Fabozzi	Yale University
Lang Gibson	First Union Securities, Inc.
Laurie Goodman	PaineWebber
Rich Gordon	First Union Securities, Inc.
Jeffrey Ho	PaineWebber
Jay Hyman	Lehman Brothers
Douglas Johnston	Lehman Brothers
Andrew Kalotay	Andrew Kalotay Associates
Robert C. Kuberek	Wilshire Associates Incorporated
Alexander Levin	The Dime Bancorp, Inc.
David Sohnen	Merrill Lynch & Co.
Stefan Szilagyi	First Union Securities, Inc.
Christopher Taylor	ING Barings
Lee R. Thomas	PIMCO
Allen Vine	Merrill Lynch & Co.
Karen Weaver	Deutsche Banc Alex. Brown
Phil Weissman	Lehman Brothers
Stephanie Whitten	Deutsche Banc Alex. Brown
Wei Wu	Lehman Brothers
Eugene Xu	Deutsche Banc Alex. Brown

Global Bond Investing in the 21st Century: Philosophy and Process

Lee R. Thomas, Ph.D
Managing Director
Senior International Portfolio Manager
PIMCO

INTRODUCTION

Investors can ill afford to neglect the opportunities available in foreign bond markets. Global integration, the end of the Cold War, and the widespread adoption of free markets mean that more and more issuers have access to the world's capital markets. At the same time portfolio managers, encouraged by increasingly cosmopolitan clients offering increasingly liberal investment mandates, are reaching out for superior risk-adjusted return wherever in the world it can be found.

 This article describes the philosophy underlying investing in global bond markets, and the process needed to implement this investment philosophy in a rapidly changing environment. It can be helpful both to plan sponsors and to the managers they hire. From an investment manager's perspective, this article's major contribution is to survey the most important sources of active return available in global bond markets. From a plan sponsor's point of view, this article offers an overview of the reasons for using foreign bonds, as well as highlighting what skills to look for when selecting a global bond manager.

 The first section surveys opportunities latent in global bond markets. After reviewing the size and composition of bond markets around the world, we discuss two ways investors can make the most of them. These two approaches, which we call *tactical* and *strategic*, are complements rather than substitutes. We wrap up the discussion on opportunities in global bond markets by considering whether the many changes that have recently occurred in global bond markets, resulting from the increasing integration of global financial markets and from the

Thanks are due to Peter van de Zilver of PIMCO, who diligently compiled many of the data used to construct the exhibits in this article. Other data were generously provided by JP Morgan and Salomon Smith Barney. Any remaining errors are my responsibility.

advent of European Monetary Union, have weakened the arguments for using global bonds. Our conclusion is that the opportunities are changing, not vanishing.

The second section elaborates on the theme of change. The global macroeconomic environment has changed radically since the volatile 1970s and 1980s. One implication is that global bond strategies that worked in the past may not work in the future. We illustrate the point with an example, and conclude with a caveat: before adopting any historically successful strategy, investors should consider *why* it worked in the past, and use that analysis to judge if it will also work going forward. In a changing world, thoughtless extrapolation could be dangerous to your financial health.

The final two sections deal with global bond investing philosophy and process. The investing philosophy we advocate recognizes that for all but a few investors, global bonds represent only a part of their much larger portfolio, which contains many classes of investments. The allocation to this particular asset class, global bonds, is predicated on its volatility and its correlations with other asset classes. The implication is that if the portfolio selected by your global bond manager strays too far from her benchmark, statistically speaking, then your overall asset allocation decisions will be made sub-optimal. Accordingly, it behooves a manager to monitor and control the tracking error between her portfolio and the benchmark. But, while she is keeping tracking error modest, the manager must simultaneously add value. The ratio of value added ("alpha") divided by tracking error, the manager's *information ratio*, can be enhanced by improving her skill or her scope. We discuss how, in principal, she can do so.

The section on process discusses how to implement the global philosophy in practice, and how the global bond portfolio manager can judge her portfolio's risks. The topics covered include approximating the parameters necessary to estimate risk, top-down sources of value added, and using bottom-up strategies such as credit analysis.

OPPORTUNITIES IN GLOBAL MARKETS

In this section we will survey the opportunities latent in global bond markets and two complementary approaches to take advantage of these opportunities.

How Large are the Foreign Markets?

What is a "foreign" bond? "Foreign" could refer to the domicile of the issuer, the domicile of the principal buyers, the market in which the bond trades, or the currency in which the bond is denominated. For the purposes of this article, foreign bonds refer to issues denominated in a currency different from that ordinarily used by the investor who owns them. A U.S. investor who buys euro denominated bonds holds "foreign" bonds. So does a German investor who buys U.S. dollar bonds. In light of this definition, exchange rate risk is unique to foreign bonds, and we will discuss managing exchange rate risks at some length.

Let us examine the world's major bond markets, by currency of denomination, to show how large the "foreign" bond market is considered from the perspectives of different investors. We will start with sovereign bonds, or those issued by governments. As estimated by the investment bank Salomon Smith Barney, at the end of 1999 the sovereign bond markets were dominated by three major blocs: the United States, representing 28% of the total market; the European Monetary Union, representing 32%; and Japan, representing 32%. Together, all other developed countries account for only 8% of the market. Accordingly, portfolio managers can think of global bond portfolio allocation largely in terms of these three blocs.

In practice many of the smaller bond markets are associated with one of the major blocs, anyway. So, for example, portfolio managers often think of Canadian, Australian, and New Zealand bonds in terms of their yield spreads to the U.S. market, while the U.K., Sweden, Denmark, and Greece would be evaluated based on their yield spreads to euro-denominated bonds. This makes the "three-bloc" approach to global bond allocation even more compelling.

The three-bloc approach to global bond markets is new, and it reflects major, recent changes in the structure of the world's bond markets. Understanding these changes will be critical to successfully managing global portfolios.

Once, managing global bond portfolios was a top down game. The major source of return was moving funds from country to country, manipulating a portfolio's interest rate and exchange rate exposures based on a manager's macroeconomic forecast. There were large yield disparities among bonds in different countries, and many countries from which to choose. Each country had its own currency, so there were many exchange rate plays to consider, too.

But the world has changed. First, yield disparities among the major economies have narrowed substantially.[1] As yield converged, the volatility of international yield spreads declined. Second, before January 1, 1999 there were 10 relatively small European markets, rather than one large euro denominated market. European Monetary Union (EMU) changed that. This change has an obvious implication for the potential for using foreign bond markets for the purpose of diversification. The creation of the EMU also reduced the opportunity for an active bond manager to generate excess return or "alpha" by managing interest rate exposures using top-down macroeconomic analysis. EMU eliminated ten currencies, so that there are far fewer exchange rates to bet on. Again, this means that top down macroeconomic analysis is becoming less important. Today there are just three major blocs to rotate into and out of, for bonds and currencies. Opportunities to make convergence trades on interest rates — betting that yields will everywhere revert towards the global average — are much less plentiful, at least when we consider the developed markets only. One implication of this is that global managers will want to range more widely, into the bonds of emerging markets.

At the same time, corporate and asset-backed bond markets have started to expand rapidly in Europe, and are likely to expand soon in Asia, too. This increases an active global bond manger's scope to add value using bottom-up, relative value analysis. (We will discuss this later in this article.)

---

[1] This is illustrated in Exhibit 18 later in this article.

Exhibit 1: The Composition of the World's Bond Markets (%) as of December 31, 1999

Category	U.S.	Eurozone	Japan	Other	Total
Sovereign Bonds	16.4	18.4	21.1	7.9	63.7
Mortgage-Backed Bonds	17.6	0.2	0.0	0.2	18.0
Other Asset-Backed Securities	0.4	0.0	0.0	0.0	0.4
Corporate Bonds	4.7	1.4	2.6	0.3	9.0
All Other	4.4	3.4	0.9	0.2	8.9
Total	43.4	23.4	24.5	8.6	100.0

So, in addition to sovereign bonds, let's consider "spread product," or non-sovereign bonds, too. When we do we see that the 25% share of the U.S. sovereign market understates the relative importance of the U.S. bond market. The United States has by far the world's largest corporate and asset-backed markets (largely mortgages). In the United States, the fixed income market is about half sovereign bonds, half other bonds. In the rest of the world, sovereign debt still dominates (see Exhibit 1). When the non-sovereign bond markets are included, the global fixed income universe is roughly equally divided between the United States and the rest of the world.

Why Use Foreign Bonds?

As will be explained in this section, foreign bonds can be used by active managers as a tactical substitute for domestic bonds. Foreign bonds add considerable tracking risk to a domestic-benchmarked portfolio, but they can contribute considerable excess return, too. Alternately, foreign bonds can be used as a permanent portion of a broader asset allocation by either active or passive investors. Consistent with modern portfolio theory (MPT), the empirical evidence is that this diversification reduces volatility, without reducing expected return. To achieve significant risk reduction, foreign bonds should be currency hedged. There is little evidence that global capital market integration is eliminating the benefits of global diversification. Until the world adapts a single currency, international bond diversification is likely to remain attractive.

There are two ways to use foreign bonds. The first is tactically, or opportunistically, as a substitute for domestic bonds. Effectively this creates a new market sector which a portfolio manager can use occasionally, to outperform a domestic benchmark. The second approach is to use foreign bonds strategically, as a separate asset class. This typically means constructing a bond portfolio that is benchmarked to one of the major global indices, such as the JP Morgan Government Bond Index, the Salomon World Government Bond Index, or the Lehman Global Aggregate Index, and including it as a permanent part of a manager's broad asset allocation. Note that these two approaches can be used in concert.

The Case for Using Foreign Bonds Tactically

Foreign markets expand the tool set a portfolio manager can use to add alpha to a domestic bogey.

Exhibit 2: Best and Worst Performing Markets 1987 to 1998
Total Hedged Return in US$

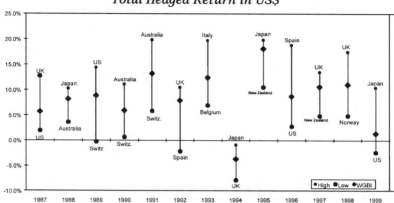

Sector rotation is a well known active technique for earning excess return. The active manager shifts funds from sector to sector, based on a forecast of prospective relative performance. Foreign bonds are a sector that can be used sporadically as a substitute for domestic bonds, just as asset-backed securities or corporate bonds are used as tactical substitutes for government bonds by active bond managers. Because economic and interest rate cycles in different countries are asynchronous, foreign bond markets may occasionally present substantial opportunities compared to an investor's domestic market.

To illustrate the potential excess return foreign bonds can offer, Exhibit 2 shows the best and worst performing major bond markets in each year from 1987 to 1999.[2] Exhibit 2 also shows the return recorded each year by the world bond market, as measured by the Salomon Smith Barney World Government Bond Index (WGBI). This can be considered to be the "average" developed bond market's performance, while the best and worst markets' returns span the range of opportunities available to an active, country-allocation specialist each year.

Notice that the typical difference in return between the world's best and the world's worst performing bond markets in any year has been substantial: it has averaged about 10%. Of course, the range of country returns would be even greater if we factored in exchange rate changes, too. The wide range of outcomes, comparing the best and worst performing markets each year, suggests that there is considerable potential to add value by using foreign bonds tactically. In fact, the yearly country bond market performance differences recorded in Exhibit 2 are not exceptional. If we look back further, to the inflationary period of the 1970s, the performance differences among national bond market returns were even greater.

---

[2] All the countries in the WGBI government bond index are included in the universe of eligible bond investments each year. To isolate pure bond market effects, the returns have been hedged into a common currency (U.S. dollars).

Exhibit 3: Growth of $1 with Perfect Foresight

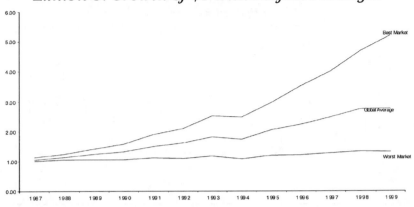

The differences among bond returns in different countries offer the opportunity for a shrewd active manager to add considerable value to his domestic bogey. Even a small allocation to a foreign bond market — if it is the right market — can add considerable excess return. A manager who can consistently select the world's best foreign markets can handily outperform a domestic benchmark. To demonstrate, Exhibit 3 shows how a wealth index would have evolved had an investor with perfect foresight improbably chosen to invest exclusively in the single best performing of all the world's bond markets every year. It also shows an investor's wealth had the investor been unfortunate enough to have chosen the worst market instead. Choosing the best performing market each year produced five times the terminal wealth, after 13 years.

Clearly, rotation into foreign bond markets can add considerable value to a domestic bogey, at least in principle. But harvesting this potential is difficult. First, the manager must choose the right foreign markets. Then the manager must time the move into foreign bonds before they outperform domestic bonds, and then rotate back into domestic bonds when foreign bonds are poised to underperform. Obviously, this requires astute active bond management and a keen sense of market timing.

It is important to recognize that Exhibit 3 shows that foreign bonds can be a two edged sword: *foreign bonds can subtract alpha just as quickly as they can add it.* More formally, the problem a manager confronts when using foreign bonds is that they often introduce substantial tracking risk when they are added to a domestic-benchmarked portfolio. For example, consider the case of a U.S. bond manager who has been assigned the Lehman Aggregate Bond Index as his bogey. A 5% excess allocation to mortgages introduces about 8 basis points of tracking risk.[3] The corresponding figure for overweighting investment-grade corporate bonds by 5% is approximately 10 basis points of tracking risk. By comparison, a well diver-

---

[3] Tracking risk is the annualized standard deviation of the difference between the return to the active manager's portfolio, and the return to the bogey.

sified, 5% overweight position in foreign bonds adds about 18 basis points of tracking risk. Notice that this is about twice the risk of an equally overweighted allocation to mortgages or corporate bonds, even when the foreign bonds are currency hedged, and even when the manager rotates into a well-diversified portfolio of foreign bonds, rather than only choosing one or two foreign markets. This means that portfolio managers will ordinarily commit only a small portion of their funds to foreign bonds when they are being evaluated against a domestic benchmark. To encourage a larger foreign allocation, the manager must be assigned a global benchmark, so that foreign bonds become a strategic part of his holdings.

The Case for Using Foreign Bonds Strategically

Using foreign bonds tactically depends on effective market timing, so it only makes sense for active managers. However, both passive and active managers can benefit from using foreign bonds strategically. In other words, the strategic benefits of international bonds do not depend on active management, though active management may enhance them. The distinctive strategic benefit afforded by foreign bonds is risk reduction; the mechanism is diversification of interest rate risk.

Foreign bonds can reduce a portfolio's volatility in two ways. First, and most obviously, *some foreign bond markets may be less volatile than a manager's domestic bond market*. If so, they represent good raw material for creating a lower risk bond portfolio. To illustrate, Exhibit 4 shows volatilities of some important national bond markets, calculated over the 1987 to 1999 period. All the returns were currency hedged (into U.S. dollars) in order to eliminate the effects of exchange rate fluctuations. The most hyperactive bond markets have been about twice as volatile as the most tranquil markets. As can be seen, dollar markets' volatilities — the U.S., Canada, Australia, and New Zealand — historically have exceeded those of most continental European markets. So it is natural to expect that a U.S. investor could reduce a bond portfolio's volatility by allocating some funds to Europe. These results are not an aberration. In fact, these volatility differences were even more marked in the 1970s and early 1980s, before economic policies in different parts of the world began to converge. But it should be recognized that it is unclear that the historic volatility of bond returns is a good predictor of future volatility in any country.

While it may be true that foreign markets are individually less risky than the domestic market for *some* investors — investors domiciled in countries with relatively volatile bond markets — that obviously cannot be the case for *all* the world's investors. Somebody must live in the countries that have relatively tranquil markets! Nevertheless, using foreign bonds can even benefit investors in countries with relatively low volatility bond markets. Why? The second reason foreign bonds can reduce a portfolio's volatility: *a global index typically has lower risk than the average of its components.*[4] This is because the correlations among bond

---

[4] Notice in Exhibit 4 that the volatility of the WGBI is 0.60% less than the volatility of the average market. The average is unweighted, while the WGBI is weighted by market capitalization, so this comparison is only indicative.

returns in different countries are often low. For example, during the period 1987-1999, the correlation between the JP Morgan U.S. Index and the JP Morgan Hedged Global (Ex-U.S.) Index — that is, between U.S. and hedged "foreign" bonds — was 54.3%. That means foreign bond markets statistically "explained" less than 30% of the variation in U.S. bond returns; more than 70% of U.S. bond market volatility was statistically unrelated to what happened in foreign markets.[5]

When we think about what drives bond returns, it should not be a surprise that bond markets in different countries are only loosely correlated. Bond yields are primarily driven by three factors: (1) secular economic forces, (2) business cycles, and (3) monetary and fiscal policies. Let's briefly consider these factors.

Structural features of economies, such as different economic factor endowments (labor, capital, and natural resources) and different population demographics, directly influence long-term growth and inflation. They also mean that global shocks have different implications for a country's business cycles. A spike in the price of oil does not affect the Japanese and U.K. economies in the same way at all. Accordingly, changes in the global economic environment will naturally cause growth and inflation to diverge in different countries.

Economic shocks will also illicit different policy responses in different countries. Moreover, policies may differ internationally quite independently of global economic shocks. In short, the fiscal and monetary policies appropriate for one country may not be appropriate or politically feasible in another.

Since structural, political, and cultural differences among countries are not likely to vanish in the early 21st century, it is unlikely that business cycles will become perfectly coordinated, replaced by a single global cycle. In fact, the scope to run independent monetary policies in different countries is one of the most important reasons cited by academic economists for using floating, rather than fixed, exchange rates. Only the adoption of a single global currency would be likely to make yields in different countries' bond markets become substantially synchronized. That is unlikely in the immediate future.

Exhibit 4: International Bond Market Volatilities (All Hedged into U.S. Dollars) 1987-1998

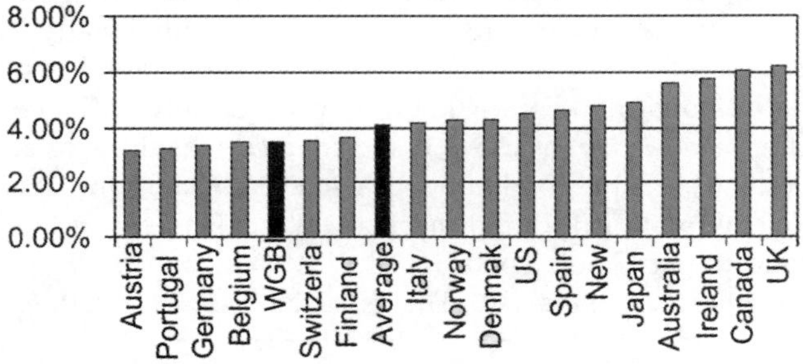

---

[5] That is, the coefficient of determination (R^2) between the U.S. and hedged foreign bond markets was about 0.30.

Exhibit 5: Foreign Bond Diversification from a U.S. Perspective

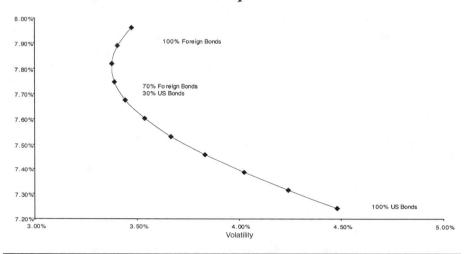

Because the returns to domestic and foreign bonds have not historically been highly correlated, substantial benefits could be realized by combining them in a globally diversified portfolio. To illustrate, we shall now examine the effect of global diversification from three perspectives: that of a U.S., a German, and a Japanese investor.

Foreign Bond Diversification: A U.S. Perspective

Exhibit 5 shows the effect of global diversification from a U.S. investor's perspective, based on 13 years of historical data (1987-1999). In Exhibit 5 we start in the lower right of the chart with a portfolio consisting of U.S. bonds alone; its historic volatility was about 4.5%. When we introduce some foreign bonds, to produce a portfolio of 90% U.S. and 10% foreign bonds, we move to the left; the volatility of the resulting portfolio falls to about 4.25%. (Each black diamond represents a 10% re-allocation to foreign bonds.) Increasing the international allocation to 30% reduces the volatility still further, to about 3.8%. In fact, the minimum variance portfolio historically consisted of 70% foreign bonds and 30% U.S. bonds, and had a volatility of 3.4%, or about three-quarters of the volatility of a U.S.-only bond portfolio.[6] Coincidentally, 30% is about the U.S. market's share in the most widely used global bond indices, the WGBI and JPM. According to Exhibit 5, the effect of this allocation has been to reduce volatility by 25% or so. But what did it do to return?

---

[6] These results use data from 1987 through 1999. The U.S. index is the JP Morgan U.S. Government Index; the foreign index is the JP Morgan Global-Ex U.S. Index, Currency Hedged.

Diversification is the only free lunch in economics; it reduces risk without necessarily reducing expected return.[7] In the case of foreign bonds there is little reason to expect the reduction in volatility associated with global diversification to be associated with a commensurate reduction in return in the future. In fact, as can be seen, from 1987-1999 a 70%/30% foreign/U.S. portfolio returned 7.7% per year, or about 0.35% per year *more*, than a U.S.-only portfolio.[8,9] Needless to say, a U.S. investor should *not* expect a globally diversified portfolio to earn more than a U.S.-only one in future years, just because it did during this particular historic period. But neither should a U.S. investor expect a globally diversified portfolio to earn less than a U.S.-only portfolio.

Diversification Potential: Foreign Bonds and U.S. Bonds Compared
The preceding section quantified the historic gains from using foreign sovereign bonds to diversify a U.S. Treasury-only bond portfolio. But, are these risk reduction results "good" or "bad"? In other words, how can we calibrate this level of historic risk reduction?[10]

One way a U.S. Treasury bond investor can evaluate the diversification benefits provided by foreign bonds is to compare what they have offered historically compared to diversifying into other categories of U.S. bonds, such as mortgage-backed securities or corporate bonds. Exhibit 6 shows the returns generated by U.S. Treasury bonds and mortgages, using monthly index data from 1986 to 1999. Exhibit 7 shows the same data for U.S. Treasury bonds and high-yield corporate bonds.

Exhibits 6 and 7 do not suggest either mortgages or high-yield bonds offered much in the way of diversification potential most of the time. Only in the tails of the distributions — in months when U.S. Treasury bond returns were extreme — do high-yield bonds, and to a lesser extent mortgages, seem to offer modest diversification. Otherwise, the monthly returns are highly correlated. In fact, the correlation between U.S. Treasury returns and mortgage-backed security returns

---

[7] See André Perold and Evan Schulman, "The Free Lunch in Currency Hedging," *Financial Analysts Journal* (May-June 1988) and Lee R. Thomas, "The Performance of Currency Hedged Foreign Bonds," *Financial Analysts Journal* (May-June 1989) for a discussion of this "free lunch" argument as applied to global bond diversification. Both of these articles are reprinted in *The Currency Hedging Debate*, Lee R. Thomas (ed.), IFR Books.

[8] Although foreign bond returns were historically higher than U.S. returns during the 1987-99 period, you should be very cautious about exaggerating the importance of this historic outperformance. There is little reason to suspect foreign bond returns will be greater in the future. The total return difference of 124 basis points between an all U.S. and an all foreign (hedged) portfolio is not statistically significant. There is little reason to suspect that it represents a stable risk premium favoring foreign bonds.

[9] In principle, we could try to predict the expected return difference between U.S. and foreign bonds using an international capital asset pricing model (CAPM). But applying the CAPM requires a number of strong simplifying assumptions that create a highly imprecise forecasts of the future outperformance of foreign bonds. To be conservative an investor should discount both historical data and CAPM-based return projections. Realistically it is not possible to say if foreign bonds or U.S. bonds have higher expected returns in the future.

[10] Thanks to Charles Dolan and Ron Leisching of Pareto Partners for suggesting this approach to calibrating the risk reduction afforded by foreign bonds.

is about 0.9. For high-yield bonds, the correlation is also about 0.9. In contrast, Exhibit 8 compares U.S. Treasury returns with the returns to foreign bonds, specifically the JP Morgan hedged, non-U.S. bond index. The correlation is only 0.6.

Diversification Benefits for Non-U.S. Investors

In principle, risk reduction from diversifying should work for bond investors anywhere, not just for U.S. investors. Let's look at diversification into "foreign" bond markets from a German or Japanese investor's perspective.

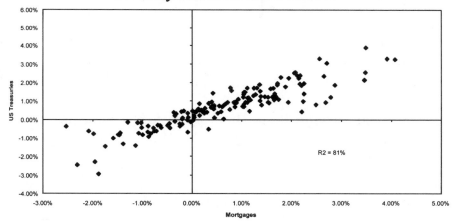

Exhibit 6: U.S. Treasuries and Mortgage Securities, Monthly Returns 1986 to 1999

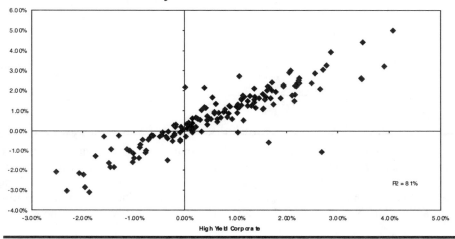

Exhibit 7: U.S. Treasury and High-Yield Corporate Bonds, Monthly Returns, 1986 to 1999

Exhibit 8: U.S. Treasuries and Hedged Foreign Bonds
Monthly Returns, 1986 to 1999

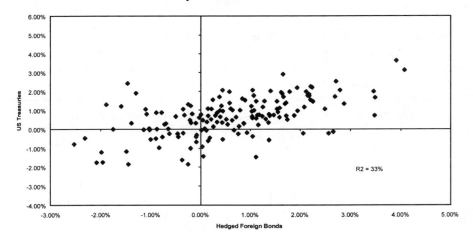

Exhibit 9: Foreign Bond Diversification from a German Investor's Perspective, 1985-1998

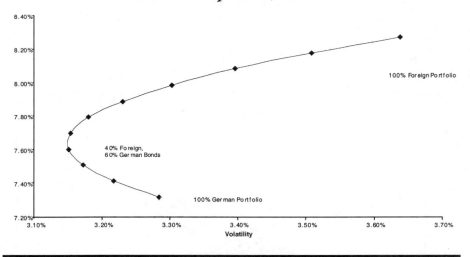

Exhibit 9 shows combinations of German and non-German bond portfolios. We start with an all German portfolio (lower right) and progress in 10%
increments to a 100% foreign (i.e., global ex-Germany) portfolio. All the bond
returns have been currency hedged into German marks. An all German portfolio
had an annual volatility of 3.3%. Adding 40% foreign bonds reduced the historic

volatility to 3.15%. The potential risk reduction from foreign diversification was only about 5%. Recall that a U.S. investor reduced his portfolio's volatility by about 25%, by adding 70% foreign bonds. But since Germany had one of the world's lowest volatility bond markets, the potential for risk reduction was much less than it was in the United States.

Exhibit 10 shows the same historic analysis from the perspective of a Japanese investor. An all-Japanese portfolio had volatility of 3.8%, while a diversified portfolio containing 70% foreign bonds had smaller volatility, 3.4%. The risk reduction was about 10%.

These historic results, and others, can be summarized as follows: *diversification into currency hedged foreign bonds reduces the volatility of a bond portfolio, when compared to investing in a domestic-only portfolio.* The historic benefits of diversification, and the risk-minimizing weight to allocate to foreign bonds, have varied considerably from country to country. It is greatest for investors who live in countries with relatively volatile bond markets. Historically, during the 1986-1999 period a U.S. bond investor could have reduced a domestic-only portfolio's volatility by about 25% using foreign bonds. The corresponding figures for German and Japanese investors were 5% and 10%, respectively. Overall, the historic data are consistent with MPT: international bond diversification reduces interest rate risk in a bond portfolio. We expect it to continue to do so in the future.

Why Use a Currency Hedged Benchmark?

So far we have looked at diversifying using *currency hedged* foreign bonds. What about using *unhedged* foreign bonds instead?

Exhibit 10: Foreign Bond Diversification from a Japanese Investor's Perspective, 1986-1999

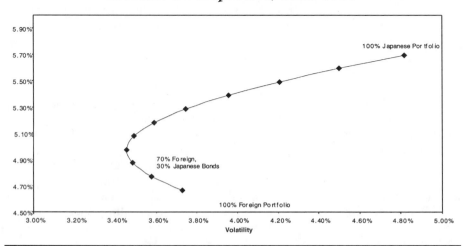

Exhibit 11: Foreign Bond Diversification from a U.S. Investor's Perspective, 1986 to 1999, Using Unhedged Foreign Bonds

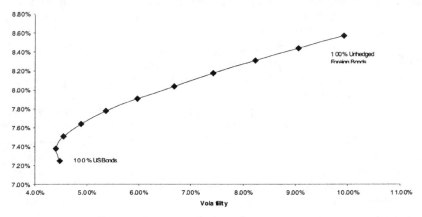

Foreign bonds provide risk reduction because their returns are imperfectly correlated with domestic bond returns. That's the good news. Unfortunately, foreign bonds also carry with them exchange rate risk. In an ideal world, that wouldn't matter: exchange rate risks would be self-diversifying. That is, if changes in different exchange rates were uncorrelated, and an investor had enough different countries represented in a bond portfolio, exchange rate risk might diversify itself away. Using the formal language of MPT, we might find that exchange rate risk was unsystematic to a global bond portfolio.

Unfortunately, it hasn't worked that way in practice. Exchange rate changes, observed from the perspective of any single base currency, are correlated. Moreover, the number of countries available to diversify into is relatively small. So foreign exchange rate risk does not just conveniently diversify itself away. Rather, as an investor adds foreign bonds, exchange rate risk accumulates in the portfolio. The result can be catastrophic if an investor's intention is to use foreign bonds to reduce risk.

Consider Exhibit 11, which shows global bond diversification from a U.S. investor's perspective *without* currency hedging. Compare it to Exhibit 5, which shows diversification from a U.S. investor's perspective *with* currency hedging. They are not at all alike. Foreign bonds offer no economically significant risk reduction. In fact, in Exhibit 11, after an investor adds only about 10% of foreign bonds to the U.S.-only portfolio, its overall volatility begins to increase. This results from the exchange rate risk embedded in the foreign bonds. That is, beyond an allocation of only 10% to foreign bonds, the disadvantage of increasing foreign exchange rate risk overwhelm the benefits of falling interest rate risk (the latter resulting from diversification). So the portfolio's total risk begins to increase.

Exhibit 12: Hedged and Unhedged Foreign Bond Returns
1987 to 1999

Investor	Unhedged Foreign Bond	Hedged Returns	Difference
U.S.	8.6%	8.0%	0.6%
German	7.8%	8.3%	−0.5%
Japanese	4.2%	4.7%	−0.5%
UK	7.0%	10.7%	−3.7%

Exchange rate risk is like toxic waste: it is an unwanted byproduct of foreign diversification. Notice in Exhibit 11 that continuing to add unhedged foreign bonds to a U.S. portfolio eventually increases its volatility substantially. Recall from Exhibit 5 that a 70% foreign/30% U.S. portfolio historically had a volatility of 3.4% when the foreign bonds were currency hedged. The same 70% foreign allocation results in portfolio volatility of 7.5% if an investor does *not* currency hedge. An all-U.S. portfolio's volatility was only 4.5%. That is, instead of volatility falling by about 25% compared to a U.S.-only bond portfolio, volatility increases by about two-thirds if an investor diversifies instead (using the same allocation) into unhedged foreign bonds.

What about returns? For a U.S. investor, foreign bond returns were higher from 1987-1999 when they were unhedged. But in examining historic data, one should be skeptical about projecting differences in hedged and unhedged returns into the future. Exhibit 12 illustrates why. From a German investor's perspective, hedged foreign bonds outperformed unhedged ones. From a Japanese investor's perspective, likewise. But a U.S. investor would have earned more by not hedging. Moreover, the results for any currency are very period-specific.

There is no general rule. Sometimes currency hedging increases a foreign bond's return, sometimes it reduces it. Ignoring transactions costs, the expected long-run return from currency hedging is probably about zero. That is, the expected return to hedged and unhedged foreign bonds is about the same.

This is the essence of the "free lunch" argument for hedging. Numerous studies of currency risk premia have found that there is a zero long-run expected return from owning foreign currency.[11] Yet foreign currency holdings clearly have significant volatility, and some of that volatility is transmitted by including foreign bonds into a portfolio if an investor fails to currency hedge. It is incumbent on any portfolio manager to secure the maximum amount of return for each unit of risk he bears. To make an investment with no expected return, but with substantial volatility — like holding a chronic, unmanaged foreign currency exposure in a bond portfolio — would be an investment management cardinal sin. Accordingly, a portfolio manager should think of currency hedging as the base case. Not hedging represents an active strategy that can only be justified if a manager thinks a partic-

---

[11] Note that in the short run, the empirical evidence is that uncovered interest rate parity has been persistently violated. This creates the opportunity to improve returns by hedging tactically, rather than all the time.

ular foreign currency will outperform its forward foreign exchange rate. If a manager is doubtful about a currency's prospects, he or she should currency hedge.

Are the Benefits of Global Diversification Declining?

This article is about global bond investing in the markets of the 21st century, not about what an investor could have done in the past. It has become conventional wisdom to observe that global markets are becoming more integrated.[12] As a result, some argue that the benefits of global bond diversification are declining. However, this is not necessarily the case in principle. "Integrated" need not mean "highly correlated." Moreover, it does not appear to be the case (yet) in practice.

The risk reduction afforded by foreign bonds depends on the correlation between foreign and domestic bonds: the smaller the better. Critics of global bond diversification are implicitly arguing that closer economic and financial integration across political borders will result in higher bond market correlations. But are domestic and foreign bond market correlations rising through time? Let's examine the evidence.

Exhibits 13, 14, and 15 do not tell a story of generally rising international bond market correlations. They show rolling 3-year correlations of "domestic" and "foreign" bond returns from 1988 to 1999, each from a different national perspective. Over this time period there have been periods of increasing correlation and periods of decreasing correlation in various markets, but there are no clear general trends, Japan is the exception: there, the domestic market's correlation with foreign bonds has been falling. In fact, upon close examination the most recent data are more consistent with *declining* bond market correlations around the world. Upon reflection, this is not surprising, in light of the markedly asynchronous business cycles in Europe, the United States and Japan from 1995 to 1998. During this period the United States was enjoying a robust expansion, Europe was experiencing a growth recession, and Japan persistently threatened to slip into a depression.

The view that bond correlations are rising around the world may be based on casual observation of the 1994-1995 period. Bond prices fell sharply during 1994, and recovered sharply during 1995, globally. However, inconveniently for the increasing correlation thesis, bond returns substantially diverged again in 1996, when the U.S. market dramatically underperformed the European markets and Japan, on a currency hedged basis (see Exhibit 2). In fact, during 1996 the return spread between the best and worst performing bond markets was unusually large. This is a reminder that a plausible story and casual anecdotes are no substitute for examining the data.

---

[12] For an interesting overview of the evolution of globally integrated markets, see Jeffrey Sachs and Andrew Warner, "Economic Reform and the Process of Global Integration," Brookings Papers on Economic Activity, 1995. They observe that economic and financial integration was probably *greater* at the end of the 19th century than it is today. The degree of integration declined during the interim, but is now rising again. While the future seems to offer more integration, at present most investors in most countries still invest most of their wealth in domestic financial markets. This is formally known as "home country bias."

Exhibit 13: Rating Three Year Correlations: U.S. and Foreign Bonds

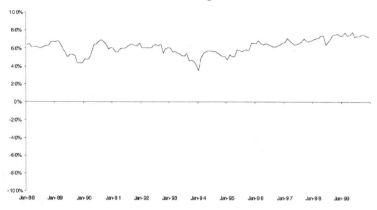

Exhibit 14: Rolling Three Year Correlations: German and Foreign Bonds

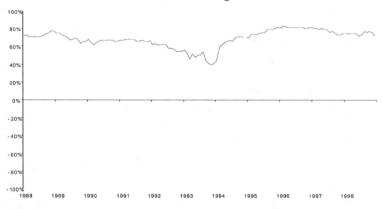

The Effect of EMU

One group of bond markets that certainly has become more correlated is those in Europe. With the advent of EMU on January 1, 1999, 11 government bond markets effectively collapsed into one: a single market for euro-denominated bonds.[13] It is widely anticipated that the U.K., Sweden, Denmark, and Greece will join the euro "club" within a decade, raising the total membership to 15 countries. Other countries in Eastern Europe are likely to follow in time.

---

[13] Various euro-denominated sovereign bonds trade at yield spreads to each other. These spreads change modestly, but for all practical purposes the Eurozone sovereign bond markets can be considered to be virtually perfectly correlated when constructing global portfolios.

Exhibit 15: Rolling Three Year Correlations: Japanese and Foreign Bonds

"Losing" foreign bond markets to EMU obviously reduces the potential efficacy of foreign diversification. One consolation is that the new euro bond market, representing 15 issuing countries, is far more liquid than any of the markets it replaces.

In this sense of creating deeper bond markets, the euro already has been a success. One of the reasons for establishing EMU was to create a competitor currency to the U.S. dollar. The economic benefits of this to Europe are small, but the political benefits are substantial. Europe wanted to assert that even though it has been in the shadow of the United States since World War II, it is now independent economically and financially. During the first nine months of EMU, 45% of all international bond issuance was denominated in euros, compared to 42% in dollars. During 1998, the component currencies of EMU together represented only 22% of international issuance, while 48% were dollar bonds.

The new euro bond market offers more diversity, including opportunities to add value using corporate bonds and asset-backed securities, in addition to its greater liquidity. Most commentators expect the euro market to become more diverse and liquid through time, becoming more like the U.S. bond market.

However, let us ignore all these benefits and ask, how much will the coming of EMU reduce the advantages of global bond diversification?

We can only guesstimate the answer to that question, and to do so let's perform the following experiment. Suppose a broad EMU had been formed in 1986. Specifically, suppose 15 countries' bond markets — Germany, France, Italy, the U.K., the Netherlands, Belgium, Luxembourg, Spain, Portugal, Denmark, Greece, Sweden, Austria, Denmark and the U.K. — had been replaced by the German market alone during the 1987 to 1999 period. From a U.S. investor's perspective, how much of the volatility reduction afforded by international diversification would have been sacrificed?

Exhibit 16: Global Bond Diversification from a U.S. Investor's Perspective (1987-1999): Assumes Broad EMU

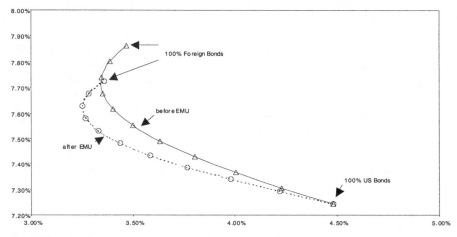

Exhibit 16 shows the risk and return combinations that historically accrued to a U.S. investor from 1987-1999 when all 15 European bond markets were available.[14] A U.S. only-portfolio had volatility of 4.5% per year. By placing 70% of the portfolio in the JP Morgan global ex-U.S. index, and 30% in the U.S., that volatility could have been reduced to 3%.[15] By way of comparison, Exhibit 16 also shows what would have happened if the 15 EMU countries' representation in the JP Morgan index had been replaced by Germany alone. The minimum volatility portfolio would have been marginally less diversified. The volatility of the minimum variance mixed portfolio, 3.4%, still reflects a substantial risk reduction compared to investing in the United States alone. The effect of broad EMU — 15 countries, including the U.K. — would have been to increase the volatility of the minimum variance portfolio from 3.3% to 3.4%.

Based on this simulation, the most likely outcome seems to be that EMU will reduce only modestly the diversification benefits of foreign bond markets; it will by no means eliminate them. Moreover, EMU will increase an active manager's opportunity to find attractive "spread product," such as corporate and asset-backed bonds, in Europe — a potentially lucrative compensation for having fewer distinct sovereign bond opportunities within Europe.

---

[14] The portfolio in Exhibit 16 uses the JP Morgan Government Bond Indices and weights. Otherwise, it is like that shown in Exhibit 4, which used the Salomon Smith Barney WGBI. Comparison of the two exhibits illustrates that the arguments for global diversification are robust to the way we measure returns.

[15] These values are similar to those shown in Exhibit 5, which was based on the Salomon Smith Barney Indices.

A Caveat: Overstating Foreign Bonds' Contribution to Risk Reduction

This article looks only at bond portfolios. Few investors own only bonds. Instead, they hold mixed portfolios containing bonds plus, at least, domestic and foreign equities. They may also hold more exotic asset classes, such as real estate, private equity, and commodities (such as gold). If we were to examine foreign bonds' diversification potential when they are held as a part of much broader portfolios of assets, we might find they offer less diversification potential. (In fact, that is exactly what we would find.) So the reader should bear in mind that this article deals with foreign bonds *only* when they are held in pure bond portfolios. It is beyond our scope to consider foreign bonds' diversification potential in a broader allocation context.

THE NEW INTERNATIONAL INVESTMENT ENVIRONMENT

As will be explained in this section, bond investors will be operating in a significantly different global environment during the early years of the 21st century, compared to much of the second half of the 20th century. An investor should not assume that investing strategies that worked in the past will also work in the future. Rather, consider each strategy in light of the changed environment. We expect bottom up, relative value strategies to become more important to global bond managers, and top down, macroeconomic strategies to become less important, if a manager wants to be successful at active management.

Let's suppose an investor has been persuaded that the risk reduction potential that comes from using hedged foreign bonds warrants a strategic allocation to that asset class. If an investor is using foreign bonds strategically, the next question the investor must address is whether to invest passively, or instead use active management in a globally diversified portfolio. Of course, if an investor is contemplating using foreign bonds tactically, he or she must consider if active management can add value at all, since if it cannot the case for using foreign bonds tactically collapses.

The objective of active management is to provide added value, or "alpha," while delivering a portfolio which has volatility similar to that of a passive benchmark (the bogey). Can an investor expect active bond management to add value? This depends, in part, on the kind of economic and financial environment an investor expect in the early years of the 21st century. In this section we make the case that the coming environment will differ significantly from the recent past, and that the changes should be reflected in a manager's active bond management philosophy and process if a manager is going to be successful at adding excess return.

Adapting to a Low Volatility World

One of my partners, Bill Gross, recently wrote a book entitled *Everything You've Heard About Investing Is Wrong*. That title didn't imply investors were naive or foolish; rather, he was observing that for most of us, our investing experience developed during the 1970s and 1980s. That was an era of unusually high inflation. It was also a period of unusually high economic and financial market volatility in the United States, and in many other countries, too.

Going forward better monetary and fiscal policies, the end of the Cold War, and the aging demographics of the populations of the United States, Japan, and Western Europe suggest that inflation will be much lower. With better economic policies and less international political tensions, we expect less financial market volatility, too. Both of these changes are, of course, good. But with them will come lower bond yields, smaller potential capital gains from active bond management, and smaller risk premia. Some investing habits and strategies that evolved in the old world, and made a bond manager successful there, will be inappropriate in the new one. In particular, in this section we will argue that it will become increasingly difficult for global bond managers to add alpha by relying exclusively on top-down, macroeconomic forecasting. Going forward, more of a manager's active return is likely to come from bottom-up bond portfolio management.

What kind of environment should bond investors anticipate in the future, and what does this imply about successful active investing? The transition period from a high inflation to a low inflation world, from the end of the 1970s to the 1990s, was characterized by tight money. Central bankers were working to reverse the inflation psychology that had taken root during the late 1960s and 1970s. Eventually, central bank policies worked: inflation fell and bond yields dropped. That provided bondholders substantial capital gains.

As a result of generally falling yields during the 1980s and 1990s, bonds' total returns were high around the world. All a manager had to do to earn them was to make a single macroeconomic bet and then stick to it: overweight duration, then hold on. But a transition period like this does not last forever; it ends when inflation and inflationary expectations have fallen and converged. Then central bankers can relax their extra cautious stance. Exhibit 17 compares U.S. inflationary expectations, as measured by survey data, to realized inflation. As can be seen, after a long period of divergence, they are now very close. In other words, the transition period is over. The Fed has successfully disinflated the U.S. economy.

There has been another important change in the global capital markets environment: once bond yield differences around the world were large, but no longer (see Exhibit 18) (Japan being an exception as of this writing). During the transition from high to low inflation, bond yields in different countries converged because inflation rates in different countries converged. Betting on international bond yield convergence was a very profitable strategy in the past. In the future, country rotation is likely to be less successful than it was in the past, because yield differences among countries no longer offer the same opportunities. Moreover, convergence trade opportunities are largely gone in the G7 markets. "Convergence trades" opportunities have moved to high quality emerging markets such as Poland, Hungary, and Korea.

Exhibit 17: Inflation and Inflation Expectations in the U.S.

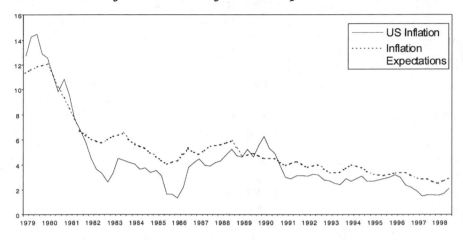

Exhibit 18: Yields Converge around the World

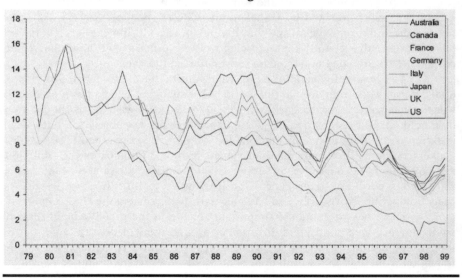

Bond investors must adopt to this changing environment. Just over-weighting duration and holding on — a successful strategy in the 1990s — won't work anymore. In the low inflation world of the early 21st century, nominal bond yields will be lower. Suppose that going forward G3 inflation averages 2%. That implies short-term interest rates of about 4%-6%, and bond yields perhaps 50 basis points above this. There is little prospect of spectacular capital gains in this environment, because bond yields will no longer experience long, one way declining trends, as they did during the 1990s. Accordingly, any top-down capital gains a manager does earn must come from successful market timing, not a buy-and-hold strategy: by buying bonds at the low end of their trading range, and selling them at the top end, rather than by riding a sustained secular change in yields. Remember, too, that the potential capital gains from moving funds from country to country will also decline, at least in the developed markets, because yield spreads will be narrower, and less volatile, in the G7 countries.

So, top-down country rotation looks less promising than it once did. But that does not mean bond managers cannot be successful at adding value. Rather, bottom-up techniques will become more important to active bond management, as more private issuers come to the world's capital markets. European and Asian investors will have to adapt to the changed environment more than U.S. investors. The United States currently has the world's best markets for "spread product," such as corporate bonds, mortgage-backed securities, and other asset-backed securities. These securities offer substantial opportunities for producing active return enhancement, and many U.S. bond managers have been intensively using bottom up, relative value strategies for years. European and Asian investors traditionally have relied more on relatively low yielding government bonds, adding value by shifting funds from country to country, because their own "spread product" markets have been undeveloped.

In summary, in a low yield environment passive management is unlikely to produce the total returns clients will demand. Portfolio managers need an active investment philosophy that can beat the benchmark, without adding too much risk. It must reflect the fact that a decreasing proportion of the alpha in a global bond portfolio will come from macroeconomic forecasting of interest rate trends and international sovereign bond yield spreads. And some specific strategies that worked historically may no longer work in the future.

An Example Reflecting How the World has Changed

Let us take a concrete example, designed to illustrate why one bond investing strategy that worked in the past may no longer work in the future. The anomaly we will consider is this: investing in countries with relatively high real bond yields has, historically, done better than investing in low-yielding bond markets.

During the 1990s high inflation countries had high nominal yields, but they also had high *real* yields. That is, nominal yields in high inflation countries seemed to overcompensate for their higher inflation rates (Exhibit 19). Higher real yields in high inflation countries could have reflected larger risk premia. But the higher real yields could have reflected the fact that in high inflation countries, central bankers had to work unusually hard to promote disinflation and convergence of bond yields towards international norms. "Working unusually hard" meant maintaining unusually high *real* interest rates wherever in the world inflation was highest.

Exhibit 19: Real Yield versus Inflation (1989-1999)

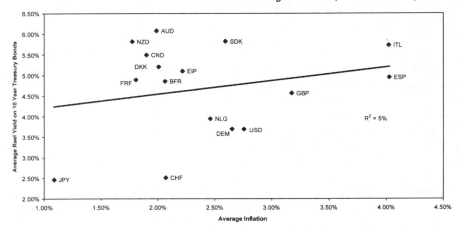

Exhibit 20: Total Return versus Real Yield (1989-1999)

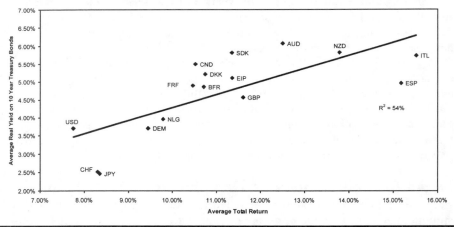

Let's suppose this process was at work during the 1980s and 1990s. That is, the higher their starting inflation rate, the more a central bank had to push up real yields to tame inflation. That would have provided one source of high real return to bondholders in high inflation countries: the high real yields themselves. In addition, the result of tight monetary policy was falling inflation, and as a result falling bond yields. That provided capital gains, too. So we would have expected bonds in high inflation countries, with relatively high real yields, to produce high total returns, too. Exhibit 20 indicates that they did.

Bond portfolio managers who are familiar with these historical data may think there is an easy strategy they can use to outperform their bogeys: just buy the bonds with the highest real yields. This *may* work in the future, as it has in the past. But it *may* not. This pattern is exactly what we would expect in a world in which central bankers pursued disinflation, and ultimately were successful, such as the 1980s and 1990s. Now that the objective of low inflation has almost everywhere been achieved, the historic relationship between high real yields and high subsequent total returns may break down.

The lesson to learn: if the global investing environment has changed, then formerly successful investing strategies may no longer work. Do not mechanically extrapolate historic simulations into the future. Rather, consider *why* particular strategies worked in the past, then decide if they will work in the future, too.

A GLOBAL BOND INVESTMENT PHILOSOPHY

The objective of a fund manager is to maximize your information ratio (defined below). A manager can do so by improving his or her skill, by finding more opportunities to earn excess return, and by making those opportunities as independent as possible. This means aggressively diversifying, not only across countries and currencies, but also across different investment styles and themes.

Risk

Let's think about risk from your client's perspective. Virtually all investors who hold foreign bonds do so as a share of a broader portfolio of securities. The allocation among different asset classes is based (in part) on assumptions the investors have made about the expected returns, volatilities, and correlations among all the asset classes they invest in. The client's global bond manager sees only a small part of the client's portfolio. Accordingly, it is important that you, as his global bond manager, produce a portfolio that conforms to your client's expectations. To construct a portfolio with very different volatility from that of the bogey, or one with very different correlations with other asset classes, would render the client's broader asset allocation decisions inefficient.

The risk objectives of a global bond manager are to construct a portfolio with bogey-like volatility and modest tracking risk. Of course, the goal of any manager also should be to produce the highest possible alpha, or excess return, consistent with these risk objectives. A manager should think of the permissible tracking risk as a "risk budget." The portfolio manager's role is to decide how best to "spend" the risk budget. Every time a manager deviates from the bogey, whether to overweight or underweight securities included in the bogey, or to add investments that are not in the bogey at all, the manager creates tracking risk. That spends part of the manager's risk budget. The manager want to get the most alpha he can for each such expenditure. Before the fact, the manager wants to maximize expected alpha, divided by tracking error. The manager's *information ratio* — actual alpha divided by realized tracking error — summarizes how well the manager has done after the fact.

Let's define investment success as achieving an *ex ante* high information ratio, or expected return per unit of risk taken. How can a manager improve his information ratio? In brief, there are two ways: (1) improve investment skill, or (2) diversify more effectively, to reduce risk. Diversifying more effectively means increasing the scope of active investments, or making active investments that are more independent. Let's briefly demonstrate why.[16]

Improving the Information Ratio

To start, let us define an *active trade* as an overweight position in one security, and equal underweight position in another security, compared to the bogey. (If we want, an active trade could contain both overweight and underweight positions in a number of securities, rather than just two. But that just complicates the explanation that follows, without adding any insight.) The overweight security may be a constituent of the bogey, but it need not be. The underweight security must be included in the bogey, unless investment guidelines permit the manager to take outright short positions. That is unusual.

Since the scale of the overweight/underweight positions constituting an active trade is arbitrary, at least for the purposes of this exposition, let us define their size so that for each active trade the average profit or loss turns out to be $P.

Each active trade represents a forecast that one asset — the one the manager is overweighting — will outperform another asset — the one the manager is underweighting. The manager's forecast will subsequently prove to be right or wrong. Suppose the manager is right 60% of the time. Then the manager is wrong 40% of the time. The difference is 20%; let's call this the manager's success rate. "Success rate" is our measure of the manager's investment skill.

A success rate of 20% means that the manager will profit, on net, on 20% of the active trades entered into. So the manager's annual active profit will be 20% of $P, multiplied by the number of different active trades the manager makes each year. (Active profit is just alpha, or the return in excess of the bogey.) Notice that the manager's active profit is proportional to the number of trades made (as well as to $P and the success rate). So a manager wants to find as many opportunities to take active trades as he can.

What is active risk? If all the active trades the manager took were statistically independent, then we could easily show that the volatility of the manager's active profit depends inversely on the square root of the number of active trades he took. The more positions the manager takes, the lower the manager's active risk will be. A manager who makes 16 independent bets each year will have only half the active risk of an equally skillful manager who makes just four independent bets per year.[17]

But what if the active trades are not strictly independent, but instead are correlated? That is likely to be the case in practice. For example, all of a man-

---

[16] See Richard Grinold and Ronald Kahn, *Active Portfolio Management: Second Edition* (New York, NY: McGraw-Hill, 1999) for the development of these ideas.

[17] The square root of 16 is 4. The square root of 4 is 2. The ratio of the square roots is 2:1.

ager's active top down positions are based on a single, integrated economic forecast. If a manager's active trades are not independent, there is less diversification benefit. Consequently, a manager's active risk rises the more correlated his active trades are. This is intuitively obvious if the manager takes the extreme case: suppose that all a manager's active trades were perfectly correlated. In that case the manager would effectively take only one active position each year, no matter how many active positions the manager thought he was taking. The square root of the number of active positions the manager took would only be one, too. The manager would enjoy no diversification benefit at all in his portfolio of active bets.

To summarize: in order to calculate a manager's information ratio, we divide the active return by the active risk. A manager's prospective success, measured by his information ratio, depends on three factors:

1. The success rate: what percentage of the active positions earn a profit, less the percentage that earn a loss. The greater the success rate, the better a manager will do. We characterize this as a manager's investment "skill."
2. The number of active positions taken each year. The more the better. We call this a manager's investment "scope."
3. How correlated the active positions are. The lower the better. We call this a manager's investment "independence."

Let us now consider each factor in turn.

Skill

Having investment skill means a manager can beat the market. If all markets were perfectly efficient all the time, then a manager would get only 50% of his bets right, and his success rate would be zero. In other words, a manager's skill would be zero, no matter how smart the manager was. So successful active management requires *at least* that the following proposition is true: even though most markets are mostly efficient most of the time, all markets are not perfectly efficient all of the time.[18] The more efficient the markets a manager chooses to participate in, the harder it will be for a manager to be skillful.

Unfortunately, we have no formal theories of market inefficiency to tell us where to look for opportunities. But we can make reasonable surmises. First, we want markets without much competition from other investors like ourselves. For example, with a little luck, taxes or government regulations may prevent some potential competitors from arbitraging away market inefficiencies. Accordingly, regulated

---

[18] Fortunately, there are good reasons to think this proposition is correct. For example, see Sanford Grossman and Joseph Stiglitz, "The Impossibility of Informationally Efficient Markets" for a technical explanation. The nontechnical explanation runs as follows: suppose that there were so many analysts devoting their time to evaluating the markets that the markets became perfectly efficient. Then, on the margin, each analyst would contribute no added value. Accordingly, he would be paid nothing. Analysts would leave the profession, seeking better jobs elsewhere. The dearth of analysts would then cause the markets to become inefficient.

markets may offer us unusual opportunities. So, too, can home country bias: the fact that many investors do not search globally for opportunities, but rather only make value comparisons within their domestic market. This means that global investors are advantaged compared to local investors. Generalizing, segmented markets are more likely to offer opportunities for managers to be skillful than are integrated markets. Finally, it is hard to believe that gross inefficiencies persist indefinitely in any financial market. The newer the market, or the more exotic, complex or unusual the instrument being traded, the more likely it is that the market will be inefficient.

Scope

A manager must find many attractive active positions each year to be successful. If a manager finds only a few, then to earn a given amount of profit he must place large wagers on the few attractive bets found. That is precisely what a manager wants to avoid doing. Instead, a manager wants to place small wagers on many different bets. This is the intemporal version of diversification. Markowitz's MPT described how placing many small bets reduces a portfolio's risk at a snapshot in time; in the same way, placing many small bets through time also reduces risk.

A global bond manager must constantly be alert to developments that may offer the chance for increasing investment scope. Currently, the most attractive opportunity to expand the scope of global bond investing is by incorporating more European credit risk into a bond portfolio. The reason is simple: the market for non-sovereign European bonds is expanding rapidly, following EMU. In fact, during the first three quarters of 1999, 51% of all new bonds issued in Europe were non-sovereigns.

Not only is the non-government sector expanding in Europe, the corporate sector is becoming a more important component of private issues. Corporate bonds represented about 20% of all non-sovereign euro bond issues during 1999. This is up from 9% in 1998. Obviously, European corporate bonds represent an attractive market segment for managers to use to expand investment scope in coming years. European corporate bond markets, because they are new, are more likely to be inefficient than the U.S. corporate bond markets are.

We will discuss evaluating corporate credit risks around the world in the next section.

Independence

Finding many bets does not really give a manager effective investment diversification if all the bets made are highly correlated. Ideally, a manager wants active bets to be as independent as possible for them to be genuinely diversifying. How can a manager make active positions independent?

One key is to diversify across countries and currencies, of course. But more subtly, a manager can increase the independence of active positions by diversifying across investment styles. For example, it seems unlikely that an active bet that the German bond market will outperform the U.K. bond market will have any correlation at all with the outcome of a basis trade made in the Japanese bond futures market. Investment styles include (1) fundamental analysis; (2) technical analysis, by which we mean evaluating other investors' positions, dealers' inventories, and flows; (3) top-down macroeconomic analysis; (4) bottom up, relative value analysis; (5) sector rotation; (6) market anomaly positioning, based on systematic inefficiencies found by the manager, related by other investors, or identified in academic studies. Use them all.

Summary

To summarize our global bond investment philosophy, a manager's investment success depends on his skill, scope, and independence. Skill depends on how well a manager's team can forecast: that is, on average how correlated is a manager's team's prediction of the prospective active return on an investment, compared to the subsequent, realized return? Skill depends on intelligence, wisdom, experience, and information. A manager's team should have all of these. But skill also depends on how efficient the markets in which a manager operates are. No matter how intelligent, wise, experienced or informed a manager's team is, if it is trying to outforecast forward prices formed in a perfectly efficient financial market, it will fail. So the flexibility to move from market-to-market, exploiting inefficiencies wherever they arise, also contributes to skill. That's one reason why global investors should have an edge compared to domestic-only investors.

The second and third factors, scope and independence, are one way of emphasizing that a successful global bond management philosophy is founded on the principal of diversification. A great latitude for investment freedom, encompassing a wide degree of diversification, is becoming increasingly important as alpha becomes harder to earn in simple ways. So our investment philosophy emphasizes diversification across bond markets, currencies, and investment styles. The latter will help to ensure that a manager's active bets are unlikely to all go wrong at the same time, as they may if a manager relies on only a top-down, macroeconomic investment approach. Global investors, with more guideline latitude, more markets and more securities to choose from, should have an edge.

Controlling Tracking Risk

A portfolio manager's expected information ratio is proportional to his skill, the square root of the number of active bets he can find per unit of time, and how independent those bets are. A successful global management team will use many sources of value added, and monitor many markets, so it can tactically exploit market inefficiencies as they arise. Of course, there is always the danger that a manager becomes too enthusiastic about all of the apparent opportunities caught in his wide net, and over extend. Careful risk management is key. Let's add *discipline* to our philosophy for global bond management.

We explained above why tracking risk is important. A manager should start with targets for the tracking risk for the portfolio. The risk target should specify the average risk to take over time, and also the maximum risk a manager is willing to bear at any one time. In other words, the risk budget should be a range, not a single number. At different times a manager will want to bear different amounts of risk, depending on how attractive the opportunities available in the financial markets are. Attractiveness is measured by the *ex ante* information ratio, or expected unit of marginal return per unit of risk borne, offered by active positions. When the prospective information ratio is great — in a target rich environment — a manager will want to be at the upper end of the risk budget. When there are few compelling active opportunities, the manager should scale back the amount of risk taken.

Next a manager must identify and select the active positions he wishes to take, and estimate the risk contributed by each one. In a global bond portfolio, typical top down, macroeconomic sources of active risk and return are duration, yield curve positioning, country allocation, and currency exposure. Pure bottom up, or relative value positions, include using futures when they are cheaply priced compared to cash instruments, identifying relatively cheap bonds on the yield curve, convergence "arbitrage" positions, and many cash management strategies. Sector rotation is both a top down and a bottom up strategy. We will expand on these alpha generating strategies in the next section, which is devoted to the global bond investment process.

One final note. A manager can identify a gross risk associated with each active position in his portfolio, as if that position was taken in isolation. But the sum of these gross risks does not equal the portfolio's total risk. Instead, the total risk in the portfolio is likely to be much smaller than the sum of the gross risks associated with each individual position, because of portfolio diversification. The magnitude of risk reduction achieved this way is great: typically, an active global bond portfolio's total risk will be only ½ to ⅓ of the sum of its individual position's risks, if a manager has diversified well. We are interested in the *incremental* risk contributed by each position, not its gross risk considered in isolation. It is beyond the scope of this article to describe various technical approaches for estimating your portfolio's value-at-risk, and the marginal contribution to value-at-risk made by each of the active positions. But it is imperative for a manager to develop the analytical tools needed to provide this information. So we will begin our discussion of the investment process by considering the role of analytics.

THE GLOBAL BOND INVESTMENT PROCESS

In this section we discuss an investment process and specific investing strategies a manager can use to implement the investment philosophy described in the previous section. We start at the final stage of the investment process, portfolio optimization. Then we work backwards to describe ways to estimate the inputs — expected returns, volatilities, and correlations — needed to construct an optimal portfolio. In the case of expected returns, we emphasize here (as we have elsewhere) the importance of diversifying the sources of a portfolio's excess return. So, we address using chronic market anomalies — apparent persistent inefficiencies — as well as transient opportunities in a portfolio, and integrating top down macroeconomic analysis, country risk assessment, and bottom up relative value techniques. We have argued in the previous section that bottom up approaches like corporate credit analysis, are likely to become more important to global bond managers in the 21st century than they have been in the past. Accordingly, we discuss applying corporate credit analysis in different bond markets. We emphasize that a common framework for corporate credit analysis applies across the globe, but that country specific differences in accounting, law, and culture must be considered, too.

Managing a global bond portfolio effectively requires using a process that is based on formal analytical tools. Of course, analytical tools are important for managing a domestic bond portfolio, too. However, good analytics are even more important for managing global portfolios, for two reasons. First, as we emphasized in the preceding section, the key to effective global bond management is exploiting the broad scope it offers to take attractive active positions wherever in the world they can be found. That means monitoring many markets simultaneously, constantly looking for opportunities around the globe. Analytical tools help a manager to continuously scan scores of markets for potential sources of alpha.

Second, analytical tools are also more important for global bond investors than they are for domestic only investors because optimization is more difficult when a manager has many potential markets, and many investing styles, to integrate into a single portfolio of active positions. In a domestic-only portfolio many bonds will be highly correlated. An unsuccessful switch from one bond to another may not have a big impact on a portfolio's performance, if the two bonds are highly correlated anyway. But a global investor is often investing across far less correlated bond markets. The potential cost of an unsuccessful active trade may be great.

This section starts by describing the global bond investment process at its final stage, portfolio construction. Then it works backwards to describe all the steps that must precede the final one of selecting the final portfolio. Essentially, these steps produce forecasts for all the inputs needed to construct an optimal portfolio: expected returns, volatilities, and correlations.

Optimization

Let us start with the obvious: when a manager has finished constructing a global bond portfolio, it should be an optimal portfolio. An *optimal portfolio* is one that has the greatest possible expected return for its level of risk. Here, "risk" means tracking risk,[19] a measure of how much a portfolio's return will probably deviate from the benchmark's return. (Recall that this is because if a manager is not sensitive to the portfolio's tracking risk, a manager will render a client's overall asset allocation decisions inefficient.) So, a manager must find a portfolio that has the greatest possible expected return, given its tracking risk.

---

[19] The terms tracking risk and tracking error are related, but not identical. The actual difference between the portfolio's return and the bogey's return, *ex post*, is called its tracking error. Tracking risk is the expected value, *ex ante*, of a portfolio's tracking error.

The basic principle of optimizing the portfolio is this: on the margin, each active position should contribute incremental expected return that is proportionate to that active position's incremental contribution to the portfolio's tracking risk.[20] An equivalent way of expressing this basic principal is that, (1) if we divide the marginal excess expected return associated with each active position by, (2) that active position's marginal expected marginal contribution to the portfolio's tracking error (MCTE), then (3) that ratio must be the same for every active position in the portfolio. If this condition does not hold, then the weights associated with active positions are not optimal. Active positions with large expected-return-to MCTE's should be scaled up, and active positions with smaller expected-return-to-MCTE's should be scaled back.

The marginal contribution to tracking error of every active position in a portfolio depends on three things: (1) the size of the active position; (2) the volatility of the active position; and, (3) the correlation of the active position with the other active positions in a portfolio. Part of a manager's job is to forecast the values of the active positions' volatilities and correlations. This part of the job is easy to neglect in favor of the "sexier" task of forecasting expected returns.

Forecasting Bond and Currency Volatilities and Correlations[21]

Volatilities can be estimated from historic data, and often they are. Usually, an algorithm is used that gives more weight to recent observations than to more distant ones. The most commonly used (sophisticated) version of this statistical approach to estimating volatilities uses GARCH-class models.

There is an alternative. Most currencies and major bond markets have active associated options markets. Options trading is substantially about forecasting future volatilities. So the implied volatilities embedded in bond and currency options prices offer the global bond portfolio manager an estimate of future volatilities of bonds and currencies. These estimates are free: all you must do is to calculate implied option volatilities, a routine task. These free estimates are made by experts (options traders) who devote much of their time and other expensive resources to forming their forecasts, and who make or lose money depending on whether their forecasts prove to be right or wrong after the fact. Implied option volatilities have another advantage over volatilities estimated from historic data: they are forward, rather than backward, looking. For estimating a portfolio's risk

---

[20] An "active position" is any difference between a portfolio and the bogey. In the last section, we characterized an active trade in terms of an overweight and an underweight compared to the bogey.

[21] The careful reader will have noticed that what we need are volatilities and correlations of a portfolio's active trades. An active trade usually consists of an overweight and an underweight position in two (or more) instruments, so the correlations and volatilities we have in mind are more complex than those used conventionally in implementing MPT. However, the correlations and volatilities of active positions easily can be built up from the "primitives" — that is, the correlations and volatilities of single instruments. Accordingly, we treat the problem of how to estimate correlations and volatilities at the single instrument level here.

and constructing the optimal portfolio, a manager needs to *predict* volatilities in the future, not measure what they were in the past.[22]

A manager must also forecast the correlations among the active positions. Correlations are generally estimated from historic data. However, since correlations frequently move substantially and abruptly, it is unsatisfactory to depend only on a mechanical, statistical methodology. A statistical estimate of a correlation, based on recent data, may be a good place to start. But a manager should go further by examining long histories of the correlations that must be forecasted. Then a manager should factor in anticipated economic and financial market changes that may mean history will not repeat itself.

That is, a manager's job is to *forecast* correlations, not to measure their historic values. Correlations are particularly unstable during periods of high market volatility — just when they can cause the most damage to a manager's estimate of portfolio risk. Accordingly, even after taking care to forecast correlations accurately, it is important to "stress test" a portfolio's tracking risk by simulating its value if volatilities and correlations change radically, as they will in a crisis.

Producing Skill: Forecasting Expected Returns

Most bond managers spend most of their time forecasting expected returns. None of the rest — how well a manager forecasts volatilities, correlations, or constructs optimal portfolios — matters if a manager is unable to identify opportunities to beat the market. If a manager cannot, he should become a passive manager.

In principle, a manager should continually forecast the expected return to every potential active position he can take. Recall, there are many of them in a global bond portfolio. Most prices are efficient most of the time, so a manager cannot afford to neglect any potential opportunity. Obviously, this is not a job that can be done by a single person. Rather, it demands a team. Managing the team is critical to its success, but the issues of organization and management of a global bond team are beyond the scope of this article. Going forward we often refer to the "global manager," but this should be understood to be a shorthand way of referring to the global management team.

No manager, no matter his skill, can produce alpha in a perfectly efficient market. A market is inefficient if the prospective returns to some investments are not commensurate with their risks.[23] The chief job of an active manager is to identify markets containing inefficiencies. Unfortunately, competitors are trying to do the same thing.

Financial theory tells us that market inefficiencies are unlikely to persist indefinitely. Soon after they appear they will be exploited by active managers. That process of exploitation serves to eliminate them. So there is no simple and

---

[22] For discussion of volatility forecasting using implied option volatilities, see Allen Poteshman, "Forecasting Future Variance from Option Prices," paper presented at the American Finance Association meetings, 2000.

[23] Specifically, their systematic risks.

stable "system" one can use to earn excess return forever. A manager's investing habits must constantly evolve, or else skill will deteriorate.

That is the bad news. The good news is that there is an increasing body of academic literature that says some markets are inefficient some of the time. For example, numerous studies have found that high yielding currencies seem persistently to outperform low yielding currencies, even after factoring in exchange rate changes.[24,25] Bond markets with high real yields and steeply upward sloping yield curves have historically outperformed bond markets with the opposite attributes.[26] Part of a manager's job is to decide if these and other chronic anomalies will persist. We will start by describing how to use chronic market anomalies to add value in the global bond portfolio management process.

A Core Anomaly Strategy

There is a serious danger with choosing one anomaly, and basing an investment process on it alone. The danger: each anomaly persists until it doesn't. A manager has no advance warning when an anomaly is going to be discovered, exploited, and eliminated by other active bond managers. For an investment boutique that has based its investment process on a single anomaly, its disappearance is likely to be catastrophic to its clients and to its business. So an investment philosophy should be to diversify across many apparent market anomalies, not to rely on one alone.

The alternative to depending on a single anomaly, consistent with the theme of aggressively diversifying sources of alpha, is taking small bets on a number of suspected market anomalies. If a manager believes high yielding currencies will systematically outperform low yielding ones in the future, as they have in the past, then *one* of the core active positions will be an overweight in a portfolio of such high yielding currencies. If a manager believes sovereign bonds with high real yields will outperform sovereign bonds with low real yields, then *one* of the core positions will be a collection of overweights in high yielders and underweights in low yielders.[27] If a manager thinks steep yield curves will be associated with abnormally high total bond returns, *one* of the core active positions should be a portfolio that is overweight of steep yield curves and underweight of flat curves. If a manager believes BBB credits will systematically outperform AAA credits, *one* of the core active positions should be a portfolio

---

[24] John Bilson, "The Speculative Efficiency Hypothesis," *Journal of Business* (July 1981) was the first to document this carefully, so this anomaly has persisted for a very long time. Many studies confirmed and expanded on his work. Among the best is Robert J. Hodrick, *The Empirical Evidence on the Efficiency of Forward and Futures Foreign Exchange Markets*, Harwood, 1987.

[25] See Antti Ilmanen, "When Do Bond Markets Reward Investors for Interest Rate Risk?" *Journal of Portfolio Management* (Winter 1996).

[26] These "inefficiencies" may represent risk premia. This article is not the place to discuss this long running debate.

[27] Earlier in this article we used this as an example to show how past anomalies may not persist in the future. Once again we urge the reader not to rely mechanistically on extrapolations of historically successful investing strategies.

overweight in a portfolio of credit exposed investment instruments. If a manager believes the total return of mortgage-backed securities will be, on average, greater than the total return on U.S. Treasury bonds, a manager should have a core active position overweight the former and underweight the latter. Will one year cash instruments systematically outperform one month cash instruments? (They have in the past.)[28] If so, a core active position is in order.

By exposing a portfolio to small active exposures to a large number of suspected anomalies, a manager eliminates the chance that the one key bet will stop performing at just the wrong time, because performance does not rely on one key bet.

A Core Anomaly Plus Strategy

Core anomalies can form the foundation of an active bond portfolio, but they do not exhaust all the opportunities the global bond and currency markets offer. Transitory security mispricings can develop for many reasons, and a manager should use them as part of an active strategy. Let's take one as an example.

Suppose a large seller temporarily depresses the price of a particular bond. Then, a manager has the chance to offer liquidity services to the market, for a fee. The manager buys the depressed bonds, holds them until the temporary oversupply has been digested, then sells at a profit. This presumes the manager has spare liquidity, but this is ordinarily the case. Typically, a manager does not need the entire portfolio to be liquid at all times: it is unlikely that all clients will withdraw all their funds simultaneously. Unneeded liquidity should be sold, so it becomes a source of alpha. Buying bonds that are in temporary oversupply is a way of selling excess liquidity. A recent trend is that brokers are less willing to supply liquidity to the bond markets, and risk their own capital to violent price swings, such as those that occurred during 1998. So the price of liquidity has risen. That makes a sell-liquidity strategy more lucrative.

Other transitory inefficiencies may be associated with "orphan securities" — bonds that have no natural home, because investors do not understand them or appreciate how they fit into a portfolio. Lets illustrate with one rather exotic U.S. bond.

TIPS — U.S. Treasury securities indexed against inflation — yield a real rate of about 4% as of this writing, plus the change in the CPI. Over the long run, the historic real return to conventional U.S. Treasury bonds has been only about 3%. By "conventional" bonds we mean nominal bonds, which are exposed to inflation risk. It seems odd that less risky bonds like TIPS, which have both negligible default risk *and* inflation risk, should offer a higher certain real yield than that produced over a long history by conventional, inflation exposed bonds that have the same obligor. The most plausible explanation for this is that TIPS are a relatively new instrument, and are not yet understood or appreciated by the general body of bond investors. In other words, they only are considered for purchase by a restricted

---

[28] See Robin Grieves and Alan Marcus, "Riding the Yield Curve: Reprise," NBER working paper No. 3511, November 1990.

clientele. This impression is reinforced by looking at inflation indexed bonds else-where in the world. Often, they appear mispriced compared to their domestic, nom-inal sovereign bonds, and also to index linked bonds in different countries.[29]

Similar transitory systematic mispricings have occurred in the past. For example, when bond futures contracts were first introduced, they chronically traded cheap to the underlying U.S. Treasury instruments. The same thing hap-pened when government bond futures contracts were introduced in Germany.

One key to unearthing transitory anomalies like these is monitoring many markets all the time. There is no predicting when and where a temporary ineffi-ciency will develop. A manager can only achieve this by organizing a global bond process as a team effort: many pairs of eyes are needed to watch all the world's major bond and currency markets. Quantitative tools are also very useful, since they can constantly scan many markets for apparent mispricings, and alert the portfolio management team of a possible opportunity.

Let us consider some of the potential transitory opportunities a global management team should be monitoring.

Of course there are many ways to add value in a global bond portfolio — that is one of the chief advantages to using all the world's bond markets. To help organize them, we can classify the opportunities as "top down" (macroeconomic) or "bottom up" (relative value). (Sector rotation involves elements of both top-down and bottom-up strategies.)

Active Top Down Positions

Let us consider some of the ways a manager can identify top down opportunities to overweight or underweight particular bond markets. Then we will consider active currency exposures.

Most international finance textbooks demonstrate that in equilibrium the yields of default free, sovereign bonds depend on (1) the level of yields available elsewhere, (2) the expected change in the appropriate exchange rate, and (3) a risk premium.[30] Alternately, this can be expressed in price deflated terms: the real yield in any sovereign bond market depends on the real yields available else-where, the expected change in the country's real exchange rate, and a risk pre-mium. The practical implication for a global bond manager is this: look for bond markets with high real yields, with undervalued currencies, and with low risk.

So there are three factors to monitor. Real yield is found by deducting expected inflation from nominal yield. The expected future inflation rate can be estimated based on historic inflation rates, time series models, formal economet-ric modeling, subjective evaluation, or a combination of these approaches. We

---

[29] See Alyce Su and Lee Thomas, "Comparing Index Linked Bonds Globally," *Investment & Pensions Europe*, July/August 1999.

[30] This description is a simplification of international capital asset pricing models (IAPM). The point is not to advocate any particular model, but to establish a simple framework we can use to identify the most important factors to consider.

will discuss exchange rate forecasting — identifying undervalued currencies — below. Conceptually, the most difficult of these three factors to deal with is the risk premium. This requires you to assess sovereign, or country risk.

Country Risk

In order to rank global bond markets according to their country risk, a manager must first ask exactly what "risk" is when investing in a country's sovereign bonds. Unlike corporate debt, sovereign debt issued in a country's own currency has little chance of defaulting. This is because the country's central bank can simply cover its Treasury's obligations by issuing new money.[31] As a result, the relevant risk associated with investing in sovereign debt is that the investor will be paid back in devalued currency, the result of inflationary monetary policy.

What might lead a central bank to pursue an inflationary monetary policy? Often inflationary monetary policy results from stresses on public budgets: the central bank covers its Treasury's obligations by issuing new money. In other words, poor economic growth (resulting in low tax revenues) or excessive spending create fissures in a government's finances which ultimately may be papered over by easy monetary policy and the inflation tax. As a result, one approach to analyzing sovereign debt is to examine a country's fundamental economic growth prospects, compared to the prospective growth rate in government spending. The implicit assumption is that success at achieving real growth in income per capita, and keeping spending controlled, will be related to a country's willingness and ability to avoid inflationary monetary policies.

This suggests that models designed to evaluate relative country risk should ascertain which factors best predict success at achieving and sustaining strong economic growth, while keeping spending under control. Solid government finances and low long run inflation will follow. But how can we predict which countries will be successful at growing?

Once we would have had little to go on except anecdotes and prejudice. Fortunately, in recent years a large body of academic research has rigorously examined exactly this question.[32] It turns out that the best predictors of a country's economic success include the openness of the economy to international trade and capital flows; prudent fiscal policies measured, for example, by debt to GDP, the deficit to GDP, and total government spending as a fraction of GDP; free and flexible labor markets; and a host of other socio-economic variables such as the levels of illiteracy and corruption.[33] These factors can be combined to produce predictive country rankings. One such set is the "competitiveness" ratings compiled annually by Havard University's Institute for Economic Development.

---

[31] EMU members are an exception to this general rule. EMU member central banks are not authorized to issue euros. Only the European Central Bank can do that.

[32] The development of the new development economies is described in Paul Krugman, "The Fall and Rise of Development Economics," in *Development Geography and Economic Theory*, MIT Press, 1997.

[33] See, for example, Robert J. Barro, *Determinants of Economic Growth: A Cross-Country Empirical Study* (Cambridge, MA: MIT Press, 1997), and Robert Barro and Xavier Sal-i-Martin, *Economic Growth* (Cambridge, MA: MIT Press, 1998).

Exhibit 21: Real 10-Year Bond Yield and Country Risk

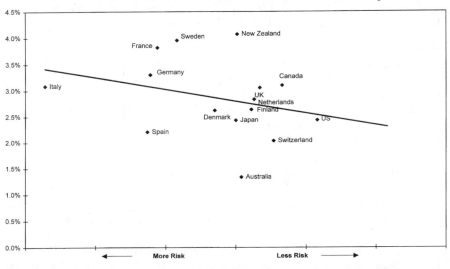

Exhibit 21 compares real yields and competitiveness — a proxy for prospective economic success — for a sample of developed and developing countries. Remember that competitiveness rankings proxy for a country's long term credit worthiness. As long run measures, these (or similar) statistics should be combined with short run factors, too, particularly an analysis of where a country is in its business cycle. Secular and cyclical factors may sometimes be at odds, and bond managers have different, and usually proprietary, ways of combining them into a single measure of a sovereign bond market's overall riskiness.

Currency Allocation

We now turn to the other major source of "top down" alpha in global bond portfolios, currency exposures. Up until this point we have not distinguished between active strategies applied to bonds and active strategies applied to currencies. In fact, failing to make this separation is conceptually flawed.

Global bond mandates entail managing both a bond portfolio and a currency portfolio. Bond and currency decisions should be analytically separated, excepting in a few instances described below. The reason: economic developments that influence bond markets often influence currency markets differently. For example, sovereign bonds respond to the business cycle by increasing in price as economic growth declines, and decreasing in price as growth picks up. That is, interest rates usually fall during a recession, and rise during expansions. Currencies behave oppositely: they tend to strengthen when a country's growth is strong. Absent the requisite investment vehicles and efficient hedging tools, it would not be possible to have exposure to a bond, but not to the currency in which it is denominated, or to have exposure to a currency, but not to the corresponding bond market. Fortunately the needed instruments exist, so that bond and currency exposures easily can be separated. The key is using currency hedging instruments, such as currency forwards and futures.

To illustrate, suppose an investor wants only bond market exposure in a particular country, without the associated currency risk. He should purchase the bond, but sell the underlying currency forward to strip away the bond's currency risk.[34] If the investor wants currency exposure, but no interest rate exposure in a country, he can simply buy the currency forward.[35] If the investor wants both currency and bond market exposure, he can buy the bond but not currency hedge. It would be purely coincidental if the desired active currency exposure in a global bond portfolio happened to correspond exactly to the desired active bond exposure in any particular country. In practice, the optimal bond and currency exposures seldom conform exactly in this way.

Since an investor can select bond exposure independently of currency exposure in any country, the portfolio selection procedure used must reflect this independence. However, even a correct principle can be exaggerated until it becomes incorrect. There are number of senses in which bond and currency decisions should not be separated, or are not separable.

For example, separating currency and bond decisions does not mean using separate macroeconomic forecasts for each. It would be absurd to choose an overweight euro bond position based on a forecast of weak European GDP growth, but use a forecast of strong European growth for a forecast of euro currency. Instead, a single macroeconomic view must separately be applied to a forecast of European interest rates and exchange rates.

Second, interest rates influence exchange rates, and exchange rates influence interest rates. In other words, interest rate and exchange rate changes are correlated. Portfolio selection should not ignore this correlation. Indeed, including such correlation is one reason why MPT potentially improves upon naïve portfolio selection rules in global bond portfolio construction.

Third, in practice bond and currency decisions may become entangled through restrictions placed by a client on the permitted portfolio. For example, if leveraging the portfolio is not allowed — certainly a common guideline restriction — then all positions usually have some degree of interdependence, since increasing the size of one position requires reducing the size of another. There are many other plausible examples of this, but one demonstration will suffice to illustrate how interdependence may arise from portfolio constraints.

---

[34] Lee Thomas, "International Bonds: Stripping Away Currency Risk," *Investing*, 1988. It should be noted that bond repos, swaps, and futures contracts all accomplish the same objective.

[35] Alternately, an investor can purchase currency futures or short duration foreign currency investments, such as foreign Treasury bills or floating-rate notes. We exaggerate slightly when we say "no" interest rate risk — i.e., duration — exists in such instruments. The interest rate duration associated with currency exposures is usually easily eliminated.

Suppose an investor is not permitted to use currency forwards or futures to establish a currency position. Instead, forwards and futures can *only* be used to hedge an exposure which was already created by a foreign bond position. (Restricting the use of forwards and futures only to hedging is common.) Now suppose that the portfolio manager wants currency exposure in Japanese yen. Since the investor cannot secure it with yen forwards or futures, he will have to buy Japanese bonds. If he does, he has not completely separated his bond and currency decisions. (In practice he will probably purchase very short duration Japanese bills or floating-rate notes, which have little interest rate risk, and so accomplish near separation of a portfolio's yen duration and yen currency exposure.)

Forecasting Currency Returns

So how do we construct a global bond portfolio's collection of active currency exposures? Whether the benchmark is hedged or unhedged, active currency exposures are potentially a powerful tool for increasing or decreasing returns. While the academic literature is rich with theoretical models for explaining exchange rate values, there are three basic approaches which empirically are most useful for predicting total currency returns. These are (1) fundamental analysis, focused on measures of relative purchasing power or fundamental equilibrium exchange rates, (2) short-term yields, and (3) market trends or technical factors.[36]

It was once thought that formal, academic models of exchange rate determination had no power to forecast exchange rates. In an influential series of academic papers, Meese and Rogoff,[37] showed that none of the major formal models of exchange rate determination could outperform a simple random walk forecast. That pathetic performance was registered even when you supplied the models with the exact future values of the exogenous variables they needed to produce their exchange rate forecasts!

It seemed then that academic economics had nothing to offer practitioners when it came to foreign exchange forecasting. Fortunately, more recent research has shown that fundamental economic analysis *is* useful for exchange rate forecasting, at least over a three year and longer forecasting horizon.[38] When examined at long forecasting horizons, currencies seem to revert towards their underlying fundamental values. The problem is, they do so very slowly.

What else can be used to forecast currency returns? In principle, short-term interest rate differences among countries should not be useful. True, one can earn more income in high yielding currencies. But the economic hypothesis called

---

[36] The treatment of forecasting currency returns here is brief. A good reference for a more comprehensive treatment is Michael R. Rosenberg, *Currency Forecasting* (Burr Ridge, IL: Irwin Professional Publishing, 1995).

[37] See Richard Meese and Kenneth Rogoff, "Empirical Exchange Rate Models of the Seventies: Do they Fit Out of Sample?" *Journal of International Economics*, 1983, and "What is Real? The Exchange Rate — Interest Rate Differential Relation over the Modern Floating Rate Period," *Journal of Finance*, 1988.

[38] See, for example, Nelson Mark, "Exchange Rates and Fundamentals: Evidence on Long Horizon Predictability," *American Economic Review* (March 1995).

"uncovered interest rate parity" asserts that high yielding currencies will, on average, depreciate at a rate just sufficient to neutralize their interest rate advantage.

As it happens, uncovered interest rate parity has been persistently violated since the 1970s. Numerous studies have found that currencies with high short-term interest rates subsequently produce higher total returns than currencies with lower short-term interest rates.[39] Consequently, all other things equal, global bond portfolio managers should avoid active exposures to low yielding currencies and favor active exposures to currencies with higher yields — that is, if they expect uncovered interest rate parity to continue to be violated in the future, as it has in the past.

Another curious anomaly exists in the currency markets: successive exchange rate changes historically have been correlated.[40] In other words, currencies trend. Central bank intervention, "leaning against the wind," may explain this curious price action.[41] But beware: during the 1990's currency trends seem to have weakened, or vanished altogether. This may represent a currency anomaly whose time has passed.[42]

Active "Bottom Up" Positions

In our discussion of the new international investment environment, we emphasized that changes in the global environment mean changes in the kinds of strategies that promise to add value in global bond portfolio. In the past, most global managers have relied largely on top-down strategies to produce alpha. International yield differences were large. Different central banks followed wildly different policies. So there were many opportunities to produce return by actively overweighting and underweighting particular countries, or by betting on exchange rate changes. Moreover, outside the United States there were few opportunities to earn much alpha using relative value approaches. The required instruments simply did not exist. In many cases, even sovereign bond markets were undeveloped, so often only a few government bonds were liquid in each country. This made it impractical even to exchange expensive bonds for cheap ones along a single, sovereign yield curve. And outside of the United States the corporate bond markets were small, because many companies in Europe and Asia relied on bank financing rather than bond financing. Moreover, mortgage- and other asset-backed markets were almost non-existent outside the United States. So sector rotation was impractical, too.

---

[39] John Bilson, "The Speculative Efficiency Hypotheses," *Journal of Business* (July 1981), and John Bilson, "Technical Currency Trading," in Lee R. Thomas (ed.), *The Currency-Hedging Debate* (IFR Publishing Ltd., 1990).

[40] Trends are documented in Richard Levich and Lee Thomas, "The Merits of Active Currency Risk Management: Evidence from International Bond Portfolios," *Financial Analysts Journal* (September-October 1993).

[41] Periods of profitability from using trend following rules are correlated with periods when Central Bankers are unusually active in the foreign exchange markets.

[42] The exception: trend following rules have continued to be profitable for the Japanese yen. The post-1990 results are based on unpublished work by Richard Levich and myself.

The bond world outside the United States is changing rapidly, particularly in Europe. EMU has created a deep, liquid market for euro denominated sovereign bonds. At the same time, regulatory and competitive pressures are reducing the role of banks as intermediaries between borrowers and lenders. This is creating new markets in Europe for corporate bonds and asset-backed securities. And liquid futures markets exist for sovereign bonds in most developed countries. So, as the opportunity to earn alpha using top-down investing techniques declines, the opportunity to earn alpha using bottom-up investing techniques is increasing. *Going forward global bond managers will rely more on relative value analysis, and less on macroeconomic analysis, than they have in the past.* And, as we have repeatedly stressed, diversification across investment styles is key to successful global bond management, anyway.

Let's consider two of the important active bottom up, or relative value strategies, global managers can use.

Convergence "Arbitrage"

Convergence arbitrage represents taking advantage of small price and yield differences between similar bonds. The return to the position takes two forms: (1) the "carry," or return in a static state, in which the bonds' yields do not change, and (2) the capital gain that accrues if the yield spread between the bonds moves favorably. Usually, favorably means a smaller yield spread, but this is not necessary; sometimes convergence "arbitrage" trades are motivated by the expectation that the spread between a pair of bonds has converged too much, and is going to increase in the future.

Convergence "arbitrage" may be executed within a single bond market. For example, selling an expensive corporate bond and replacing it with a similar, but cheap one, is a form of convergence arbitrage. Convergence "arbitrage" can also be an international strategy.

We will illustrate how an international convergence arbitrage strategy works using an actual market opportunity available in late 1999. The yield on 30-year U.K. gilts (sovereign bonds) was 4.46%; the yield on 30-year German bunds (sovereign bonds) was 5.91%. The difference was 1.45%. At some point during the coming five or six years, it was generally expected that the U.K. would enter the EMU. At that time its bonds will be redenominated in euros. As a result, they would become much more fungible with other euro denominated sovereign bonds. The yield spread between gilts and bunds would then collapse, probably approaching zero.

For purposes of illustration, assume that this convergence is expected to occur in six years, and when it does the bonds' yield spread is expected to fall to zero. What is the profit potential on a convergence "arbitrage" position that is long the 30-year bund, and underweight a duration equivalent position in 30-year gilts?

Suppose the precise timing of the convergence from a spread of 145 bp to a spread of 0 bp is unknown. Having no timing information, we will therefore suppose convergence occurs at a constant rate of 2 bp per month (145 bp divided by 72 months). That spread narrowing represents a capital gain of about 0.24% per month, in price terms, once we factor in duration.

Now we must calculate carry, or the return that accrues if the yield spread does not change. The "carry" on the position reflects the yield difference between the bonds, as well as the cost of financing the bund and gilt positions. The yield difference, 1.45% per year, is in an investor's favor. Moreover, gilt financing costs are greater than bund financing costs: the difference is about 9 bp per month. So the financing difference, about 2.30% per year, is also in your favor. As a result, an investor will earn income — so called *positive carry* — by holding the over-weight bund/underweight gilt position. If nothing changes — financing costs or bond yields — the long bund/short gilt position will earn 31 bp per month in carry. If the spread converges smoothly, it will earn an additional 24 bp per month in capital gains. If all these "ifs" come to fruition, the position will produce a profit of 56 bp per month, or about 1.9% per year. A 1% active convergence position, overweight of 30-year Bunds and underweight of 30-year gilts would generate alpha of approximately ½ bp each month for a global bond portfolio.

This makes international convergence "arbitrage" trades seem easy, but don't try this at home, kids, unless your parents are around.[43] One risk is that the yield spread between 30-year gilts and bunds does not converge, but diverges further. What, for example, if the U.K. never enters EMU?

Convergence trades usually work well in calm markets, when they produce small, consistent profits. The risks come from unusual events, such as default or market disruption. These events are infrequent, but can produce large losses. Accordingly, many bottom up convergence "arbitrage" trades have a payoff pattern like that of selling an option: a large chance of a small gain, offset by a small chance of a large loss. Obviously, these are exactly the kind of active positions that can cause a catastrophe when they go wrong. Accordingly, a manager wants to diversify convergence "arbitrage" trades aggressively by taking small positions in many uncorrelated trades.

Using Corporate Bonds in a Global Portfolio

The other most important relative value strategy global bond investors will use in the early 21st century is sector rotation: selling sovereign bonds, and replacing them with higher yielding alternatives, such as corporate bonds. Let's consider how a global bond manager might value corporate bonds compared to sovereign bonds, and why this comparison might have to be adapted to be used in different countries around the world.

Crafting the corporate exposures in a bond portfolio involves making three decisions. First, you must decide how much corporate credit exposure you want to include, in total, in the portfolio. In other words, a manager must decide how much of the risk budget to allocate to corporate credit risk. Then a manager must decide which countries and which sectors (such as financials; industrials; or utilities) to concentrate your corporate credit exposures in. These are the top down

---

[43] Long Term Capital Management, a well known hedge fund that almost failed spectacularly in 1998, was known for its shrewd use of convergence "arbitrage" positions. Its staff included some of the most sophisticated bond investors and risk managers in the business, including two Nobel laureates.

credit decisions. Then you must evaluate companies from the bottom up, to decide which particular names to choose to "spend" her corporate credit risk budget on.

Corporate credit used to be largely a U.S. game, but recently the European corporate markets have begun to expand rapidly. Most observers expect the rapid expansion of European corporate bond markets to continue, and even accelerate, during the early part of the 21st century. Asian corporate bond markets are likely to expand, too. In the context of European or Asian bonds, credit decisions require a process that is similar to, but not necessarily identical to, the one a manager would use in the United States. U.S. skills are useful, but they must be coupled with knowledge of the idiosyncrasies of non-U.S. markets. And applying the same credit evaluation process does not imply a manager will come to the same conclusions in the United States and abroad.

Corporate Sector Allocation

Let's start by considering the first top down credit decision — setting the target for corporate credit risk in a global portfolio.

Why include any corporate credit risk in a portfolio at all? The reason is that bonds that are exposed to credit risk offer higher yields than otherwise identical government bonds. The yield advantage is called the *credit spread*. The credit spread compensates for the possibility that a bond will default — fail to make a promised interest or principal payment, or make one late — during the bond's life. Government bonds, with no (or very low) credit risk, are the safe play; corporate bonds are a more aggressive, but potentially more lucrative, alternative.

A manager can think of assigning a budget to corporate credit risk as balancing extra yield against the extra default risk in corporate bonds. In practice a manager can use a simple approach to decide how much credit exposure to include in a portfolio: forecast the prospective change in corporate bond spreads in the immediate future. If a manager believes credit spreads soon will widen — the yield premium offered for taking credit risk will become greater — obviously a manager should delay buying corporate bonds. After all, a manager will be better compensated for taking credit risk by waiting. If a manager expects corporate spreads to tighten — in the future it is expected to be offered less of a yield premium to bear corporate credit risk — then a manager should lock in the current spread by buying corporate bonds immediately. Of course, a manager may expect credit spreads to widen in some countries, and narrow simultaneously in others. So let's consider what moves corporate credit spreads in general.

What Makes Credit Spreads Move?

Let's start with corporate credit basics that apply anywhere in the world.[44] Suppose a company issues two classes of security, equity shares and bonds. The bonds promise to pay a certain sum of cash in the future. Further suppose that,

---

[44] This framework for evaluating credit risk was first developed in Robert Merton, "On the Pricing of Corporate Debt: The Risk Structure of Interest Rates," *Journal of Finance* (May 1974).

according to law, if the bondholder's promised cash is not paid to him in full, then he has the right to seize the company's assets. That makes the equity shares like a call option written on the value of the corporation's assets. When the bond matures, if the corporation's assets are worth more than the cash required to service the bondholders' claims, shareholders exercise their call option by paying off the bonds and keeping the remainder of the corporate assets. But if the corporate assets turn out to be worth less than the cash required to service the bonds, then the shareholders don't exercise their right to receive the corporation's assets. Instead, the corporate assets go to the bondholders in lieu of the cash promised by their bonds. We would call that event a default.

Notice we have barely begun, but we have already implicitly introduced country-specific elements of law and culture. For example, what if local bankruptcy laws do *not* require shareholders always and immediately to turn over all the corporation's assets to bondholders if its bonds are in default? (Governments in some countries are very sensitive to the social disruptions that may result from laying off workers if a corporation is declared bankrupt.) Or, what if by tradition shareholders in some countries prefer to protect their reputations — to "save face" — by paying off bondholders in full, rather than permitting a bond issue to default, even if they are not strictly required to do so by law? Already we can see that a global bond manager in one country may have to adapt his corporate credit evaluation process to reflect different cultures and legal environments in different countries.

If the shares of a corporation represent a call option on the corporation's assets, what do the corporation's bonds represent? Owning a corporate bond is like (1) lending default-risk free, and simultaneously (2) selling a put option on the corporation's assets. If the corporation prospers, the corporate bondholder will receive interest and principal payments in full and on time. The corporate bondholder will be paid more than just making a default-risk free loan alone would produce (i.e., if an investor just bought a sovereign bond). In other words, one can think of interest and principal payments as including an embedded premium for the put option sold. That premium is the credit spread.

But what if the corporation does not prosper? In this event an investor may be sorry to have sold a put option on the corporation's assets. The owners of that put (the shareholders) may exercise it. Instead of paying the bond's promised interest and principal, the bond may default. In that event, instead of the cash promised the investor will receive the corporation's assets, and those assets will be worth less than the cash the investor was promised by buying the bond. The investor will lose the difference between the cash expected to be received and the market value of the corporate assets. To add insult to injury, the corporation's assets may have to be sold at "fire sale" prices, and the investor may have to pay substantial legal fees, too!

Now let's climb down from this abstract world and see what all this implies for forecasting corporate credit spread changes in different countries, so a manager can use corporate bonds to add alpha to a global portfolio.

Since credit spreads represent the value of a put option on a corporation's assets, we can simply ask what would cause the value of such a put option to change. There are two classes of factors: those that change the expected market value of a corporation's assets, and those that change the volatility of the market value of the corporation's assets.

One factor that can change the expected market value of corporate assets is the rate of economic growth in its home country. In a robustly growing economy, corporations generally will prosper. That is, they will earn a lot of cash, compared to what they would earn if the economy was in recession. The expected value of a representative corporation's assets will be rising, so the odds of corporate bonds defaulting declines. Accordingly, expected future economic growth is one factor that influences economy-wide corporate bond spreads. If a manager expects economic growth prospects in a country to improve, corporate yield spreads should tighten, so a manager may wish to rotate out of government bonds and into corporate bonds in part of a global portfolio.

A second factor that changes the expected value of corporate assets is the level of interest rates. Interest payments must be made before any dividends are paid to shareholders. And if interest payments are so high that they exceed the value of a corporation's assets even if it pays no dividends at all, then it must default on its bonds. Putting it another way, when interest rates are high corporate cash flows need also to be high to satisfy bondholders' demands. If a country hikes interest rates sharply, corporate credit spreads may widen to reflect the prospect of corporate distress. A manager doesn't want to be overweighted in corporate bonds in countries where rates rise unexpectedly. Best to be underweighted in those countries anyway, of course, but in particular a manager wants to eschew corporates.

The third important factor to consider is the volatility of the market value of corporate assets. In general, any option is worth more when volatility is high. Corporate bondholders have implicitly sold options on the value of a corporation's assets. Since they have effectively sold options, corporate bondholders hope for gentle winds and smooth sailing. If volatility rises instead, then the value of the options corporate bondholders have sold rises, to the bondholders' detriment. To put it another way, if the volatility of the value of a corporation's assets rises, corporate bonds become riskier. Credit spreads should become wider to compensate.

The value of a company's assets may become more volatile for either of two reasons. First, the intrinsic volatility of corporate assets may rise if gross disposable product (GDP) growth becomes more volatile. So a manager should beware of corporate bonds wherever she expects a country to pursue destabilizing monetary and fiscal policies. Corporate asset values can also be volatile because companies use a lot of financial leverage. The amount of financial leverage commonly used by corporations may be quite different in different countries, because tax laws are different and because business cultures encourage or discourage using debt financing.

Earlier in this article we mentioned that the economic environment is changing rapidly, and that these changes may have profound implications for investors. One example: the New Economy is a winner takes all arena, where some companies do spectacularly well, while others fail. That means future corporate cash flows for a particular company are harder to predict — will it be a winner or loser? Corporate spreads should be wider to compensate.

A final, and important note, regarding corporate credit analysis for global bond portfolio: the output of any credit analysis is only as good as the quality of the inputs. Different countries have vastly different regulations governing corporate accounting. U.S. Generally Accepted Accounting Principles (GAAP) are not the same as International Accounting Standards (IAS), and various national accounting standards differ from both. In general, an analyst cannot compare corporate data and ratios derived from balance sheets and income statements prepared using different accounting standards. Most practitioners consider it difficult *or even impossible* to reconcile GAAP and IAS data, and the problems are likely to be far worse when evaluating bonds issued by companies that use neither GAAP or IAS.

CONCLUSION

Global bond management is changing rapidly, because it is highly sensitive to two of the most powerful forces influencing the investment management industry today: (1) the increasing sophistication of investing, in terms of the complexity of the instruments used and the analytical power needed to evaluate them and combine them into efficient portfolios, and (2) the globalization of all financial markets. That means that bond portfolio managers have had to acquire new skills, and the future promises no relief from this trend.

Global bond investors must consider all the nuances of domestic bond investing: duration, slope exposure, convexity, and credit issues. In addition they must also understand currencies, sovereign risks, and the differing legal and accounting frameworks that exist in different countries. And they must do all this in an environment that is in a state of flux. Investors should anticipate that the significant changes that occurred in the financial markets during the late years of the 20th century will have a major impact on the philosophy and process of global bond portfolio management during the early years of the 21st century. The most profound changes in the economic and financial landscape have occurred in Europe, but similar changes are occurring in Asia, too.

The first year of EMU was 1999; yet in that year alone merger and acquisition activity in Europe doubled in value to about U.S. $1,200 billion. Initially merger activity was largely intranational: Olivetti trying to take over Telecom Italia; Banque National de Paris trying to take over Paribas and Societe Generale. But by the end of 1999, merger and acquisition activity had already spilled across borders — witness Vodafone of the U.K.'s hostile takeover offer for the German firm Mannesmann. That is a trend that is going to accelerate. It will cause new bond issuance, and changing corporate credit risks throughout Europe.

The creation of a single European market, without internal exchange rate risk, means there will be fewer, larger companies. Banks, hobbled by the Basle Capital adequacy regulations and competitive pressures of their own, are lending less. The result is an explosion of corporate bond issuance in Europe.

At the same time, a single European currency and European Central Bank has meant the opportunity to earn an excess return from forecasting interest rates and exchange rates has diminished. Global bond managers really have three currency blocs — dollar, euro, and yen — to choose from, plus emerging markets. The plethora of bond and currency choices that existed before EMU is gone. The implications for bond investors are clear. In the future, global managers will depend far less on top down macroeconomic forecasts, and far more on bottom up relative value analysis (including credit analysis) than they ever have in the past. Global bond investors will, in style anyway, begin more and more to look like U.S. bond investors.

EMU is only one global change that will radically change how global bond portfolios are managed. The late 1960s and 1970s were the era of the Great Inflation, worldwide. The 1980s and 1990s represented the corresponding Great Disinflation. The world now has lower interest rates, and more stable ones. Bond investment strategies that were successful during the inflationary 1970s or the disinflationary 1990s, may no longer work. But new strategies will replace them as the investing environment evolves.

As the world's markets become more integrated in the 21st century — a return to the conditions that prevailed at the beginning of the 20th century — foreign bonds are likely to be seen less and less as "exotic" instruments, and more and more as part of the investment mainstream. Active managers will use foreign bonds tactically, as substitutes for domestic bonds when they manage against a domestic bogey. Or, foreign bonds will be used strategically, as a permanent part of an investor's asset allocation, to diversify across the world's three major currencies to secure the benefits of interest rate risk reduction.

To date it has been more common for investors to choose a domestic bond bogey, and permit their active managers to use foreign bonds tactically to add alpha to that bogey. But in the future as clients become accustomed to seeing foreign bonds in their portfolios broader global bogeys are likely to become more common.

In addition to diversification, the main attraction of foreign bonds is that they expand a manager's investment universe. The information ratio achievable by a manager depends on his skill, on his scope to range over many investment opportunities, and on how correlated the active bets he takes are. Most financial markets are mostly efficient most of the time. Inefficiencies — opportunities to add excess return — develop sporadically and unpredictably. The lesson is clear: for a manager to improve his information ratio, he must search for opportunities anywhere in the world they can be found. A manager must be able to use whatever bond investing style is appropriate for the moment — top down macroeconomic forecasting, bottom up relative value analysis, sector rotation, credit analysis, and convergence trades, to name just a few. A manager with more tools in his toolbox is likely to outperform a competitor who knows how to use only a few, even if that specialist knows how to use his few tools very well. That means neglecting foreign bonds, a whole world of potential opportunities, will almost certainly condemn a manager to the "also ran" category of bond managers in the 21st century.

The Active Decisions in the Selection of Passive Management and Performance Bogeys

Chris P. Dialynas
Managing Director
Pacific Investment Management Company

INTRODUCTION

In this article, the active bond management process will be explored and contrasted with the "passive management" option. We will also examine the differences in index composition. Performance references will be made based exclusively on the index composition and the future economic environment. We will see that successful bond management, whether active or passive, depends on good long-term economic forecasting and a thorough understanding of the mathematical dynamics of fixed income obligations. Likewise, selection of a performance bogey depends on similar considerations as well as the liability structure of the client.

ACTIVE BOND MANAGEMENT

Active management of bond portfolios capitalizes on changing relations among bonds to enhance performance. Volatility in interest rates and changes in the amount of volatility induce divergences in the relative prices between bonds. Since volatility, by definition, allows for opportunity, the fact that during the first half of 1986 and the second half of 1998 active bond managers as a class underperformed the passive indexes in two of the most volatile bond markets in the past 50 years seems counter-intuitive. What went wrong then? What should we expect in the future?

The author expresses his gratitude to his associate at PIMCO, Mark Kiesel, for his considerable contribution, and to the research department at Lehman Brothers for their effort in providing data.

Exhibit 1: LBGC Characteristics

	6/80	6/84	6/89	6/94	6/98	9/98	6/99	12/99
US Government	59.0	72.3	73.3	76.8	70.0	69.7	68.0	66.0
Corporates	41.0	27.7	26.7	23.2	30.0	30.3	32.0	34.0
Duration	5.04	4.02	4.67	4.98	5.46	5.61	5.47	5.30
Yield-to-Maturity	10.25	13.59	8.48	7.12	5.87	5.08	6.29	6.96

Active bond managers each employ their own methods for relative value analysis. Common elements among most managers are historical relations, liquidity considerations, and market segmentation. Market segmentation allegedly creates opportunities, and historical analysis provides the timing cue. The timing of strategic moves is important because there is generally an opportunity cost associated with every strategy. Unfortunately, since the world is in perpetual motion and constant evolution, neither market segmentation nor historical analysis is able to withstand the greater forces of change. Both methods, either separately or jointly, are impotent.

The dramatic changes in interest rates and the volatility of interest rates experienced in the past few decades implies the world is changing and evolving more quickly. Paradoxically, many active managers are using methods voided by volatility to try to capitalize on volatility.

The mistakes of active bond managers have been costly. As a result, a significant move from active to passive (or indexed) management has occurred. Does this move make sense? To understand relative performance differentials between passive and active managers, we need to dissect the active and passive portfolios and reconstruct the macroeconomic circumstances. We will see that composition of the indexes and the circumstances produced by a dynamic combination that was most difficult to beat in 1986 and in the second half of 1998.

MARKET INDEXES

While a variety of bond market indexes are popular today, only two have been notable throughout the present business cycle. The Lehman Brothers Government Corporate (LBGC) bond index was the most popular and the Salomon High Grade Long Term Bond Index was the traditional measure. Since the high-grade index sees little use today, our focus will be primarily on the LBGC index and the Lehman Brothers Aggregate Index (LBAG), which includes mortgage securities and became the industry standard in the late 1980s. We will conclude with a comparison of the different indexes and their respective performance expectations given various interest-rate movements, as well as a review of historical performance comparisons.

The LBGC Index

The LBGC is primarily composed of government and agency securities. The composition of the index is detailed in Exhibit 1. It also includes investment grade corporate bonds.

The LBGC is constructed such that its composition is representative of the relative distribution of securities in the market exclusive of the mortgage market. Because the government issues the vast majority of debt, it is not surprising that the index holds such a high proportion of government securities. It is noteworthy that, after a period of stability, government debt will represent a smaller proportion of the index. The index must, by definition, "buy" the debt. With the exception of some of the 30-year government bonds issued during this period, virtually all of the government and most agency debt held in the index is noncallable. Because of this, between 1980 and 1989 the index has become increasingly call-protected. We will see that the callable/noncallable distribution is an important distinguishing feature between the index and active managers.

The transition from government fiscal deficit to government fiscal surplus during the latter half of the 1990s has reversed the growing influence of noncallable higher-quality debt in the index. In fact, Exhibit 1 demonstrates that, in the time intervals evaluated, the distribution of government debt increased from 59% in 1980 to a peak of 76.8% in 1994. It has subsequently declined to 66% in 1999. Similarly, the percentage of corporate bonds decreased and has subsequently increased. These changes in index character have important implications for asset allocation models and relative performance expectations. The distributional changes in sector composition translate into more subtle changes in index callability, quality and sensitivity to the volatility of interest rates, and the usual increase in volatility that accompanies significant changes in rates.

The LBAG Index

The primary difference between the LBGC and the LBAG is the inclusion of mortgage-related securities in the LBAG. Mortgage-related securities provide the most uncertain distribution of cash flows among conventional fixed income securities and can exhibit substantial negative convexity. The degree of convexity differential between the LBGC and the LBAG is largely determined by the concentration of mortgages below par. The greater the percentage of mortgages below par is, the greater the relative convexity of the LBAG will be. Relative index performance expectations along the yield curve spectrum are sensitive to the relative coupon distribution of mortgages in the market at any point in time. That distribution, reported in Exhibit 2, will largely influence subsequent duration differences between the indexes and, therefore, subsequent performance differences as well.

Exhibit 2: LBAG Characteristics

	6/80	6/84	6/89	6/94	6/98	9/98	6/99	12/99
US Government	53.8	60.6	53.9	53.6	48.2	48.0	43.4	42.0
Corporates	36.0	23.2	19.6	17.7	21.6	21.0	22.0	22.0
Mortgages	10.2	16.2	26.5	28.7	30.2	31.0	34.6	36.0
Duration	5.26	4.24	4.52	4.87	4.47	4.29	4.89	4.92
Yield	10.34	13.78	8.77	7.41	5.88	5.37	6.55	7.16

Exhibit 3: Expected Performance Characteristics of Callable and Noncallable Bonds Under Difference Market Environments

			Direction of Interest Rates		
			Increase in Rates	No Change	Decrease in Rates
Increase		NC	+	+	⊕
		C	Amb+	−	⊖
No Change		NC	i	i	⊕
		C	+	i	⊖
Decrease		NC	−	− i	+Amb
		C	⊕	+	−Amb

Volatility Changes (vertical axis label)

Performance Expectations
Relative to Comparable Duration
Govt. Securities Portfolios

i	Income advantage	⊕	Big winner
⊖	Big loser	−	Loser
Amb	Ambiguous	NC	Noncallable portfolio
+	Winner	C	Callable portfolio

The Salomon Brothers High Grade Index

The Salomon Brothers high-grade, long-term index was a popular bond market bogey during the 1970s and early 1980s. The index is comprised primarily of high-quality, long-term (10 years and longer) corporate bonds. Its reported duration approximated 8.5. The performance of the index was very poor during this period of increasing rates and increasing volatility in interest rates. The rate increases were so great that call options were driven well out of the money, reducing the localized cushioning effect normally associated with rate increases. The increase in volatility was tremendous and directly reduced the value of corporate bonds. Naturally, the high-grade index became perceived as too risky and not representative of the market's distribution of bonds. The LBGC was adopted as the market index. Its shorter duration allowed it to better weather the bear market. The LBAG index is most representative of the market and gained popularity during the latter half of the 1980s. Ironically, the shift to shorter and shorter duration market bogeys coincided with a substantial decline in long-term interest rates.

PERFORMANCE CHARACTERISTICS
OF CALLABLE AND NONCALLABLE BONDS

Exhibit 3 characterizes the expected performance characteristics of callable and noncallable bonds under different market environments. The market environments are described by two parameters: the direction of interest rates and the volatility of rates.

Callable bonds do well in rising rate environments and decreasing volatility environments. Decreases in volatility have the profound direct effect of reducing the value of the call option embedded within the callable bond. Since the bond-holder has effectively sold the option, as its value is reduced by the lower volatility, the total value of the bond increases independent of any interest-rate movement.

Callable bonds do better than noncallable bonds in increasing rate environments because the higher rates cause the option to go out of the money. As the option goes out of the money, its value diminishes and the bond's value increases. The option value decline cushions the bond price decline induced by higher rates, thereby reducing the *market duration* of the bond. The perceived duration of the bond decreases as rates increase, and the callable bond outperforms the noncallable bond, whose duration is relatively inelastic. However, this phenomenon is only true for small changes in interest rates. The callable bond's duration can extend quite substantially with large interest rates causing it to perform very poorly if relative durations are not managed.

Noncallable bonds perform better than callable bonds in decreasing rate and increasing volatility environments. Their effective duration[1] increases in decreasing rate environments because, exclusive of credit-risk considerations, the noncallable bonds are more convex;[2] that is, their rate of price increase outpaces that of the comparable duration callable bonds. As the volatility of interest rates increases, noncallable bonds will command a premium and, because the noncallable bonds are more convex, they will appreciate exclusively because of their relative convexity advantage.

The call features of the bond universe are summarized in Exhibit 4.

Exhibit 4: Call Features of the Bond Universe

Issue Type	Refunding Protection	Call Protection	Refunding Price	Current Call Price
Treasury	Maturity[1]	Maturity	NA	NA
Traditional Agency	Maturity	Maturity	NA	NA
Traditional Industrial	10 Years	None	Premium	Premium
Traditional Utility	5 Years	None	Premium	Premium
Traditional Finance	10 Years[2]	None	Premium	Premium
GNMA Pass-Through	None	None	100	100
FNMA Pass-Through	None	None	100	100
FHLMC PC	None	None	100	100
CMO	None	None	100	100
Title XI	None[3]	None[3]	100[3]	100[3]
PAC CMO	Within Prepayment Range	None Outside Range		
TAC CMO	Within Prepayment Range[4]	None Outside Range	100	100

[1] Some 30-year government bonds were issued with 25 years of call protection.
[2] A decline in receivables may permit an immediate par call.
[3] Default negates any refunding or call protection.
[4] Call protected within a prespecified range of prepayment rates on the collateral.

[1] In this instance, effective duration refers to the expected percentage price change in the market. It is not used here in a volatility adjusted duration context.
[2] Convexity is the measure of how a bond's price change as yields change differs relative to the price change expected from its duration. Convexity is a measure of duration elasticity.

Exhibit 5: Volatility
6-Month Moving Average, 12-Month Standard Deviation of TR
on 30-Year Treasury

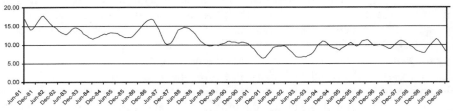

Change in Volatility

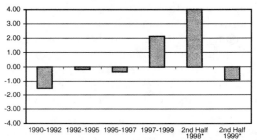

*3-year and 4-year periods are change in Treasury volatility. 2nd Half 1998 and
2nd Half 1999 periods are change in 3-year volatility on 10-year swap rates.

Period	Volatility	Relative Benchmark Performance
1990-1992	Declined	LBAG outperforms LBGC
1992-1995	High volatility in wide range	LBGC outperforms LBAG
1995-1997	Rangebound, volatility of volatility calm	LBAG outperforms LBGC
1997-1999	Increased; sharp pick-up in late '98	LBGC outperforms LBAG
2nd Half 1998	Increased sharply	LBGC outperforms LBAG
2nd Half 1999	Declined	LBAG outperforms LBGC

A LOOK AT MARKET VOLATILITY

It is helpful to examine the volatility of the bond market to make inferences about
performance attributes. Exhibit 5 displays the volatility of the bond market as
described by the 6-month moving average of the 12-month standard deviation of
total return on 30-year U.S. Treasury bonds.

Unprecedented, high volatility had been experienced in the bond market
during the 1980s. Not only was volatility high, but the degree of variation in volatility was high as well. It is *volatility change* that influences the changes in the
value of options, which, in turn, causes relative performance differences between
callable and noncallable portfolios. The 1990s experienced a period of lower absolute volatility but percentage changes in the volatility of volatility remained high.

Exhibit 6: 30-Year Treasury Yields

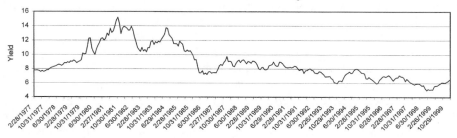

Change in Rates: 30-Year Treasury

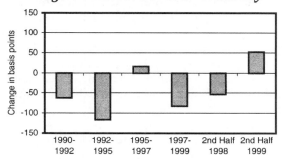

Period	Volatility	Relative Benchmark Performance
1990-1992	Gradual decline	LBAG outperforms LBGC
1992-1995	Lower and volatile	LBGC outperforms LBAG
1995-1997	Modestly higher	LBAG outperforms LBGC
1997-1999	Down	LBGC outperforms LBAG
2nd Half 1998	Sharp fall	LBGC outperforms LBAG
2nd Half 1999	Significant increase	LBAG outperforms LBGC

A LOOK AT INTEREST RATES

The most important piece of the puzzle is the direction of interest rates. Exhibit 6 depicts the movement of rates for the period February 1977 to December 1999. We observe dramatic changes in the absolute level of rates. As such changes occur, the relative values of callable and noncallable bonds change. Lower rates work to the advantage of noncallable bonds, and higher rates to the advantage of callable bonds. With extreme increases in rates, ironically, U.S. government non-callable bonds perform best. This is generally because of the importance of liquidity and credit considerations of corporate bonds (credit risk is also an option the investor sells with the purchase of a corporate bond) and the fact that their duration change is influenced exclusively by interest rates since there are few embedded options. Virtually all callable bonds suffer the joint problem of effective duration variability based upon both interest rates and volatility.

A Look at Recent History

The volatility of the bond market increased from about 4% in 1976 to about 20% in 1982. It averaged about 8% during the 1990s. In the period from 1976 to 1982, the volatility of return on 30-year Treasury bonds ranged between 2% and 20%. In the period from 1982 to 1986, volatility was never less than 7%. Over the complete period from 1976 to 1986, average volatility tripled. Volatility declined substantially after 1986 and hit a low of about 6% in 1992. It ranged from 6% to 12% for the balance of the 1990s. Therefore, as we can see from Exhibit 5, volatility levels rose and then fell, but the volatility of volatility remains. The information from 1976-1986 alone would favor bond portfolios containing the *fewest* callable securities. However, all else equal, we would prefer noncallable portfolios during the period from 1976 to 1982 and callable ones during the 1982-1986 period. Subsequently, all else equal, we would prefer callable portfolios during the dramatic reduction in volatility. In essence, noncallable portfolios "buy" volatility and callable portfolios "sell" volatility.

Yields on long-term government bonds increased from 8% in 1976 to 14.5% in 1982. In the 1982-1986 period, rates dropped from 14.5% to 7.25%. The 1986-1989 period was one within which rates increased from 7.25% to 8.625%. The range in rates from 1976 to 1982 was 8% to 14.5%. The range for the period was 7.25% to 14.5%. Rates changed from 7.25% to 10% during the latter period. We would naively expect portfolios containing callable securities to do best during the first period, portfolios containing noncallable bonds to do best during the middle period, and portfolios containing callable bonds to excel during the latter period. Of course, these inferences assume constant conditions in credit, volatility, and yield-curve shape.

Thirty-year interest rates subsequently fell to 6% in 1993 but increased substantially to 8% in 1994. The 1994 rate increase was coincident with a dramatic increase in volatility from about 6% to 12% — a 100% increase. Interest rates subsequently fell to a low of about 5% in 1998 but rebounded to 6½% in 1999 — a 30% increase representing a price change of −20 points on a 30-year bond.

The performance differences between callable and noncallable bonds for these periods are summarized in Exhibit 7.

A Review of the Second Half of 1998

The latter half of 1998 is one of the most interesting intervals in recent bond market history. Exhibit 8 provides a review of the vital statistics of the Lehman Brothers Aggregate Index and Lehman Brothers Government/Corporate Index.

Exhibit 7: Historical Review: LBAG versus LBGC

1976-1982

Interest-rate change from 8% to 14.5% moved the call features out of the money. However, the change in interest rates was so large that the duration of callable bonds increased substantially. This, combined with a substantial increase in volatility, led to the outperformance of noncallable portfolios.

1982-1986

The steep decline in interest rates and the virtually unchanged level of high volatility favored noncallable over callable portfolios by a wide margin. The options became in the money and shortened the duration of the callable portfolio, revealing the dramatic effects of negative convexity.

1976-1986

While interest rates declined only modestly, the tremendous increase in volatility served to make the option more valuable. A countervailing effect of callable issues' income advantage did not offset their decrease in principal value created by the option over short investment horizons.

1986-1989

During the first half of this period, the increase in interest rates swamped the increase in volatility. Callable bonds outperformed noncallables during this subperiod. During the second half of the period rates declined and volatility declined. The drop in rates dominated and callables performed best. There were ambiguous results for the full period. Rates increased modestly and volatility was largely unchanged.

1990-1992

Intermediate interest rates declined gradually throughout the period. Despite the Gulf War and a U.S. recession in 1991, volatility declined causing callable bonds to outperform noncallable bonds. The relatively range-bound path of interest rates helped the LBAG outperform the LBGC during the period. While the Fed Funds rate was lowered 525 basis points from 8.25% in June of 1990 to 3.00% in September of 1992, 10-year Treasury rates remained primarily in a 6¾% to 8¼% range. As a result, mortgage repayments remained benign. Fortunately, the LBAG started the decade with solid convexity due to a mortgage pool that was the least negatively convex in June of 1990 than at any point in the 1990s (65% of the GNMA mortgage universe traded at or below par).

1992-1995

Interest rates moved down and then up and then down again in this highly volatile period which was marked by a U.S. recovery and the Fed's aggressive monetary stance against inflation. By June of 1992, only 3.5% of the GNMA mortgage universe was priced at or below par. The negative convexity of the mortgage universe during this timeframe caused the LBGC to sharply outperform the LBAG as interest rates fell and volatility increased from 1992-1993. Throughout 1994, the Fed was vigilant in its fight against inflation causing volatility to remain high. Long-term interest rates moved up in 1994 but then fell in 1995 once inflation was no longer a threat to the U.S. economy. The LBGC continued to lead the LBAG near the end of this period due to its longer duration.

1995-1997

Ten-year interest rates remained range-bound between 5½% and 6½%. Volatility remained calm. The LBAG outperformed the LBGC due to the range-bound nature of interest rates during the period and a more positively convex mortgage universe (by June of 1996, 52% of the GNMA mortgage universe was priced at or below par).

Exhibit 7 (Continued)

1997-1999

This period was marked by the Asian Contagion, the IMF's bailout of Russia, the LTCM crisis, and a liquidity scare which lead to the decade's low in interest rates, rising risk premiums, soaring volatility, and widening credit spreads. Mortgage prepayments surged and the mortgage universe became its most negatively convex ever in the decade with only 3% of the GNMA mortgage universe trading at or below par by December of 1998. The Fed lowered the Fed Funds rate to 4.75% and 10-year Treasury rates approached 4½% by the end of 1998. The LBGC outperformed the LBAG throughout this period due to a sharp rise in volatility.

1999

Interest rates moved up sharply throughout 1999 as the Fed took away its 75bp of easing in 1998 by tightening 75bp in 1999, taking the Fed Funds rate back up to 5.50%. Ten-year Treasury rates soared almost 2% to end the decade at 6.44%. While interest rates rose, volatility came down. Fears of a Y2K induced liquidity crush were contained by the Fed's aggressive actions. The LBAG outperformed the LBGC due to a shorter duration and callable bonds outperformed noncallable bonds as volatility declined.

Exhibit 8: Statistics of Lehman Brothers Indexes to 1998
Lehman Brothers Aggregate Index

	Duration	% Government	% Corporate	% Mortgage	% Callable	% ≤ 7-Yr.	% Mortgages Below Par
6/98	4.47	48.2	21.6	30.2	8.1	80.9	17.2
9/98	4.29	43.3	17.5	39.2	8.0	79.8	3.0
12/98	4.44	46.3	23.0	30.7	7.9	79.6	6.4

Lehman Brothers Government/Corporate Index

	Duration	% Government	% Corporate	% Mortgage	% Callable	OAD % ≤ 7-Yr.	% Mortgages Below Par
6/98	5.46	70.0	30.0	0.0	11.8	72.3	0.0
9/98	5.61	69.7	30.3	0.0	11.6	70.5	0.0
12/98	5.58	68.0	32.0	0.0	11.6	70.2	0.0

	30-Yr.	10-Yr.	Change In Volatility	Change In
6/98-9/98	−66 bp	−104 bp	+20 bp*	−55 bp Steeper
9/98-12/98	+136 bp	+24 bp	+380 bp*	−146 bp Flatter

* Change in UDS swaption volatility (3-yr. Option on 10-yr. Swap rates)

Performance

	6/98-9/98	9/98-12/98	6/98-12/98
LBAG	4.23	0.34	4.58
LBGC	4.95	0.13	5.08
LBGC - LBAG	+72 bp	−21 bp	+50 bp

A series of events, including a Russian default on its debt and the disso-
lution of Long-Term Capital Management Hedge Fund, resulted in a tremendous
increase in volatility and incredible decline in interest rates and a coincident but
unprecedented increase in liquidity premiums. This set of circumstances favored
the LBGC over the LBAG in all respects except yield curve exposure. However,
the combination of substantially lower rates and substantial increased volatility
swamped the yield curve effort. For example, MBS underperformed Treasuries by
−180 basis points in the third quarter of 1998 alone as interest rates fell and prepayments surged. The call-protected LBGC outperformed the LBAG by 1.01%
through 9/98 and by 0.78% through 12/98.

The Exclusion of Treasury Inflation Protected Securities

Treasury Inflation Protected Securities (TIPS) are bonds issued by the U.S. government. TIPS provide a fixed coupon that is added to the rate of inflation to render a static return expectation. In 1999, these securities represented 7% of the U.S.
Treasury's issuance of debt. They were originally included in the Lehman Brothers
indexes and subsequently excluded. Presumably, this exclusion is a result of the
difficulty in computation of durations. This, however, is not a robust reason. Arguably, the calculation of the duration of mortgage securities is even more uncertain.

A consistent application of the standard that the index contains those
investment grade bonds which are supplied in the market would suggest that TIPS
should be included in the indexes. It seems appropriate to include these securities
and extraordinary to exclude them. For our purposes, it is important to understand
that the addition of these securities to the indexes would alter the investment
dynamics. The indexes would:

1. increase direct exposure to real interest rates
2. increase quality
3. increase call protection
4. become less volatile
5. cause the risk parameter of the LBGC and the LBAG to diverge

The inclusion of TIPS, while complicating the dynamics, would be an appropriate
and necessary choice given the volume of supply of these securities.

The Budget Surplus Trend

The recent trend toward continued fiscal budget surpluses will have a profound
influence on the risk parameters of the respective indexes. The LBGC index will
contain a lower percentage of government securities. The LBGC will become less
call-protected and its quality will diminish both absolutely and relative to the
LBAG. We should expect the LBGC to become dominated by corporate securities
and to find that its volatility sensitivity merge with the LBAG and its credit sensitivity to diverge from the LBAG.

THE IMPLICIT FORECASTS OF
VOLATILITY AND INTEREST RATES

Most active bond managers are sector managers, or sector rotators. They hold portfolios composed of a high proportion of nongovernment securities. These portfolios are short the call options or, viewed alternatively, long portfolios of callable bonds. Few managers seem to have anticipated the magnitude of the change in interest rates and the profound increase in realized volatility that occurred during the 1980s. Both of these forecast errors were important detractors from performance. Even those managers who correctly forecasted the changes in interest rates terribly underestimated the combined impact of increased volatility and declining rates on the value of the option. Thus, their selection of bonds was inconsistent with their forecast.

Bond management necessarily requires an interest-rate forecast, a volatility forecast, and a set of analytical models that calculate the future value of individual securities and portfolios of securities based upon those forecasts. It is the confluence of volatility movement and interest rate movement that largely affects bond values.[3]

Similarly, the decision to move from active to passive management, or from passive to active, is necessarily predicated upon an implicit forecast of interest rates, volatility, and perceived investment manager consciousness. Moreover, the choice of index as a bogey for active managers or as a source of investment value contains within it an implicit forecast of both interest rates and volatility. Bogey selection may be a plan sponsor's most important decision. The plan sponsor should be careful interpreting statistical data. The pack mentality in the industry may distort the fundamental economics of investment risk.

The choice of indexes as of this writing (long government rates at 6.75%) is a choice, as is generally the case, of buying or selling convexity and duration. Convex portfolios, such as the LBGC, hold a high percentage of noncallable bonds. Portfolios with little convexity, such as the Lehman Brothers Aggregate Index (LBAG) hold many callable bonds. Thus, the durations of convex portfolios change inversely with market rates, whereas the durations of nonconvex portfolios may, perversely, change in the same direction as rates.

Simply stated, in today's world, the LBGC is a more convex portfolio than the LBAG.[4] However, the fact that a high proportion of mortgages securities in the LBAG are at a discounted price provides for a reasonably convex portfolio over relatively short interest rate changes. Moreover, the percentage of corporate bonds in the LBGC index has increased rendering it less convex. The approxi-

---

[3] See Chris P. Dialynas and David H. Edington, "Bond Yield Spreads Revisited," *Journal of Portfolio Management* (Fall 1992), for a rigorous discussion.

[4] The importance of coupon concentration in the relative performance of these two indexes is explained in the next section.

mate 10% duration differential between the two indexes is an important issue. As such, the LBGC yields less than the LBAG and is much more sensitive to changes in interest rates. However, if rates decline substantially, the LBAG index will underperform the LBGC by a significant margin because its duration will not increase and may actually decrease and it starts with a lower duration. The LBAG will outperform the LBGC in a mild bear market but will run into problems in an extreme bear market within which volatility also increases. Exhibit 9 compares the expected performance characteristics of the LBGC and LBAG.

Implicit Forecasts

The LBAG portfolio seeks yield in place of convexity. The style is one that does well in stable yield environments. In Exhibit 10, we can observe relative bogey performance. The LBAG index is the higher-yielding, less convex index. The respective duration proxies are missing so it is hard to be completely precise. However, for the first half of 1986, second half of 1988, first half of 1993, first half of 1995, and the second half of 1998, volatilities increased dramatically. We would expect, duration assumed constant, the LBAG to underperform the LBGC and, in fact, it happened.

Portfolios described in terms of both duration and convexity have greater explanatory power because risk parameters are more fully defined. Implicit within a move to passive management and the selection of a bogey is both a volatility and an interest-rate forecast. The move to passive management reinforces Say's Law, which holds that supply creates its own demand. Passive investment portfolios have done well in spite of their main investment criterion: Buy that which is produced independent of price or value considerations. Passive management relies upon the market forces to ensure that asset values are appropriately priced. Passive, narrow indexes, such as the LBGC, have even done very well at times because of the circumstances — radically lower rates and increased volatility, both of which benefited call-protected portfolios. The past is prologue: today's investment choice will be judged by tomorrow's circumstances.

Exhibit 9: Comparison of the Expected Performance of the LBGC and LBAG

Interest Rates	UNCH	Rise	Fall	UNCH	UNCH	Rise	Rise	Fall	Fall
Volatility	UNCH	UNCH	UNCH	Rises	Falls	Rises	Falls	Rises	Falls
Index That Performs Best	LBAG	LBAG	LBGC	LBGC	LBAG	Ambiguous (LBAG)*	LBAG	LBGC	Ambiguous (LBGC)*

* Interest-rate movements are usually the prevailing force. The index in parentheses would therefore dominate unless the interest-rate movement was very small and the volatility movement great.

Exhibit 10: Index Performance (%) (6-Month Periods)

End Date	LBGC	LBAG	AG-GC Difference	Ratio GC to AG%
Dec-78	0.99	1.26	0.27	78.57
Jun-79	6.62	6.50	−0.12	101.85
Dec-79	−4.05	−4.29	−0.24	94.41
Jun-80	8.22	8.44	0.22	97.39
Dec-80	−4.77	−5.29	−0.52	90.17
Jun-81	0.70	0.15	−0.55	466.67
Dec-81	6.51	6.09	−0.42	106.90
Jun-82	6.41	6.84	0.43	93.71
Dec-82	23.20	24.13	0.93	96.15
Jun-83	4.82	4.91	0.09	98.17
Dec-83	3.03	3.29	0.26	92.10
Jun-84	−1.02	−1.68	−0.66	60.71
Dec-84	16.42	17.11	0.69	95.97
Jun-85	10.56	10.95	0.39	96.44
Dec-85	9.72	10.05	0.33	96.72
Dec-86	5.14	5.70	0.56	90.18
Jun-87	−0.44	−0.17	0.27	258.82
Dec-87	2.74	2.93	0.19	93.52
Jun-88	4.60	4.98	0.38	92.37
Dec-88	2.85	2.77	−0.08	102.89
Jun-89	9.23	9.20	−0.03	100.33
Dec-89	4.58	4.89	0.31	93.66
Jun-90	2.42	2.82	0.40	85.82
Dec-90	5.73	5.96	0.23	96.14
Jun-91	4.25	4.47	0.22	95.08
Dec-91	11.38	11.04	−0.34	103.08
Jun-92	2.49	2.71	0.22	91.88
Dec-92	4.87	4.57	−0.30	106.58
Jun-93	7.79	6.89	−0.90	113.06
Dec-93	3.01	2.67	−0.34	112.73
Jun-94	−4.34	−3.87	0.47	112.14
Dec-94	0.66	0.99	0.33	66.67
Jun-95	11.80	11.44	−0.36	103.15
Dec-95	6.66	6.31	−0.35	105.55
Jun-96	−1.88	−1.21	0.67	155.37
Dec-96	4.88	4.90	0.02	99.59
Jun-97	2.74	3.09	0.35	88.67
Dec-97	6.83	6.36	−0.47	107.39
Jun-98	4.17	3.93	−0.24	106.11
Dec-98	5.09	4.58	−0.51	111.14
Jun-99	−2.28	−1.37	0.91	166.42

Exhibit 11: Index Returns (%) (2-Year Periods)

End Date	LBGC	LBAG	AG-GC Difference	Ratio GC To AG%
Jun-80	11.81	11.92	0.11	99.08
Jun-82	8.70	7.51	−1.19	115.85
Jun-84	31.45	32.25	0.80	97.52
Jun-86	55.29	55.94	0.65	98.84
Jun-88	12.50	14.02	1.52	89.16
Jun-90	20.33	21.03	0.70	96.67
Jun-92	25.84	26.24	0.40	98.48
Jun-94	11.50	10.33	−1.17	111.33
Jun-96	18.01	18.19	0.18	99.01
Jun-98	19.91	19.55	−0.36	101.84
Oct-99	2.16	2.94	0.78	73.47

The compositional and structural differences between the narrow and aggregate indexes are much more similar today than they were in September 1998. Previously, while compositionally distinct, their structural similarities caused highly correlated performance results. (See Exhibits 10 and 11.) The performance characteristics of the two indexes differed to a degree that had been previously experienced infrequently. In fact, the aggregate index, with very few securities below par (3%), was at the risk of experiencing a gradual, unpredictable lengthening in duration as the high percentage of low-duration premium mortgages are prepaid and refinanced with current coupon longer duration mortgages. This lengthening would occur quite independently of any changes in interest rates and as long as rates do not drop considerably. A big drop in rates will most likely cause the LBAG duration to decrease, and its performance would lag behind the performance of the LBGC substantially. The differential would probably exceed most market participants' expectations.

In fact, since September 1998, interest rates on 10-year bonds have risen from 5% to 6.25% in June 2000. The LBAG duration lengthened from 4.29 to approximately 5. Meanwhile, the duration of the LBGC dropped to 5.4 from 5.61. Therefore, as of this writing (June 2000), absent very large changes in interest rates, we should expect the two indexes to perform very similarly. Duration differences between the bogeys will dominate performance considerations if interest rate changes are large.

Those who are required to select a performance bogey for their fund have a difficult choice. The bogey performs the role of directing the risk of the assets. The choice involves a trade-off between a bogey that (1) replicates the proportional distribution of bonds in the market, (2) has risk characteristics complementary to the liability structure of the assets, and (3) has a relatively neutral market bias associated with it. Unfortunately, no bogey satisfies all of these requirements, and the trade-offs can be costly. It is important to fully understand what the bogey represents to ensure the robustness of the asset allocation decision.

Exhibit 12: Percentage of Outstanding GNMAs Priced at or Below Par

Date	Percentage
6/78	96.8
6/80	97.4
6/82	97.1
6/84	95.7
6/86	34.9
6/88	83.0
6/90	65.1
6/92	3.5
6/94	58.7
6/96	52.2
6/98	13.1
6/90	37.1
12/99	77.7

The choices are difficult. Ultimately, correct macroeconomic forecasts will dominate the active/passive choice. Will volatility increase or diminish and when? Will rates go up or down and when? What influences volatility? How do interest rates and volatility changes trade off? When does the volatility/interest-rate forecast favor one index over the other? These are the tough questions you should be asking your active manager or your passive index.

THE IMPORTANCE OF COUPON CONCENTRATION IN RELATIVE LBGC/LBAG PERFORMANCE

The LBAG and LBGC have exhibited a high historical correlation. The high correlation was violated during the second half of 1998. It is important to understand why the high correlation existed and why it diverges to better understand tomorrow's expected correlation.

It was previously noted that the major distinction between the LBGC and the LBAG is the inclusion of mortgages in the LBAG. As such, we must determine whether these securities' options were at the money, in the money, or out of the money to establish their effect on portfolio convexity. The simplest framework we can utilize to evaluate the effect on convexity is a pricing framework. Mortgages selling at a discount exhibit positive convexity and higher durations, whereas other mortgages exhibit low or negative convexity and lower durations.

Exhibit 12 shows the percentage of outstanding GNMAs priced at or below par for selected time periods. We observe that in 1982 all mortgages were at par or a discount. In 1984, most mortgages were at a discount. The situation differed in June 1986 in that very few mortgages were priced at a discount. The bear market into 1988 caused most mortgages to be at a discount. The bull market in 1998 caused most mortgages to be at a premium. As of this writing, most mortgages are at a discount but only a modest discount. A bear market will cause more mortgages to be discounted and improve the convexity of the index.

Exhibit 13 provides combined coupon distribution data of GNMA, FHLMC, and FNMA mortgage pass-throughs. The greater percentage of discount mortgage securities will cause the durations of the two indexes to converge.

In a modest bull market, the LBAG index duration will decline and it will increase in a bear market. A radical bull or bear market in interest rates will magnify these phenomenons. The opposite response will occur within the LBGC index. As such, at prevailing yield levels, the relative performance differentials between the indexes will be meaningful given some meaningful level of interest rate volatility.

Lower yields will increase performance differentials as index character diverges; higher yields will mitigate expected performance differentials because index character will merge.

THE IMPORTANCE OF CHANGES IN THE SHAPE OF YIELD CURVE

Changing yield-curve shapes represent the other important first-order determinant of relative performance differentials. The indices are represented by various distributional holdings along the yield curve. Distributional differences between the LBGC and the LBAG,[5] and bond managers' portfolios will be important when yield-curve shapes are frequently variable and/or when changes in shape are of substantial magnitude. Generally speaking, the LBAG index contains a set of cash flows heavily weighted in the intermediate portion of the yield curve relative to the LBGC. Therefore, all other factors equal, yield curve steepening favors the LBAG and flattening yield curves favor the LBGC. Yield-curve shape changes also change expected returns relative to those expected *a priori* because of the effects upon duration, call and put option values, prepayment behavior, and other more subtle effects.

Exhibit 13: GNMA Pass-Through Prices

Coupon	6/30/98	9/30/98	12/31/98	% Of Market
5.5	97.47	97.25	96.63	0.35%
6.0	97.47	100.34	99.13	6.79%
6.5	99.78	102.16	101.00	23.43%
7.0	101.56	103.16	102.31	27.98%
7.5	102.72	103.59	103.00	19.16%
8.0	103.65	104.16	103.88	12.33%
8.5	105.56	105.63	105.88	3.64%
9.0	107.06	106.63	106.72	3.37%

Prices of 10-Year Treasury Securities

	6/30/98	9/30/98	12/31/98
Treasury	101.34	109.36	100.80

[5] Changes in the shape of the yield curve directly affect mortgage values. Coupon distribution relative to prevailing interest rates will influence the LBAG asset distribution along the yield curve.

The yield-curve effect is not included in this analysis. The difficulty in bond investment analysis is extremely complex when yield-curve shape changes are included. These complexities, including the potential correlation between interest rates and volatility, are beyond the scope of this article. Professional bond portfolio managers must understand these uncertain linkages if they hope to succeed.

INDEX CONSCIOUSNESS

The extraordinary increased volatility of interest rates during the 1970s and 1980s and the reduction in volatility in the 1990s has resulted in considerable volatility in returns. Durational differences between portfolios result in substantially different returns when interest rates are volatile. The historical return differences between the LBGC and the Salomon High Grade Index illustrate this point. Many market participants were apparently surprised by the amount of price volatility that their bond portfolios experienced in the 1960s and 1970s. In an effort to control portfolio return variability relative to the "market," some bond managers have adopted portfolio constraints wherein the durational risk relative to the market index is bound. The movement to this new investment strategy helped control variability but nullifies the relative advantages achievable through expert macroeconomic analysis and interest-rate forecasting. The movement to this policy is an admission of a flawed investment theory, risk aversion, and/or an uncertain conviction in forecasting of quantitative capability. This article has emphasized the importance of the contribution of good interest-rate and volatility forecasts with consistent period-dependent asset selection.

SOME IMPORTANT MISCELLANEOUS COMMENTS ABOUT INDEXES

The well-educated community requires and understands rigorous modern finance statistical methods. A compelling risk/reward statistical argument resulted in the transition from the Long Salomon Bond Index to the LBGC just after interest rates hit a historical high. At the time, the high interest rates caused, oddly enough, the durational difference (risk) of long bonds and 10-year bonds to approach each other. The subsequent transition to the LBAG occurred shortly thereafter, resulting in a further reduction in duration and call protection at a time when interest rates were very high.

Presently, there is a movement to a "core-plus" concept represented by the Lehman Universal Index (LUNV). This concept more closely coincides with the end of one of the most remarkable growth decades in U.S. history. A move to the LUNV implies a further reduction in: (1) duration, (2) call protection, and (3) quality. I remain skeptical of the "historically blind" but, empirically rigorous, approach of the herd. A study of financial history over longer periods of time reveals gradual transitions to greater risk followed by abrupt periods of wealth destruction and risk aversion. It is because all agents in the process — especially plan sponsors and investment managers — are judged over relatively short time periods. However, that decision-making is dominated by studies subjugated by recent data. These short periods are incongruent with the life of the plans.

Important macroeconomic and microeconomic phenomena result from the choices clients such as plan sponsors make with respect to bogeys. These are described in Exhibit 14.

The herd move from one bogey to another initially results in shifting demand curves for a sector that is soon followed by a shift in the supply curve. The demand curve shift reinforces the asset allocation realignment as prices of the newly added asset class are bid up. When more and more of the herd enter, assets are bid up ever more, further reinforcing the original statistical analysis and creating a more powerful updated statistical study. Eventually, supply catches up to the fresh demand, resulting in a more leveraged economy and a reduced quality of plan assets. Present U.S. Treasury debt retirement will accelerate the transition to lower quality holdings.

Exhibit 14: Important Macroeconomic and Microeconomic Phenomena

	Micro	Macro
1. Salomon Long Index → LBGC	Substitution of issuance of intermediate debt in lieu of longer bonds.	More risky capital structure
2. LBGC → LBAG	Financing of mortgage industry from banking industry to longer-term investors. Securitization of asset markets.	Cheaper cost of debt to consumers. Results in more robust housing industry, consumer demand, and household leverage. Potential moral hazard risk in loan origination.
3. LBAG → LUNV	Financing of emerging market and high yield debt market.	Reduces cost of debt to highly leveraged producers. Encourages more debt and leverage. Increases risk of plan assets and reduces value of bond portfolio as deflationary hedge.

Active Portfolio Management Against an Index

Rich Gordon
Director
Fixed-Income Research
First Union Securities, Inc.

Lang Gibson
Vice President
Fixed-Income Research
First Union Securities, Inc.

INTRODUCTION

There are essentially two types of index managers. The most common category is the set of insurance companies, pension funds, foundations and endowments that consider their liabilities (or spending profiles for the latter two) in choosing their market indices. This category of investor has two benchmarks — liabilities and market indices — against which performance is judged. The other category of index manager is asset managers who have no liabilities. These investors only have to outperform the market index. Nevertheless, as evidenced by managed portfolio averages, most institutional investors underperform their market indices. In this article, we evaluate the three broad methods of fixed-income portfolio management used by both types of index managers.

THE THREE BROAD METHODS OF PORTFOLIO MANAGEMENT

There are three broad methods of managing a portfolio against a benchmark that can be employed. Investors typically manage to their own personal strengths. To the extent investors have the staff and means to understand all the markets, they may use a combination of all three methods. The two most common strategic initiatives are duration trading and relative value sector rotation. An emerging method is spread management, which attempts to time exposure to spreads.

Duration Management

At its core, duration management is the purest form of market-directional trading. Some investors have an intuitive feel for guessing the short-term direction of interest rates. Markets invariably get oversold or overbought in the short term. Some portfolio managers are able to consistently exploit these conditions. In a cross-sector portfolio, the spread sectors are constructed so as to mirror as closely as possible the structure of the market index. Duration is then adjusted by the trading of Treasurys or, in some cases, benchmark agency debentures. Duration management can also be used as the primary driver of returns over a longer time frame. Under this method, duration adjustments versus the benchmarks are made infrequently, usually no more than several times a year, but in greater increments. The effective duration of the portfolio may be significantly shorter or longer than that of the benchmark index. The portfolio manager depends on his or her ability to guess the longer-term general trend of interest rates, usually based on Federal Reserve Board actions and the interpretation of macroeconomic data. Most important, the government market remains a relatively liquid market, and therefore the strategy is executable in application as well as in theory.

Relative Value Sector Rotation

Money managers with specific industry expertise commonly use relative value sector rotation. The sector rotator feels far more comfortable discerning relative value in specific securities or sectors rather than guessing the short or intermediate direction of interest rates. The sector rotator typically positions a cross-sector portfolio that is duration and curve neutral. The manager overweights cheap sectors and underweights rich sectors (i.e., mortgage-backed securities (MBS) versus corporates) or trades relative value intrasector (i.e., autos versus equipment). Portfolio managers with specific credit expertise often look to buy undervalued story bonds further down the credit spectrum, which will be unwound when the story plays out over time.

On a risk-adjusted basis, sector rotation theoretically has the greater appeal. The effects of new issuance and investor psychology do, in fact, cause dislocation and create pockets of value, which can be exploited by savvy and nimble investors. However, deteriorating liquidity in the fixed-income markets poses a serious threat to the portfolio manager who relies on sector rotation to enhance returns. The problem has become particularly acute in the corporate bond market. Lack of transparency, wide bid/ask spreads and inconsistent execution have increased risk factors underlying the strategy because liquidity can all but evaporate at precisely the times when technical indicators dictate that certain trades or rotations are appropriate.

Spread Management

We believe a third method of general portfolio management is increasing in importance and in time will become as common as the first two strategies described above. We call this third strategy spread management. It essentially consists of going long spreads (overweighting) before spreads contract and going short spreads (underweighting) before they widen. Swap spreads then become the proxy for the overall general movement of spreads in the cash fixed-income markets. Under a spread management portfolio philosophy, a cross-sector portfolio is set up to be essentially duration and curve neutral. Return enhancement is accomplished by shifting allocations between the most liquid spread sectors and duration-matched Treasurys, and vice versa. In spread sectors, the most liquid markets are usually considered to be agency debentures (benchmarks and reference notes), card and auto asset-backed securities (ABS), and commercial mortgage-backed securities (CMBS). Following are several reasons why we believe this method of management will become increasingly predominant:

- *Spread sectors are more tightly correlated with swaps and each other than with Treasurys.* Exhibit 1 summarizes what most observers have known for more than two years. (We discuss the results reported in this exhibit in more detail later in this article.) The correlations of spread products are much higher versus swap yields and other spread products than versus Treasury yields. Many analysts have persuasively argued that because of these increasing correlations, swaps have become the key analytical benchmark, as opposed to Treasurys. The problem for a cross-sector portfolio manager is Treasurys remain a substantial sector and are often the single largest discrete fixed-income sector in which a manager is involved. That characteristic makes them, de facto, a benchmark (obviously, swaps do not figure into market indices). If it is the case that spread products correlate tightly with swaps and other spread sectors, and poorly with Treasurys, then it is important to be overweighted to spread products when swap spreads are generally tightening, and underweighted when swap spreads are generally widening. The choice of spread sector becomes far less important because it can only bring minor performance enhancement. The major enhancement comes from being on the right side of swap spread movements, as there is greater volatility and play in the swap yield/Treasury yield basis than the intersector yield basis.

- *Liquidity has become a paramount factor in portfolio management.* Since 1998, it has become clear to investors that shorting liquidity as a broad strategy has become difficult and risky. Obviously, lack of liquidity can impede rotation timing. However, lack of liquidity raises a more insidious issue, that of the lack of transparency of information. To properly assess the richness/cheapness of spread sectors relative to each other, a portfolio manager needs to get accurate pricing on bellwether issues. Absent this information, decision making becomes increasingly risky and random. We believe that by properly modeling the swap basis, an investor can guess with reasonable accuracy the general direction of swap spread movements. One can essentially trade spreads by trading bullet agencies or similarly liquid spread products versus Treasurys. Not only are swaps and agencies highly fungible but they are also the two most liquid sectors of the dollar fixed-income markets. We believe this type of portfolio strategy will become more prevalent, owing to the confluence of factors described above and because the Treasury and agency markets are liquid enough to allow execution of this broad strategy.

DURATION MANAGEMENT

Many managers refuse to be tied to a rigid standard of duration-neutral portfolio management. Particularly when an investor is not tied to managing against the duration of an institution's liabilities, he or she is free to take views on the slope and direction of interest rates. In Exhibits 2 and 3, we show simplified examples of how a manager uses intermediate and long Treasurys and agencies to manage the duration of his portfolio. In this example, the manager maintains neutral weightings to the Lehman Aggregate Index's spread sectors (see the appendix for an overview of the performance and makeup of the Lehman Aggregate from January 1, 2000 to October 20, 2000). Alternatively, the manager could alter the duration profile with bonds in a spread sector to achieve similar results. In reality, the duration manager takes more complicated views on the shape of the curve. For instance, in late October's market, a manager might have built a barbell along the Treasury curve, speculating that technical factors would continue to drive down long Treasury rates and short Treasury rates would back up, betting the economy will have a soft as opposed to a hard landing.

Exhibit 1: Quarterly R-Squares for Five-Year Spread Product Yields Through 10/20/00*

Spread Sector	Versus			Improvement over Treasurys	
	Swap	Agency	Treasury	Swap	Agency
Agencies	0.99	1.00	0.90	0.09	0.10
Cards (AAA)	0.99	0.99	0.90	0.09	0.09
CMBS (AAA)	0.98	0.98	0.86	0.12	0.13
Banks (A)	0.97	0.95	0.93	0.04	0.02
Home Equities (AAA)	0.95	0.95	0.82	0.13	0.13
Agency Collateral	0.94	0.96	0.80	0.15	0.16
Whole-Loan CMOs (AAA)	0.94	0.93	0.90	0.03	0.03
CMO PACs (AAA)	0.91	0.91	0.91	0.00	−0.01
Agency CMO SEQs (AAA)	0.87	0.86	0.93	−0.05	−0.07

CMBS: Commercial mortgage-backed securities; CMO: Collateralized mortgage obligation; PACs: Planned amortization classes; SEQs: Sequentials.
* Sorted by swap R-squares.

Source: First Union Securities, Inc.

Exhibit 2: Duration Management with Treasurys

Scenario	Long Treasury % of Total	Annualized Return	Return Pickup	Duration	Return/ Duration
1	0%	9.1%	−0.94%	4.1	2.2
2	25%	9.8%	−0.27%	4.6	2.1
3-Base	*35%*	*10.1%*	*0.00%*	*4.8*	*2.1*
4	50%	10.5%	0.40%	5.1	2.0
5	75%	11.1%	1.07%	5.7	2.0
6	100%	11.8%	1.74%	6.2	1.9

Source: First Union Securities, Inc.

Exhibit 3: Duration Management with Agencies

Scenario	Long Agency % of Total	Annualized Return	Return Pickup	Duration	Return/ Duration
1	0%	10.0%	−0.11%	4.7	2.1
2-Base	*16%*	*10.1%*	*0.00%*	*4.8*	*2.1*
3	25%	10.1%	0.07%	4.9	2.1
4	50%	10.3%	0.25%	5.1	2.0
5	75%	10.5%	0.43%	5.3	2.0
6	100%	10.7%	0.61%	5.5	1.9

Source: First Union Securities, Inc.

Exhibit 2 shows the impact of varying allocations between long and intermediate Treasurys. Scenario 3, the base case, represents the current 35% allocation to long Treasurys as a percent of all Treasurys in the Aggregate as of September 29, 2000. The remaining five scenarios show various allocations to long Treasurys in increments of 25 percentage points. In all scenarios, allocations to spread sectors are unaltered. Due to the outperformance of long Treasurys over the year, larger allocations to long Treasurys boost the portfolio's returns significantly and detract from the portfolio's risk-adjusted performance marginally. For instance, if 100% of Treasurys are allocated to the long Treasury subsector, there is a 174 bps improvement in annualized return and 0.2 subtraction in the return/duration ratio. Furthermore, the portfolio's duration increases 1.4. By contrast, if all Treasurys are allocated to the intermediate sector, the portfolio's return declines 94 bps and the duration falls 0.7.

When we use agencies to manage the portfolio's duration and maintain neutral weightings to the remaining five sectors, we get less exaggerated results. The primary reason for the minimal impact on duration and return is that agencies represent only slightly more than one-third of Treasurys in the Aggregate. An additional reason agencies are not as ideal as Treasurys for duration management is that agencies include a spread component. For this reason, managers often use agencies for spread management, our third asset allocation methodology. Exhibit 3 shows the impact of varying the allocation between long and intermediate agencies. The portfolio return pickup ranges between negative 11 bps and 61 bps as the duration swings from 4.7 to 5.5.

Exhibit 4: Intersector Rotation

Scenario	ABS	MBS	Agencies	CMBS	Corporate	Annual Return	Return Pickup	Duration	Return/ Duration
1	17.3%	18.0%	0.0%	1.6%	35.0%	9.6%	−0.56%	4.83	1.98
2-Base	1.7%	34.6%	10.2%	1.6%	23.9%	10.1%	0.00%	4.83	2.10
3	10.0%	40.0%	10.2%	5.0%	6.7%	10.4%	0.28%	4.54	2.29
4	15.0%	36.7%	10.2%	10.0%	0.0%	10.6%	0.46%	4.46	2.37
5	10.0%	23.5%	28.4%	10.0%	0.0%	10.6%	0.51%	4.62	2.30

ABS: Asset-backed securities; CMBS: Commercial mortgage-backed securities; MBS: Mortgage-backed securities.

Source: First Union Securities, Inc.

Exhibit 5: Intrasector Rotation

Scenario	Autos	Cards	Home Equities	RRB	MH	CMBS	Annual Return	Return Pickup	Duration	Return/ Duration
1-Base	7.4%	24.2%	5.4%	7.3%	7.4%	48.3%	10.0%	0.00%	4.12	2.61
2	10.0%	10.0%	10.0%	10.0%	10.0%	50.0%	10.0%	−0.02%	4.17	2.60
3	0.0%	31.0%	0.0%	30.0%	0.0%	39.0%	10.2%	0.23%	4.12	2.56
4	28.5%	0.0%	0.0%	0.0%	0.0%	71.5%	9.9%	−0.10%	4.12	2.82
5	0.0%	48.5%	0.0%	0.0%	0.0%	51.5%	10.1%	0.12%	4.12	2.57

CMBS: Commercial mortgage-backed securities; MH: Manufactured housing; RRB: Rate-reduction bond.

Source: First Union Securities, Inc.

RELATIVE VALUE SECTOR ROTATION

Many portfolio managers choose their benchmarks in accordance with an institution's liabilities. Duration is the major variable that goes into the market index selection. Particularly for outside managers, there is some apprehension to tinker with the duration of the assets, which have already been defined by the liabilities. Consequently, these managers choose to keep the portfolio's duration and curve position fairly neutral to the market index and trade relative value between spread sectors. In Exhibits 4 and 5, we show the two major sector rotation strategies. In practice, managers also trade relative value between specific bonds, a third strategy. We will demonstrate that index outperformance is most obtainable using intersector rotation as opposed to intrasector rotation because correlations are lower in the former.

Exhibit 4 shows five intersector rotation strategies. We show hypothetical alterations to the Aggregate's base case spread sector weightings holding a neutral weighting to Treasurys. As corporates have the longest duration of all spread sectors, decreasing weightings in corporates implies a lower portfolio duration. Therefore, scenarios 3-5 have slightly lower durations than the Aggregate. In reality, a pure-sector rotator would adjust durations within spread sectors to maintain a neutral bias to the duration and curve shape. In Scenario 1, we increase our weighting to corporates and keep duration constant by balancing allocations to ABS and MBS. The result is a 56 bps annualized reduction from the Aggregate's year-to-date return. Clearly, a strategy of overweighting corporates would have been detrimental so far this year. Scenarios 3-5 slowly pump up the portfolio return by significantly underweighting corporates. Because durations also decline, the return/duration ratios improve considerably from 2.10 in the base case to 2.37 in Scenario 4. In Scenario 3, the manager earns an additional 28 bps by substantially underweighting corporates and increasing weightings in all sectors but agencies. By exiting corporates altogether, the pickup is 46 bps (Scenario 4). In Scenario 5, the manager increases his allocation to agencies and picks up 51 bps.

To illustrate intrasector rotation strategies, we picked a portfolio benchmarked against ABS and commercial mortgage-backed securities (CMBS). In Exhibit 5, Scenario 1 represents the Aggregate's implied weighting for such a portfolio; 48.3% of the portfolio is CMBS, whereas all five ABS sectors represent the remaining 51.7%. The return/duration ratio has meaningful improvement of 0.54 over that of the Aggregate due to the decline in duration. In Scenario 2, the manager chooses to weight 50% in CMBS and equally weight the remaining 50% in the five ABS sectors. As expected, the impact on performance is negligible, because cards — which represent almost half the ABS sector — have similar risk-adjusted return characteristics to the median performance of the ABS sector. Scenarios 3-5 represent different intrasector bets that maintain durations equivalent to the base case. The allocation in Scenario 3 reflects the manager's preference for cards, rate-reduction bonds and CMBS. As these three subsectors have relatively favorable risk-adjusted return characteristics, the portfolio's return is improved 23 bps. Scenario 4 shows 10 bps underperformance using a duration barbell strategy of CMBS and autos. Finally, Scenario 5 shows 12 bps improvement in return investing in only cards and CMBS. The high correlation between the subsectors means it is more difficult to outperform using intrasector rotation versus intersector rotation.

SPREAD MANAGEMENT

As in the sector rotation method, spread management implies a duration and curve neutral portfolio. The difference is that proxies for general credit spreads are used instead of securities in the numerous underlying subsectors. With spread products increasingly correlated with swaps and agencies, these instruments are often used to express a view on the direction of spreads. Furthermore, because these tools are significantly more liquid, the strategy allows for lower transaction costs as the manager enters and exits the market. Similar to the duration manager expressing a view on the direction of interest rates, the spread manager expresses a view on the general direction of credit spreads. Market timing can account for the major portion of performance relative to the index. In addition to transaction cost savings, the spread manager requires substantially less industry expertise. Consequently, he has more time to focus on market-timing strategies and the implications of general macroeconomic data.

Exhibit 6: Spread Management with Treasurys and Agencies

Scenario	Treasurys	Agencies	Annual Return	Return Pick-up	Duration	Return/ Duration
1	0.0%	100.0%	10.2%	−0.50%	4.56	2.23
2	25.0%	75.0%	10.6%	−0.06%	4.84	2.20
3-Base	*28.1%*	*71.9%*	*10.7%*	*0.00%*	*4.87*	*2.19*
4	50.0%	50.0%	11.1%	0.39%	5.12	2.16
5	75.0%	25.0%	11.5%	0.83%	5.40	2.13
6	100.0%	0.0%	12.0%	1.28%	5.68	2.11

Source: First Union Securities, Inc.

In Exhibit 6, we show portfolios composed of only Treasurys and agencies. Agencies replace all of the Aggregate's spread sectors, which account for 71.9% of the Aggregate. The year-to-date result is a base-case portfolio return of 10.7% and a duration of 4.87. In Scenario 1, agencies make up the entire portfolio. This 100% allocation to spreads results in a 50 bps subtraction from the base case. Over 2000, the dislocation of the Treasury market from the general fixed-income market made the allocation to Treasurys vis-à-vis spread products a key driver of portfolio performance. However, Scenario 1 has a higher risk-adjusted return, because duration is minimized. In Scenario 4, the allocation to Treasurys is almost double that in the base case. The result is a 39 bps return pickup. A portfolio fully indexed to the Aggregate's Treasury sector would have experienced a 128 bps pickup over the base-case portfolio of Treasurys and agencies.

Swaps and Agencies as a Spread Management Tool

The spread management method depends greatly on the high correlation of spread product to swaps, agencies and any other highly liquid fixed-income securities (e.g., cards, autos, CMBS) the manager may use. Of course, the highest correlations are found in the higher-rated, more liquid spread sectors. However, the efficacy of spread management is unaltered if the manager desires to go down in credit where correlations are weaker. The spread manager would simply use a combination of the most liquid spread product and lower-rated, less liquid bonds. Therefore, the manager could put on "liquidity barbells" if his view is that less liquid sectors have been oversold. Most large investors are permitted to invest in agency debentures, CMBS and ABS. Many can also use swaps and eurodollar futures contracts, which permit the manager to leverage his or her views on the direction of spreads.

Exhibit 1 provides regression data demonstrating the higher year-to-date R-squares between five-year spread products and swaps and agencies vis-à-vis Treasurys. The regressions are calculated from quarterly yield changes staggered weekly to create a sample size of 45.

As indicated by the 0.99 R-square, swaps and agencies are virtually fungible. Except for agency collateralized mortgage obligation (CMO) sequentials, the

R-square with both swaps and agencies is comfortably above 0.90 in all sectors. As expected, ABS, CMBS and bank paper have the highest correlation with swaps and agencies. In these sectors, the R-square improvement of swaps over Treasurys ranges between 0.04 and 0.12. The four MBS sectors have R-squares with swaps ranging between 0.87 and 0.94. The R-square for agency CMO sequentials is relatively low due to their average-life variability versus other structured products. Treasurys actually have the best R-square with agency CMO sequentials and PACs, mostly because CMOs are still priced off the Treasury curve.

CONCLUSION

Few portfolios are truly passively managed against a market index, despite the evidence that the average manager underperforms the market index. However, the range of active portfolio management strategies is wide and depends on a number of exogenous factors. For example, the sophistication and size of the manager's staff are the primary determinants of the complexity of a manager's asset allocation strategy. Clearly, industry regulations, such as ERISA requirements and NAIC guidelines, define the range of permissible investments. However, the combination of the three basic styles presented here — duration, sector rotation and spread — primarily depends on whether the assets are benchmarked against liabilities. If the manager does not manage against liabilities, there is considerably more freedom to manage his or her portfolio. By contrast, managers who must consider the duration profile of an institution's liabilities in their choice of market indices are more constrained. Such managers will favor either sector rotation or spread management because the liabilities more or less define the portfolio's duration profile.

Intersector rotation is more effective than intrasector rotation strategies because there are lower correlations between sectors than bonds within a sector. On the other hand, intrasector rotation requires specialized knowledge on fewer securities. Spread management is an evolving style that requires the least specific security knowledge. The spread manager can focus more on market-timing opportunities for the general direction of credit spreads. Clearly, market timing is riskier, but the rewards can be great. It is the increasingly stronger correlations between all spread products that make spread management appealing. Furthermore, the superior liquidity and relatively low transaction costs of swaps, agencies and certain structured products minimizes spread market dislocation risk and transaction costs.

APPENDIX: YEAR-TO-DATE FIXED-INCOME INDEX PERFORMANCE

To illustrate our three portfolio management methods, we use the most broadly followed Lehman Aggregate Index. Lehman Brothers has been a pioneer in the development of broad-based fixed-income market indices for more than 25 years. Lehman's indices are all rule-based, which means inclusion in the index depends on satisfying clearly specified criteria, and represent the fixed-income market as a whole. For these reasons, roughly 70% of index users•mostly asset managers, plan sponsors and insurance companies•choose this benchmark against which to measure their performance.

Exhibit 7 shows the annualized risk-adjusted performance of the Aggregate's six major sectors year to date as of October 20, 2000. Weightings and durations are as of September 29, 2000. The annualized return for the Aggregate is 10.1%, and the duration was 4.8 as of September 29, 2000. However, using weightings as of September 29, 2000, the return is 10.0%. The six sectors are presented in descending order according to the return/duration ratio, a measure of risk-adjusted performance. Three of the six major sectors — MBS, Treasurys and corporates — represent 86.6% of the Aggregate. Agencies' 10.2% weighting is the fastest-growing portion of the index and is increasingly catching up with Treasurys as the large Treasury buyback programs continue. ABS and CMBS represent only 1.7% and 1.6%, respectively, of the Aggregate. However, managers active in these sectors normally concentrate between 6% and 15% of their portfolios in these sectors. On a year-to-date basis, ABS and MBS have the highest risk-adjusted returns with return/duration ratios of 2.92 and 2.63, respectively. Treasurys and CMBS have the highest annualized returns of 12.0% and 10.8%, respectively. The outperformance of long Treasurys spurred by the Treasury buybacks and falling swap yields have been the key drivers behind this performance.

Exhibit 7: Lehman Aggregate Major Sectors[1]

Sector	Return/ Duration	Annualized Return[2]	Duration[3]	Weighting[3]
ABS	2.92	9.3%	3.2	1.7%
MBS	2.63	10.1%	3.8	34.6%
Agency	2.23	10.2%	4.6	10.2%
CMBS	2.12	10.8%	5.1	1.6%
Treasury	2.11	12.0%	5.7	28.1%
Corporate	1.37	7.5%	5.5	23.9%
Total	2.07	10.0%	4.8	100.0%

ABS: Asset-backed securities; CMBS: Commercial mortgage-backed securities; MBS: Mortgage-backed securities.
[1] Sorted by the return/duration ratio in descending order.
[2] Total returns year-to-date Oct. 20, 2000.
[3] Sector weightings/durations as of Sept. 29, 2000.
Source: Lehman Brothers Holdings Inc. and First Union Securities, Inc.

Exhibit 8: Lehman Aggregate Subsectors 1

Sector	Subsector	Return/ Duration	Annualized Return[2]	Duration[3]	Weighting[3]
ABS	Autos	4.6	7.5%	1.6	0.2%
	Cards	3.1	9.4%	3.1	0.8%
	Home Equities	3.0	8.7%	2.9	0.2%
	Rate-Reduction Bonds	2.6	10.4%	3.9	0.2%
	Manufactured Housing	2.1	9.7%	4.6	0.2%
MBS	Convertible Balloons	3.4	8.3%	2.4	0.3%
	GNMA 15-Year	3.1	9.2%	3.0	0.3%
	Convertible 15-Year	3.0	9.2%	3.1	5.4%
	Convertible 20-Year	2.7	10.2%	3.8	0.6%
	GNMA 30-Year	2.6	10.5%	4.0	8.1%
	Convertible 30-Year	2.5	10.2%	4.0	19.9%
Agency	Intermediate Agencies	2.7	9.1%	3.4	8.6%
	Long Agencies	1.5	16.2%	11.2	1.6%
CMBS	CMBS	2.1	10.8%	5.1	1.6%
Treasury	Intermediate Treasurys	2.9	8.9%	3.1	18.3%
	Long Treasurys	1.8	18.4%	10.5	9.8%
Corporate	Other	1.8	9.2%	5.1	3.3%
	Financials	1.6	7.4%	4.5	7.6%
	Utilities	1.5	8.8%	5.7	2.0%
	Industrials	1.1	6.8%	6.2	11.0%
Total		2.1	10.1%	4.8	100.0%

ABS: Asset-backed securities; CMBS: Commercial mortgage-backed securities; MBS: Mortgage-backed securities.
[1] Sorted by the return/duration ratio within each major sector.
[2] Total returns year-to-date Oct. 20, 2000.
[3] Sector weightings/durations as of Sept. 29, 2000.
Source: Lehman Brothers Holdings Inc. and First Union Securities, Inc.

Exhibit 8 breaks out the Aggregate's six major sectors into 20 subsectors. Within each major sector, subsectors are ranked in descending order on a risk-adjusted basis. Within ABS, autos have the highest risk-adjusted return, and rate-reduction bonds have the highest year-to-date return. Within MBS, conventional balloons have the highest risk-adjusted return, and 30-year Ginnie Maes have the highest return. In agencies, the long agency subsector performed considerably better than intermediate agencies. The former has a duration of 11.2 and an annualized return of 16.2%, whereas the latter has a duration of 3.4 and a return of 9.1%. In Treasurys, we see even better performance in the longer-duration subsector. Long Treasurys have a duration of 10.5 and an annualized return of 18.4%; whereas intermediate Treasurys have a duration of 3.1 and an annualized return of 8.9%. In corporates, utilities and the other category had good performance but were outweighed by the poor returns in financial and industrial paper.

Exhibit 9: Unweighted FUSI Structured Product Index[1]

Subsector	Sector	Return/Duration	Return[2]	Duration[3]	Weighting
Autos	ABS	5.2	7.2%	1.4	10%
Equipment	ABS	4.9	7.0%	1.4	10%
Cards	ABS	4.2	7.7%	1.8	10%
Callables	Agencies	2.7	10.7%	3.9	10%
Collateral	MBS	2.6	11.3%	4.4	10%
CMBS	CMBS	2.5	12.3%	5.0	10%
CMO PACs	MBS	2.3	8.7%	3.8	10%
Home Equities	ABS	2.0	8.4%	4.2	10%
Whole-Loan CMOs	MBS	1.7	10.2%	6.1	10%
CMO SEQs	MBS	1.6	9.2%	5.7	10%
Totals		3.0	9.3%	3.8	100%

ABS: Asset-backed securities; CMBS: Commercial mortgage-backed securities; CMO: Collateralized mortgage obligation; MBS: Mortgage-backed securities; PACs: Planned amortization classes; SEQs: Sequentials.
[1] Sorted by the return/duration ratio in descending order.
[2] Total returns year-to-date Oct. 20, 2000.
[3] Sector durations as of Oct. 20, 2000.
Source: First Union Securities, Inc. (FUSI).

For comparison purposes, Exhibit 9 presents January 1 to October 20, 2000 performance results for First Union Securities, Inc.'s (FUSI) Structured Product Index (SPI). Although there is some overlap, the SPI's focus on structured products produces five sectors excluded from the Aggregate — equipment, callable agencies, CMO PACs, whole-loan CMOs and CMO sequentials. Mostly due to the SPI's exclusion of Treasurys and agencies, the SPI's annualized return of 9.3% is 0.8 percentage point less than the Aggregate's return.

ABS Portfolio Management

Karen Weaver, CFA
Managing Director
Global Head of Securitization Research
Deutsche Banc Alex. Brown

Stephanie Whitten
Associate
Deutsche Banc Alex. Brown

Eugene Xu, Ph.D.
Director
Deutsche Banc Alex. Brown

INTRODUCTION

Asset-backed securities (ABS) are securities backed by a pool of assets, typically loans or accounts receivable originated by banks, specialty finance companies, or other credit providers. ABS have grown from a niche market product in the 1980s to a mainstay of today's fixed income portfolios. ABS have one of the broadest investor bases of any spread product. Investors employ ABS to suit a spectrum of needs — from a cash or Treasury surrogate in their most liquid forms, to a yield enhancer in their more esoteric ones. Here, after an overview of some of the common ABS investor types, we'll discuss constraints, guidelines and risks in ABS investing, as well as relative value assessment and methods used to monitor and measure ABS performance.

INVESTOR TYPES AND STRATEGIES

Investment advisors and money managers often benchmark the performance of their portfolios against an index, such as the Lehman Aggregate or Salomon Broad Index. "Indexers" are those who seek to match the index's performance. Definitionally, a portfolio constructed to exactly mimic the index will perform in line with the index (i.e., no better and no worse). Other portfolio managers seek to *beat* an index's performance. Portfolio managers typically try to outperform an index by one of several ways. They can underweight portions of the index they think are rich, or overweight portions they think are cheap. They may even buy something that is not in the index because they expect it to perform better than the index. In addition, a portfolio manager may choose a longer or shorter duration than the index, based on a belief about the direction of interest rates. Lastly, a portfolio manager might chose a higher or lower credit profile than the index against which he or she is measured, based on a belief about credit spreads and/or the economy.

In any event, the starting point is a portfolio that mimics the index. Portfolio managers either try to match the index with the starting portfolio, or make adjustments to it in hopes that, by placing slightly different bets, they will outperform the index benchmark. For example, ABS currently represent a very small fraction of most fixed-income indices (e.g., 2% or less). Many argue that ABS are underrepresented in the indices, in part due to the quirks of the index guidelines relating to minimum deal and/or tranche sizes. As a result, most managers who use ABS are substantially overweighted (e.g., with 8 or 10% or more of their portfolios in ABS versus the 2% in the index). Historically, such an overweighting has proven beneficial.

Because performance is measured on a total return basis, these investors may trade actively and are concerned not just about credit, but also about price performance. They often invest in liquid ABS with AAA ratings, although money managers are active across the spectrum.

Federal agencies, like FNMA and FHLMC, use their expertise in the mortgage market to assess mortgage-related ABS, e.g., home equities and manufactured housing. They are one of the largest investors in this sector. The yields on these mortgage-related ABS products are typically higher than the agencies' traditional mortgage investments. Because the agencies' own credit quality is so strong, they are especially important buyers in market crises, because they can still fund themselves at attractive levels and use the proceeds to buy what they perceive to be "cheap" ABS.

FNMA and FHLMC also run what are referred to as "liquidity portfolios." As the name might suggest, these portfolios are used as a place to hold cash and cash substitutes for general purposes. In their liquidity portfolios, FNMA and FHLMC are unlikely to hold mortgage-related assets, and generally buy large, highly-rated on-the-run ABS deals, especially credit cards and autos.

Insurance companies and *pension funds* invest to meet a stream of future liabilities (death benefits, annuity benefits, pension benefits, etc.) Generally these investors try to "match" the assets they buy to their liabilities. If they "cash flow match," they simply buy assets with cash flows scheduled to be paid when the liability is due. For example, assume an insurance company actuarially estimates that it will pay out $1 million per quarter in death benefits. The cash flow matched portfolio would include assets with quarterly sinking fund payments of $1 million. This approach to selecting investments is difficult and cost prohibitive, not to mention that liability cash flows can sometimes be dynamic and generally involve some estimation error. For this reason, most insurance companies and pension funds do not use cash flow matching. They either "horizon match" or "immunize." "Immunization," refers to matching the duration of their investments (assets) with the duration of their products (liabilities). "Horizon matching" is a hybrid approach, whereby the first few years of liabilities are cash flow matched, with the remaining years of liabilities immunized.

Both insurance companies and pension funds tend to be "buy-and-hold" investors. That is, once they find an investment that suits their liabilities, they are less likely to actively trade. Their main objective is to find the best relative value that funds their liabilities and, in the case of insurance companies, allows them to sell competitive products.

As the ABS market has matured, the product has evolved to, in floater form, a cash surrogate and, in fixed rate form, often a Treasury surrogate. Many *corporate treasuries* and *monetary authorities* use ABS in this way. The extraordinary credit quality and liquidity of the most commoditized ABS (credit card floaters especially) provides a higher yielding substitute for other liquid assets. Corporate treasuries and monetary authorities usually buy ABS product in maturities of five years and in.

The goal of a *leveraged fund* is to maximize the difference between the yield on its portfolio and its funding cost. A significant portion of a leveraged fund's portfolio is usually invested in ABS because of their spread relative to other investment options. Leveraged funds invest mostly in investment-grade securities, and historically the credit risk of their portfolios has been, on average, AA. The portfolios are fully hedged to protect against interest rate and currency related risks. The high quality and liquidity of the underlying assets, diversification, and the funds' equity capital enable the funds to issue AAA paper to fund themselves. Leveraged funds raise financing through the issuance of rated commercial paper (CP), medium-term notes (MTNs), and bonds.

Securities lenders lend out clients' investment portfolios, typically portfolios of Treasuries and agencies. The cash they receive is then invested in accordance with guidelines agreed upon with the clients, and the returns are shared with the clients. These guidelines typically stipulate very high credit quality and maturities of 2 to 3 years (though in some cases as long as 5 years). In the early stages of the ABS market, these guidelines were stipulated in legal final maturity terms. This initially precluded the use of many ABS products. In recent years, most investors have come to accept the expected final maturity as the true final maturity. Today, ABS floaters are very popular with securities lenders. Because the clients of securities lenders generally preclude securities lenders from taking credit risk, the only alternatives to ABS floaters are highly rated bank floating-rate notes (FRNs). As long as floating ABS continue to offer a pick-up to these alternatives, securities lenders will continue to be a major force, particularly in floater ABS inside of 3 years.

Hedge funds are partnerships that involve speculative investing. They generally are yield-driven, which makes them willing to go out the curve, down in credit, and buy esoteric asset types. In addition, hedge funds use leverage and so their ability to finance ABS at attractive levels is paramount. Hedge funds are most active in ABS floaters with maturities of 5 years or longer, and are primarily interested in lower-rated tranches.

Asset-backed commercial paper (ABCP) conduit facilities buy ABS for various reasons. Some conduits are considered arbitrage programs and participate in spread investing. These conduits purchase assets, including ABS and other debt securities, that meet a number of criteria to be considered eligible under various capital monitoring, hedging, and other calculations. The assets are bought with the proceeds raised by the issuance of ABCP and/or MTNs. The pool of assets securitizes the conduits' issuance, and hedge contracts are used to limit the change in the value of the pool. Conduits can also purchase hard-to-place tranches (i.e., subordinate classes) of asset-backed deals, funding them temporarily until another investor can be found.

Companies who issue *guaranteed investment contracts* (GICs) often use ABS for "cash flow matching." A GIC is a secured obligation of a limited liability company that pays holders a specified rate of return over the life of the contract. The GICs can be secured by an investment portfolio, sometimes containing ABS, that is hedged to match the investment contract's liability.

Some ABS investors seek to maximize their total return on investments. This "total return" strategy is concerned not just with income, but price performance as well. These investors are opportunistic and may speculate on price movements by purchasing bonds with the intent of flipping them for a profit. This strategy obviously is used when it is anticipated that an issue will be in great demand. Many investors who do not trade per se will still mark-to-market their portfolios in order to measure performance.

CONSTRAINTS AND GUIDELINES

Portfolio managers all have different constraints impacting their use of ABS. These constraints are often dictated externally, by industry or government regulation, by prospectus or by client directive. When selecting securities for investment, portfolio managers must consider questions with regard to diversification, duration, credit risk, liquidity, and cash flow variability, among others.

Some investors (insurance companies, for example) must take into consideration the duration of their liabilities, and when investing select ABS whose own durations roughly match their liabilities. Other types of portfolio managers, like investment advisors, try to match an index and choose ABS with durations comparable to their benchmark, thereby attempting to use their portfolios to achieve results similar to, or better than, the index.

Portfolio managers who are able to take a certain degree of credit risk can make credit plays by collateral, originator or tranche. By investing in ABS secured by sub-prime collateral or in subordinate pieces, portfolio managers can often achieve a significant spread pick-up versus competing products. Moreover, ABS issued by out-of-favor or financially weak seller/servicers offer spread pick-ups.

Exhibit 1: Types of Constraints and Guidelines in ABS Portfolios

Characteristic	Comment
Exposure Limits	By issuer, by wrapper and by sector
Duration	Versus an index or versus a liability
Credit Quality	Weighted average or absolute minimum
Form of Offering	Public, Private, 144A, Reg. S
Size of Each Investment	Minimum size to efficiently manage portfolio and for trading liquidity
Sovereign Risk Limitations	Some structures ameliorate exposure
Currency	Both at the collateral level and the bond level (if swapped)
Bullet vs. Amortizers	Z-spread analysis; systems issues
Risk Weighting	Varies in jurisdictions
Asset Type	Based on perceived risk/reward
Tax Issues	Withholding tax can apply for some investors in junior tranches
Senior vs. Subordinated	Subordinated bonds not always ERISA-eligible and are less liquid
Hybrid (corporate guaranty bonds, credit-linked notes)	Some portfolio managers prefer "pure" ABS
Legal jurisdiction	"Bankruptcy remoteness" and other bedrock legal ABS concepts are not universal
Financing	Repo-able or not, and at what level?

Source: DB Global Markets Research

The need for liquidity factors into a portfolio manager's investment decisions. Does a manager need to have the ability to raise cash quickly, or does he operate under a "buy-and-hold" strategy? Corporate treasurers, for example, often invest in credit card floaters as a cash substitute. On the other hand, insurance companies are more willing to buy less liquid paper because their long-lived liabilities do not require them to actively trade.

Portfolio managers vary in their ability and/or willingness to accept cash flow variability. Broadly speaking, there are two types of cash flow variability. Cash flow variability that is correlated with interest rates (for example, the risk that cash will be returned early if rates fall and a mortgage borrower refinances) is more difficult to manage than random cash flow variability. Interest rate-related variability is more damaging because the portfolio manager gets money back early to reinvest at a time when rates are low. Investors typically require additional spread to take on cash flow variability, particularly if the variability is correlated to interest rate movements.

Of course, portfolio managers are sensitive to their customers. Some customers may be very averse to headline or credit risk, therefore a portfolio manager's investments may be limited to AAA-rated, plain-vanilla ABS. The size of a portfolio manager's staff also plays a role in dictating ABS selected for investment. A portfolio management team with a large staff devoted to analyzing, monitoring, and trading ABS can more easily invest in complex, off-the-run securities than can a smaller team.

Exhibit 1 provides a summary of the types of constraints and guidelines in ABS portfolios.

IDENTIFYING ABS RISKS

The risks in ABS investing, as with investing in any spread product, include *fundamental risks* as well as *technical risks*. "Technicals" are largely supply and demand factors and do not directly impact the securitized collateral, whereas the "fundamentals" largely relate to collateral performance. Fundamentals can be broken up into credit quality and cash flow considerations.

Fundamentals

The most obvious credit quality fundamentals are *collateral risk* and *structural protection*. Although the rating agencies perform extensive analysis when assigning a rating, portfolio managers should perform their own analyses as well. To assess collateral risk, a portfolio manager should look at past performance of previous deals. For deals secured by installment loans (auto loans and leases, home equity and manufactured housing loans, and student loans), *static pool analysis* gives the best indication of past loss experience. Static pool analysis isolates a particular pool of collateral and plots the cumulative net loss experience (gross losses or defaults net of recoveries) over time. This is preferable to an "income statement" approach, whereby losses are expressed simply as a percent of the outstanding portfolio, because rapid portfolio growth can mask losses. The past performance should then be compared to future expectations to see if the expectations are reasonable. However, comparisons must take into account differences in underwriting, servicing, and the economy.

The structural protection in a transaction, or its "credit enhancement," protects ABS investors from losses on the underlying collateral and thus allows the securities to achieve credit ratings as high as AAA. Credit enhancement is determined by the rating agencies such that the collateral pool can experience many multiples of the expected level of losses before the senior bonds experience any loss of principal. The higher the rating, the greater the multiple of expected losses the bond can withstand. Credit enhancement can take many forms, including subordinated notes or certificates, cash reserve funds, overcollateralization, excess servicing, and surety bonds. The riskier the underlying collateral, the greater the credit enhancement required to earn a given rating.

Although the cornerstone premise of ABS has been bankruptcy-remoteness (i.e., achieving structures whose creditworthiness is separate and insulated from the seller/servicer's credit risk), the seller/servicer can have both a technical and a fundamental impact. On the fundamental side, deteriorating quality and stability of the seller/servicer can translate into *operational risk* and negatively impact collateral performance. When assessing servicer risk, portfolio managers should consider the servicer's operations and financial health. A wrapped transaction, for example, is insulated from servicer impact on fundamentals, since the wrap provider backs up the collateral performance, but the bond might still trade poorly if the seller/servicer falters (technical risk). The seller/servicer has the greatest impact on fundamentals for servicing-intensive assets, for unusual assets (where back-up servicers are hard to find), and in subordinated investments (because the servicer's skills can have a bigger impact for investors who are disproportionately exposed to collateral losses).

ABS structures do contemplate the transfer of servicing in the event the original servicer is unable to fulfill its duties. A specified stream of funds is allocated in a transaction's waterfall that is sized by the rating agencies to be sufficient to attract another party to service. Oftentimes arrangements are made to employ the Trustee as a back-up servicer. If the Trustee is not acting as back-up servicer, the Trustee will usually control a bidding process to sell the servicing rights of a troubled portfolio to a new servicer. Portfolio managers should also perform due diligence with respect to a servicer's operations (size, employee training, technology, specialization) and financial statements.

Surety bonds (or wraps) are bond insurance policies purchased from third parties, which guarantee the timely payment of interest and the ultimate full recovery of principal. Wraps are common in home equity, manufactured housing, and sub-prime auto ABS. Wrapped ABS are subject to surety provider risk, a unique type of credit risk. In some ways the business risk of wrappers is similar to a bank's in that they invest in a portfolio of credits. However, unlike a bank, or any corporate credit for that matter, their credit rating is their livelihood. A financial guarantor that loses its AAA rating is, arguably, out of business. For this reason, the interests of management are uniquely aligned with the interests of AAA bond investors. Although the possibility of a downgrade does exist, a wrapper's credit risk is tied to a diversified portfolio of not just ABS, but other credits as well, and that risk is further buffered by their substantial capital.

Prior to 1998, downgrades in the ABS world were very rare (analysis of corporate downgrades shows that, in the past decade, anywhere from 5% to 15% of the corporate universe was downgraded annually), and downgrades due to collateral performance were virtually unheard of. In fact, an analysis of downgrades (as measured by the Moody's rated universe) shows that there were only seven collateral-related ABS downgrades for the entire period 1986-1997. Collateral-related downgrades increased to 45 in 1998, and downgrades for external reasons (servicer or guarantor downgrades) numbered 115.[1] Taken together, ABS downgrades as a percentage of the ABS universe amounted to 3.20%[2] in 1998 versus 0.45% on average in the prior 5 years. The marked increase in collateral-related downgrades in 1998 was primarily due to the performance of sub-prime auto ABS and CBOs with emerging market content. For 1999, the percentage of downgrades amounted to 1.61%. There is significant precedent for major ABS issuers to protect their programs prior to a rating agency action. Issuers have protected imperiled ABS transactions prior to a downgrade by adding/removing collateral, adding credit enhancement, buying out loans and transferring servicing. Exhibit 2 outlines ABS downgrade activity by year.

---

[1] Each tranche downgraded equals one downgrade. An issuer may have multiple series and each series may have multiple tranches which may be downgraded multiple times. Historically, the number of tranches per downgrade averages 1.8.

[2] This is calculated by dividing the total number of downgrades by the difference of ratings outstanding as of January 1 and ½ of ratings withdrawn. By subtracting ½ of ratings withdrawn, Moody's assumes the ratings were withdrawn (i.e., the issues matured) at a steady pace throughout the year.

Exhibit 2: Moody's ABS Downgrade Activity by Year (Based on Number of Ratings)

Year	Ratings O/S as of Jan. 1	Downgrade Reason		Total Downgrades		Comments
		Collateral	External	Number	Percentage*	
1986	4	0	0	0	0.00%	
1987	25	0	0	0	0.00%	
1988	63	0	15	15	25.21%	13 GMAC deals due to GM downgrade (corporate guarantee structure) and 2 Household deals due to downgrade of third party enhancer
1989	126	0	0	0	0.00%	
1990	194	0	13	13	7.05%	All related to downgrade of third party enhancer
1991	357	0	12	12	3.53%	All related to downgrade of third party enhancer
1992	528	2	30	32	6.30%	2 classes of a CBO downgraded for collateral. All others related to downgrade of third party enhancer
1993	726	0	12	12	1.76%	All related to downgrade of third party enhancer
1994	1,009	0	3	3	0.31%	All related to downgrade of third party enhancer
1995	1,551	1	0	1	0.07%	Long Beach subordinated home equity bond downgraded due to California housing market
1996	2,361	0	0	0	0.00%	
1997	3,524	4	0	4	0.12%	3 separate subprime auto deals (one deal had 2 tranches downgraded)
1998	5,320	45	115	160	3.20%	101 of the external-downgrade incidents related to two waves of Green Tree corporate downgrades. 17 of the collateral-related downgrades related to CBOs, primarily those with emerging markets exposure. The remaining 29 collateral-related downgrades were related mainly to subprime autos and charged-off credit cards
1999	6,892	98	8	106	1.61%	The 8 external downgrades related to Oakwood corporate downgrades. 28 and 15 of the collateral-related downgrades were due to poor performance of UCFC and BankAmerica MH transactions, respectively. 26 were CBO-related and the remainder were related to subprime auto, home equity, charged-off credit card, and other MH deals

* Calculated by dividing the total number of downgrades by the difference of ratings outstanding as of January 1 and ½ of ratings withdrawn. By subtracting ½ of ratings withdrawn, Moody's assumes the ratings were withdrawn (i.e., the issues matured) at a steady pace throughout the year

Source: Compiled from Moody's Investors Service, "Rating Changes in the U.S. Asset-Backed Securities Market: 1999 Second Half Update," July 14, 2000

Cash flow risks include *early amortization/payout risk, prepay and extension risk, cap risk*, and *basis risk*. Although rare (only two credit card pay-outs, totalling 0.2% of outstandings, have occurred in the market's 15-year history), early amortization/payout risk is particularly applicable to revolvers, such as credit card ABS. Early amortization occurs when the revolving period ends ahead of schedule and the transaction begins to pay out early. Generally, early amortization/payout can happen when there is negative excess spread in the transaction, when the seller's interest falls below the minimum amount required, when the seller/servicer goes bankrupt or declares insolvency or when there is a breach of contract. The early amortization/payout feature is actually a protection for investors, acting as a *de facto* credit "put." If a portfolio is deteriorating, principal collections should not be reinvested in new receivables, but should be returned to the investor to reduce the risk of loss. Issuers can (and have) taken steps to prevent early amortization.

Mortgage-related ABS (home equity and manufactured housing) entail some degree of prepayment risk. When interest rates fall, home equity borrowers can refinance into a new, lower rate loan and prepay their old loan — and the investor is left to find an alternate investment in a lower yield environment. The extent of this risk (i.e., borrowers' sensitivity to changes in interest rates) varies considerably among different types of collateral and at different points in time. The yield paid to investors in mortgage-related ABS compensates for this risk (and its corollary, extension risk, when rates back up).

Although cap risk is not common in ABS, it does exist in some transactions, usually in the home equity and manufactured housing sectors. Types of caps found in ABS include *available funds caps*[3] and *nominal caps*. When investing in capped ABS, portfolio managers must understand the caps and price them in. Portfolio managers should also be aware of basis risk, occurring in transactions where the underlying collateral pays off one benchmark but the securities issued pay off another benchmark. Credit enhancement and/or the use of swaps usually mitigate basis risk.

Technicals

While not directly affecting a deal's underlying collateral, technical risks should not be discounted. Technicals include supply and demand, headline risk and liquidity. Supply and demand affect prices in all markets. As it relates to ABS, investors try to understand supply and demand dynamics for ABS and competing products in order to predict price movements. On the supply side, there are seasonal patterns to consider (quarter-ends have traditionally been a popular time for issuers who wish to maximize quarterly gain-on-sale earnings). More broadly,

---

[3] Available funds caps, often found in student loan ABS, are caps tied to the blended average coupon of the loans, less servicing fees. To the extent that the cap is less than the bond coupon in any given period, an interest shortfall results, and is recouped in future periods, usually from excess spread.

ABS supply forecasts are a function of the growth of the underlying collateral (i.e., rising new car sales translates into more auto ABS, refinancing booms equate to more home equity ABS, etc.) and the financing choices of the seller/servicers. The decisions of seller/servicers to fund themselves by issuing ABS will depend on cost, control, structural ease, and their funding alternatives.

ABS demand is a function of competing supply as well as the breadth of the investor base. Investors who wish to assess demand for a particular ABS need to understand who buys the bonds and why, as well as understand flow of funds. If a particular investor type encounters troubles (e.g., many hedge funds faltered in the 1998 liquidity crisis), an investor might expect spreads to widen in the products the investor type favored (in that instance, subordinated bonds). On the other hand, regulatory changes (risk weightings, for example) can broaden the demand.

Increasingly, performance in ABS has been affected by the perceived quality and stability of the issuer. Part of this has been due to "headline risk," (i.e., news events regarding the issuer and not necessarily directly impacting the collateral). Transaction liquidity is another technical risk. Tranche size, frequency of issuance, the form of offering (public, private, or 144A) and the size of the underwriting group are all factors unrelated to collateral that affect a transaction's liquidity. The most liquid transactions are those issued in the public market by frequent issuers with large underwriting groups and sizable tranches. Credit cards have historically been viewed by investors as the most liquid asset class in the ABS market.

Exhibit 3 summarizes fundamental and technical risks by major asset type.

MONITORING ABS PORTFOLIOS AND MEASURING PERFORMANCE

ABS are more fungible than corporates and as such, may be easier to monitor. Portfolio managers should review the remittance reports produced on a regular basis by the servicers of the ABS deals in which they invest. The rating agencies also offer regularly updated summaries of deal collateral performance. Other information sources exist (e.g., Bloomberg, Passport, Lewtan) and many issuers are starting to put electronic copies of their remittance reports on the Web. Tracking actuals and trends in excess spread, losses, and delinquencies (and, for revolving ABS, payment rates and portfolio yields as well) provides important information about the performance of the ABS in a manager's portfolio. Analyzing these percentages on a 3-month rolling average basis, rather than a straight monthly basis, will help smooth any month-to-month volatility and distinguish between noise and a meaningful trend. Exhibit 4 lists website addresses for various sources of ABS information.

Exhibit 3: Different Asset Classes Have Varying Degrees of Risk

Risk	Credit Card	Auto	MH	HE	Student Loan	CBO	CLO (Delinked)
Fundamental-Credit Quality							
Collateral Risk	High	Variable	High	Moderate	Minimal*	High	Usually Low
Structural Protection	Excellent; Triggered**	Very Good	Very Good	Very Good	Very Good	Excellent; Triggered**	Excellent; Triggered**
Servicer Risk (i.e., intensity of servicing)	Moderate	Prime-Low Sub-prime-High	High	Moderate	Moderate	Moderate	Low
Wrapper Risk	NA	Sub-prime-Yes	Some	Some	NA	NA	NA
Downgrade Risk	Lowest, due to early am	Low	Moderate	Low	Low	Low	Low
Fundamental-Cash Flow							
Early Amortization/Payout Risk	Yes	NA	NA	NA	NA	Generally Low	Generally Low
Prepay Risk	NA	NA	Generally Low	Low to Moderate	Very Low	NA	NA
Extension Risk	Very Low	Very Low	Moderate	Low to Moderate	Very Low	NA	NA
Cap Risk	NA	Generally NA	Generally NA	Variable	Variable	NA	NA
Basis Risk	Some	NA	Generally NA	Minimal	Some	Minimal	Minimal
Technical							
Liquidity	Excellent	Excellent	Fair	Good	Excellent	Fair	Fair
Headline Risk	Moderate	Variable	High	High	Low	Low	Low

* Assumes government guaranteed loans

** In order to reduce the risk of loss to investors, credit card ABS can amortize early (i.e., the revolving period ends ahead of schedule and the deal begins to pay out) if a portfolio is deteriorating. For cash flow CBO/CLOs, failure of a transaction's portfolio tests can lead to early payout.

Source: DB Global Markets Research

Exhibit 4: General Data Sources on the Web

Selected Issuers

Credit Card		Auto	
www.americanexpress.com	www.discovercard.com	www.americredit.com	www.mitsubishicars.com
www.bankofamerica.com	www.firstusa.com	www.bmwusafs.com	www.nissan-usa.com
www.bankone.com	www.fleet.com	www.chryslerfinancial.com	www.onyxacceptance.com
www.capitalone.com	www.mbna.com	www.fordcredit.com	www.toyota.com
www.chase.com	www.providian.com	www.gm.com	www.unionacceptance.com
www.citibank.com	www.wachovia.com	www.honda.com	www.wfsfinancial.com

Equipment		Home Equity	
www.cat.com	www.dvi-inc.com	www.advanta.com	www.irwinfinancial.com
www.cit.com	www.hellerfinancial.com	www.conseco.com	www.provident-bank.com
www.cnh.com	www.ikon.com	www.countrywide.com	www.rfc.com
www.copelco.com	www.sierracities.com	www.equicredit.com	www.saxonmortgage.com
www.deere.com	www.unicapitalcorp.com	www.gmacmortgage.com	www.superiorbank.com

Manufactured Housing	Student Loan
www.bombardiernv.com	www.keybank.com
www.clayton.net	www.salliemae.com
www.conseco.com	www.slfc.com
www.greenpoint.com	www.usagroup.com
www.oakwoodhomes.com	

Rating Agencies		Other	
Fitch	www.fitchibca.com	American Bankruptcy Institute	www.abiworld.org
Moody's	www.moodysresearch.com	ABSNet (Lewtan)	www.absnet.net
Standard & Poor's	www.standardandpoors.com	EDGAR	www.sec.gov/edaux/formlynx.htm
		Federal Reserve	www.bog.frb.fed.us
		Securitizaton.net	www.securitization.net

Trustee	
Bankers Trust	www.apps.gis.deutsche-bank.com/invr
Bank of New York	www.mbsreporting.com
Bank One	www.bankone.com/commercial/invest/corporate
Chase Manhattan	www.chase.com/sfa
First Union	www.firstunion.com/corptrust
Norwest Bank	www.ctslink.com
U.S. Bank	www.usbank.com/corp_trust/inv_info_reporting.html

Source: DB Global Markets Research

Assembling a *loss curve* from historical data can provide one of the most important tools for monitoring a portfolio of installment loans. A loss curve shows the timing as well as the magnitude of losses and allows the portfolio manager to create a baseline stress scenario for examining the sufficiency of loss protection in a given bond. One should start by graphing the loss curves for as many issues as possible (again using rating agency data or remittance reports). Varying degrees of sophistication can be employed to fit a base curve, from simple hand-drawn curves to spreadsheet-based curve fitting techniques, like nonlinear regression analysis. Exhibit 5 shows the loss experience of a set of collateral pools of different vintages, and a representative curve chosen to analyze an actual issue. For the example in Exhibit 5, to build a representative curve, we weighted the experience of more recent deals more heavily, because we felt that that experience reflected shifts in collateral quality that best matched the bond we were analyzing.

One of the most important parts of curve-fitting is in developing the shape of the curve. Once a reasonable shape exists, modifying the amplitude of the curve (i.e., 1.25×, 1.5×, etc.) is easily done. Portfolio managers should pay special attention to any deal that is not "tracking" along the expected curve.

As mentioned earlier, headline risk is a concern of many ABS investors. Some find it helpful to track issuers' equity performance as a possible early warning indicator of difficulties. Leaving tickers up on the Bloomberg screen is a quick and easy way check up on stock performance. Also important to note is the issuer's credit rating (if such rating exists). Higher rated companies usually have greater funding flexibility than lower rated companies. Diversification of funding is often reflected in an ABS issuer's pricing and trading levels.

In addition to monitoring the performance of a portfolio manager's specific ABS investments, a manager should monitor industry trends within each sector. By reading available research reports and attending conferences, portfolio managers can keep up to date on sector growth and change as well as overall ABS market performance. While these trends may or may not affect a portfolio manager's outstanding portfolio, on a going-forward basis, they may cause portfolio managers to rethink their strategies with regard to ABS.

Portfolio managers who invest in ABS transactions enhanced by surety bonds should pay special attention to credit quality trends of wrap providers. The major rating agencies provide periodic updates on their financial strength.

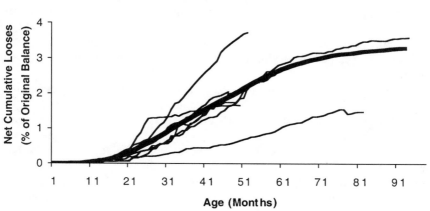

Exhibit 5: Projected Loss Curve for a Representative Collateral Pool

Source: DB Global Markets Research

Exhibit 6: Correlation Between ABS Spreads and Swap Spreads is Strong and Rising (October 1997 and June 2000)

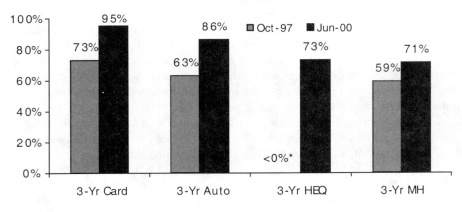

* Negatively correlated.

Source: DB Global Markets Research

Measuring ABS Performance

Part of monitoring a portfolio includes measuring its performance. Several dealers compile and distribute spread information on a weekly basis. Many portfolio managers mark-to-market their portfolios on a regular basis. Various pricing services exist that will mark to market portfolios for a fee. Dealers can provide this information to investors as well. With the mark-to-market information, a portfolio manager can compare his ABS portfolio to other debt products, such as corporates or Treasuries, and he can also compare his ABS portfolio to the ABS universe. In this way, the portfolio manager can evaluate his security selection and his sector selection.

Portfolio managers should obviously be on the watch for decomposing portfolio performance. As Exhibit 6 shows, most ABS move closely in tandem with swap spreads.

An ABS portfolio that moves dramatically versus swap spreads may be experiencing difficulties. Also important to note is the bid/ask on the securities in a portfolio. A widening bid/ask usually indicates a less liquid and/or troubled security. Additionally, home equity investors should track prepayment trends in their portfolio to assess the likelihood of shortening or lengthening, and possibly evaluate trading. Home equity ABS prepaying at a faster speed than expected, for example, may force the portfolio manager to reinvest in a lower-yielding instrument. Extending ABS will cause poor price performance in positive-sloped yield curve environments.

QUANTITATIVE TECHNIQUES FOR ABS PORTFOLIO MANAGERS

Below, we discuss three quantitative techniques often used by ABS portfolio managers.

Measuring Exposure to Guarantors: Wrap or Surety Providers

The third-party credit risk from the surety bond provider in a wrapped deal can be quantified using a joint probability approach. For a surety-wrapped bond to default, both of the following two events have to occur: the guarantor defaults and the internal credit enhancement of the deal fails to provide enough protection. (It is important to note that in many wrapped transactions with sequential payment structures, front tranches often can sustain high levels of losses without having to invoke the guarantee. This is primarily because the front tranches may be paid down before losses in the collateral can completely obliterate the deal's internal credit enhancement.)

Of course, for some guarantors, ABS insurance is a significant part of the guarantors' business. In a distressed case, in which a general deterioration of consumer credit occurs, the collateral of many consumer finance transactions may perform poorly, and the insurance companies that provide guarantees to these transactions may also come under severe financial pressures. Therefore, financial guarantor default and severe deterioration in collateral performance may be positively correlated. However, structured finance insurance generally consists of less than 20%[4] of the surety bond providers' portfolios. Therefore, if we assume collateral performance variance to be uniform in overall fixed income markets, the correlation of the two above-mentioned events can be reasonably estimated to be below 15%.

If we denote the probability of the guarantor default to be a, the probability of the internal credit enhancement of the bond being exhausted to be b, and the correlation of two events to be c, the probability that the bond incurs actual losses is then

$$P = a \times b + c \times \sqrt{a - a^2} \times \sqrt{b - b^2}$$

In the extreme case, where we assume that structure alone cannot insulate the bond from losses (i.e., it entirely relies on the financial guarantee to avoid a write-down), $b = 1$. Then $P = a$. That is, the probability of the bond incurring losses is the same as that of the surety provider defaulting.

In a more realistic case, let's assume a 5-year wrapped bond can earn an A2 rating solely on its *internal* credit enhancement (wrapped deals generally must earn at least a Baa3 rating before the wrap). According to Moody's[5] default probability matrix for corporate bonds, the probability of a 5-year A2-rated corporate bond defaulting over its life is 0.6%. (Note that, although historically, structured

---

[4] Moody's Investors Service, "Financial Guaranty Industry Outlook," October 1999.
[5] Moody's Investors Service, "Historical Default Rates of Corporate Bond Issuers, 1920-1999," January 2000.

finance transactions had better performance than corporate bonds, we will still use corporate default probabilities for this purpose.) Also according to Moody's, the probability of a Aaa-rated guarantor defaulting in five years is 0.2%. Using the 15% correlation number, the probability that this wrapped bond will incur losses within 5 years is about one thousandth of 1%, or[6]

$$P = 0.002 \times 0.006 + 0.15 \times \sqrt{0.002 - 0.002^2} \times \sqrt{0.006 - 0.006^2}$$
$$\approx 0.000014$$

As we can see, the exposure of the bond to the guarantor is largely mitigated by the bond's internal credit enhancement. This implies that an investor who limits exposure to any one AAA issuer to $100 million, for example, would be comfortable with a staggering $14.3 billion of exposure to the guarantor using the above example ($100 million × 0.002/0.000014).

Calculation of Z-Spreads

Although the traditional nominal spread over a benchmark gives a convenient and succinct measure of a bond's pricing, it doesn't address the issue of the relationship between the yield curve and amortizing principal. Amortizing, rather than bullet principal repayment, is common in many types of structured finance transactions. Because the principal of an amortizing bond is paid over a period of time, and the yields of various benchmarks pertaining in the time span may vary substantially, to measure the spread of the bond against *all these benchmarks*, instead of against just one of them, seems to be a logical extension to the nominal spread. One method to do this is known as the *zero-volatility spread* or simply *Z-spread*.

In a Z-spread calculation, one first constructs a zero-coupon curve from a benchmark curve. (Some quantitative analysts argue that the zero-coupon curve is a better benchmark curve to calculate spreads, because the yield distortion caused by the various coupons of the benchmarks can be theoretically cleansed away by using zero-coupon instruments. In practice, however, there are many ways to construct a zero-coupon curve, with results that often differ.) The interest and principal payments are then discounted by the zero-coupon rates for the corresponding periods plus a spread. The formula for this is

$$P = \sum_i \frac{FP_i + FI_i}{\left(1 + \dfrac{r_i + z}{D}\right)^{\frac{D \times i}{N}}}$$

where P is the present value of all future cash flows, D is the annual discounting frequency, N is the annual payment frequency, i is the index for payment periods (for a bond that matures in M years, the index runs from 1 to $M \times N$), FP_i and FI_i

---

[6] A more rigorous method can be developed using a stochastic model, but that is beyond the scope of this discussion.

are the principal payment in period i, respectively, r_i is the zero-coupon rate for period i, and z is the spread. The spread, z, that makes P equal to the price of the bond is called the "Z-spread." As shown in the above formula, each cash flow is discounted with the spread over the zero-coupon rate for the corresponding period.

Z-spread is sometimes also called zero-volatility spread. This is because, in an option-adjusted spread calculation, if one sets the volatility of rates to be 0, the option-adjusted spread (OAS) would equal the Z-spread solved from the formula.

Break-Even Holding Period for Liquidity Premium

Less liquid assets often carry premiums to compensate holders for investing in them. A bond may be less liquid for various reasons. The collateral type may be more esoteric, the issuer may issue infrequently or be viewed as a lesser player in the market, the structure of the transaction may involve some unique feature, the bond may not publicly registered, or the bond may not be rated by all major rating agencies, etc. The degree of illiquidity of a bond is generally reflected in the bond's "bid-ask spread" (the difference, in basis points, between where a bond is offered and where it is bid). The more illiquid a bond, the wider the spread. For example, for a frequent credit card issuer, the bid-ask spread of a 5-year bond may only be 1bp, whereas the bid-ask spread for 5-year bond of a less frequent private label issuer may be 5bp. For a total-rate-of-return investor, the extra bid-ask spread means that the selling price at the horizon will be lower for the less liquid bond, thus the lack of liquidity would adversely affect the rate of return. However, this may be offset by the liquidity premium provided by the less liquid bond (in the form of higher returns) on the cash flows received within the horizon. The longer the holding period (horizon), the better the result for the less liquid bond.

To illustrate this, suppose there are two 5-year bullet credit card bonds issued at the same time. Both are quarterly pay, issued at par. Issuer A is a highly recognized player, and its bond is issued with a 5.75% coupon (corresponding to a semiannual yield at 5.79%). Issuer B is lesser known, and its bond carries a 5.95% coupon (corresponding to a semi-annual yield of 5.99%). Thus, there is a 20bp liquidity premium on Issuer B's bond. However, because Issuer B's bond is less liquid, the bid-ask spread on it is 5bp, which is wider than Issuer A's (1bp). Exhibit 7 shows the return on both bonds, and the excess (or deficiency) of return on Issuer B's bond against Issuer A's, with different horizons. As shown in the exhibit, when the holding horizon is set at 2.9 quarters, Issuer A's bond and Issuer B's bond should have the same return. This makes 2.9 quarters the break-even holding horizon.

Exhibit 8 shows the return curves for the bonds of Issuer A and Issuer B in terms of annualized return rates. It should be noted that in the exhibit, we have assumed that the yield roll-downs[7] for both bonds are the same. In reality, less liquid bonds often have a steeper credit spread curve. That means the actual return for Issuer B's bond could be higher than shown in the example, if a separate, steeper roll-down for it is used. That would result in a shorter break-even horizon.

---

[7] A yield roll-down refers to the fact that as a bond ages, it "rolls down" the credit spread curve.

Exhibit 7: Rate of Return Comparison

Holding Quarters	Roll Down	Bond A Return (Simple Rate)	Bond B Return (Simple Rate)	Excess (Deficiency) for Bond B Investors
1	1 bp	1.438%	1.326%	(0.112%)
2	2 bp	2.932%	2.878%	(0.054%)
2.9	3 bp	4.329%	4.329%	Break-even
3	3 bp	4.440%	4.445%	0.004%
4	4 bp	5.963%	6.027%	0.064%
5	5 bp	7.501%	7.625%	0.124%
6	6 bp	9.053%	9.238%	0.185%
7	7 bp	10.620%	10.867%	0.247%
8	8 bp	12.202%	12.511%	0.309%
9	9 bp	13.799%	14.172%	0.373%
10	10 bp	15.411%	15.848%	0.437%

Source: DB Global Markets Research

Exhibit 8: Annualized Rates of Return

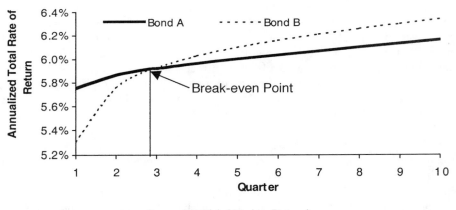

Source: DB Global Markets Research

CONCLUSIONS

Asset-backed securities are now a common part of all types of investors' fixed income portfolios. ABS offer many different types of opportunities, from the most liquid, highest quality, least volatile bonds (AAA credit card floaters, for example) to esoteric, complex high-yield instruments (subordinates bonds, future flow deals, etc.). ABS continue to offer investors — rating for rating — incremental spread, inherent diversification, and stable ratings.

Multi-Factor Risk Models and Their Applications

Lev Dynkin
Managing Director
Lehman Brothers

Jay Hyman
Senior Vice President
Lehman Brothers

Wei Wu
Vice President
Lehman Brothers

INTRODUCTION

The classical definition of investment risk is uncertainty of returns, measured by their volatility. Investments with greater risk are expected to earn greater returns than less risky alternatives. Asset allocation models help investors choose the asset mix with the highest expected return given their risk constraints (for example, avoid a loss of more than 2% per year in a given portfolio).

Once investors have selected a desired asset mix, they often enlist specialized asset managers to implement their investment goals. The performance of the portfolio is usually compared with a benchmark that reflects the investor's asset selection decision. From the perspective of most asset managers, risk is defined by performance relative to the benchmark rather than by absolute return. In this sense, the least-risky investment portfolio is one that replicates the benchmark. Any portfolio deviation from the benchmark entails some risk. For example, to the manager of a bond fund benchmarked against the High Yield Index, investing 100% in U.S. Treasuries would involve a much greater long-term risk than investing 100% in high yield corporate bonds. In other words, benchmark

The authors would like to thank Jack Malvey for his substantial contribution to this paper and Ravi Mattu, George Williams, Ivan Gruhl, Amitabh Arora, Vadim Konstantinovsky, Peter Lindner, and Jonathan Carmel for their valuable comments.

risk belongs to the plan sponsor, while the asset manager bears the risk of deviating from the benchmark.

In this article we discuss a risk model developed at Lehman Brothers that focuses on portfolio risk relative to a benchmark. The risk model is designed for use by fixed-income portfolio managers benchmarked against broad market indices.

QUANTIFYING RISK

Given our premise that the least-risky portfolio is the one that exactly replicates the benchmark, we proceed to compare the composition of a fixed-income portfolio to that of its benchmark. Are they similar in exposures to changes in the term structure of interest rates, in allocations to different asset classes within the benchmark, and in allocations to different quality ratings? Such portfolio versus benchmark comparisons form the foundation for modern fixed-income portfolio management. Techniques such as "stratified sampling" or "cell-matching" have been used to construct portfolios that are similar to their benchmarks in many components (i.e., duration, quality etc.). However, these techniques can not answer quantitative questions concerning portfolio risk. How much risk is there? Is portfolio A more or less risky than portfolio B? Will a given transaction increase or decrease risk? To best decrease risk relative to the benchmark, should the focus be on better aligning term structure exposures or sector allocations? How do we weigh these different types of risk against each other? What actions can be taken to mitigate the overall risk exposure? Any quantitative model of risk must account for the magnitude of a particular event as well as its likelihood. When multiple risks are modeled simultaneously, the issue of correlation also must be addressed.

The risk model we present in this article provides quantitative answers to such questions. This multi-factor model compares portfolio and benchmark exposures along all dimensions of risk, such as yield curve movement, changes in sector spreads, and changes in implied volatility. Exposures to each *risk factor* are calculated on a bond-by-bond basis and aggregated to obtain the exposures of the portfolio and the benchmark.

Tracking error, which quantifies the risk of performance difference (projected standard deviation of the return difference) between the portfolio and the benchmark, is projected based on the differences in risk factor exposures. This calculation of overall risk incorporates historical information about the volatility of each risk factor and the correlations among them. The volatilities and correlations of all the risk factors are stored in a covariance matrix, which is calibrated based on monthly returns of individual bonds in the Lehman Brothers Aggregate Index dating back to 1987. The model is updated monthly with historical information. The choice of risk factors has been reviewed periodically since the model's introduction in 1990. The model covers U.S. dollar-denominated securities in most Lehman

Brothers domestic fixed-rate bond indices (Aggregate, High Yield, Eurobond). The effect of non-index securities on portfolio risk is measured by mapping onto index risk categories. The net effect of all risk factors is known as systematic risk.

The model is based on historical returns of individual securities and its risk projections are a function of portfolio and benchmark positions in individual securities. Instead of deriving risk factor realizations from changes in market averages (such as a Treasury curve spline, sector spread changes, etc.) the model derives them from historical returns of securities in Lehman Indices. While this approach is much more data and labor intensive, it allows us to quantify residual return volatility of each security after all systematic risk factors have been applied. As a result, we can measure non-systematic risk of a portfolio relative to the benchmark based on differences in their diversification. This form of risk, also known as concentration risk or security-specific risk, is the result of a portfolio's exposure to individual bonds or issuers. Non-systematic risk can represent a significant portion of the overall risk, particularly for portfolios containing relatively few securities, even for assets without any credit risk.

PORTFOLIO MANAGEMENT WITH THE RISK MODEL

Passive portfolio managers, or "indexers," seek to replicate the returns of a broad market index. They can use the risk model to help keep the portfolio closely aligned with the index along all risk dimensions. Active portfolio managers attempt to outperform the benchmark by positioning the portfolio to capitalize on market views. They can use the risk model to quantify the risk entailed in a particular portfolio position relative to the market. This information is often incorporated into the performance review process, where returns achieved by a particular strategy are weighed against the risk taken. Enhanced indexers express views against the index, but limit the amount of risk assumed. They can use the model to keep risk within acceptable limits and to highlight unanticipated market exposures that might arise as the portfolio and index change over time. These management styles can be associated with approximate ranges of tracking errors. Passive managers typically seek tracking errors of 5 to 25 basis points per year. Tracking errors for enhanced indexers range from 25 to 75 bp, and those of active managers are even higher.

WHY A MULTI-FACTOR MODEL?

With the abundance of data available in today's marketplace, an asset manager might be tempted to build a risk model directly from the historical return characteristics of individual securities. The standard deviation of a security's return in the upcoming period can be projected to match its past volatility; the correlation between any two securities can be determined from their historical performance.

Despite the simplicity of this scheme, the multi-factor approach has several important advantages. First of all, the number of risk factors in the model is much smaller than the number of securities in a typical investment universe. This greatly reduces the matrix operations needed to calculate portfolio risk. This increases the speed of computation (which is becoming less important with gains in processing power) and, more importantly, improves the numerical stability of the calculations. A large covariance matrix of individual security volatilities and correlations is likely to cause numerical instability. This is especially true in the fixed-income world, where returns of many securities are very highly correlated. Risk factors may also exhibit moderately high correlations with each other, but much less so than for individual securities.[1]

A more fundamental problem with relying on individual security data is that not all securities can be modeled adequately in this way. For illiquid securities, pricing histories are either unavailable or unreliable; for new securities, histories do not exist. For still other securities, there may be plenty of reliable historical data, but changes in security characteristics make this data irrelevant to future results. For instance, a ratings upgrade of an issuer would make future returns less volatile than those of the past. A change in interest rates can significantly alter the effective duration of a callable bond. As any bond ages, its duration shortens, making its price less sensitive to interest rates. A multi-factor model estimates the risk from owning a particular bond based not on the historical performance of that bond, but on historical returns of all bonds with characteristics similar to those currently pertaining to the bond.

In this article, we present the risk model by way of example. In each of the following sections, a numerical example of the model's application motivates the discussion of a particular feature.

THE RISK REPORT

For illustration, we apply the risk model to a sample portfolio of 57 bonds benchmarked against the Lehman Brothers Aggregate Index. The model produces two important outputs: a tracking error summary report and a set of risk sensitivities reports that compare the portfolio composition to that of the benchmark. These various comparative reports form the basis of our risk analysis, by identifying structural differences between the two. Of themselves, however, they fail to quantify the risk due to these mismatches. The model's anchor is therefore the tracking error report, which quantifies the risks associated with each cross-sectional comparison. Taken together, the various reports produced by the model provide a complete understanding of the risk of this portfolio versus its benchmark.

---

[1] Some practitioners insist on a set of risk factors that are uncorrelated to each other. We have found it more useful to select risk factors that are intuitively clear to investors, even at the expense of allowing positive correlations among the factors.

Exhibit 1: Top-Level Statistics Comparison
Sample Portfolio versus Aggregate Index, 9/30/98

	Portfolio	Benchmark
Number of Issues	57	6,932
Average Maturity/Average Life (years)	9.57	8.47
Internal Rate of Return (%)	5.76	5.54
Average Yield to Maturity (%)	5.59	5.46
Average Yield to Worst (%)	5.53	5.37
Average Option-Adjusted Convexity	0.04	−0.22
Average OAS to Maturity (bp)	74	61
Average OAS to Worst (bp)	74	61
Portfolio Mod. Adjusted Duration	4.82	4.29
Portfolio Average Price	108.45	107.70
Portfolio Average Coupon (%)	7.33	6.98
Risk Characteristics		
Estimated Total Tracking Error (bp/year)	52	
Portfolio Beta	1.05	

From the overall statistical summary shown in Exhibit 1, it can be seen that the portfolio has a significant term structure exposure, as its duration (4.82) is longer than that of the benchmark (4.29). In addition, the portfolio is over-exposed to corporate bonds and under-exposed to Treasuries. We will see this explicitly in the sector report later; it is reflected in the statistics in Exhibit 1 by a higher average yield and coupon. The overall annualized tracking error, shown at the bottom of the statistics report, is 52 bp. Tracking error is defined as one standard deviation of the difference between the portfolio and benchmark annualized returns. In simple terms, this means that with a probability of about 68% the portfolio return over the next year will be within +/- 52 bp of the benchmark return.[2]

Sources of Systematic Tracking Error

What are the main sources of this tracking error? The model identifies market forces influencing all securities in a certain category as *systematic risk factors.* Exhibit 2 divides the tracking error into components corresponding to different categories of risk. Looking down the first column, we see that the largest sources of systematic tracking error between this portfolio and its benchmark are the differences in sensitivity to term structure movements (36.3 bp) and to changes in credit spreads by sector (32 bp) and quality (14.7 bp). The components of systematic tracking error correspond directly to the groups of risk factors. A detailed report of the differences in portfolio and benchmark exposures (sensitivities) to the relevant set of risk factors illustrates the origin of each component of systematic risk.

---

[2] This interpretation requires several simplifying assumptions. The 68% confidence interval assumes that returns are normally distributed, which may not be the case. Second, this presentation ignores differences in the expected returns of portfolio and benchmark (due, for example, to a higher portfolio yield). Strictly speaking, the confidence interval should be drawn around the expected outperformance.

Exhibit 2: Tracking Error Breakdown for Sample Portfolio
Sample Portfolio versus Aggregate Index, 9/30/98

	Tracking Error (bp/year)		
	Isolated	Cumulative	Change in Cumulative*
Tracking Error Term Structure	36.3	36.3	36.3
Non-Term Structure	39.5		
Tracking Error Sector	32.0	38.3	2.0
Tracking Error Quality	14.7	44.1	5.8
Tracking Error Optionality	1.6	44.0	−0.1
Tracking Error Coupon	3.2	45.5	1.5
Tracking Error MBS Sector	4.9	43.8	−1.7
Tracking Error MBS Volatility	7.2	44.5	0.7
Tracking Error MBS Prepayment	2.5	45.0	0.4
Total Systematic Tracking Error			45.0
Non-Systematic Tracking Error			
Issuer-specific	25.9		
Issue-specific	26.4		
Total	26.1		
Total Tracking Error			52

	Systematic	Non-systematic	Total
Benchmark Return Standard Deviation	417	4	417
Portfolio Return Standard Deviation	440	27	440

* Isolated Tracking Error is the projected deviation between the portfolio and benchmark return due to a single category of systematic risk. Cumulative Tracking Error shows the combined effect of all risk categories from the first one in the table to current.

Sensitivities to risk factors are called *factor loadings*. They are expressed in units that depend on the definition of each particular risk factor. For example, for risk factors representing volatility of corporate spreads factor loadings are given by spread durations, for risk factors measuring volatility of prepayment speed (in units of PSA) factor loadings are given by "PSA Duration." The factor loadings of a portfolio or an index are calculated as a market-value weighted average over all constituent securities. Differences between portfolio and benchmark factor loadings form a vector of *active portfolio exposures*. A quick comparison of the magnitudes of the different components of tracking error highlights the most significant mismatches.

Because the largest component of tracking error is due to term structure, let us examine the term structure risk in our example. Risk factors associated with term structure movements are represented by the fixed set of points on the theoretical Treasury spot curve shown in Exhibit 3. Each of these risk factors exhibits a certain historical return volatility. The extent to which the portfolio and the benchmark returns are affected by this volatility is measured by factor loadings (exposures). These exposures are computed as percentages of the total present value of the portfolio and benchmark cash flows allocated to each point on the curve. The risk of the portfolio performing differently from the benchmark due to term structure movements is due to the differences in the portfolio and benchmark exposures to these risk factors and to their volatilities and correlations. Exhibit 3 compares the term structure exposures of the portfolio and benchmark for our example. The Difference column shows the portfolio to be overweighted in the 2-year section of the curve, underweighted in the 3- to 10-year range, and over-weighted at the long end. This makes the portfolio longer than the benchmark and more barbelled.

Exhibit 3: Term Structure Report
Sample Portfolio versus Aggregate Index, 9/30/98

Year	Cash Flows Portfolio	Benchmark	Difference
0.00	1.45%	1.85%	−0.40%
0.25	3.89	4.25	−0.36
0.50	4.69	4.25	0.45
0.75	4.34	3.76	0.58
1.00	8.90	7.37	1.53
1.50	7.47	10.29	−2.82
2.00	10.43	8.09	2.34
2.50	8.63	6.42	2.20
3.00	4.28	5.50	−1.23
3.50	3.90	4.81	−0.92
4.00	6.74	7.19	−0.46
5.00	6.13	6.96	−0.83
6.00	3.63	4.67	−1.04
7.00	5.77	7.84	−2.07
10.00	7.16	7.37	−0.21
15.00	4.63	3.88	0.75
20.00	3.52	3.04	0.48
25.00	3.18	1.73	1.45
30.00	1.22	0.68	0.54
40.00	0.08	0.07	0.01

The tracking error is calculated from this vector of differences between portfolio and benchmark exposures. However, mismatches at different points are not treated equally. Exposures to factors with higher volatilities have a larger effect on tracking error. In this example, the risk exposure with the largest contribution to tracking error is the overweight of 1.45% to the 25-year point on the curve. While other vertices have larger mismatches (e.g., –2.07% at 7 years), their overall effect on risk is not as strong because the longer duration of a 25-year zero causes it to have a higher return volatility. It should also be noted that the risk caused by overweighting one segment of the yield curve can sometimes be offset by underweighting another. Exhibit 3 shows the portfolio to be underexposed to the 1.50-year point on the yield curve by –2.82% and overexposed to the 2.00-year point on the curve by +2.34%. Those are largely offsetting positions in terms of risk because these two adjacent points on the curve are highly correlated and almost always move together. To eliminate completely the tracking error due to term structure, differences in exposures to each term structure risk factor need to be reduced to zero. To lower term structure risk, it is most important to focus first on reducing exposures at the long end of the curve, particularly those that are not offset by opposing positions in nearby points.

The tracking error due to sector exposures is explained by the detailed sector report shown in Exhibit 4. This report shows the sector allocations of the portfolio and the benchmark in two ways. In addition to reporting the percentage of market value allocated to each sector, it shows the contribution of each sector to the overall spread duration.[3] These contributions are computed as the product of the percentage allocations to a sector and the market-weighted average spread duration of the holdings in that sector. Contributions to spread duration (factor loadings) measure the sensitivity of return to systematic changes in particular sector spreads (risk factors) and are a better measure of risk than simple market allocations. The rightmost column in this report, the difference between portfolio and benchmark contributions to spread duration in each sector, is the exposure vector that is used to compute tracking error due to sector. A quick look down this column shows that the largest exposures in our example are an underweight of 0.77 years to Treasuries and an overweight of 1.00 years to consumer non-cyclicals in the industrial sector. (The fine-grained breakdown of the corporate market into industry groups corresponds to the second tier of the Lehman Brothers hierarchical industry classification scheme.) Note that the units of risk factors and factor loadings for sector risk differ from those used to model the term structure risk.

---

[3] Just as traditional duration can be defined as the sensitivity of bond price to a change in yield, spread duration is defined as the sensitivity of bond price to a change in spread. While this distinction is largely academic for bullet bonds, it can be significant for other securities, such as bonds with embedded options and floating-rate securities. The sensitivity to spread change is the correct measure of sector risk.

Exhibit 4: Detailed Sector Report
Sample Portfolio versus Aggregate Index, 9/30/98

Detailed Sector	Portfolio			Benchmark			Difference	
	% of Portf.	Adj. Dur.	Contrib. to Adj. Dur.	% of Portf.	Adj. Dur.	Contrib. to Adj. Dur.	% of Portf.	Contrib. to Adj. Dur.
Treasury								
Coupon	27.09	5.37	1.45	39.82	5.58	2.22	−12.73	−0.77
Strip	0.00	0.00	0.00	0.00	0.00	0.00	0.00	0.00
Agencies								
FNMA	4.13	3.40	0.14	3.56	3.44	0.12	0.57	0.02
FHLB	0.00	0.00	0.00	1.21	2.32	0.03	−1.21	−0.03
FHLMC	0.00	0.00	0.00	0.91	3.24	0.03	−0.91	−0.03
REFCORP	3.51	11.22	0.39	0.83	12.18	0.10	2.68	0.29
Other Agencies	0.00	0.00	0.00	1.31	5.58	0.07	−1.31	−0.07
Financial Inst.								
Banking	1.91	5.31	0.10	2.02	5.55	0.11	−0.11	−0.01
Brokerage	1.35	3.52	0.05	0.81	4.14	0.03	0.53	0.01
Financial Cos.	1.88	2.92	0.06	2.11	3.78	0.08	−0.23	−0.02
Insurance	0.00	0.00	0.00	0.52	7.47	0.04	−0.52	−0.04
Other	0.00	0.00	0.00	0.28	5.76	0.02	−0.28	−0.02
Industrials								
Basic	0.63	6.68	0.04	0.89	6.39	0.06	−0.26	−0.01
Capital Goods	4.43	5.35	0.24	1.16	6.94	0.08	3.26	0.16
Consumer Cycl.	2.01	8.37	0.17	2.28	7.10	0.16	−0.27	0.01
Consum. Non-cycl.	8.88	12.54	1.11	1.66	6.84	0.11	7.22	1.00
Energy	1.50	6.82	0.10	0.69	6.89	0.05	0.81	0.05
Technology	1.55	1.58	0.02	0.42	7.39	0.03	1.13	−0.01
Transportation	0.71	12.22	0.09	0.57	7.41	0.04	0.14	0.04
Utilities								
Electric	0.47	3.36	0.02	1.39	5.02	0.07	−0.93	−0.05
Telephone	9.18	2.08	0.19	1.54	6.58	0.10	7.64	0.09
Natural Gas	0.80	5.53	0.04	0.49	6.50	0.03	0.31	0.01
Water	0.00	0.00	0.00	0.00	0.00	0.00	0.00	0.00
Yankee								
Canadians	1.45	7.87	0.11	1.06	6.67	0.07	0.38	0.04
Corporates	0.49	3.34	0.02	1.79	6.06	0.11	−1.30	−0.09
Supranational	1.00	6.76	0.07	0.38	6.33	0.02	0.62	0.04
Sovereigns	0.00	0.00	0.00	0.66	5.95	0.04	−0.66	−0.04
Hypothetical	0.00	0.00	0.00	0.00	0.00	0.00	0.00	0.00
Cash	0.00	0.00	0.00	0.00	0.00	0.00	0.00	0.00
Mortgage								
Conventnl. 30-yr.	12.96	1.52	0.20	16.60	1.42	0.24	−3.64	−0.04
GNMA 30-yr.	7.53	1.23	0.09	7.70	1.12	0.09	−0.16	0.01
MBS 15-yr.	3.52	1.95	0.07	5.59	1.63	0.09	−2.06	−0.02
Balloons	3.03	1.69	0.05	0.78	1.02	0.01	2.25	0.04
OTM	0.00	0.00	0.00	0.00	0.00	0.00	0.00	0.00
European & International								
Eurobonds	0.00	0.00	0.00	0.00	0.00	0.00	0.00	0.00
International	0.00	0.00	0.00	0.00	0.00	0.00	0.00	0.00
Asset Backed	0.00	0.00	0.00	0.96	3.14	0.03	−0.96	−0.03
CMO	0.00	0.00	0.00	0.00	0.00	0.00	0.00	0.00
Other	0.00	0.00	0.00	0.00	0.00	0.00	0.00	0.00
Totals	100.00		4.82	100.00		4.29	0.00	0.54

Exhibit 5: Quality Report
Sample Portfolio versus Aggregate Index, 9/30/98

Quality	Portfolio			Benchmark			Difference	
	% of Portf.	Adj. Dur.	Cntrb. to Adj. Dur.	% of Portf.	Adj. Dur.	Cntrb. to Adj. Dur.	% of Portf.	Cntrb. to Adj. Dur.
Aaa+	34.72	5.72	1.99	47.32	5.41	2.56	−12.60	−0.57
MBS	27.04	1.51	0.41	30.67	1.37	0.42	−3.62	−0.01
Aaa	1.00	6.76	0.07	2.33	4.84	0.11	−1.33	−0.05
Aa	5.54	5.67	0.31	4.19	5.32	0.22	1.35	0.09
A	17.82	7.65	1.36	9.09	6.23	0.57	8.73	0.80
Baa	13.89	4.92	0.68	6.42	6.28	0.40	7.47	0.28
Ba	0.00	0.00	0.00	0.00	0.00	0.00	0.00	0.00
B	0.00	0.00	0.00	0.00	0.00	0.00	0.00	0.00
Caa	0.00	0.00	0.00	0.00	0.00	0.00	0.00	0.00
Ca or lower	0.00	0.00	0.00	0.00	0.00	0.00	0.00	0.00
NR	0.00	0.00	0.00	0.00	0.00	0.00	0.00	0.00
Totals	100.00		4.82	100.00		4.29	0.00	0.54

The analysis of credit quality risk shown in Exhibit 5 follows the same approach. Portfolio and benchmark allocations to different credit rating levels are compared in terms of contributions to spread duration. Once again we see the effect of the overweighting of corporates: there is an overweight of 0.80 years to single As and an underweight of −0.57 years in AAAs (U.S. government debt). The risk represented by tracking error due to quality corresponds to a systematic widening or tightening of spreads for a particular credit rating, uniformly across all industry groups.

As we saw in Exhibit 2, the largest sources of systematic risk in our sample portfolio are term structure, sector, and quality. We have therefore directed our attention first to the reports that address these risk components; we will return to them later. Next we examine the reports explaining optionality risk and mortgage risk, even though these risks do not contribute significantly to the risk of this particular portfolio.

Exhibit 6 shows the optionality report. Several different measures are used to analyze portfolio and benchmark exposures to changes in the value of embedded options. For callable and putable bonds, the difference between a bond's static duration[4] and its option-adjusted duration, known as "reduction due to call," gives one measure of the effect of optionality on pricing. This "reduction" is positive for bonds trading to maturity and negative for bonds trading to a call. These two categories of bonds are represented by separate risk factors. The exposures of the portfolio and benchmark to this "reduction," divided into option categories, constitute one set of factor loadings due to optionality. The model also looks at option delta and gamma, the first and second derivatives of option price with respect to security price.

---

[4] "Static duration" refers to the traditional duration of the bond assuming a fixed set of cash flows. Depending on how the bond is trading, these will be the bond's natural cash flows either to maturity or to the most likely option redemption date.

Exhibit 6: Optionality Report
Sample Portfolio versus Aggregate Index, 9/30/98

Optionality	% of Portfolio	Duration	Contrib to Duration	Adjusted Duration	Contrib. to Adj. Dur.	Reduction Due to Call
PORTFOLIO						
Bullet	63.95	5.76	3.68	5.76	3.68	0.00
Callable Traded to Matur	4.74	10.96	0.52	10.96	0.52	0.00
Callable Traded to Call	4.26	8.43	0.36	4.97	0.21	0.15
Putable Traded to Matur.	0.00	0.00	0.00	0.00	0.00	0.00
Putable Traded to Put	0.00	0.00	0.00	0.00	0.00	0.00
MBS	27.04	3.28	0.89	1.51	0.41	0.48
ABS	0.00	0.00	0.00	0.00	0.00	0.00
CMO	0.00	0.00	0.00	0.00	0.00	0.00
Others	0.00	0.00	0.00	0.00	0.00	0.00
Totals	100.00		5.45		4.82	0.63
BENCHMARK						
Bullet	57.53	5.70	3.28	5.70	3.28	0.00
Callable Traded to Matur.	2.66	9.06	0.24	8.50	0.23	0.01
Callable Traded to Call	7.06	6.93	0.49	3.56	0.25	0.24
Putable Traded to Matur.	0.35	11.27	0.04	9.64	0.03	0.01
Putable Traded to Put	0.78	11.59	0.09	5.77	0.04	0.05
MBS	30.67	3.25	1.00	1.37	0.42	0.58
ABS	0.96	3.14	0.03	3.14	0.03	0.00
CMO	0.00	0.00	0.00	0.00	0.00	0.00
Others	0.00	0.00	0.00	0.00	0.00	0.00
Totals	100.00		5.17		4.29	0.88

	Option Delta Analysis							
	Portfolio			Benchmark			Difference	
Option Delta	% of Portf.	Delta	Cntrb. to Delta	% of Portf.	Delta	Cntrb. to Delta	% of Portf.	Cntrb. to Delta
Bullet	63.95	0.000	0.000	57.53	0.000	0.000	6.43	0.000
Callable Traded to Matur.	4.74	0.000	0.000	2.66	0.057	0.002	2.08	−0.002
Callable Traded to Call	4.26	0.474	0.020	7.06	0.584	0.041	−2.80	−0.021
Putable Traded to Matur.	0.00	0.000	0.000	0.35	0.129	0.001	−0.35	−0.001
Putable Traded to Put	0.00	0.000	0.000	0.78	0.507	0.004	−0.78	−0.004
Totals	72.96		0.020	68.38		0.047	4.58	−0.027

	Option Gamma Analysis							
	Portfolio			Benchmark			Difference	
Option Gamma	% of Portf.	Delta	Cntrb. to Delta	% of Portf.	Delta	Cntrb. to Delta	% of Portf.	Cntrb. to Delta
Bullet	63.95	0.0000	0.0000	57.53	0.0000	0.0000	6.43	0.0000
Callable Traded to Matur.	4.74	0.0000	0.0000	2.66	0.0024	0.0001	2.08	−0.0001
Callable Traded to Call	4.26	0.0059	0.0002	7.06	0.0125	0.0009	−2.80	−0.0006
Putable Traded to Matur.	0.00	0.0000	0.0000	0.35	−0.0029	−0.0000	−0.35	0.0000
Putable Traded to Put	0.00	0.0000	0.0000	0.78	−0.0008	−0.0000	−0.78	0.0000
Totals	72.96		0.0002	68.38		0.0009	4.58	−0.0007

The risks particular to mortgage-backed securities consist of spread risk, prepayment risk, and convexity risk. The underpinnings for MBS sector spread risk, like those for corporate sectors, are found in the detailed sector report shown in Exhibit 4. Mortgage-backed securities are divided into four broad sectors based on a combination of originating agency and product: conventional 30-year; GNMA 30-year; all 15-year; and all balloons. The contributions of these four sectors to the portfolio and benchmark spread durations form the factor loadings for mortgage sector risk. Exposures to prepayments are shown in Exhibit 7. This group of risk factors corresponds to systematic changes in prepayment speeds by sector. Thus, the factor loadings represent the sensitivities of mortgage prices to changes in prepayment speeds (PSA durations). Premium mortgages will show negative prepayment sensitivities (i.e., prices will decrease with increasing prepayment speed), while those of discount mortgages will be positive. To curtail the exposure to sudden changes in prepayment rates, the portfolio should match the benchmark contributions to prepayment sensitivity in each mortgage sector. The third mortgage-specific component of tracking error is due to MBS volatility. Convexity is used as a measure of volatility sensitivity because volatility shocks will have the strongest impact on prices of those mortgages whose prepayment options are at the money (current coupons). These securities tend to have the most negative convexity. Exhibit 8 shows the comparison of portfolio and benchmark contributions to convexity in each mortgage sector, which forms the basis for this component of tracking error.

Sources of Non-Systematic Tracking Error

In addition to the various sources of systematic risk, Exhibit 2 indicates that the sample portfolio has 26 bp of non-systematic tracking error, or special risk. This risk stems from portfolio concentrations in individual securities or issuers. The portfolio report in Exhibit 9 helps elucidate this risk. The rightmost column of the exhibit shows the percentage of the portfolio's market value invested in each security. As the portfolio is relatively small, each bond makes up a noticeable fraction. In particular, there are two extremely large positions in corporate bonds, issued by GTE Corp. and Coca-Cola. With $50 million apiece, each of these two bonds represents more than 8% of the portfolio. A negative credit event associated with either of these firms (i.e., a downgrade) would cause large losses in the portfolio, while hardly affecting the highly diversified benchmark. The Aggregate Index consisted of almost 7,000 securities as of September 30, 1998, so that the largest U.S. Treasury issue accounts for less than 1%, and most corporate issues contribute less than 0.01% of the index market value. Thus, any large position in a corporate issue represents a material difference between portfolio and benchmark exposures that must be considered in a full treatment of risk.

Exhibit 7: MBS Prepayment Sensitivity Report
Sample Portfolio versus Aggregate Index, 9/30/98

MBS Sector	Portfolio			Benchmark			Difference	
	% of Portfolio	PSA Sens.	Cntrb. to PSA Sens.	% of Portfolio	PSA Sens.	Cntrb. to PSA Sens.	% of Portfolio	Cntrb. to PSA Sens.
COUPON < 6.0%								
Conventional	0.00	0.00	0.00	0.00	1.28	0.00	0.00	0.00
GNMA 30-yr.	0.00	0.00	0.00	0.00	1.03	0.00	0.00	0.00
15-year MBS	0.00	0.00	0.00	0.14	0.01	0.00	−0.14	0.00
Balloon	0.00	0.00	0.00	0.05	−0.08	0.00	−0.05	0.00
6.0% ≤ COUPON < 7.0%								
Conventional	2.90	−1.14	−0.03	5.37	−1.05	−0.06	−2.48	0.02
GNMA 30 yr.	0.76	−1.19	−0.01	1.30	−1.11	−0.01	−0.53	0.01
15-year MBS	3.52	−0.86	−0.03	3.26	−0.88	−0.03	0.26	0.00
Balloon	3.03	−0.54	−0.02	0.48	−0.73	0.00	2.55	−0.01
7.0% ≤ COUPON < 8.0%								
Conventional	4.93	−2.10	−0.10	8.32	−2.79	−0.23	−3.39	0.13
GNMA 30-yr.	4.66	−3.20	−0.15	3.90	−2.82	−0.11	0.76	−0.04
15-year MBS	0.00	0.00	0.00	1.83	−1.92	−0.04	−1.83	0.04
Balloon	0.00	0.00	0.00	0.25	−1.98	−0.01	−0.25	0.01
8.0% ≤ COUPON < 9.0%								
Conventional	5.14	−3.91	−0.20	2.26	−4.27	−0.10	2.87	−0.10
GNMA 30-yr.	0.00	0.00	0.00	1.71	−4.71	−0.08	−1.71	0.08
15-year MBS	0.00	0.00	0.00	0.31	−2.16	−0.01	−0.31	0.01
Balloon	0.00	0.00	0.00	0.00	−2.38	0.00	0.00	0.00
9.0% ≤ COUPON < 10.0%								
Conventional	0.00	0.00	0.00	0.54	−6.64	−0.04	−0.54	0.04
GNMA 30-yr.	2.11	−7.24	−0.15	0.62	−6.05	−0.04	1.49	−0.12
15-year MBS	0.00	0.00	0.00	0.04	−1.61	0.00	−0.04	0.00
Balloon	0.00	0.00	0.00	0.00	0.00	0.00	0.00	0.00
COUPON ≥ 10.0%								
Conventional	0.00	0.00	0.00	0.10	−8.14	−0.01	−0.10	0.01
GNMA 30-yr.	0.00	0.00	0.00	0.17	−7.49	−0.01	−0.17	0.01
15-year MBS	0.00	0.00	0.00	0.00	0.00	0.00	0.00	0.00
Balloon	0.00	0.00	0.00	0.00	0.00	0.00	0.00	0.00
Subtotals								
Conventional	12.96		−0.34	16.6		−0.43	−3.64	0.09
GNMA 30-yr.	7.53		−0.31	7.70		−0.26	−0.16	−0.06
15-year MBS	3.52		−0.03	5.59		−0.07	−2.06	0.04
Balloon	3.03		−0.02	0.78		−0.01	2.25	−0.01
Totals	27.04		−0.70	30.67		−0.76	−3.62	0.07

Exhibit 8: MBS Convexity Analysis
Sample Portfolio versus Aggregate Index, 9/30/98

MBS Sector	Portfolio			Benchmark			Difference	
	% of Portfolio	Convexity	Cntrb. to Convexity	% of Portfolio	Convexity	Cntrb. to Convexity	% of Portfolio	Cntrb. to Convexity
COUPON < 6.0%								
Conventional	0.00	0.00	0.00	0.00	−0.56	0.00	0.00	0.00
GNMA 30-yr.	0.00	0.00	0.00	0.00	−0.85	0.00	0.00	0.00
15-year MBS	0.00	0.00	0.00	0.14	−0.88	0.00	−0.14	0.00
Balloon	0.00	0.00	0.00	0.05	−0.48	0.00	−0.05	0.00
6.0% ≤ COUPON < 7.0%								
Conventional	2.90	−3.52	−0.10	5.37	−3.19	−0.17	−2.48	0.07
GNMA 30-yr.	0.76	−3.65	−0.03	1.30	−3.13	−0.04	−0.53	0.01
15-year MBS	3.52	−1.78	−0.06	3.26	−2.06	−0.07	0.26	0.00
Balloon	3.03	−1.50	−0.05	0.48	−1.11	−0.01	2.55	−0.04
7.0% ≤ COUPON < 8.0%								
Conventional	4.93	−3.39	−0.17	8.32	−2.60	−0.22	−3.39	0.05
GNMA 30-yr.	4.66	−2.40	−0.11	3.90	−2.88	−0.11	0.76	0.00
15-year MBS	0.00	0.00	0.00	1.83	−1.56	−0.03	−1.83	0.03
Balloon	0.00	0.00	0.00	0.25	−0.97	0.00	−0.25	0.00
8.0% ≤ COUPON < 9.0%								
Conventional	5.14	−1.27	−0.07	2.26	−1.01	−0.02	2.87	−0.04
GNMA 30-yr.	0.00	0.00	0.00	1.71	−0.56	−0.01	−1.71	0.01
15-year MBS	0.00	0.00	0.00	0.31	−0.93	0.00	−0.31	0.00
Balloon	0.00	0.00	0.00	0.00	−0.96	0.00	0.00	0.00
9.0% ≤ COUPON < 10.0%								
Conventional	0.00	0.00	0.00	0.54	−0.80	0.00	−0.54	0.00
GNMA 30-yr.	2.11	−0.34	−0.01	0.62	−0.36	0.00	1.49	−0.01
15-year MBS	0.00	0.00	0.00	0.04	−0.52	0.00	−0.04	0.00
Balloon	0.00	0.00	0.00	0.00	0.00	0.00	0.00	0.00
COUPON ≥ 10.0%								
Conventional	0.00	0.00	0.00	0.10	−0.61	0.00	−0.10	0.00
GNMA 30-yr.	0.00	0.00	0.00	0.17	−0.21	0.00	−0.17	0.00
15-year MBS	0.00	0.00	0.00	0.00	0.00	0.00	0.00	0.00
Balloon	0.00	0.00	0.00	0.00	0.00	0.00	0.00	0.00
Subtotals								
Conventional	12.96		−0.33	16.6		−0.42	−3.64	0.08
GNMA 30-yr.	7.53		−0.15	7.70		−0.16	−0.16	0.02
15-year MBS	3.52		−0.06	5.59		−0.10	−2.06	0.04
Balloon	3.03		−0.05	0.78		−0.01	2.25	−0.04
Totals	27.04		−0.59	30.67		−0.69	−3.62	0.10

Exhibit 9: Portfolio Report: Composition of Sample Portfolio, 9/30/98

#	Cusip	Issuer Name	Coup	Maturity	Moody	S&P	Sect	DurW	DurA	Par Val	%
1	057224AF	BAKER HUGHES	8.000	05/15/04	A2	A	IND	4.47	4.47	5,000	0.87
2	097023AL	BOEING CO	6.350	06/15/03	Aa3	AA	IND	3.98	3.98	10,000	1.58
3	191219AY	COCA-COLA ENTERPRISES I	6.950	11/15/26	A3	A+	IND	12.37	12.37	50,000	8.06
4	532457AP	ELI LILLY CO	6.770	01/01/36	Aa3	AA	IND	14.18	14.18	5,000	0.83
5	293561BS	ENRON CORP	6.625	11/15/05	Baa2	BBB+	UTL	5.53	5.53	5,000	0.80
6	31359MDN	FEDERAL NATL MTG ASSN	5.625	03/15/01	Aaa+	AAA+	USA	2.27	2.27	10,000	1.53
7	31359CAT	FEDERAL NATL MTG ASSN-G	7.400	07/01/04	Aaa+	AAA+	USA	4.66	4.66	8,000	1.37
8	FGG06096	FHLM Gold 7-Years Balloon	6.000	04/01/26	Aaa+	AAA+	FHg	2.55	1.69	20,000	3.03
9	FGD06494	FHLM Gold Guar Single F.	6.500	08/01/08	Aaa+	AAA+	FHd	3.13	1.95	23,000	3.52
10	FGB07098	FHLM Gold Guar Single F.	7.000	01/01/28	Aaa+	AAA+	FHb	3.68	1.33	32,000	4.93
11	FGB06498	FHLM Gold Guar Single F.	6.500	02/01/28	Aaa+	AAA+	FHb	5.00	2.83	19,000	2.90
12	319279BP	FIRST BANK SYSTEM	6.875	09/15/07	A2	A-	FIN	6.73	6.73	4,000	0.65
13	339012AB	FLEET MORTGAGE GROUP	6.500	09/15/99	A2	A+	FIN	0.92	0.92	4,000	0.60
14	FNA08092	FNMA Conventional Long T.	8.000	05/01/21	Aaa+	AAA+	FNa	2.56	0.96	33,000	5.14
15	31364FSK	FNMA MTN	6.420	02/12/08	Aaa+	AAA+	USA	2.16	3.40	8,000	1.23
16	345397GS	FORD MOTOR CREDIT	7.500	01/15/03	A1	A	FIN	3.62	3.62	4,000	0.65
17	347471AR	FORT JAMES CORP	6.875	09/15/07	Baa2	BBB-	IND	6.68	6.68	4,000	0.63
18	GNA09490	GNMA I Single Family	9.500	10/01/19	Aaa+	AAA+	GNa	2.69	1.60	13,000	2.11
19	GNA07493	GNMA I Single Family	7.500	07/01/22	Aaa+	AAA+	GNa	3.13	0.75	30,000	4.66
20	GNA06498	GNMA I Single Family	6.500	02/01/28	Aaa+	AAA+	GNa	5.34	3.14	5,000	0.76
21	362320AQ	GTE CORP	9.375	12/01/00	Baa1	A	TEL	1.91	1.91	50,000	8.32
22	458182CB	INT-AMERICAN DEV BANK-G	6.375	10/22/07	Aaa	AAA	SUP	6.76	6.76	6,000	1.00
23	459200AK	INTL BUSINESS MACHINES	6.375	06/15/00	A1	A+	IND	1.58	1.58	10,000	1.55
24	524909AS	LEHMAN BROTHERS INC	7.125	07/15/02	Baa1	A	FIN	3.20	3.20	4,000	0.59
25	539830AA	LOCKHEED MARTIN	6.550	05/15/99	A3	BBB+	IND	0.59	0.59	10,000	1.53
26	563469CZ	MANITOBA PROV CANADA	8.875	09/15/21	A1	AA-	CAN	11.34	11.34	4,000	0.79
27	58013MDE	MCDONALDS CORP	5.950	01/15/08	Aa2	AA	IND	7.05	7.05	4,000	0.63
28	590188HZ	MERRILL LYNCH & CO.-GLO	6.000	02/12/03	Aa3	AA-	FIN	3.77	3.77	5,000	0.76
29	638585BE	NATIONSBANK CORP	5.750	03/15/01	Aa2	A+	FIN	2.26	2.26	3,000	0.45

Exhibit 9 (Continued)

#	Cusip	Issuer Name	Coup	Maturity	Moody	S&P	Sect	DurW	DurA	Par Val	%
30	650094BM	NEW YORK TELEPHONE	9.375	07/15/31	A2	A+	TEL	2.43	3.66	5,000	0.86
31	654106AA	NIKE INC	6.375	12/01/03	A1	A+	IND	4.30	4.30	3,000	0.48
32	655844AJ	NORFOLK SOUTHERN CORP	7.800	05/15/27	Baa1	BBB+	IND	12.22	12.22	4,000	0.71
33	669383CN	NORWEST FINANCIAL INC.	6.125	08/01/03	Aa3	AA–	FIN	4.12	4.12	4,000	0.62
34	683234HG	ONT PROV CANADA-GLOBA	7.375	01/27/03	Aa3	AA–	CAN	3.67	3.67	4,000	0.65
35	744567DN	PUB SVC ELECTRIC + GAS	6.125	08/01/02	A3	A–	ELU	3.36	3.36	3,000	0.47
36	755111AF	RAYTHEON CO	7.200	08/15/27	Baa1	BBB	IND	12.61	12.61	8,000	1.31
37	761157AA	RESOLUTION FUNDING CORP	8.125	10/15/19	Aaa+	AAA+	USA	11.22	11.22	17,000	3.51
38	88731EAF	TIME WARNER ENT	8.375	03/15/23	Baa2	BBB–	IND	11.45	11.45	5,000	0.90
39	904000AA	ULTRAMAR DIAMOND SHAM	7.200	10/15/17	Baa2	BBB	IND	10.06	10.06	4,000	0.63
40	912810DB	US TREASURY BONDS	10.375	11/15/12	Aaa+	AAA+	UST	6.30	6.38	10,000	2.17
41	912810DS	US TREASURY BONDS	10.625	08/15/15	Aaa+	AAA+	UST	9.68	9.68	14,000	3.43
42	912810EQ	US TREASURY BONDS	6.250	08/15/23	Aaa+	AAA+	UST	13.26	13.26	30,000	5.14
43	912827XE	US TREASURY NOTES	8.875	02/15/99	Aaa+	AAA+	UST	0.37	0.37	9,000	1.38
44	912827F9	US TREASURY NOTES	6.375	07/15/99	Aaa+	AAA+	UST	0.76	0.76	4,000	0.61
45	912827R4	US TREASURY NOTES	7.125	09/30/99	Aaa+	AAA+	UST	0.96	0.96	17,000	2.59
46	912827Z9	US TREASURY NOTES	5.875	11/15/99	Aaa+	AAA+	UST	1.06	1.06	17,000	2.62
47	912827T4	US TREASURY NOTES	6.875	03/31/00	Aaa+	AAA+	UST	1.42	1.42	8,000	1.23
48	9128273D	US TREASURY NOTES	6.000	08/15/00	Aaa+	AAA+	UST	1.75	1.75	11,000	1.70
49	912827A8	US TREASURY NOTES	8.000	05/15/01	Aaa+	AAA+	UST	2.31	2.31	9,000	1.50
50	912827D2	US TREASURY NOTES	7.500	11/15/01	Aaa+	AAA+	UST	2.72	2.72	10,000	1.67
51	9128272P	US TREASURY NOTES	6.625	03/31/02	Aaa+	AAA+	UST	3.12	3.12	6,000	0.96
52	9128273G	US TREASURY NOTES	6.250	08/31/02	Aaa+	AAA+	UST	3.45	3.45	10,000	1.60
53	912827L8	US TREASURY NOTES	5.750	08/15/03	Aaa+	AAA+	UST	4.22	4.22	1,000	0.16
54	912827T8	US TREASURY NOTES	6.500	05/15/05	Aaa+	AAA+	UST	5.33	5.33	1,000	0.17
55	9128273E	US TREASURY NOTES	6.125	08/15/07	Aaa+	AAA+	UST	6.90	6.90	1,000	0.17
56	949740BZ	WELLS FARGO + CO	6.875	04/01/06	A2	A–	FIN	5.89	5.89	5,000	0.80
57	961214AD	WESTPAC BANKING CORP	7.875	10/15/02	A1	A+	FOC	3.34	3.34	3,000	0.49

Exhibit 10: Calculation of Variance Due to Special Risk (Issue-Specific Model) *

	Portfolio Weights	Benchmark Weights	Contribution to Issue-Specific Risk
Issue 1	w_{P_1}	w_{B_1}	$(w_{P_1} - w_{B_1})^2 \sigma_{\varepsilon_1}^2$
Issue 2	w_{P_2}	w_{B_2}	$(w_{P_2} - w_{B_2})^2 \sigma_{\varepsilon_2}^2$
. . .			
Issue $N-1$	$w_{P_{N-1}}$	$w_{B_{N-1}}$	$(w_{P_{N-1}} - w_{B_{N-1}})^2 \sigma_{\varepsilon_{N-1}}^2$
Issue N	w_{P_N}	w_{B_N}	$(w_{P_N} - w_{B_N})^2 \sigma_{\varepsilon_N}^2$
Total Issue-specific Risk			$\displaystyle\sum_{i=1}^{N} (w_{P_i} - w_{B_i})^2 \sigma_{\varepsilon_i}^2$

* w_{P_i} and w_{B_i} are weights of security i in the portfolio and in the benchmark as a percentage of total market value. $\sigma_{\varepsilon_i}^2$ is the variance of residual returns for security i. It is obtained from historical volatility of security-specific residual returns unexplained by the combination of all systematic risk factors.

The magnitude of the return variance that the risk model associates with a mismatch in allocations to a particular issue is proportional to the square of the allocation difference and to the residual return variance estimated for the issue. This calculation is shown in schematic form in Exhibit 10 and illustrated numerically for our sample portfolio in Exhibit 11. With the return variance based on the square of the market weight, it is dominated by the largest positions in the portfolio. The set of bonds shown includes those with the greatest allocations in the portfolio and in the benchmark. The large position in the Coca-Cola bond contributes 21 bp of the total non-systematic risk of 26 bp. This is due to the 8.05% overweighting of this bond relative to its position in the index and the 77 bp monthly volatility of non-systematic return that the model has estimated for this bond. (This estimate is based on bond characteristics such as sector, quality, duration, age, and amount outstanding.) The contribution to the annualized tracking error is then given by

$$\sqrt{12 \times (0.0805 \times 77)^2} = 21$$

While the overweighting to GTE is larger in terms of percentage of market value, the estimated risk is lower due to the much smaller non-systematic return volatility (37 bp). This is mainly because the GTE issue has a much shorter maturity (12/2000) than the Coca-Cola issue (11/2026). For bonds of similar maturities, the model tends to assign higher special risk volatilities to lower-rated issues. Thus, mismatches in low-quality bonds with long duration will be the biggest contributors to non-systematic tracking error. We assume independence of the risk from individual bonds, so the overall non-systematic risk is computed as the sum of the contributions to variance from each security. Note that mismatches also arise due to bonds that are underweighted in the portfolio. Most bonds in the index do not appear in the portfolio, and each missing bond contributes to tracking error. However, the percentage of the index each bond represents is usually very small. Besides, their contributions to return variance are squared in the calculation of tracking error. Thus, the impact of bonds not included in the portfolio is usually insignificant. The largest contribution to tracking error stemming from an underweighting to a security is due to the 1998 issuance of FNMA 30-year 6.5% pass-throughs, which represents 1.16% of the benchmark. Even this relatively large mismatch contributes only a scant 1 bp to tracking error.

Exhibit 11: Illustration of the Calculation of Non-Systematic Tracking Error

CUSIP	Issuer	Coupon	Maturity	Spec. Risk Vol. (bp/mo.)	% of Portf.	% of Bnchmrk.	Diff.	Contrib. Tracking Error (bp/mo.)
097023AL	BOEING CO	6.350	06/15/03	44	1.58	0.01	1.58	2
191219AY	COCA-COLA ENTERPRISES INC.	6.950	11/15/26	77	8.06	0.01	8.05	21
362320AQ	GTE CORP	9.375	12/01/00	37	8.32	0.01	8.31	11
532457AP	ELI LILLY CO	6.770	01/01/36	78	0.83	0.01	0.82	2
563469CZ	MANITOBA PROV CANADA	8.875	09/15/21	73	0.79	0.01	0.79	2
655844AJ	NORFOLK SOUTHERN CORP	7.800	05/15/27	84	0.71	0.02	0.70	2
755111AF	RAYTHEON CO	7.200	08/15/27	85	1.31	0.01	1.30	4
761157AA	RESOLUTION FUNDING CORP	8.125	10/15/19	19	3.51	0.12	3.39	2
88731EAF	TIME WARNER ENT	8.375	03/15/23	80	0.90	0.02	0.88	2
912810DS	U.S. TREASURY BONDS	10.625	08/15/15	17	3.43	0.18	3.25	2
912810EC	U.S. TREASURY BONDS	8.875	02/15/19	18	0.00	0.49	−0.49	0
912810ED	U.S. TREASURY BONDS	8.125	08/15/19	18	0.00	0.47	−0.47	0
912810EG	U.S. TREASURY BONDS	8.750	08/15/20	18	0.00	0.54	−0.54	0
912810EL	U.S. TREASURY BONDS	8.000	11/15/21	17	0.00	0.81	−0.81	0
912810EQ	U.S. TREASURY BONDS	6.250	08/15/23	19	5.14	0.46	4.68	3
912810FB	U.S. TREASURY BONDS	6.125	11/15/27	20	0.00	0.44	−0.44	0
FGB07097	FHLM Gold Guar. Single Fam. 30-yr.	7.000	04/01/27	16	0.00	0.56	−0.56	0
FGB07098	FHLM Gold Guar. Single Fam. 30-yr.	7.000	01/01/28	15	4.93	0.46	4.47	2
FNA06498	FNMA Conventional Long T. 30-yr.	6.500	03/01/28	15	0.00	1.16	−1.16	1
FNA07093	FNMA Conventional Long T. 30-yr.	7.000	07/01/22	16	0.00	0.65	−0.65	0
FNA07097	FNMA Conventional Long T. 30-yr.	7.000	05/01/27	16	0.00	0.69	−0.69	0
FNA08092	FNMA Conventional Long T. 30-yr.	8.000	05/01/21	17	5.14	0.24	4.90	3
GNA07493	GNMA I Single Fam. 30-yr.	7.500	07/01/22	16	4.66	0.30	4.36	2

This non-systematic risk calculation is carried out twice, using two different methods. In the issuer-specific calculation, the holdings of the portfolio and benchmark are not compared on a bond-by-bond basis, as in Exhibits 10 and 11, but are first aggregated into concentrations in individual issuers. This calculation is based on the assumption that spreads of bonds of the same issuer tend to move together. Therefore, matching the benchmark issuer allocations is sufficient. In the issue-specific calculation, each bond is considered an independent source of risk. This model recognizes that large exposures to a single bond can incur more risk than a portfolio of all of an issuer's debt. In addition to credit events that affect an issuer as a whole, individual issues can be subject to various technical effects. For most portfolios, these two calculations produce very similar results. In certain circumstances, however, there can be significant differences. For instance, some large issuers use an index of all their outstanding debt as an internal performance benchmark. In the case of a single-issuer portfolio and benchmark, the issue-specific risk calculation will provide a much better measure of non-systematic risk. The reported non-systematic tracking error of 26.1 bp for this portfolio, which contributes to the total tracking error, is the average of the results from the issuer-specific and issue-specific calculations.

Combining Components of Tracking Error

Given the origins of each component of tracking error shown in Exhibit 2, we can address the question of how these components combine to form the overall tracking error. Of the 52 bp of overall tracking error (TE), 45 bp correspond to systematic TE and 26 bp to non-systematic TE. The net result of these two sources of tracking error does not equal their sum. Rather, the squares of these two numbers (which represent variances) sum to the variance of the result. Next we take its square root to obtain the overall TE ($[45.0^2 + 26.1^2]^{0.5} = 52.0$). This illustrates the risk-reducing benefits of diversification from combining independent (zero correlation) sources of risk.

When components of risk are not assumed to be independent, correlations must be considered. At the top of Exhibit 2, we see that the systematic risk is composed of 36.3 bp of term structure risk and 39.5 bp from all other forms of systematic risk combined (non-term structure risk). If these two were independent, they would combine to a systematic tracking error of 53.6 bp ($[36.3^2 + 39.5^2]^{0.5} = 53.6$). The combined systematic tracking error of only 45 bp reflects negative correlations among certain risk factors in the two groups.

The tracking error breakdown report in Exhibit 2 shows the sub-components of tracking error due to sector, quality, etc. These sub-components are calculated in two different ways. In the first column, we estimate the isolated tracking error due to the effect of each group of related risk factors considered alone. The tracking error due to term structure, for example, reflects only the portfolio/benchmark mismatches in exposures along the yield curve, as well as the volatilities of each of these risk factors and the correlations among them.

Exhibit 12: Illustration of "Isolated" and "Cumulative" Calculations of Tracking Error Subcomponents*

a. Isolated Calculation of Tracking Error Components

$Y \times Y$	$Y \times S$	$Y \times Q$
$S \times Y$	$S \times S$	$S \times Q$
$Q \times Y$	$Q \times S$	$Q \times Q$

b. Cumulative Calculation of Tracking Error Components

$Y \times Y$	$Y \times S$	$Y \times Q$
$S \times Y$	$S \times S$	$S \times Q$
$Q \times Y$	$Q \times S$	$Q \times Q$

* Y – Yield curve risk factors; S – Sector spread risk factors; Q – Credit Quality spread risk factors.

Similarly, the tracking error due to sector reflects only the mismatches in sector exposures, the volatilities of these risk factors, and the correlations among them. However, the correlations between the risk factors due to term structure and those due to sector do not participate in either of these calculations. Exhibit 12 depicts an idealized covariance matrix containing just three groups of risk factors relating to the yield curve (Y), sector spreads (S), and quality spreads (Q). Exhibit 12a illustrates how the covariance matrix is used to calculate the sub-components of tracking error in the isolated mode. The three shaded blocks represent the parts of the matrix that pertain to: movements of the various points along the yield curve and the correlations among them ($Y \times Y$); movements of sector spreads and the correlations among them ($S \times S$); and movements of quality spreads and the correlations among them ($Q \times Q$). The unshaded portions of the matrix, which deal with the correlations among different sets of risk factors, do not contribute to any of the partial tracking errors.

The next two columns of Exhibit 2 represent a different way of subdividing tracking error. The middle column shows the *cumulative tracking error*, which incrementally introduces one group of risk factors at a time to the tracking error calculation. In the first row, we find 36.3 bp of tracking error due to term structure. In the second, we see that if term structure and sector risk are considered together, while all other risks are ignored, the tracking error increases to 38.3 bp. The rightmost column shows that the resulting "change in tracking error" due to the incremental inclusion of sector risk is 2.0 bp. As additional groups of risk factors are included, the calculation converges toward the total systematic tracking error, which is obtained with the use of the entire matrix. Exhibit 12b illustrates the rectangular section of the covariance matrix that is used at each stage of the calculation. The incremental tracking error due to sector reflects not only the effect of the $S \times S$ box in the diagram, but the $S \times Y$ and $Y \times S$ cross terms as well. That is, the partial tracking error due to sector takes into account the correlations between sector risk and yield curve risk. It answers the question, "Given the exposure to yield curve risk, how much more risk is introduced by the exposure to sector risk?"

The incremental approach is intuitively pleasing because the partial tracking errors (the "Change in Tracking Error" column of Exhibit 2) add up to the total systematic tracking error. Of course, the order in which the various partial tracking errors are considered will affect the magnitude of the corresponding terms. Also, note that some of the partial tracking errors computed in this way are negative. This reflects negative correlations among certain groups of risk factors. For example, in Exhibit 2, the incremental risk due to the MBS Sector is −1.7 bp.

The two methods used to subdivide tracking error into different components are complementary and serve different purposes. The isolated calculation is ideal for comparing the magnitudes of different types of risk to highlight the most significant exposures. The cumulative approach produces a set of tracking error sub-components that sum to the total systematic tracking error and reflect the effect of correlations among different groups of risk factors. The major drawback of the cumulative approach is that results are highly dependent on the order in which they are computed. The order currently used by the model was selected based on the significance of each type of risk; it may not be optimal for every portfolio/benchmark combination.

Other Risk Model Outputs

The model's analysis of portfolio and benchmark risk is not limited to the calculation of tracking error. The model also calculates the absolute return volatilities (sigmas) of portfolio and benchmark. *Portfolio sigma* is calculated in the same fashion as tracking error, but is based on the factor loadings (sensitivities to market factors) of the portfolio, rather than on the differences from the benchmark. Sigma represents the volatility of portfolio returns, just as tracking error represents the volatility of the return difference between portfolio and benchmark. Also like tracking error, sigma consists of systematic and non-systematic components, and the volatility of the benchmark return is calculated in the same way. Both portfolio and benchmark sigmas appear at the bottom of the tracking error report (Exhibit 2). Note that the tracking error of 52 bp (the annualized volatility of return difference) is greater than the difference between the return volatilities (sigmas) of the portfolio and the benchmark (440 bp − 417 bp = 23 bp). It is easy to see why this should be so. Assume a benchmark of Treasury bonds, whose entire risk is due to term structure. A portfolio of short term, high-yield corporate bonds could be constructed such that the overall return volatility would match that of the Treasury benchmark. The magnitude of the credit risk in this portfolio might match the magnitude of the term structure risk in the benchmark, but the two would certainly not cancel each other out. The tracking error in this case might be larger than the sigma of either the portfolio or the benchmark.

In our example, the portfolio sigma is greater than that of the benchmark. Thus, we can say that the portfolio is "more risky" than the benchmark — its longer duration makes it more susceptible to a rise in interest rates. What if the portfolio was shorter than the benchmark and had a lower sigma? In this sense, we could consider the portfolio to be less risky. However, tracking error could be just as big given its capture of the risk of a yield curve rally in which the portfolio would lag. To reduce the risk of underperformance (tracking error), it is necessary to match the risk exposures of portfolio and benchmark. Thus, the reduction of tracking error will typically result in bringing portfolio sigma nearer to that of the bench-mark; but sigma can be changed in many ways that will not necessarily improve the tracking error.

It is interesting to compare the non-systematic components of portfolio and benchmark risk. The first thing to notice is that, when viewed in the context of the overall return volatility, the effect of non-systematic risk is negligible. To the precision shown, for both the portfolio and benchmark, the overall sigma is equal to its systematic part. The portfolio-level risk due to individual credit events is very small when compared to the total volatility of returns, which includes the entire exposure to all systematic risks, notably yield changes. The portfolio also has significantly more non-systematic risk (27 bp) than does the benchmark (4 bp), because the latter is much more diversified. In fact, because the benchmark exposures to any individual issuer are so close to zero, the non-systematic tracking error (26 bp) is almost the same as the non-systematic part of portfolio sigma. Notice that the non-systematic risk can form a significant component of the tracking error (26.1 bp out of a total of 52 bp) even as it is a negligible part of the absolute return volatility.

Another quantity calculated by the model is beta, which measures the risk of the portfolio relative to that of the benchmark. The beta for our sample portfolio is 1.05, as shown at the bottom of Exhibit 1. This means that the portfolio is more risky (volatile) than the benchmark. For every 100 bp of benchmark return (positive or negative), we would expect to see 105 bp for the portfolio. It is common to compare the beta produced by the risk model with the ratio of portfolio and benchmark durations. In this case, the duration ratio is 4.82/4.29 = 1.12, which is somewhat larger than the risk model beta. This is because the duration-based approach considers only term structure risk (and only parallel shift risk at that), while the risk model includes the combined effects of all relevant forms of risk, along with the correlations among them.

RISK MODEL APPLICATIONS

In this section we explore several applications of the model to portfolio management.

Quantifying Risk Associated with a View

The risk model is primarily a diagnostic tool. Whatever position a portfolio manager has taken relative to the benchmark, the risk model will quantify how much risk has been assumed. This helps measure the risk of the exposures taken to express a market view. It also points out the potential unintended risks in the portfolio.

Many firms use risk-adjusted measures to evaluate portfolio performance. A high return achieved by a series of successful but risky market plays may not please a conservative pension plan sponsor. A more modest return, achieved while maintaining much lower risk versus the benchmark, might be seen as a healthier approach over the long term. This point of view can be reflected either by adjusting performance by the amount of risk taken or by specifying in advance the acceptable level of risk for the portfolio. In any case, the portfolio manager should be cognizant of the risk inherent in a particular market view and weigh it against the anticipated gain. The increasing popularity of risk-adjusted performance evaluation is evident in the frequent use of the concept of an *information ratio* — portfolio outperformance of the benchmark per unit of standard deviation of observed outperformance. Plan sponsors often diversify among asset managers with different styles, looking for some of them to take more risk and for others to stay conservative, but always looking for high information ratios.

Risk Budgeting

To limit the amount of risk that may be taken by its portfolio managers or a plan sponsor can prescribe a maximum allowable tracking error. In the past, an asset management mandate might have put explicit constraints on deviation from the benchmark duration, differences in sector allocations, concentration in a given issuer, and total percentage invested outside the benchmark. Currently, we observe a tendency to constrain the overall risk versus the benchmark and leave the choice of the form of risk to the portfolio manager based on current risk premia offered by the market. By expressing various types of risk in the same units of tracking error, the model makes it possible to introduce the concept of opportunistic risk budget allocation. To constrain specific types of risk, limits can be applied to the different components of tracking error produced by the model. As described above, the overall tracking error represents the best way to quantify the net effect of multiple dimensions of risk in a single number.

With the model-specific nature of tracking error, there may be situations where the formal limits to be placed on the portfolio manager must be expressed in more objective terms. Constraints commonly found in investment policies include limits on the deviation between the portfolio and the benchmark, both in terms of Treasury duration and in spread duration contributions from various fixed-income asset classes. Because term structure risk tends to be best understood, many organizations have firm limits only for the amount of duration deviation allowed. For example, a portfolio manager may be limited to ±1 around benchmark duration. How can this limit be applied to risks along a different dimension?

The risk model can help establish relationships among risks of different types by comparing their tracking errors. Exhibit 13 shows the tracking errors achieved by several different blends of Treasury and spread product indices relative to the Treasury Index. A pure Treasury composite (Strategy 1) with duration one year longer than the benchmark has a tracking error of 85 bp per year. Strategies 2 and 3 are created by combining the investment-grade Corporate Index with both intermediate and long Treasury Indices to achieve desired exposures to spread duration while remaining neutral to the bench-mark in Treasury duration. Similar strategies are engaged to generate desired exposures to spread duration in the MBS and high-yield markets. As can be seen in Exhibit 13, an increase in pure Treasury duration by 1 (Strategy 1) is equivalent to an extension in corporate spread duration by 2.5, or an extension in high-yield spread duration by about 0.75. Our results with MBS spreads show that an MBS spread duration of 1 causes a tracking error of 58 bp, while a duration of 1.5 gives a tracking error of 87 bp. A simple linear interpolation would suggest that a tracking error of 85 bp (the magnitude of the risk of an extension of duration by 1) thus corresponds to an extension in MBS spread duration of approximately 1.47.

Of course, these are idealized examples in which spread exposure to one type of product is changed while holding Treasury duration constant. A real portfolio is likely to take risks in all dimensions simultaneously. To calculate the tracking error, the risk model considers the correlations among the different risk factors. As long as two risks along different dimensions are not perfectly correlated, the net risk is less than the sum of the two risks. For example, we have established that a corporate spread duration of 2.5 produces roughly the same risk as a Treasury duration of 1, each causing a tracking error of about 85 bp. For a portfolio able to take both types of risk, an investor might allocate half of the risk budget to each, setting limits on Treasury duration of 0.5 and on corporate spread duration of 1.25. This should keep the risk within the desired range of tracking error. As shown in Exhibit 13, this combination of risks produces a tracking error of only 51 bp. This method of allocating risk under a total risk budget (in terms of equivalent duration mismatches) can provide investors with a method of controlling risk that is easier to implement and more conservative than a direct limit on tracking error. This macro view of risk facilitates the capablity to set separate but uniformly expressed limits on portfolio managers responsible for different kinds of portfolio exposures.

Exhibit 13: "Risk Budget": An Example Using Components of Treasury and Spread Indices Relative to a Treasury Benchmark

Index	Treasury	Intermediate Treasury	Long Treasury	Corporate	MBS	High Yield
Duration	5.48	3.05	10.74	5.99	3.04	4.68
Spread Duration	0.00	0.00	0.00	6.04	3.46	4.58

Strategy No.	Risk Strategy	Tsy Dur. Diff.	Spread Dur. Diff.	% Interm. Treasury	% Long Treasury	% Sprd. Sector	Tracking Error vs. Tsy. Index (bp/yr)
	Treasury Index			68.40	31.60	0.00	0
1	Treasury Duration	1.0	0.00	55.40	44.60	0.00	85
2	Corp. Spread Duration	0.0	1.00	58.17	25.27	16.56	34
3		0.0	2.50	42.83	15.78	41.39	85
4	Tsy. Dur. & Corp. Sprd. Dur	0.5	1.25	49.12	30.19	20.70	51
5	MBS Spread Duration	0.0	1.00	39.46	31.64	28.90	58
6		0.0	1.47	25.99	31.65	42.36	85
7		0.0	1.50	24.99	31.66	43.35	87
8	High Yield Spread Duration	0.0	0.75	55.50	28.13	16.38	84
9		0.0	1.00	51.19	26.97	21.83	119

Exhibit 14: A Simple Diversification Trade: Cut the Size of the Largest Position in Half

	Issuer	Coupon	Maturity	Par Value ($000s)	MV ($000s)	Sector	Quality	Dur Adj.
Sell:	Coca-Cola Enterprises Inc.	6.95	11/15/2026	25000	27053	IND	A3	12.37
Buy:	Anheuser-Busch Co.,inc.	6.75	12/15/2027	25000	26941	IND	A1	12.86

Projecting the Effect of Proposed Transactions on Tracking Error

Proposed trades are often analyzed in the context of a 1-for-1 (substitution) swap. Selling a security and using the proceeds to buy another may earn a few additional basis points of yield. The risk model allows analysis of such a trade in the context of the portfolio and its benchmark. By comparing the current portfolio versus benchmark risk and the pro forma risk after the proposed trade, an asset manager can evaluate how well the trade fits the portfolio. Our portfolio analytics platform offers an interactive mode to allow portfolio modifications and immediately see the effect on tracking error.

For example, having noticed that our sample portfolio has an extremely large position in the Coca-Cola issue, we might decide to cut the size of this position in half. To avoid making any significant changes to the systematic risk profile of the portfolio, we might look for a bond with similar maturity, credit rating, and sector. Exhibit 14 shows an example of such a swap. Half the position in the Coca-Cola 30-year bond is replaced by a 30-year issue from Anheuser-Busch, another single-A rated issuer in the beverage sector. As shown later, this transaction reduces non-systematic tracking error from 26 bp to 22 bp. While we have unwittingly produced a 1 bp increase in the systematic risk (the durations of the two bonds were not identical), the overall effect was a decrease in tracking error from 52 bp to 51 bp.

Optimization

For many portfolio managers, the risk model acts not only as a measurement tool but plays a major role in the portfolio construction process. The model has a unique optimization feature that guides investors to transactions that reduce portfolio risk. The types of questions it addresses are: What single transaction can reduce the risk of the portfolio relative to the benchmark the most? How could the tracking error be reduced with minimum turnover? The portfolio manager is given an opportunity to intervene at each step in the optimization process and select transactions that lead to the desired changes in the risk profile of the portfolio and are practical at the same time.

As in any portfolio optimization procedure, the first step is to choose the set of assets that may be purchased. The composition of this investable universe, or bond swap pool, is critical. This universe should be large enough to provide flexibility in matching all benchmark risk exposures, yet it should contain only securities that are acceptable candidates for purchase. This universe may be created by querying a bond database (selecting, for instance, all corporate bonds with more than $500 million outstanding that were issued in the last three years) or by providing a list of securities available for purchase.

Once the investable universe has been selected, the optimizer begins an iterative process (known as *gradient descent*), searching for 1-for-1 bond swap transactions that will achieve the investor's objective. In the simplest case, the objective is to minimize the tracking error. The bonds in the swap pool are ranked in terms of reduction in tracking error per unit of each bond purchased. The system indicates which bond, if purchased, will lead to the steepest decline in tracking error, but leaves the ultimate choice of the security to the investor. Once a bond has been selected for purchase, the optimizer offers a list of possible market-value-neutral swaps of this security against various issues in the portfolio (with the optimal transaction size for each pair of bonds), sorted in order of possible reduction in tracking error. Investors are free to adjust the model's recommendations, either selecting different bonds to sell or adjusting (e.g., rounding off) recommended trade amounts.

Exhibit 15 shows how this optimization process is used to minimize the tracking error of the sample portfolio. A close look at the sequence of trades suggested by the optimizer reveals that several types of risk are reduced simultaneously. In the first trade, the majority of the large position in the Coca-Cola 30-year bond is swapped for a 3-year Treasury. This trade simultaneously changes systematic exposures to term structure, sector, and quality; it also cuts one of the largest issuer exposures, reducing non-systematic risk. This one trade brings the overall tracking error down from 52 bp to 29 bp. As risk declines and the portfolio risk profile approaches the benchmark, there is less room for such drastic improvements. Transaction sizes become smaller, and the improvement in tracking error with each trade slows. The second and third transactions continue to adjust the sector and quality exposures and fine-tune the risk exposures along the curve. The fourth transaction addresses the other large corporate exposure, cutting the position in GTE by two-thirds. The first five trades reduce the tracking error to 16 bp, creating an essentially passive portfolio.

An analysis of the tracking error for this passive portfolio is shown in Exhibit 16. The systematic tracking error has been reduced to just 10 bp and the non-systematic risk to 13 bp. Once systematic risk drops below non-systematic risk, the latter becomes the limiting factor. In turn, further tracking error reduction by just a few transactions becomes much less likely. When there are exceptionally large positions, like the two mentioned in the above example, non-systematic risk can be reduced quickly. Upon completion of such risk reduction transactions, further reduction of tracking error requires a major diversification effort. The critical factor that determines non-systematic risk is the percentage of the portfolio in any single issue. On average, a portfolio of 50 bonds has 2% allocated to each position. To reduce this average allocation to 1%, the number of bonds would need to be doubled.

The risk exposures of the resulting passive portfolio match the benchmark much better than the initial portfolio. Exhibit 17 details the term structure risk of the passive portfolio. Compared with Exhibit 3, the overweight at the long end is reduced significantly. The overweight at the 25-year vertex has gone down from 1.45% to 0.64%, and (perhaps more importantly) it is now offset partially by underweights at the adjacent 20- and 30-year vertices. Exhibit 18 presents the sector risk report for the passive portfolio. The underweight to Treasuries (in contribution to duration) has been reduced from −0.77% to −0.29% relative to the initial portfolio (Exhibit 4), and the largest corporate overweight, to consumer non-cyclicals, has come down from +1.00% to +0.24%.

Exhibit 15: Sequence of Transactions Selected by Optimizer Showing Progressively Smaller Tracking Error, $000s

Initial Tracking Error: 52.0 bp

Transaction # 1		
Sold:	31000 of COCA-COLA ENTERPRISES	6.950 2026/11/15
Bought:	30000 of U.S. TREASURY NOTES	8.000 2001/05/15
Cash Leftover:	−17.10	
New Tracking Error:	29.4 bp	
Cost of This Transaction:	152.500	
Cumulative Cost:	152.500	
Transaction # 2		
Sold:	10000 of LOCKHEED MARTIN	6.550 1999/05/15
Bought:	9000 of U.S. TREASURY NOTES	6.125 2007/08/15
Cash Leftover:	132.84	
New Tracking Error:	25.5 bp	
Cost of This Transaction:	47.500	
Cumulative Cost:	200.000	
Transaction # 3		
Sold:	4000 of NORFOLK SOUTHERN CORP	7.800 2027/05/15
Bought:	3000 of U.S. TREASURY BONDS	10.625 2015/08/15
Cash Leftover:	−8.12	
New Tracking Error:	23.1 bp	
Cost of This Transaction:	17.500	
Cumulative Cost:	217.500	
Transaction # 4		
Sold:	33000 of GTE CORP	9.375 2000/12/01
Bought:	34000 of U.S. TREASURY NOTES	6.625 2002/03/31
Cash Leftover:	412.18	
New Tracking Error:	19.8 bp	
Cost of This Transaction:	167.500	
Cumulative Cost:	385.000	
Transaction # 5		
Sold:	7000 of COCA-COLA ENTERPRISES	6.950 2026/11/15
Bought:	8000 of U.S. TREASURY NOTES	6.000 2000/08/15
Cash Leftover:	−304.17	
New Tracking Error:	16.4 bp	
Cost of This Transaction:	37.500	
Cumulative Cost:	422.500	

Exhibit 16: Tracking Error Summary
Passive Portfolio versus Aggregate Index, 9/30/98

	Tracking Error (bp/year)		
	Isolated	Cumulative	Change
Tracking Error Term Structure	7.0	7.0	7.0
Non-Term Structure	9.6		
Tracking Error Sector	7.4	10.5	3.5
Tracking Error Quality	2.1	11.2	0.7
Tracking Error Optionality	1.6	11.5	0.3
Tracking Error Coupon	2.0	12.3	0.8
Tracking Error MBS Sector	4.9	10.2	−2.1
Tracking Error MBS Volatility	7.2	11.1	0.9
Tracking Error MBS Prepayment	2.5	10.3	−0.8
Total Systematic Tracking Error		10.3	
Non-systematic Tracking Error			
Issuer-specific	12.4		
Issue-specific	3.0		
Total	12.7		
Total Tracking Error Return		16	

	Systematic	Non-systematic	Total
Benchmark Sigma	417	4	417
Portfolio Sigma	413	13	413

Exhibit 17: Term Structure Risk Report for Passive Portfolio, 9/30/98

	Cash Flows		
Year	Portfolio	Benchmark	Difference
0.00	1.33%	1.85%	−0.52%
0.25	3.75	4.25	−0.50
0.50	4.05	4.25	−0.19
0.75	3.50	3.76	−0.27
1.00	8.96	7.37	1.59
1.50	7.75	10.29	−2.54
2.00	8.30	8.09	0.21
2.50	10.30	6.42	3.87
3.00	5.32	5.50	−0.19
3.50	8.24	4.81	3.43
4.00	6.56	7.19	−0.63
5.00	5.91	6.96	−1.05
6.00	3.42	4.67	−1.24
7.00	5.75	7.84	−2.10
10.00	6.99	7.37	−0.38
15.00	4.00	3.88	0.12
20.00	2.98	3.04	−0.05
25.00	2.37	1.73	0.64
30.00	0.47	0.68	−0.21
40.00	0.08	0.07	0.01

Exhibit 18: Sector Risk Report for Passive Portfolio, 9/30/98

Detailed Sector	Portfolio			Benchmark			Difference	
	% of Portfolio	Adj. Dur.	Contrib. to Adj. Dur.	% of Portfolio	Adj. Dur.	Contrib. to Adj. Dur.	% of Portfolio	Contrib. to Adj. Dur.
Treasury								
Coupon	40.98	4.72	1.94	39.82	5.58	2.22	1.16	−0.29
Strip	0.00	0.00	0.00	0.00	0.00	0.00	0.00	0.00
Agencies								
FNMA	4.12	3.40	0.14	3.56	3.44	0.12	0.56	0.02
FHLB	0.00	0.00	0.00	1.21	2.32	0.03	−1.21	−0.03
FHLMC	0.00	0.00	0.00	0.91	3.24	0.03	−0.91	−0.03
REFCORP	3.50	11.22	0.39	0.83	12.18	0.10	2.68	0.29
Other Agencies	0.00	0.00	0.00	1.31	5.58	0.07	−1.31	−0.07
Financial Institutions								
Banking	1.91	5.31	0.10	2.02	5.55	0.11	−0.11	−0.01
Brokerage	1.35	3.52	0.05	0.81	4.14	0.03	0.53	0.01
Financial Cos.	1.88	2.92	0.05	2.11	3.78	0.08	−0.23	−0.02
Insurance	0.00	0.00	0.00	0.52	7.47	0.04	−0.52	−0.04
Other	0.00	0.00	0.00	0.28	5.76	0.02	−0.28	−0.02
Industrials								
Basic	0.63	6.68	0.04	0.89	6.39	0.06	−0.26	−0.01
Capital Goods	2.89	7.88	0.23	1.16	6.94	0.08	1.73	0.15
Consumer Cycl.	2.01	8.37	0.17	2.28	7.10	0.16	−0.27	0.01
Consum. Non-cycl.	2.76	12.91	0.36	1.66	6.84	0.11	1.10	0.24
Energy	1.50	6.82	0.10	0.69	6.89	0.05	0.81	0.05
Technology	1.55	1.58	0.02	0.42	7.39	0.03	1.13	−0.01
Transportation	0.00	0.00	0.00	0.57	7.41	0.04	−0.57	−0.04
Utilities								
Electric	0.47	3.36	0.02	1.39	5.02	0.07	−0.93	−0.05
Telephone	3.69	2.32	0.09	1.54	6.58	0.10	2.15	−0.02
Natural Gas	0.80	5.53	0.04	0.49	6.50	0.03	0.31	0.01
Water	0.00	0.00	0.00	0.00	0.00	0.00	0.00	0.00
Yankee								
Canadians	1.45	7.87	0.11	1.06	6.67	0.07	0.38	0.04
Corporates	0.49	3.34	0.02	1.79	6.06	0.11	−1.30	−0.09
Supranational	1.00	6.76	0.07	0.38	6.33	0.02	0.62	0.04
Sovereigns	0.00	0.00	0.00	0.66	5.95	0.04	−0.66	−0.04
Hypothetical	0.00	0.00	0.00	0.00	0.00	0.00	0.00	0.00
Cash	0.00	0.00	0.00	0.00	0.00	0.00	0.00	0.00
Mortgage								
Conventional 30-yr.	12.96	1.52	0.20	16.60	1.42	0.24	−3.64	−0.04
GNMA 30-yr.	7.53	1.23	0.09	7.70	1.12	0.09	−0.17	0.01
MBS 15-yr.	3.52	1.95	0.07	5.59	1.63	0.09	−2.07	−0.02
Balloons	3.02	1.69	0.05	0.78	1.02	0.01	2.24	0.04
OTM	0.00	0.00	0.00	0.00	0.00	0.00	0.00	0.00
European & International								
Eurobonds	0.00	0.00	0.00	0.00	0.00	0.00	0.00	0.00
International	0.00	0.00	0.00	0.00	0.00	0.00	0.00	0.00
Asset Backed	0.00	0.00	0.00	0.96	3.14	0.03	−0.96	−0.03
CMO	0.00	0.00	0.00	0.00	0.00	0.00	0.00	0.00
Other	0.00	0.00	0.00	0.00	0.00	0.00	0.00	0.00
Totals	100.00		4.35	100.00		4.29	0.00	0.00

Minimization of tracking error, illustrated above, is the most basic application of the optimizer. This is ideal for passive investors who want their portfolios to track the benchmark as closely as possible. This method also aids investors who hope to outperform the benchmark mainly on the basis of security selection, without expressing views on sector or yield curve. Given a carefully selected universe of securities from a set of favored issuers, the optimizer can help build security picks into a portfolio with no significant systematic exposures relative to the benchmark.

For more active portfolios, the objective is no longer minimization of tracking error. When minimizing tracking error, the optimizer tries to reduce the largest differences between the portfolio and benchmark. But what if the portfolio is meant to be long duration or overweighted in a particular sector to express a market view? These views certainly should not be "optimized" away. However, unintended exposures need to be minimized, while keeping the intentional ones.

For instance, assume in the original sample portfolio that the sector exposure is intentional but the portfolio should be neutral to the benchmark for all other sources of risk, especially term structure. The risk model allows the investor to keep exposures to one or more sets of risk factors (in this case, sector) and optimize to reduce the components of tracking error due to all other risk factors. This is equivalent to reducing all components of tracking error but the ones to be preserved. The model introduces a significant penalty for changing the risk profile of the portfolio in the risk categories designated for preservation.

Exhibit 19 shows the transactions suggested by the optimizer in this case.[5] At first glance, the logic behind the selection of the proposed transactions is not as clear as before. We see a sequence of fairly small transactions, mostly trading up in coupon. Although this is one way to change the term structure exposure of a portfolio, it is usually not the most obvious or effective method. The reason for this lies in the very limited choices we offered the optimizer for this illustration. As in the example of tracking error minimization, the investable universe was limited to securities already in the portfolio. That is, only rebalancing trades were permitted. Because the most needed cash flows are at vertices where the portfolio has no maturing securities, the only way to increase those flows is through higher coupon payments. In a more realistic optimization exercise, we would include a wider range of maturity dates (and possibly a set of zero-coupon securities as well) in the investable universe to give the optimizer more flexibility in adjusting portfolio cash flows. Despite these self-imposed limitations, the optimizer succeeds in bringing down the term structure risk while leaving the sector risk almost unchanged. Exhibit 20 shows the tracking error breakdown for the resulting portfolio. The term structure risk has been reduced from 36 bp to 12 bp, while the sector risk remains almost unchanged at 30 bp.

---

[5] Tracking error does not decrease with each transaction. This is possible because the optimizer does not minimize the tracking error itself in this case, but rather a function that includes the tracking error due to all factors but sector, as well as a penalty term for changing sector exposures.

Exhibit 19: *Sequence of Transactions Selected by Optimizer, Keeping Exposures to Sector, $000s*

Initial Tracking Error: 52.0 bp

Transaction # 1		
Sold:	2000 of COCA-COLA ENTERPRISES	6.950 2026/11/15
Bought:	2000 of NORFOLK SOUTHERN CORP	7.800 2027/05/15
Cash Leftover:	−235.19	
New Tracking Error:	52.1 bp	
Cost of This Transaction:	10.000	
Cumulative Cost:	10.000	
Transaction # 2		
Sold:	2000 of COCA-COLA ENTERPRISES	6.950 2026/11/15
Bought:	2000 of NEW YORK TELEPHONE	9.375 2031/07/15
Cash Leftover:	−389.36	
New Tracking Error:	50.1 bp	
Cost of This Transaction:	10.000	
Cumulative Cost:	20.000	
Transaction # 3		
Sold:	10000 of U.S. TREASURY BONDS	6.250 2023/08/15
Bought:	10000 of NEW YORK TELEPHONE	9.375 2031/07/15
Cash Leftover:	−468.14	
New Tracking Error:	47.4 bp	
Cost of This Transaction:	50.000	
Cumulative Cost:	70.000	
Transaction # 4		
Sold:	2000 of COCA-COLA ENTERPRISES	6.950 2026/11/15
Bought:	2000 of FHLM Gold Guar. Single Fam.	7.000 2028/01/01
Cash Leftover:	−373.47	
New Tracking Error:	46.0 bp	
Cost of This Transaction:	10.000	
Cumulative Cost:	80.000	
Transaction # 5		
Sold:	6000 of U.S. TREASURY BONDS	6.250 2023/08/15
Bought:	6000 of GNMA I Single Fam.	7.500 2022/07/01
Cash Leftover:	272.43	
New Tracking Error:	47.2 bp	
Cost of This Transaction:	30.000	
Cumulative Cost:	110.000	
Transaction # 6		
Sold:	1000 of NORFOLK SOUTHERN CORP	7.800 2027/05/15
Bought:	1000 of U.S. TREASURY NOTES	6.125 2007/08/15
Cash Leftover:	343.44	
New Tracking Error:	46.4 bp	
Cost of This Transaction:	5.000	
Cumulative Cost:	115.000	
Transaction # 7		
Sold:	2000 of NORFOLK SOUTHERN CORP	7.800 2027/05/15
Bought:	2000 of ANHEUSER-BUSCH CO.,INC.	6.750 2027/12/15
Cash Leftover:	587.60	
New Tracking Error:	45.7 bp	
Cost of This Transaction:	10.000	
Cumulative Cost:	125.000	

Exhibit 20: Summary of Tracking Error Breakdown for Sample Portfolios

Tracking Error Due to:	Original Portfolio	Swapped Coca-Cola	Passive	Keep Sector Exposures
Term Structure	36	37	7	12
Sector	32	32	7	30
Systematic Risk	45	46	10	39
Non-systematic	26	22	13	24
Total	52	51	16	46

Proxy Portfolios

How many securities does it take to replicate the Lehman Corporate Index (containing about 4,500 bonds) to within 25 bp/year? How close could a portfolio of $50 million invested in 10 MBS securities get to the MBS index return? How many high yield securities does a portfolio need to hold to get sufficient diversification relative to the High Yield Index? How could one define "sufficient diversification" quantitatively? Investors asking any of these questions are looking for "index proxies" — portfolios with a small number of securities that nevertheless closely match their target indices.

Proxies are used for two distinct purposes: passive investment and index analysis. Both passive portfolio managers and active managers with no particular view on the market at a given time might be interested in insights from index proxies. These proxy portfolios represent a practical method of matching index returns while containing transaction costs. In addition, the large number of securities in an index can pose difficulties in the application of computationally intensive quantitative techniques. A portfolio can be analyzed against an index proxy of a few securities using methods that would be impractical to apply to an index of several thousand securities. As long as the proxy matches the index along relevant risk dimensions, this approach can speed up many forms of analysis with only a small sacrifice in accuracy.

There are several approaches to the creation of index proxies. Quantitative techniques include stratified sampling or cell-matching, tracking error minimization, and matching index scenario results. (With limitations, replication of index returns can also be achieved using securities outside of indices, such as Treasury futures contracts.[6] An alternative way of getting index returns is entering into an index swap or buying an appropriately structured note.) Regardless of the means used to build a proxy portfolio, the risk model can measure how well the proxy is likely to track the index.

In a simple cell-matching technique, a benchmark is profiled on an arbitrary grid that reflects the risk dimensions along which a portfolio manager's allocation decisions are made. The index contribution to each cell is then matched by

---

[6] *Replicating Index Returns with Treasury Futures*, Lehman Brothers, November 1997.

one or more representative liquid securities. Duration (and convexity) of each cell within the benchmark can be targeted when purchasing securities to fill the cell. We have used this technique to produce proxy portfolios of 20-25 MBS passthroughs to track the Lehman Brothers MBS Index. These portfolios have tracked the index of about 600 MBS generics to within 3 bp per month.[7]

To create or fine-tune a proxy portfolio using the risk model, we can start by selecting a seed portfolio and an investable universe. The tracking error minimization process described above then recommends a sequence of transactions. As more bonds are added to the portfolio, risk decreases. The level of tracking achieved by a proxy portfolio depends on the number of bonds included. Exhibit 21a shows the annualized tracking errors achieved using this procedure, as a function of the number of bonds, in a proxy for the Lehman Brothers Corporate Bond Index. At first, adding more securities to the portfolio reduces tracking error rapidly. But as the number of bonds grows, the improvement levels off. The breakdown between systematic and non-systematic risk explains this phenomenon. As securities are added to the portfolio, systematic risk is reduced rapidly. Once the corporate portfolio is sufficiently diverse to match index exposures to all industries and credit qualities, non-systematic risk dominates, and the rate of tracking error reduction decreases.

Exhibit 21b illustrates the same process applied to the Lehman Brothers High-Yield Index. A similar pattern is observed: Tracking error declines steeply at first as securities are added; tracking error reduction falls with later portfolio additions. The overall risk of the high-yield proxy remains above the investment-grade proxy. This reflects the effect of quality on our estimate of non-systematic risk. Similar exposures to lower-rated securities carry more risk. As a result, a proxy of about 30 investment-grade corporates tracks the Corporate Index within about 50 bp/year. Achieving the same tracking error for the High-Yield Index requires a proxy of 50 high-yield bonds.

To demonstrate that proxy portfolios track their underlying indices, we analyze the performance of three proxies over time. The described methodology was used to create a corporate proxy portfolio of about 30 securities from a universe of liquid corporate bonds (minimum $350 million outstanding). Exhibit 22 shows the tracking errors projected at the start of each month from January 1997 through September 1998, together with the performance achieved by portfolio and benchmark. The return difference is sometimes larger than the tracking error. (Note that the monthly return difference must be compared to the monthly tracking error, which is obtained by scaling down the annualized tracking error by $\sqrt{12}$.) This is to be expected. Tracking error does not constitute an upper bound of return difference, but rather one standard deviation. If the return difference is normally distributed with the standard deviation given by the tracking error, then the return difference should be expected to be within ±1 tracking error about 68%

---

[7] *Replicating the MBS Index Risk and Return Characteristics Using Proxy Portfolios*, Lehman Brothers, March 1997.

of the time, and within ±2 tracking errors about 95% of the time. For the corporate proxy shown here, the standard deviation of the return difference over the observed time period is 13 bp, almost identical to the projected monthly tracking error. Furthermore, the result is within ±1 tracking error in 17 months out of 24, or about 71% of the time.

Exhibit 21: Corporate Proxy—Tracking Error as a Function of Number of Bonds (Effect of Diversification)
a. Proxy for Corporate Bond Index

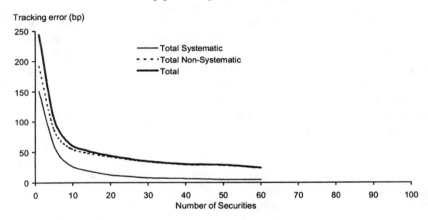

b. Proxy for High Yield Index

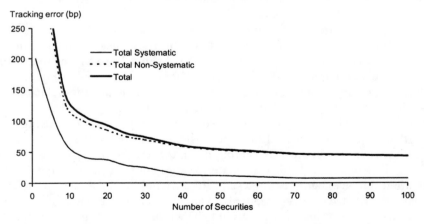

Exhibit 22: Corporate Proxy Portfolio: Comparison of Achieved Results with Projected Tracking Errors

Date	Annual Tracking Error (bp)	Monthly Tracking Error (bp)	Return (%/mo.) Proxy	Return (%/mo.) Index	Return Difference (bp/mo.)	Ret. Diff./ Monthly Tracking Error
Jan-97	48	14	0.15	0.14	0	0.03
Feb-97	48	14	0.37	0.42	−5	−0.34
Mar-97	48	14	−1.60	−1.56	−4	−0.30
Apr-97	47	14	1.60	1.52	8	0.60
May-97	48	14	1.14	1.13	1	0.04
Jun-97	48	14	1.42	1.42	0	0.03
Jul-97	47	14	3.62	3.66	−4	−0.27
Aug-97	48	14	−1.48	−1.48	0	−0.01
Sep-97	47	14	1.65	1.75	−10	−0.72
Oct-97	48	14	1.43	1.27	16	1.13
Nov-97	49	14	0.60	0.57	4	0.25
Dec-97	49	14	1.33	1.06	27	1.88
Jan-98	49	14	1.36	1.19	17	1.19
Feb-98	46	13	0.05	−0.03	8	0.59
Mar-98	46	13	0.39	0.37	2	0.16
Apr-98	45	13	0.75	0.63	12	0.93
May-98	44	13	1.22	1.19	3	0.24
Jun-98	45	13	0.79	0.74	6	0.42
Jul-98	45	13	−0.18	−0.10	−8	−0.63
Aug-98	44	13	0.76	0.47	29	2.26
Sep-98	44	13	3.62	3.24	38	2.99
Oct-98	46	13	−1.40	−1.54	15	1.11
Nov-98	45	13	2.04	1.88	16	1.20
Dec-98	47	14	0.17	0.29	−12	−0.87
Std. Dev.:					13	

	Number	Percentage
Observations within +/− 1 × tracking error	17	71%
Observations within +/− 2 × tracking error	22	92%
Total number of observations	24	

Exhibit 23 summarizes the performance of our Treasury, corporate, and mortgage index proxies. The MBS Index was tracked with a proxy portfolio of 20-25 generics. The Treasury index was matched using a simple cell-matching scheme. The index was divided into three maturity cells, and two highly liquid bonds were selected from each cell to match the index duration. For each of the three proxy portfolios, the observed standard deviation of return difference is less than the tracking error. The corporate portfolio tracks as predicted by the risk model, while the Treasury and mortgage proxies track better than predicted. The corporate index proxy was generated by minimizing the tracking error relative to the Corporate Index using 50-60 securities. Being much less diversified than the index of about 4,700 securities, the corporate proxy is most exposed to non-systematic risk. In the difficult month of September 1998, when liquidity in the credit markets was severely stemmed, this resulted in a realized return difference three times the projected tracking error.

A proxy portfolio for the Lehman Brothers Aggregate Index can be constructed by building proxies to track each of its major components and combining them with the proper weightings. This exercise clearly illustrates the benefits of diversification. The aggregate proxy in Exhibit 24 is obtained by combining the government, corporate, and mortgage proxies shown in the same exhibit. The tracking error achieved by the combination is smaller than that of any of its constituents. This is because the risks of the proxy portfolios are largely independent.

Exhibit 23: Summary of Historical Results of Proxy Portfolios for Treasury, Corporate, and MBS Indices, in bp per month

	Treasury		Corporate		MBS	
	Tracking Error	Return Difference	Tracking Error	Return Difference	Tracking Error	Return Difference
Jan-97	5.5	−1.7	13.9	0.4	4.3	0.8
Feb-97	5.2	−0.6	13.9	−4.7	4.3	−0.3
Mar-97	5.5	−1.8	13.9	−4.2	4.0	2.9
Apr-97	5.5	1.7	13.6	8.2	4.3	−3.3
May-97	5.8	−0.3	13.9	0.6	4.0	1.6
Jun-97	6.6	3.5	13.9	0.4	4.0	−0.5
Jul-97	6.6	3.8	13.6	−3.7	4.0	−2.5
Aug-97	6.9	−3.8	13.9	−0.1	4.3	1.5
Sep-97	6.4	1.5	13.6	−9.8	4.3	−1.2
Oct-97	6.4	3.2	13.9	15.7	4.0	−0.6
Nov-97	6.1	−2.3	14.1	3.5	4.0	0.8
Dec-97	6.6	6.0	14.1	26.6	4.0	−2.4
Jan-98	6.6	1.0	14.1	16.9	4.3	1.8
Feb-98	6.6	−1.8	13.3	7.8	4.9	2.2
Mar-98	6.6	1.8	13.3	2.1	4.0	−1.9
Apr-98	6.6	−1.8	13.0	12.1	4.6	−0.9
May-98	6.6	3.8	12.7	3.1	4.6	−0.3
Jun-98	7.8	−1.4	13.0	5.5	4.9	0.4
Jul-98	7.5	−1.7	13.0	−8.2	4.3	−1.3
Aug-98	7.5	−0.6	12.7	28.7	4.3	−3.4
Sep-98	8.1	−6.1	12.7	38.0	4.0	−1.7
Oct–98	7.8	5.4	13.3	14.7	4.0	3.4
Nov-98	7.8	−4.9	13.0	15.6	4.6	−1.8
Dec-98	6.1	−2.7	13.6	−11.8	4.3	−1.6
Mean	6.6	0.0	13.5	6.6	4.3	−0.3
Std. Dev.		3.2		12.5		1.9
Min		−6.1		−11.8		−3.4
Max		6.0		38.0		3.4

Exhibit 24: Effect of Diversification — Tracking Error versus Treasury, Corporate, MBS, and Aggregate

Index	No. of Bonds in Proxy	No. of Bonds in Index	Tracking Error (bp/year)
Treasury	6	165	13
Government	39	1,843	11
Corporate	51	4,380	26
Mortgage	19	606	15
Aggregate	109	6,928	10

When using tracking error minimization to design proxy portfolios, the choice of the "seed" portfolio and the investable universe should be considered carefully. The seed portfolio is the initial portfolio presented to the optimizer. Due to the nature of the gradient search procedure, the path followed by the optimizer will depend on the initial portfolio. The seed portfolio will produce the best results when it is closest in nature to the benchmark. At the very least, asset managers should choose a seed portfolio with duration near that of the benchmark. The investable universe, or bond swap pool, should be wide enough to offer the optimizer the freedom to match all risk factors. But if the intention is to actually purchase the proxy, the investable universe should be limited to liquid securities.

These methods for building proxy portfolios are not mutually exclusive, but can be used in conjunction with each other. A portfolio manager who seeks to build an investment portfolio that is largely passive to the index can use a combination of security picking, cell matching, and tracking error minimization. By dividing the market into cells and choosing one or more preferred securities in each cell, the manager can create an investable universe of candidate bonds in which all sectors and credit qualities are represented. The tracking error minimization procedure can then match index exposures to all risk factors while choosing only securities that the manager would like to purchase.

Benchmark Selection: Broad versus Narrow Indices

Lehman Brothers' development has been guided by the principle that benchmarks should be broad-based, market-weighted averages. This leads to indices that give a stable, objective and comprehensive representation of the selected market. On occasion, some investors have expressed a preference for indices composed of fewer securities. Among the rationales, transparency of pricing associated with smaller indices and a presumption that smaller indices are easier to replicate have been most commonly cited.

We have shown that it is possible to construct proxy portfolios with small numbers of securities that adequately track broad-based benchmarks. Furthermore, broad benchmarks offer more opportunities for outperformance by low-risk security selection strategies.[8] When a benchmark is too narrow, each security rep-

---

[8] *Value of Security Selection versus Asset Allocation in Credit Markets: A "Perfect Foresight" Study,* Lehman Brothers, March 1999.

resents a significant percentage, and a risk-conscious manager might be forced to own nearly every issue in the benchmark. Ideally, a benchmark should be diverse enough to reduce its non-systematic risk close to zero. As seen in Exhibit 2, the non-systematic part of sigma for the Aggregate Index is only 4 bp.

Defining Spread and Curve Scenarios Consistent with History

The tracking error produced by the risk model is an average expected performance deviation due to possible changes in all risk factors. In addition to this method of measuring risk, many investors perform "stress tests" on their portfolios. Here scenario analysis is used to project performance under various market conditions. The scenarios considered typically include a standard set of movements in the yield curve (parallel shift, steepening, and flattening) and possibly more specific scenarios based on market views. Often, though, practitioners neglect to consider spread changes, possibly due to the difficulties in generating reasonable scenarios of this type. (Is it realistic to assume that industrial spreads will tighten by 10 bp while utilities remain unchanged?) One way to generate spread scenarios consistent with the historical experience of spreads in the marketplace is to utilize the statistical information contained within the risk model.

For each sector/quality cell of the corporate bond market shown in Exhibit 25, we create a corporate sub-index confined to a particular cell and use it as a portfolio. We then create a hypothetical Treasury bond for each security in this sub-index. Other than being labeled as belonging to the Treasury sector and having Aaa quality, these hypothetical bonds are identical to their corresponding real corporate bonds. We run a risk model comparison between the portfolio of corporate bonds versus their hypothetical Treasury counterparts as the benchmark. This artificially forces the portfolio and benchmark sensitivity to term structure, optionality and any other risks to be neutralized, leaving only sector and quality risk. Exhibit 25 shows the tracking error components due to sector and quality, as well as their combined effect. Dividing these tracking errors (standard deviations of return differences) by the average durations of the cells produces approximations for the standard deviation of spread changes. The standard deviation of the overall spread change, converted to a monthly number, can form the basis for a set of spread change scenarios. For instance, a scenario of "spreads widen by one standard deviation" would imply a widening of 6 bp for Aaa utilities, and 13 bp for Baa financials. This is a more realistic scenario than an across-the-board parallel shift, such as "corporates widen by 10 bp."

Hedging

Since the covariance matrix used by the risk model is based on monthly observations of security returns, the model cannot compute daily hedges. However, it can help create long-term positions that over time perform better than a naïve hedge. This point is illustrated by a historical simulation of a simple barbell versus bullet strategy in Exhibit 26, in which a combination of the 2- and 10-year on-the-run

Treasuries is used to hedge the on-the-run 5-year. We compare two methods of calculating the relative weights of the two bonds in the hedge. In the first method, the hedge is rebalanced at the start of each month to match the duration of the 5-year Treasury. In the second, the model is engaged on a monthly basis to minimize the tracking error between the portfolio of 2- and 10-year securities and the 5-year benchmark. As shown in Exhibit 26, the risk model hedge tracks the performance of the 5-year bullet more closely than the duration hedge, with an observed tracking error of 19 bp/month compared with 20 bp/month for the duration hedge.

Exhibit 25: Using the Risk Model to Define Spread Scenarios Consistent with History

		Dur.	Annual Tracking Error (%)			Spread Volatility (bp)			
		(years)	Sector	Quality	Both	Sector	Quality	Both	Monthly
U.S. Agencies	Aaa	4.54	0.26	0.00	0.26	6	0	6	2
Industrials	Aaa	8.42	2.36	0.00	2.36	28	0	28	8
	Aa	6.37	1.72	0.57	2.03	27	9	32	9
	A	6.97	1.89	0.82	2.43	27	12	35	10
	Baa	6.80	1.87	1.36	2.96	27	20	43	13
Utilities	Aaa	7.34	1.62	0.13	1.65	22	2	22	6
	Aa	5.67	1.21	0.45	1.39	21	8	25	7
	A	6.03	1.33	0.63	1.67	22	10	28	8
	Baa	5.68	1.36	1.01	2.07	24	18	36	11
Financials	Aaa	4.89	1.41	0.00	1.41	29	0	29	8
	Aa	4.29	1.31	0.34	1.50	30	8	35	10
	A	4.49	1.31	0.49	1.65	29	11	37	11
	Baa	4.86	1.58	0.86	2.14	32	18	44	13
Banking	Aa	4.87	1.23	0.44	1.40	25	9	29	8
	A	5.68	1.43	0.62	1.72	25	11	30	9
	Baa	5.06	1.27	1.13	2.11	25	22	42	12
Yankees	Aaa	6.16	1.23	0.06	1.26	20	1	20	6
	Aa	5.45	1.05	0.49	1.27	19	9	23	7
	A	7.03	1.62	0.89	2.17	23	13	31	9
	Baa	6.17	1.51	1.36	2.60	24	22	42	12

Exhibit 26: Historical Performance of a Two-security Barbell versus the 5-year On-the-run Treasury Bullet; Duration-based Hedge versus a Tracking Error-based Hedge, January 1994-February 1999

		Difference				
		Duration Hedge		Tracking Error Hedge		% of Months
		Return	Duration	Return	Duration	Tracking Improved
2-10 vs. 5	Mean	0.03	0.00	0.03	0.10	59%
	Std. Dev.	0.20	0.00	0.19	0.02	
2-30 vs. 5	Mean	0.04	0.00	0.04	0.36	62%
	Std. Dev.	0.36	0.00	0.33	0.03	

The duration of the 2- and 10-year portfolio built with the minimal tracking error hedging technique is consistently longer than that of the 5-year. Over the study period (1/94–2/99), the duration difference averaged 0.1 years. This duration extension proved very stable (standard deviation of 0.02) and is rooted in the shape of the historically most likely movement of the yield curve. It can be shown that the shape of the first principal component of yield curve movements is not quite a parallel shift.[9] Rather, the 2-year will typically experience less yield change then the 5- or 10-year. To the extent that the 5- and 10-year securities experience historically similar yield changes, a barbell hedge could benefit from an underweighting of the 2-year and an overweighting of the 10-year security. Over the 62 months analyzed in this study, the risk-based hedge performed closer to the 5-year than the duration-based hedge 59% of the time.

A similar study conducted using a 2- and 30-year barbell versus a 5-year bullet over the same study period (1/94-2/99) produced slightly more convincing evidence. Here, the risk-based hedge tracked better than the duration hedge by about 3 bp/month (33 bp/month tracking error versus 36 bp/month) and improved upon the duration hedge in 60% of the months studied. Interestingly, the duration extension in the hedge was even more pronounced in this case, with the risk-based hedge longer than the 5-year by an average of 0.36 years.

Estimating the Probability of Portfolio Underperformance

What is the probability that a portfolio will underperform the benchmark by 25 basis points or more over the coming year? To answer such questions, we need to make some assumptions about the distribution of the performance difference. We assume this difference to be distributed normally, with the standard deviation given by the tracking error calculated by the risk model. However, the risk model does not provide an estimate of the mean outperformance. Such an estimate may be obtained by a horizon total return analysis under an expected scenario (e.g., yield curve and spreads unchanged), or by simply using the yield differential as a rough guide. In the example of Exhibit 1, the portfolio yield exceeds that of the benchmark by 16 bp, and the tracking error is calculated as 52 bp. Exhibit 27 depicts the normal distribution with a mean of 16 bp and a standard deviation of 52 bp. The area of the shaded region, which represents the probability of underperforming by 25 bp or more, may be calculated as

$$N[(-25) - 16)/52] = 0.215 = 21.5\%$$

where $N(x)$ is the standard normal cumulative distribution function. As the true distribution of the return difference may not be normal, this approach must be used with care. It may not be accurate in estimating the probability of rare events such as the "great spread sector crash" in August 1998. For example, this calculation would assign a probability of only 0.0033 or 0.33% to an underperformance of -125 bp or worse. Admittedly, if the tails of the true distribution are slightly different than normal, the true probability could be much higher.

---

[9] *Managing the Yield Curve with Principal Component Analysis*, Lehman Brothers, November 1998.

Exhibit 27: Projected Distribution of Total Return Difference (in bp/year) between Portfolio and Benchmark, Based on Yield Advantage of 16 bp and Tracking Error of 52 bp, Assuming Normal Distribution

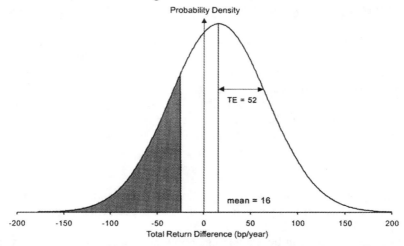

Measuring Sources of Market Risk

As illustrated in Exhibit 2, the risk model reports the projected standard deviation of the absolute returns (sigma) of the portfolio and the benchmark as well as that of the return difference (tracking error). However, the detailed breakdown of risk due to different groups of risk factors is reported only for the tracking error. To obtain such a breakdown of the absolute risk (sigma) of a given portfolio or index, we can measure the risk of our portfolio against a riskless asset, such as a cash security. In this case, the relative risk is equal to the absolute risk of the portfolio, and the tracking error breakdown report can be interpreted as a breakdown of market sigma.

Exhibit 28 illustrates the use of this technique to analyze the sources of market risk in four Lehman Brothers indices: Treasury, (investment grade) Corporate, High-Yield Corporate, and MBS. The results provide a clear picture of the role played by the different sources of risk in each of these markets. In the Treasury Index, term structure risk represents the only significant form of risk. In the Corporate Index, sector and quality risk add to term structure risk, but the effect of a negative correlation between spread risk and term structure risk is clearly visible. The overall risk of the Corporate Index (5.47%) is less than the term structure component alone (5.81%). This reflects the fact that when Treasury interest rates undergo large shocks, corporate yields often lag, moving more slowly in the same direction. The High Yield Index shows a marked increase in quality risk and in non-systematic risk relative to the Corporate Index. But, the negative correlation between term structure risk and quality risk is large as well, and the overall risk (4.76%) is less than the term structure risk (4.98%) by even more than it is for corporates. The effect of negative correlations among risk factors is also very strong in the MBS Index, where the MBS-specific risk factors bring the term structure risk of 3.25% down to an overall risk of 2.69%.

MODELING THE RISK OF NON-INDEX SECURITIES

The risk model calculates risk factor exposures for every security in the portfolio and the benchmark. As the model supports all securities in the Lehman Brothers Aggregate Index, the risk of the benchmark usually is fully modeled. Portfolios, however, often contain securities (and even asset classes) not found in the Aggregate Index. Our portfolio analytics platform has several features designed to represent out-of-index portfolio holdings. In addition, modeling techniques can be used to synthesize the risk characteristics of non-index securities through a combination of two or more securities.

Bonds

The analytics platform supports the modeling of all types of government and corporate bonds. User-defined bonds may contain calls, puts, sinking fund provisions, step-up coupon schedules, inflation linkage, and more. Perpetual-coupon bonds (and preferred stock) can be modeled as bonds with very distant maturity dates. Floating-rate bonds are represented by a short exposure to term structure risk (as though the bond would mature on the next coupon reset date) and a long exposure to spread risk (the relevant spread factors are loaded by the bond's spread duration, which is based on the full set of projected cash flows through maturity).

Exhibit 28: Risk Model Breakdown of Market Risk (Sigma) to Different Categories of Risk Factors (Isolated Mode) for Four Lehman Brothers Indices, as of 9/30/98, in percent per year

Index:	Treasury	Corporate	High Yield	MBS
Duration (years)	5.58	6.08	4.74	1.37
Convexity	0.69	0.68	0.20	−2.19
Term Structure Risk	5.25	5.81	4.98	3.25
Non-term Structure Risk	0.17	2.14	5.20	2.28
Risk Due to:				
Corp. Sector	0.00	1.50	1.21	0.00
Quality	0.00	0.84	4.67	0.00
Optionality	0.01	0.08	0.15	0.00
Coupon	0.17	0.01	0.19	0.00
MBS Sector	0.00	0.00	0.00	1.15
MBS Volatility	0.00	0.00	0.00	1.27
MBS Prepayment	0.00	0.00	0.00	0.73
Total Systematic Risk	5.26	5.47	4.75	2.69
Non-systematic Risk	0.04	0.08	0.17	0.09
Total Risk (std. dev. of annual return)	5.26	5.47	4.76	2.69

Mortgage Passthroughs

The Lehman Brothers MBS Index is composed of several hundred "generic" securities. Each generic is created by combining all outstanding pools of a given program, pass-through coupon, and origination year (e.g., FNMA conventional 30-year 8.0% of 1993).[10] The index database contains over 3000 such generics, offering comprehensive coverage of the agency passthrough market, even though only about 600 meet the liquidity requirements for index inclusion. In addition to this database of MBS generics and their risk factor loadings, the analytics platform contains a lookup table of individual pools. This allows portfolios that contain mortgage pools to be bulk loaded based on either the pool CUSIP or the agency and pool number. For portfolio analytics, the characteristics of the appropriate generic are used as a proxy for the pool. This can lead to some inaccuracy for esoteric pools that differ considerably from the generic to which they are mapped, but adequately represents most mortgage portfolios in our experience.

CMOs

CMOs are not included in the Lehman Brothers MBS Index because their collateral has already been included as passthroughs. At present, the portfolio analytics recognize and process structured securities as individual tranches, but do not possess deal-level logic to project tranche cash flows under different assumptions. Thus, each tranche is represented in the system by a fixed set of cash flows, projected using the Lehman Brothers prepayment model for the zero-volatility interest rate path calibrated to the forward curve. Risk factor loadings for these securities are calculated as a hybrid between the characteristics of the tranche and the underlying collateral. Term structure risk is assumed to follow the cash flows of the tranche.

For PAC securities with less than 3 years to maturity (WAM), the model assigns no mortgage sector risk. For PACs with WAM greater than 10 years and for other types of tranches, the mortgage sector risk is assumed to be equal to that of a position in the underlying collateral with the same dollar duration. For PACs with WAM between 3 and 10 years, we use a prorated portion of the mortgage risk exposure of the collateral. This set of assumptions well represents tranches with stable cash flows, such as PACs trading within their bands. Tranches with extremely volatile cash flows, such as IOs and inverse floaters, cannot be represented adequately in the current system. The mechanism of defining a "cash flow bond" (with an arbitrary fixed cash flow stream), with or without the additional treatment of mortgage risk, can be used to model many kinds of structured transactions.

Futures

A bond futures contract may be represented as a combination of a long position in the Treasury security that is the cheapest-to-deliver issue (CDI) and a short position in a cash instrument. To match the dollar duration of a Treasury futures posi-

---

[10] For a discussion of MBS Index composition and the relationship between pools and generics, see the Lehman Brothers report, "MBS Index Returns: A Detailed Look," August 1998.

tion with a notional market value of N_f, the size of the position N_t in the CDI Treasury bond should satisfy

$$(P_t + A_t)N_tD_t = P_fN_fD_f$$

where D_f is the option-adjusted duration of the futures contract. The negative holding N_c in the cash instrument has to offset the market value of the CDI:

$$(P_c + A_c)N_c + (P_t + A_t)N_t = 0$$

If the cash instrument is priced at par and has no accrued interest, the amount needed is simply

$$N_c = -(P_t + A_t)N_t$$

If the option-adjusted duration of the futures contract is not known, one could approximate N_t for a given CDI using the conversion factor CF_t:

$$N_t = N_f/CF_t$$

The disadvantage of a representation using a single CDI is that the notional values N_t and N_c need to be regularly maintained in order to properly reflect the risk of an unchanged position in futures. As yields change, the resulting changes in the delivery probabilities of different bonds will change the futures duration. A failure to update the portfolio frequently enough can lead to a discontinuity, especially around a switch in the CDI. A more sophisticated synthetic representation of a futures contract may involve more than one deliverable instrument weighted by the probability of delivery.

Index Swaps

The analytics platform provides a mechanism for including index swaps in portfolios. An individual security can be defined as paying the total return of a particular index, and a specific face amount of such a security can be included in a portfolio, corresponding to the notional value of the swap. These special securities have been created for all widely used Lehman Indices and are stored in the standard security database. Swaps written on other custom indices or portfolios can be modeled in a similar fashion. These capabilities, in conjunction with the dollar-based risk reporting described below, allow a comprehensive risk analysis of a portfolio of index swaps versus a hedge portfolio.

SUMMARY

In this article, we described a risk model for dollar-denominated government, corporate, and mortgage-backed securities. The model quantifies expected deviation in performance ("tracking error") between a portfolio of fixed-income securities and an index representing the market, such as the Lehman Brothers Aggregate, Corporate, or High Yield Index.

The forecast of the return deviation is based on specific mismatches between the sensitivities of the portfolio and the benchmark to major market forces ("risk factors") that drive security returns. The model uses historical variances and correlations of the risk factors to translate the structural differences of the portfolio and the index into an expected tracking error. The model quantifies not only this systematic market risk, but security-specific (non-systematic) risk as well.

Using an illustrative portfolio, we demonstrated the implementation of the model. We showed how each component of tracking error can be traced back to the corresponding difference between the portfolio and benchmark risk exposures. We described the methodology for the minimization of tracking error and discussed a variety of portfolio management applications.

Term Structure Factor Models

Robert C. Kuberek
Vice President and Principal
Wilshire Associates Incorporated

INTRODUCTION

Quantitative models of risk provide portfolio managers with valuable tools in the construction and maintenance of investment portfolios that meet specific performance objectives. Fixed income portfolio management is especially amenable to quantitative risk modeling because so much structure is present in the pricing of fixed income securities and because the returns of investment grade fixed income securities are so highly correlated with one another. Factor models provide a particularly powerful technique for modeling fixed income portfolio risk. Moreover, because the main sources of risk (and correlation) in the returns of investment grade fixed income portfolios relate to the shape and position of the yield curve, *term structure* factor models represent the most important of these models.

The purpose of this article is to review some of the leading approaches to term structure factor modeling. However, to understand how term structure factor models work and how they fit into the risk management landscape it is useful first to define this important class of risk models and to put their development in historical perspective. This is the objective of the next section. Succeeding sections discuss the application of factor models to risk management, identify the major types of term structure factor models, describe leading examples of each type of term structure model, and discuss the advantages and disadvantages of each.

FACTOR MODELS DEFINED AND HISTORICAL BACKGROUND

Whether risk is measured in terms of standard deviation of return, standard deviation of tracking error relative to a benchmark, value-at risk or probability of underperforming some target, a useful first step in building a factor model is to develop a quantitative description of returns that relates returns meaningfully to other quantities and that has statistical moments that can be estimated easily and reliably. One of the simplest descriptions of return that meets these requirements is the market model for common stocks.[1] In this model, asset returns are generated by the process

---

[1] The market model follows from the assumption that stock returns are multi-variate normal. See Eugene F. Fama, *Foundations of Finance* (New York: Basic Books, 1976).

$$\tilde{R}_i = a_i + b_i \tilde{R}_m + \tilde{e}_i \tag{1}$$

where

R_i = the total return of asset i

R_m = the total return of the market portfolio

e_i = a random error term that is uncorrelated with the market return

and the tilde ($\sim$) denotes a random variable.

If it is further assumed that the residual error terms in equation (1) are uncorrelated *across* assets after taking out the influence of the single index return R_m, then this model is an example of a simple "factor" model where the single factor is the return of the market portfolio. It is also a *linear* factor model because it is linear in the factor return R_m. The particular description of the return-generating process in (1) is closely identified with the Capital Asset Pricing Model (CAPM) of William Sharpe[2] and John Lintner.[3]

Another well-known example of a linear factor model for risky assets underlies the Arbitrage Pricing Theory (the APT) of Stephen Ross.[4] This type of return model, which is very general, assumes that it is not possible to completely eliminate the correlations of residuals across assets with a single index. In this more general model, returns are generated by the following process:

$$\tilde{r}_i = a_i + b_{i1}\tilde{f}_1 + b_{i2}\tilde{f}_2 + \ldots + b_{ik}\tilde{f}_k + \tilde{e}_i \tag{2}$$

where

r_i = the excess return of asset i over the risk-free rate

f_j = the return to risk factor j

e_i = a mean-zero random residual error term that is uncorrelated with the factor returns and uncorrelated across assets

In the APT model, excess returns are generated by a linear process which is the sum of a risk premium a, a set of random factor effects bf, and a random, asset-specific residual. Examples of factors include index returns, unexpected changes in GNP, changes in corporate bond yield spreads, beta, and the ratio of earnings to price. It often simplifies matters further to assume that the factor returns and the residuals are normally distributed.

---

[2] William F. Sharpe, "Capital Asset Prices: A Theory of Market Equilibrium under Conditions of Risk," *Journal of Finance* (September 1964), pp. 425-442.

[3] John Lintner, "The Valuation of Risk Assets and the Selection of Risk Investments in Stock Portfolios and Capital Budgets," *Review of Economics and Statistics* (February 1965), pp. 13-37.

[4] Stephen A. Ross, "The Arbitrage Theory of Capital Asset Pricing," *Journal of Economic Theory* (December 1976), pp. 341-360.

USING FACTOR MODELS TO MEASURE RISK

The moments of a linear factor model are the means, variances and covariances of the factor returns, and the variances of the residuals (one for each asset).[5] The usefulness and power of factor models in risk management lie in the fact that once the values of the moments are determined together with the exposures of the risky assets to the factors, it becomes possible to compute portfolio risk using any one of a number of definitions.

For example, suppose that the k factors f in equation (2) have $k \times k$ covariance matrix Ψ. Furthermore, suppose that a particular portfolio holds n ($>k$) assets with the $n \times 1$ weight vector $\mathbf{x}$. The portfolio excess return can be written in matrix form as

$$\tilde{r}_p = x'a + x'\mathbf{B}\tilde{f} + x'\tilde{e} \tag{3}$$

where $\mathbf{B}$ is an $n \times k$ matrix of exposures in which the ith row consists of the b's in equation (2).

Equation (3) gives the portfolio return for a portfolio of assets whose returns are generated by equation (2). The first term in equation (3) is the average risk premium in the portfolio, which is a weighted average of the risk premiums of the individual holdings. The second term is the part of the return that is explained by the k common factors f, and the third term is the aggregate residual return, the unexpected return or noise in the portfolio return that is not explained by the risk factors.

The variance, or total risk, of the portfolio return then is

$$\text{var}(\tilde{r}_p) = x'\mathbf{B}\Psi\mathbf{B}'x + x'\mathbf{D}x \tag{4}$$

where $\mathbf{D}$ is an $n \times n$ diagonal matrix whose non-zero elements are the variances of the residuals in equation (2).[6] Decomposition of return variance in this way has important computational benefits. By reducing the size of the non-diagonal covariance matrix from $n \times n$ to $k \times k$, for example, portfolio optimization can be performed using significantly less cpu time and computer memory.[7]

---

[5] Factor models have moments and parameters. Moments are the means, variances and covariances of the factor returns. Parameters are used in defining and measuring the factors. For example, the *variance* of a factor is a moment, while the *weights* of the stocks in the index that represents the factor are parameters. The number of moments (means, variances and covariances) in a factor model is a function of the number of factors. The number of parameters in the model, on the other hand, depends on the specification of the model.

[6] The decomposition of return variance in this manner is traceable to William F. Sharpe, "A Simplified Model for Portfolio Analysis," *Management Science* (January 1963), pp. 277-293.

[7] In their original paper, which studied single and multiple index portfolios in portfolio selection, Kalman J. Cohen and Jerry A. Pogue ("An Empirical Evaluation of Alternative Portfolio Selection Models," *Journal of Business* 40 (1967), pp. 166-193), reported that a single optimization involving only 150 securities required 90 minutes of processing time on an IBM 7090 computer using the full $n \times n$ covariance matrix. While computers presumably have gotten faster in the years since Cohen and Pogue did their work, the relative advantage of equation (4) in computational time surely remains.

Equation (4) decomposes portfolio risk into two components. The first component represents the contribution to total risk from the exposures to the common risk factors while the second represents the contribution from residuals. The contributions to return variance can be separated in this way because of the assumption in equation (2) that the factor returns are uncorrelated with the residual returns. Moreover, the residual variance matrix $\mathbf{D}$ has the especially simple diagonal form because of the assumption in equation (2) that the residuals are uncorrelated *across* assets. An important feature of this measure of risk is that the second term, the residual variance, tends to shrink with the number of assets in the portfolio. Thus, portfolio managers can diversify away the residual risk in their portfolios but not the systematic, factor risk.

Furthermore, since equation (3) applies to any portfolio, including a benchmark portfolio, the variance of the tracking error of a portfolio relative to a benchmark can be written as

$$\text{var}(\tilde{r}_p - \tilde{r}_b) = [x_p - x_b]'\mathbf{B}\Psi\mathbf{B}'[x_p - x_b] + [x_p - x_b]'\mathbf{D}[x_p - x_b] \qquad (5)$$

where the weighting vectors x are now subscripted to denote whether they relate to the portfolio or to the benchmark. The reader will notice that in equation (5) the variance of the tracking error goes to zero as the weight differences from the benchmark go to zero — if one holds the index, the tracking error variance is zero.

TYPES OF FACTOR MODELS

In terms of equation (2), factor models can be categorized according to how the factor exposures and factor returns are measured. In this regard, it is customary to classify factor models as macroeconomic, statistical or fundamental.

Macroeconomic Factor Models

In macroeconomic factor models, the factor returns in equation (2) represent unexpected changes in quantities that are observable. Quantities that are commonly employed as macroeconomic factors include the returns of specified indexes of common stocks, such as capital goods or materials and services indexes, as well as unexpected changes in measures of aggregate economic activity, such as industrial production, personal income or employment. Since the factor returns are directly observable, the moments of the factor model (the means, variances, and covariances of the factor returns) can be estimated directly from the *time series* of factor returns. Assets are differentiated by their exposures to these variables, which are the b's in equation (2). These exposures can be estimated by regressing time series of individual stock returns (or of portfolios of similar stocks) on the observed factor returns, using equation (2), with the stock returns as the dependent variable and the observed factor returns f as the independent variables. Examples of macroeconomic factor models include the single and multiple index models of Cohen and Pogue[8] and the APT model of Chen, Roll, and Ross.[9]

Macroeconomic factor models have the great advantage that because the factors are observable, they are easy to relate to the performance of individual stocks in an intuitive way. One can imagine (whether it is true or not), for example, that airline stocks would tend to do well in an economic upturn, while drug stocks might be relatively insensitive to general economic conditions. A disadvantage of this approach is that with only a small number of factors it may be difficult to eliminate correlation of residuals across assets. A second disadvantage of this type of factor model is that it may be difficult to measure either the exposures of the assets to the macroeconomic variables or the returns to these variables using data of arbitrary frequency. For example, one could identify a factor with the Federal Reserve's Industrial Production index, but this statistic is published only monthly, making it impossible to estimate and use the model in this form with daily returns data.

Statistical Factor Models

The second traditional type of factor model is the statistical model. In this type of model a statistical procedure, such as factor analysis or principal components analysis, is used both to identify the factors and to measure the factor returns. In principal components analysis, for example, a factor model is constructed using a multivariate time series of individual stock returns. The covariance (or correlation) matrix of stock returns is factored by identifying some small number of linear combinations (the principal components) of stock returns that account for most of the return variance in the sample. Thus the factor returns end up being linear combinations of individual stock returns and the factor exposures are the multiple regression coefficients of individual stock returns with these principal components.[10]

An advantage of this method relative to pure macroeconomic factor models is that one can remove as much of the correlation in residuals as one likes by including as many principal components as desired, all the way up to the number of stocks (or stock portfolios) in the original sample. A second advantage relative to macroeconomic factor models is that returns are the only inputs and thus frequency is not an issue: the model can be estimated with any frequency for which the individual stock returns are available.

A disadvantage of the statistical approach is that the factors are not observable in the sense that one cannot make measurements of the factor returns independently of the stock returns themselves and in the sense that the factors do not always correspond to quantities that can be related easily to stock returns.

A disadvantage of both the pure macroeconomic factor models (when the factor returns are observed and the exposures are estimated) and the statistical

---

[8] Cohen and Pogue, "An Empirical Evaluation of Alternative Portfolio Selection Models."

[9] Nai-Fu Chen, Richard Roll, and Stephen A. Ross, "Economic Forces and the Stock Market," *Journal of Business* (1986), pp. 383-404.

[10] For an early application of this approach, see Benjamin King, "Market and Industry Factors in Stock Price Behavior," *Journal of Business* 39 (1966), pp. 139-190.

approaches is that the exposure of a given stock to a factor can, and probably does, change over time as the company's business mix and capital structure change. Because of their reliance on *time series* estimates of factor exposure, neither of these approaches handles this problem gracefully. A related disadvantage of both pure macroeconomic factor models and statistical factor models is that new securities are difficult to fit in a portfolio because there is no history with which to estimate the exposures.

Fundamental Factor Models

The fundamental approach combines some of the advantages of macroeconomic factor models and statistical factor models while avoiding certain of their difficulties.[11] The fundamental approach identifies the factors with a stock's exposures to a set of attributes, which can include the stock's beta, its ratio of earnings-to price (e/p), its economic sector (e.g., capital goods), and its industry classification (e.g., automotive). In this type of factor model the factor exposures are the exposures to the economic variables, the actual (or normalized) values of the fundamentals (e.g., the actual e/p ratio) and, in the case of a classification factor, simply a dummy variable that has a value of one if the stock falls into the category or zero otherwise. Factor returns are not observed directly but are inferred by regressing *cross-sections* of stock returns against their exposures to the set of factors.[12]

An important advantage of the fundamental approach relative to the macroeconomic and statistical approaches is that as the exposure of a stock to a given factor changes over time, these exposure changes can be tracked immediately so that measures of portfolio risk correctly reflect the current condition of the portfolio's underlying assets. By the same token it is easy to include new securities in a portfolio because no history is required to estimate their factor exposures.

TYPES OF TERM STRUCTURE FACTOR MODELS

The general framework of equation (2) can be applied to fixed income securities easily. However, for investment grade fixed income securities, the main sources of risk relate to the level and shape of the yield curve. Thus, the appropriate factor models are term structure factor models, where the factors in equation (2) are defined specifically to explain the returns of default free bonds, such as Treasuries or stripped Treasuries, and thus describe changes in yield curve level and shape.[13]

---

[11] Examples of this approach include, Eugene F. Fama and James MacBeth, "Risk, Return and Equilibrium: Empirical Tests," *Journal of Political Economy* (1973), pp. 607-636, and Eugene F. Fama and Kenneth R. French, "The Cross-Section of Expected Stock Returns," *Journal of Finance* (June 1992), pp. 427-465.

[12] In this case the beta, if it is included as a factor, is estimated or modeled using *a prior* time series.

[13] For non-Treasury securities additional factors can be important in determining portfolio risk. See, for example, Robert C. Kuberek, "Common Factors in Bond Portfolio Returns," Wilshire Associates Incorporated (1989).

An important feature of term structure factor models is that, because the factors mainly explain the risk of yield changes, in each model there is a characteristic yield curve shift associated with each factor. Still, as will be seen, each of the models described here bears a resemblance to one or another of the common stock models already described. Along these lines, term structure factor models can be classified in four types, as follows:

1. arbitrage models
2. principal components models
3. spot rate models
4. functional models

Term structure factor models that use equilibrium or arbitrage methods, especially Cox, Ingersoll, and Ross[14] and Richard[15] are analogous to macroeconomic factor models for common stocks. These models work by postulating dynamics for a set of observable state variables that are assumed to underlie interest rates and deriving (in the case of equilibrium models) or assuming (in the case of arbitrage models) some equilibrium condition for expected returns, then *deriving* the term structure.[16] Examples of state variables underlying these models include the short-term nominal interest rate, the short-term "real" rate of interest, the rate of inflation, and the unexpected component of the change in the Consumer Price Index. A unique feature of the equilibrium/arbitrage approach, relative to other types of term structure factor models, is that the equilibrium/arbitrage approach produces term structure factor models that are rigorously consistent with security valuation. In other words, these models provide both bond prices and dynamics.

Term structure factor models based on principal components or factor analysis, such as Gultekin and Rogalski[17] and Litterman and Scheinkman,[18] are

---

[14] John C. Cox, Jonathan E. Ingersoll, and Stephen A. Ross, "A Theory of the Term Structure of Interest Rates," Working Paper (August 1978) and John C. Cox, Jonathan E. Ingersoll, and Stephen A. Ross, "A Theory of the Term Structure of Interest Rates," *Econometrica* (1985), pp. 385-407.

[15] Scott F. Richard, "An Arbitrage Model of the Term Structure of Interest Rates," *Journal of Financial Economics* (1978), pp.33-57.

[16] In distinguishing the arbitrage approach from their own equilibrium approach, Cox, Ingersoll, and Ross write, "An alternative to the equilibrium approach taken here is based purely on arbitrage considerations. Here is a brief summary of this argument. Assume that all uncertainty is described by some set of state variables. If there are no pure arbitrage opportunities in the economy, then there exists a (not necessarily unique) set of state-space prices which support current contingent claim values... By assuming that the state variables follow an *exogenously* specified diffusion process, one obtains a valuation equation of the same general form as [CIR (1978) eq.] (25). However, the resulting equation contains *undetermined* coefficients which depend on both preferences and production opportunities and *can be identified only in a general equilibrium setting*" (italics supplied). Notwithstanding this criticism, however, as Richard and others have shown, arbitrage models are powerful, easy to develop, and, providing one is willing and has the means to solve them numerically, reasonably practical.

[17] N. Bulent Gultekin and Richard J. Rogalski, "Government Bond Returns, Measurement of Interest Rate Risk and the Arbitrage Pricing Theory," *Journal of Finance* (1985), pp. 43-61.

[18] Robert Litterman and José Scheinkman, "Common Factors Affecting Bond Returns," *Journal of Fixed Income* (June 1991), pp. 54-61.

analogous to the statistical factor models for common stocks described previously. In this type of model, factor analysis or principal components analysis is used to identify the factors underlying the returns of bonds of different maturities or, almost equivalently, to identify the factors underlying the movements of yields at different maturities. As with the common stock return models, the factor returns typically are linear combinations of the returns of zero-coupon bonds and the factor exposures are the multiple regression coefficients of individual bond returns with these principal components.

Two other approaches, spot rate models and polynomial models, bear some resemblance to fundamental models for common stocks in that the factors are most naturally identified with different measures of exposure. Spot rate models identify the term structure factors directly with the durations of zero-coupon bonds at specified points along the term structure. An important example of this type of model is J. P. Morgan's RiskMetrics™ model,[19] which identifies factors with the durations of zero coupon bonds at ten points along the yield curve, 3-months, 1-year, 2 years, 3-years, 5-years, 7-years, 10-years, 15-years, 20-years, and 30 years. Duration for coupon bonds can be calculated either directly from the cash flows, if the cash flows are well defined, using so-called cash-flow mapping techniques, or with the aid of a yield-curve-based valuation model (e.g., an option-adjusted-spread, or OAS, model), in the case of bonds with embedded options and payment contingencies.[20] The RiskMetrics™ model and approach are in wide use in a variety of risk management applications, but especially in applications focusing on value-at-risk.

Functional models, for example Kuberek[21] and Willner,[22] seek to represent yield curve risk using approximating functions that are based on, or related, to polynomials. These models fit smooth curves to actual yield curve movements, where the fitted shifts represent a composite of a basic set of yield curve shift components, reflecting, for example, change in yield curve level, change in slope, and change in curvature. Factors are identified with the durations of zero-coupon Treasuries with respect to these pre-specified shift components. Superficially, the basic yield curve shift components resemble principal components shifts, but are generated not by a historical data sample but by some underlying mathematical reasoning.

---

[19] For a comprehensive description of this approach, see "RiskMetrics — Technical Document," J.P. Morgan/Reuters, 1996.

[20] See, for example, Robert C. Kuberek and Prescott C. Cogswell, "On the Pricing of Interest Rate Contingent Claims in a Binomial Lattice," Wilshire Associates Incorporated (May 1990). These term-structure-based OAS models are prerequisite for measuring exposures to term-structure factors for any but the simplest fixed income securities. The general approach is to fit the model to the quoted price of a bond by iterating on a spread over the initial term structure, then numerically to compute the factor exposure by shifting the starting term structure and re-calculating the model value of the bond at the same spread.

[21] Robert C. Kuberek, "An Approximate Factor Model for U.S. Treasuries," *Proceedings of the Seminar on the Analysis of Security Prices* (November 1990), The University of Chicago Center for Research in Securities Prices, pp. 71-106.

[22] Ram Willner, "A New Tool for Portfolio Managers: Level, Slope and Curvature Durations," *Journal of Fixed Income* (June 1996), pp. 48-59.

In fact, as will be seen, all of the term structure factor models described here can be represented as a form of equation (2). Moreover, all of the term structure factor models described here share the property that the factor returns in the model represent the amounts and direction of each characteristic yield curve shift allowed in the model, and the exposures, the b's in equation (2), are the durations of the bonds with respect to these yield curve shifts. From this perspective, a useful way to distinguish the models is in the number of characteristic yield curve movements that each model implies and in the forms of these characteristic yield curve movements.

The remainder of this article will explore a leading example of each of the four term structure factor models described above. The examples that will be used are (1) for arbitrage models, the one-factor equilibrium term structure model of Cox, Ingersoll, and Ross; (2) for principal components models, Litterman and Scheinkman; (3) for spot rate models, J. P. Morgan's RiskMetrics™ model; and, (4) for functional models, Kuberek. To facilitate the comparison of the different models, each of the models is recast to describe yield curve risk at the same 12 points along the yield curve — 9 months, 1 year, 1.5 years, 2 years, 3 years, 4 years, 5 years, 7 years, 10 years, 15 years, 20 years, and 30 years.

ARBITRAGE MODELS

The Cox, Ingersoll, and Ross equilibrium term structure model (CIR) is developed fully within the context of a single-good production economy with stochastic production possibilities and uncertain technological change. However, the model can be developed using arbitrage arguments, providing that the specification of the equilibrium condition for expected bond returns is consistent with their general equilibrium formulation.[23]

Assume that there is one factor, which is represented by the short-term interest rate r. Further, assume that this rate evolves according to the process

$$dr = \kappa(\mu - r)dt + \sigma\sqrt{r}dz \qquad (6)$$

where

μ = long-term average value of the short-term interest rate r

κ = rate of reversion of the short-term interest rate r toward its long-term average value

$\sigma r^{1/2}$ = standard deviation of unexpected changes in the short-term interest rate

dz = a standard Brownian motion

---

[23] The CIR model is constructed for an economy where money does not play a role and therefore the short-term interest rate in the model is a "real" rate. Nevertheless, by convention the one-factor CIR model is applied to the nominal term structure, where the short-term rate in the model is regarded as a nominal rate.

Equation (6) says that the change in the short-term interest rate r over the period dt is the sum of two components, a drift component, which represents the expected reversion of the short-term rate toward the mean, and a surprise term that reflects unexpected changes in interest rates. This description of interest rate dynamics has several important properties. These include mean reversion, volatility of interest rates that increases with the level of interest rates, and the fact that the future behavior of the interest rate depends only on it current value and not on the history of its movements.

If the price $P(r,T)$ of a zero-coupon bond paying \$1 in T years depends only on the short-term interest rate r and the maturity T, it follows from Ito's lemma[24] that the return over a period dt of a zero-coupon bond with maturity T is

$$\tilde{r}_T = \left\{ (P_r/P)k(\mu-r) + P_t/P + \frac{1}{2}(P_{rr}/P)\sigma^2 r - r \right\} dt + (P_r/P)\sigma\sqrt{r}dz \quad (7)$$

The first term on the right hand side of equation (7) is the expected excess return of the T-year maturity zero-coupon bond. It consists of four components. The first is that part of the return due to the expected movement of the short-term rate r toward its long-term average value μ. The second component is due to accretion toward par. The third component is that part of the expected return that is due to convexity. The fourth component is the current value of the short-term rate, subtracted to obtain the expected excess return.

The second term on the right hand side of equation (7) is the effect of the unexpected component of the change in the short-term interest rate.

If it is assumed that the expected excess return of the T-year zero-coupon bond in equilibrium is proportional to the bond's "duration" with respect to the short-term interest rate by a risk premium λr, that represents the price of interest rate risk per unit of duration, then equation (7) becomes

$$\tilde{r}_T = (P_r/P)\lambda r dt + (P_r/P)\sigma\sqrt{r}dz \quad (8)$$

Equation (8) says that the excess return on a zero coupon bond of maturity T is the sum of two components, a risk premium that is proportional to the product of the bond's duration with respect to r and the risk premium λr, and a surprise that is the product of the bond's duration and the unexpected change in the interest rate r.

Careful inspection of equation (8) shows that it has exactly the form of equation (2) where

$$a = (P_r/P)\lambda r dt \quad (9a)$$

and

---

[24] For a discussion of the application of Ito's lemma to the pricing of bonds, see S. Fischer, "The Demand for Index Bonds," *Journal of Political Economy* (1975), pp. 509-534.

$$b = (P_r/P) \tag{9b}$$

Under these conditions CIR provide a closed-form expression for the duration P_r/P of a zero-coupon bond maturity T. This is given by the following formula:

$$\frac{P_r(r, T)}{P} = -\frac{2(e^{\gamma T} - 1)}{(\gamma + k + \lambda)(e^{\gamma T} - 1) + 2\gamma} \tag{10}$$

where

$$\gamma = \sqrt{(\kappa + \lambda)^2 + 2\sigma^2}$$

The CIR model produces a single characteristic yield shift as illustrated in Exhibit 1. The shift, which resembles a twist at the short end of the curve, describes yield curve behavior when yield changes are perfectly correlated and when short-term yields tend to move more than long-term yields. This tendency for short-term interest rates to be more volatile than long rates is a result of the mean reversion in the short rate assumed for the model and described in equation (6). For example, suppose that the values of the parameters in equation (10) for this example are as follows: $\kappa = 0.1$, $\lambda = -0.04$ (a negative value corresponds to a positive term premium), and $\sigma = 0.03578$. These parameter values are consistent with a 10-year mean reversion time, a term premium of 20 basis points per year of duration, and an annual standard deviation of short-term interest rate changes of 80 basis points. Given these values for the parameters, if the short rate increases by 100 basis points, the 30-year zero-coupon rate will increase by only just over 20 basis points.

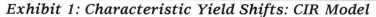

Exhibit 1: Characteristic Yield Shifts: CIR Model

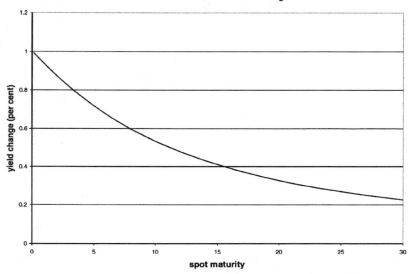

Exhibit 2: Bond Durations: CIR Model

Time to Maturity	b_1
0.75	−0.71
1.00	−0.93
1.50	−1.35
2.00	−1.74
3.00	−2.45
4.00	−3.05
5.00	−3.58
7.00	−4.43
10.00	−5.32
15.00	−6.16
20.00	−6.56
30.00	−6.84

As can be seen in Exhibit 2, for this combination of parameter values the CIR durations of zero-coupon bonds do not increase as rapidly as their ordinary durations, which are just the times-to-maturity of the bonds. This is a reflection of the tendency for long rates to rise by less than short rates, when short rates rise, and for long rates to fall by less than short rates, when short rates fall. Thus, CIR durations suggest that ordinary durations overstate the risk of long maturity bonds relative to short maturity bonds.

The CIR model has several advantages over other approaches. First, it is rigorously consistent with the valuation of fixed income securities. In other words, the model produces both prices and returns. A second advantage is that the model is defined continuously in maturity: exposures can be calculated for zero-coupon bonds of any maturity without recourse to approximation or interpolation. A third advantage, which has already been mentioned, is that the moments — the mean and variance of the (single) factor return — can be estimated directly by observing the time series of factor returns, in this case the time series of changes in the short-term interest rate.

A disadvantage of this model is that it allows only one type of yield curve shift and is thus very limited in the variety of actual yield curve behaviors that it can describe. This is not a shortcoming of the general approach, however. CIR also present a two-factor model, with uncertain short-term interest rates and uncertain inflation, within the context of their general equilibrium model, and Richard and others have proposed other two-factor and multi-factor models based on arbitrage arguments. However, for the variety of interest rate dynamics that have known solutions like equation (10), the models tend to have a large number of parameters and very complicated forms.

A second minor disadvantage of the one-factor CIR model as a factor model is evident from inspection of equation (8), namely, that the coefficients in the factor model depend on the level of interest rates. This dependence of the coefficients on the level of interest rates is plausible on the grounds that it is consistent with the presumption that interest rates tend to be more volatile when interest rate levels are higher. However, it means that this model cannot be implemented by regressing cross sections of bond returns on their durations, then averaging over time to obtain the moments, without first normalizing the exposures for the level of interest rates.

PRINCIPAL COMPONENTS MODELS

A second major category of term structure factor models is based on principal components analysis. In this approach, the returns of zero coupon bonds of different maturities are factor analyzed to extract a (hopefully small) set of characteristic yield curve shifts, defined at discreet maturities, that together explain a large proportion of the total variance of returns in the sample. The factors are thus the amounts and direction of each type of characteristic yield curve shift that combine to explain the returns of a cross-section of bond returns for a given performance period. Gultekin and Rogalski use this technique on coupon Treasuries, while Litterman and Scheinkman use the method to factor analyze the returns of Treasury implied zero-coupon bonds.[25] Because the use of implied zeros is more consistent with generalizations of equation (2) for any bond, the focus here will be on the approach of Litterman and Scheinkman (LS).

To illustrate the LS model, suppose that returns are available for implied zeros at twelve maturities, as follows: 9 months, 1 year, 1.5 years, 2 years, 3 years, 4 years, 5 years, 7 years, 10 years, 15 years, 20 years, and 30 years. With principal components one can specify any number of factors up to the number of securities in the data sample — in this case 12. Typically, a number is chosen such that most of the variance in the sample is explained by the factors selected. For the example here, the first three principal components typically explain more than 98% of the variance in the data sample, so three is chosen as the number of factors. The characteristic yield curve shifts that correspond to the first three yield curve factors are shown in Exhibit 3.

The first yield curve factor is the relatively flat curve near the top of Exhibit 3. This corresponds to a yield shift that is roughly, but not exactly, uniform. The second shift is a pivoting shift for which short rates fall and long rates rise. This shift is almost uniform for maturities greater than 15 years. The third shift is a change in curvature, with short rates rising, intermediate rates falling and long rates rising. Actual yield curve shifts are represented as composites of these three characteristic yield shifts. The principal components procedure works

---

[25] Implied zero-coupon bonds, or implied zeros, are hypothetical bonds that are priced using discount factors that are consistent with the discount factors that the market uses to price actual coupon Treasuries. While these bond prices cannot be observed directly, their existence is somewhat validated by the possibility of creating them synthetically by constructing hedge portfolio of coupon Treasuries. Also, a closely related security, the Treasury strip, does actually exist. The reason for using implied zeros in preference to actual Treasury strips to build a factor model is the availability of more history for backtesting: Treasury strips did not exist before the early 1980s, whereas Treasury prices are widely available back to 1974 and implied zero curves are available back even further.

in such a way that the factors are uncorrelated in the data sample that was used to generate them. This uncorrelatedness of the factors is a consequence of the property of principal components referred to as orthogonality.

The exposures or "durations" of the implied zeros with respect to each of these factors, the b's in equation (2) are shown in Exhibit 4. As with the analogous common stock models, factor returns are produced by the principal components procedure itself but, alternatively, can be estimated by regressing the returns of cross-sections of zero-coupon bonds on the durations implied by the characteristic yield shifts that are produced by the principal components analysis (Exhibit 4). The durations are scaled to the characteristic yield shifts themselves, so that, for example, one unit of return for the second factor corresponds to a yield shift of 0.38% at 30 years. Thus, to obtain the return of the 5-year zero coupon bond resulting from one half unit of return for the second factor, assuming the factor returns for the other factors are zero for a given period, it is only necessary to multiply the duration (−0.20) by the factor return (0.50) to get −0.10%. In practice, the realized factor returns will all be non-zero, but then the effects are computed in the same way for each factor and the results added together to get the total excess return predicted for that security, as in equation (2).[26]

Exhibit 3: Characteristic Yield Curve Shifts: Principal Components Model

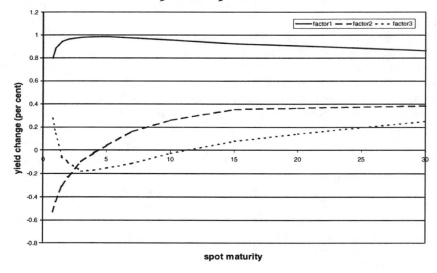

[26] The scaling of principal components models is pretty arbitrary. Thus, for example, the model here could have been scaled so that the characteristic yield shift of the second factor was 1.00% at 30 years instead of 0.38% (see Exhibit 2). In this case the duration of the 30-year bond with respect to the second factor would have had to have been scaled up accordingly. The content and explanatory power of the complete factor model would remain the same, however. In particular, the returns predicted for a bond, given its exposures and given the realized factor returns estimated for the performance period, would be identical.

Exhibit 4: Bond Durations: Principal Components Model

Time to Maturity	b_1	b_2	b_3
0.75	−0.60	0.40	−0.21
1.00	−0.88	0.44	−0.14
1.50	−1.41	0.46	0.08
2.00	−1.93	0.46	0.20
3.00	−2.93	0.29	0.53
4.00	−3.93	0.10	0.67
5.00	−4.92	−0.20	0.75
7.00	−6.83	−1.13	0.77
10.00	−9.56	−2.60	0.24
15.00	−13.84	−5.33	−1.17
20.00	−18.10	−7.35	−2.81
30.00	−25.89	−11.58	−7.51

An advantage of the principal components approach in term structure factor modeling is that the actual data provide guidance in defining the factors. A disadvantage of the principal components model, which is inherent in the approach, is the large number of parameters required. In the example here with three principal components, 36 parameters are required. These are the parameters required to describe the characteristic yield curve shift for each of the three factors at each of 12 maturities. A second disadvantage is that the exact definition of the factors, and therefore of the exposures, depends on the data sample used to extract the principal components. As experience is accumulated, the data change and the definition of the factors, and thus the durations of bonds, change.

A third disadvantage of this approach is that the model is not defined continuously on maturity. Thus, to calculate factor exposures for bonds with maturity or cash flow dates different from the maturities of the zeros used to define the factors, some interpolation of the characteristic yield curve shifts must be performed. The larger the number of maturities used to define the factors, the less interpolation is needed, but the more parameters are required. Of course, there is no guarantee that once the factors are defined, using a particular historical data sample, the factor returns still will be uncorrelated out of sample.

SPOT RATE MODELS

Spot rate models identify factors with the durations of zero-coupon bonds at each of a number of points along the yield curve. The factors thus can be interpreted as changes in the yields of these hypothetical zero-coupon bonds. Moreover, any number of yield curve points can be used to define the model, so the portfolio manager has wide latitude in defining the model to suit the specific application. Spot rate models have the least content in terms of economic assumptions and, correspondingly, the fewest parameters.

One of the leading examples of spot rate models is J. P. Morgan's Risk-Metrics™ model.[27] This model defines ten points along the yield curve and provides the variance-covariance matrix, the Ψ in equation (4), of spot rate changes for 13 countries including the United States. The RiskMetrics™ model is widely applied in measuring value-at-risk. The portfolio's "value-at-risk" is the largest *dollar* loss (or loss in terms of some other reference currency) that a portfolio will suffer "ordinarily." For example, if a portfolio will lose not more than $100, 95% of the time, then the value at-risk is said to be $100. Value-at-risk can be computed from equation (4), as follows:

$$\text{Value-at-Risk} = 1.65 \text{ (Portfolio Value) } [\text{var}(r_p)]^{\frac{1}{2}}$$

As with all the term structure factor models described here, however, spot rate models can be estimated in at least two ways. The time series of factor returns can be estimated by measuring the yield changes at each yield curve point in the model, as with a macroeconomic factor model for common stocks. Alternatively, one may calculate the durations of the bonds with respect to the spot rate changes and regress bond returns cross-sectionally on these durations to create a time-series of factor returns. Typically, the second method is more direct because, by using this method, the yield curve itself does not need to be estimated.

Exhibit 5 shows the characteristic yield curve shifts for the first four spot rate factors in the 12-factor formulation. As the exhibit makes clear, the characteristic yield curve movements of spot rate models have a very extreme appearance. A yield change is either zero, off a given yield curve point, or 100 basis points, on the yield curve point. Yield changes are interpolated between adjacent points. In other words, if one of the bond's cash flows falls between the stipulated yield curve points, that cash flow has *some* duration with respect to both the adjacent points. Spot rate factors can be scaled, as in the example here, so that the duration of a zero-coupon bond to a given spot rate change is just equal to that bond's time to maturity.

Exhibit 6 shows durations for the first four factors in the 12-factor spot rate model. A feature of spot rate models is that because of the way the models are defined, the spot rate durations of a bond, if scaled this way, add up approximately to the ordinary duration of the bond.

A major advantage of spot rate models over principal components models is that fewer parameters are required. Where principal components models imply that spot rate changes at various maturities can combine only in the ways implied by the principal components, in spot rate models spot rate changes can combine in any way that is possible using the number of spot rates in the model. Like arbitrage models and unlike principal components models, the factors in spot rate models are not required to be orthogonal.

---

[27] For a discussion this approach as compared with the principal components approach, see Bennett W. Golub and Leo M. Tilman, "Measuring Yield Curve Risk Using Principal Components Analysis, Value at Risk and Key Rate Durations," *Journal of Portfolio Management* (Summer 1997), pp. 72 84.

Exhibit 5: Characteristic Yield Shifts: Spot Rate Model

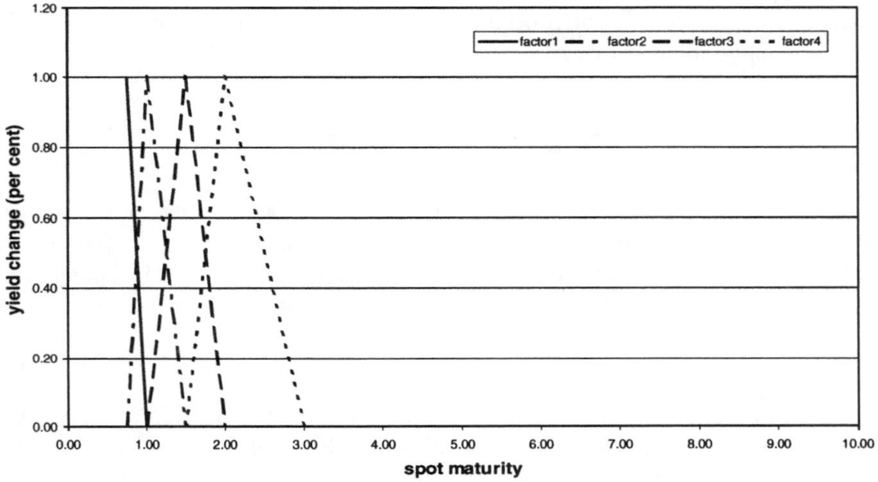

Exhibit 6: Bond Durations: Spot Rate Model

Time to Maturity	b_1	b_2	b_3	b_4
0.75	−0.75	0.00	0.00	0.00
1.00	0.00	−1.00	0.00	0.00
1.50	0.00	0.00	−1.50	0.00
2.00	0.00	0.00	0.00	−2.00
3.00	0.00	0.00	0.00	0.00
4.00	0.00	0.00	0.00	0.00
5.00	0.00	0.00	0.00	0.00
7.00	0.00	0.00	0.00	0.00
10.00	0.00	0.00	0.00	0.00
15.00	0.00	0.00	0.00	0.00
20.00	0.00	0.00	0.00	0.00
30.00	0.00	0.00	0.00	0.00

A disadvantage of the spot rate approach is the fact that the characteristic yield curve shifts in the spot rate model, as illustrated in Exhibit 3, do not correspond with yield curve movements that actually take place. Nor are the characteristic yield curve shifts defined continuously on maturity. Thus, as with principal components models, some interpolation of yield changes is required to apply the model to bonds with cash flows (or yield curve exposures) at times other than the points defined in the model.

A third disadvantage of spot rate models is the fact that a large number of factors are required to model yield curve risk accurately. To use an example, suppose that one wanted to reproduce with spot rate changes the characteristic yield curve movements of a principal components model as described in Exhibit 3. To accomplish this it would be necessary to combine 12 spot rate shifts in the appropriate proportions to recover the information in just one principal components shift. As a consequence, portfolio managers need to use a large number of durations to manage interest rate risk effectively using this approach.

FUNCTIONAL MODELS

Functional models combine the advantages of arbitrage models, continuity and consistency with equilibrium pricing, with the parsimony of principal components models. Functional models assume that zero-coupon yield changes are defined continuously in maturity, for example with a shift function $f(T)$:

$$f(T) = \Delta y(T) \tag{11}$$

where $\Delta y(T)$ is the change in the zero-coupon yield at maturity T. Then, a Taylor series or some other approximating function can be applied to the function $f(T)$, retaining the number of terms are sufficient to describe actual yield curve movements adequately. Durations are computed from the approximating function directly. For example, the yield shift function $f(T)$ can be approximated by a Taylor series, as follows:

$$f(T) = c_0 + c_1 T + c_2 T^2 + \dots \tag{12}$$

The factors are identified with the resulting durations, which can be derived easily from equation (12).

Chambers, Carleton, and McEnally employ this idea to devolop risk measures for use in immunization and hedging, but do not explore the implications of this approach for developing term structure factor models.[28] Similarly, Nelson and Siegel use exponentials to fit yield levels at the short end of the yield curve, but do not extend their approach to the long end of the curve, except to test extrapolations of the model as fitted to Treasury bills, nor to the identification of a factor model.[29]

Kuberek uses the functionals that are proposed by Nelson and Siegel, to model the short-end of the forward rate curve, for the purpose of approximating the shift function given by equation (11) for zero-coupon yields. This three-factor model has the following form:

$$f(T) \approx c_0 + c_1 e^{-T/q} + c_2 (T/q) e^{1-T/q} \tag{13}$$

---

[28] D. R. Chambers, W. T. Carleton, and R. W. McEnally, "Immunizing Default free Bond Portfolios with a Duration Vector," *Journal of Financial and Quantitative Analysis* (1988), pp. 89-104. See also, D. R. Chambers and W. T. Carleton, "A More General Duration Approach," Unpublished Manuscript (1981).

[29] Charles R. Nelson and Andrew F. Siegel, "A Parsimonious Modeling of Yield Curves," *Journal of Business* (October 1987), pp. 473-489.

where q is a parameter.[30] The model given by equation (13) resembles equation (12) except that the second and third terms contain an exponential decay. This exponential form has the benefit that, in contrast to equation (12), changes in yield curve level and shape will not become unbounded in maturity.

With this formulation, the zero-coupon bond durations, the b's in equation (2), take the very simple form

$$b_{ij} = w_j(T_i)T_i \tag{14}$$

where

$$w_1 = -1$$
$$w_2 = -e^{-T/q}$$
$$w_3 = -T/q\,e^{1-T/q}$$

and where the b_{ij} are the exposures of the ith zero-coupon bond to the jth factor.

Thus, the first factor in this three-factor model represents the effect of a precisely uniform change in the level of interest rates, the second factor represents the effect of a change in slope of the yield curve, and the third factor represents the effect of a change in curvature of the yield curve. Factor returns can be estimated by regressing cross-sections of zero-coupon bond returns on these durations.

Exhibit 7 shows these characteristic yield curve movements for the three-factor functional model in equation (13). In this exponential form the characteristic yield shifts represent changes in level (factor 1), slope (factor 2), and curvature (factor 3). The model is specified so that changes in slope affect short rates more than long rates. This is consistent with the behavior of the yield curve at certain times, where short rates are more volatile than long rates. To reproduce yield curve movements where long rates change by more than short rates, factors 1 and 2 can be combined. For example, an upward shift of one unit of factor 2 (100 basis points at the short end) combined with a downward shift of one unit of factor 1 (100 basis points uniformly) produces a flattening of 100 basis points at the long end, with short rates unchanged. Additional complexity in yield curve movements, including various combinations of change in slope and curvature, can be achieved by including factor 3.

The zero-coupon bond durations are given in Exhibit 8. As can be seen, the durations at various maturities with respect to the first factor are equivalent to the ordinary (effective) duration of the bonds. The durations with respect to the second factor, which represents a change in slope, increase in magnitude with maturity to seven years, then decrease. The third factor's durations increase in magnitude to 14 years, then decrease.

---

[30] The value of the single parameters q, which represents the location of the maximum in the third shift component and simultaneously determines the rate of decay in the second, can be chosen in any convenient way. Kuberek ("An Approximate Factor Model for U.S. Treasuries") uses the value of q that maximizes the ability of the three-factor model to describe a wide variety of yield curve shifts under diffuse priors.

Exhibit 7: Characteristic Yield Curve Shifts: Functional Model

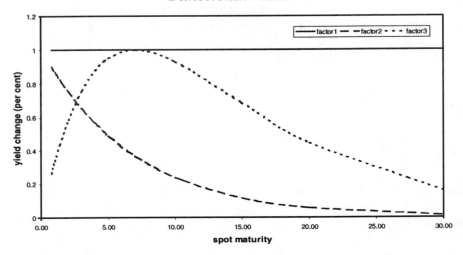

Exhibit 8: Bond Durations: Functional Model

Time to Maturity	b_1	b_2	b_3
0.75	−0.75	−0.67	−0.20
1.00	−1.00	−0.87	−0.34
1.50	−1.50	−1.21	−0.71
2.00	−2.00	−1.50	−1.17
3.00	−3.00	−1.95	−2.28
4.00	−4.00	−2.26	−3.51
5.00	−5.00	−2.45	−4.75
7.00	−7.00	−2.58	−7.00
10.00	−10.00	−2.40	−9.31
15.00	−15.00	−1.76	−10.25
20.00	−20.00	−1.15	−8.92
30.00	−30.00	−0.41	−4.81

The model described here, which is based on approximating functions, has several significant advantages. Most usefully, ordinary (effective) duration, as conventionally defined, is the first factor. Second, unlike the principal components models and spot rate models, the model is inherently consistent with rigorous equilibrium or arbitrage term structure models that imply yield changes that are continuous in maturity, including the CIR model already described. Third, it has only one parameter (and it has no more *moments* than any other three-factor model). Finally, the yield shifts implied by this model correspond with yield curve movements that portfolio managers can easily imagine occurring, namely, changes in level, slope, and curvature.

Because of the particularly simple form of equation (14), the durations of coupon bonds also have a very simple form, as follows:

$$b_j = \sum_h w_j(T_h)s_h T_h / \sum_h s_h \tag{15}$$

where s_h is the present value of the hth cash flow and where the w's are as given in equation (14). Equation (15) is simply the formula for ordinary duration, with an added weighting term $w(T)$. For the first factor, w has a value of unity for all maturities T equation (14), so the associated duration is simply the ordinary (effective) duration. More generally, bond durations in this model are calculated in the same way as ordinary (effective) duration, except that cash flows are weighted differently to reflect the differential exposure to various alternative yield curve shifts.

Like the arbitrage and spot rate models, the factors in functional models are not required to be orthogonal. However, if uncorrelatedness of factor returns is desired, the three factors in equation (14) can easily be rotated to have this property, for example, by estimating the factor returns and extracting the principal components.

CONCLUSION

Term structure factor models can be classified in one of four categories: arbitrage models, principal components models, spot rate models, and functional models. Examples of these reviewed here are the models of Cox, Ingersoll and Ross (arbitrage), Litterman and Scheinkman (principal components), J. P. Morgan's Risk-Metrics™ (spot rate), and Kuberek (functional). Each approach resembles, in some important way, one or another of the traditional types of factor models for common stocks, macroeconomic, statistical, and fundamental.

As with common stock models, the approaches to term structure factor models reviewed here differ primarily in the identification of the factors and in how the factor exposures and factor returns are measured. Arbitrage models assume some underlying set of state variables, then derive the term structure and its dynamics. Principal components models extract factor returns from the excess returns of zero-coupon bonds at specified maturities using statistical techniques. Spot rate models associate factors with yield changes at every point (of a specified set) along the yield curve, and functional models use pre-specified yield curve shifts to fit actual yield curve movements, where the shift components are motivated by equilibrium considerations.

At the extremes, the one-factor model of Cox, Ingersoll, and Ross is most rigorously consistent with equilibrium pricing, but is also the most restrictive in describing actual yield curve movements, while spot rate models are most descriptive, but have the most factors (and thus, the most durations) of any approach.

Principal components and functional models find a middle ground, compromising between the structure and rigorousness of arbitrage models, with few factors, and the explanatory power of spot rate models, with many. Principal components models have the advantage that actual data guide in the identification of the factors, but suffer from the defect that the durations are sample dependent. Functional models have the advantage that the factors can be pre specified in a manner that is convenient to the portfolio manager, for example by defining the factors in such a way that ordinary duration, as conventionally defined, is the first factor.

An important common feature of the models reviewed here relates to the fact that each one associates factors with characteristic yield curve movements. Specifically, factor exposures can be estimated in these models by subjecting a bond to each of the characteristic yield shifts, using a term-structure-based valuation model, or OAS model, to see how much return results. Indeed, the application of term structure factor models crucially depends on the availability and usability of these ancillary valuation models.

The power and usefulness of term structure factor models lie in their application to risk management. Once the moments of the model are determined together with the exposures of the portfolio to each of the factors, it becomes possible to measure portfolio risk in any number of ways, including return variance, tracking error relative to a benchmark, and value-at-risk. By further assuming that the factor returns are normally distributed, it becomes possible to characterize the distribution of portfolio return fully, regardless of its composition.

Hedging Mortgage Products with Swaps and Agencies

Laurie Goodman, Ph.D.
Managing Director
Mortgage Strategy Group
PaineWebber

Jeffrey Ho
Senior Vice President
Mortgage Strategy Group
PaineWebber

INTRODUCTION

With the Treasury universe shrinking so dramatically since mid-1998, all spread product has experienced higher absolute spreads versus Treasuries, and the correlation of spreads among spread product is also higher. This has lead market participants to conclude that hedging mortgages with Treasuries is useless, as the tracking error is huge. However, many investors have the impression that tracking error can be reduced to near-zero if they hedge mortgages with Agency debentures, or with swaps. In this article, we examine the effectiveness of hedging mortgages with Treasuries, swaps, and agency debentures. We show that hedging mortgages with Treasuries is much less effective than it was prior to mid-1998. By contrast, the tracking error of mortgages versus other spread product is now very similar to what it was versus Treasuries prior to the summer of 1998.

A WHOLE NEW BALLGAME

After years of budget deficits, the United States is now in surplus. As a matter of fact, 1998-1999 were the first back-to-back budget surpluses since 1956-1957. Because of these surpluses, the need for Treasury borrowings has been decreased, and Treasury debt is actually being paid down. As a result of the Treasury surpluses and the net reduction in Treasury debt, the debt world is a very different place. Treasury securities now constitute a much smaller proportion of the fixed income universe than they used to. Consequently, spreads on all spread products are wider than they used to be, as scarcity has driven up Treasury prices. Spreads on spread product are also much more volatile than before. Top that off with all spread product being much more highly correlated.

Exhibit 1 shows average spreads on spread product for four periods: 11/1/95-6/30/98, 7/1/98-3/14/00, 9/1/99-3/14/00, and 11/1/95-3/14/00. The first period (11/1/95-6/30/98) is the period before Treasury scarcity became an issue. We refer to this as "the earlier period." The second period reflects the period in which Treasury scarcity was a problem. We refer to this as "the later period." The third period is the most recent sub-set of the second period, a period in which mortgages are believed to have traded more closely with swaps and with agency debentures. We refer to this as "the last six months" or as "the most recent period." It takes out the October of 1998 and August of 1999 spread widenings. The final period used for this analysis is the entire period 11/1/95-6/30/98 (referred to as "the whole period").

As a proxy for the mortgage universe, we used the perfect current coupon FNMA (the mortgage selling at par for corporate settlement). To characterize Agency product, we employed the 10-year benchmark FNMA issue. For swaps, we applied data provided by Telerate. The exhibit shows that spreads on all spread product are higher in the later period than they were in the earlier period. For example, mortgage spreads (the spread between the current coupon mortgage and the 10-year Treasury) averaged 110 basis points in the earlier period but 147 basis points in the later period. Swap spreads averaged 41 basis points in the earlier period, then doubled to 81 basis points.

The exhibit also evidences that not only are swap spreads higher, they are also more volatile. We display the detrended standard deviation of spreads for each of the two periods. The standard deviation of mortgage spreads averaged 6 basis points in the earlier period, then expanded to 20 basis points in the second period. Swap spreads and spreads on Agency debentures show a more extreme change. The standard deviation on Agency debentures was 2 basis points in the earlier period, and then it blew out to 10 basis points.

Exhibit 1: Volatility of Selected Spreads

Begin	End	\multicolumn{6}{c}{Average Spreads}
Begin	End	Mtg/Tsy	Agy/Tsy	Swap/Tsy	Mtg/Agy	Mtg/Swap	Swap/Agy
11/1/95	6/30/98	110	28	41	82	69	13
7/1/98	3/14/00	147	61	81	85	66	19
9/1/99	3/14/00	144	67	85	77	58	19
11/1/95	3/14/00	123	40	56	83	68	15

Begin	End	\multicolumn{6}{c}{Standard Deviation of Spread (bps)*}
Begin	End	Mtg/Tsy	Agy/Tsy	Swap/Tsy	Mtg/Agy	Mtg/Swap	Swap/Agy
11/1/95	6/30/98	6	2	3	5	5	2
7/1/98	3/14/00	20	10	12	13	11	4
9/1/99	3/14/00	13	11	12	4	4	1
11/1/95	3/14/00	13	7	8	9	8	3

* 6-month moving average detrended std dev of spread level.

Exhibit 2: Correlation of Selected Yields and Spreads

		Correlation Among Spreads					
Begin	End	Corp/Mtg	Agy/Mtg	Swap/Mtg	Agy/Swap	Corp/Swap	Agy/Corp
11/1/95	6/30/98	8.1%	14.8%	18.4%	29.8%	22.9%	20.0%
7/1/98	3/14/00	51.5%	70.0%	69.4%	84.7%	62.3%	60.3%
9/1/99	3/14/00	63.7%	76.8%	76.3%	97.5%	92.3%	89.1%
11/1/95	3/14/00	40.6%	53.0%	53.5%	67.4%	52.0%	50.1%

		Correlation Among Yields						
Begin	End	Mtg/Tsy	Mtg/Agy	Mtg/Swap	Mtg/Corp	Agy/Swap	Corp/Tsy	Agy/Tsy	Swap/Tsy
11/1/95	6/30/98	97.4%	99.6%	99.3%	99.5%	99.2%	99.5%	99.6%	99.3%
7/1/98	3/14/00	85.2%	95.1%	93.7%	90.0%	97.9%	90.0%	95.1%	93.7%
9/1/99	3/14/00	76.5%	90.1%	89.2%	87.6%	99.5%	87.6%	90.1%	89.2%
11/1/95	3/14/00	91.2%	97.2%	96.4%	94.6%	98.6%	94.6%	97.2%	96.4%

Note that average spreads between mortgages and Agencies, mortgages and swaps, and swaps and Agencies are all roughly the same between the two periods. For example, mortgage-Agency spreads averaged 82 basis points in the 11/1/95-6/30/98 period and 85 basis points in the 7/1/98-3/14/00 period. However, the detrended standard deviation of the later period is much higher — 5 basis points over 11/1/95-6/30/98, then out to 13 basis points during 7/1/98-3/14/00. However, when looking at standard deviations of spreads between mortgage and Agency debentures, the last six months were approximately as volatile as was the 11/95-1/98 period — 4 basis points from 9/1/99-3/14/00, versus 5 basis points between 11/1/95 and 6/30/98. Mortgage-Agency and mortgage-swap spreads are now, at best, as volatile as mortgage-Treasury spreads used to be.

HIGHER SPREAD CORRELATIONS

Exhibit 2 shows that not only are all spreads more volatile versus Treasury securities, but that spread product is also more highly correlated with other spread product than ever before. The top panel of Exhibit 2 illustrates that during the 11/1/95-6/30/98 period, correlation between Agencies and mortgages rose from 14.8% to 70%, while that between swaps and mortgages increased from 18.4% to 69.4% (exactly the pattern that would be expected).

The bottom panel of Exhibit 2 shows correlation among yields. Here we find results that many will consider surprising. Note that in the earlier period, correlation of the mortgage-Treasury yield was 97.4%; then in the later period it slipped to 85.2%, which is in line with intuition. However, correlation between mortgage and Agency yields also dropped, albeit by less (from 99.6% to 95.1%). Note that the correlations between mortgage-Agency yields and mortgage-swap yields (95.1% and 93.7%, respectively) are weaker in the later period than the mortgage-Treasury yield correlation was during the earlier period (97.4%).

Increased spread volatility outweighs the higher spread correlations, and yield correlations have actually dropped.

Now, it's naturally tough to "see" yield correlations, as they are inherently unintuitive for most of us. Moreover, the doubting Thomases are apt to murmur that this analysis has been "rigged" by our use of the perfect current coupon mortgage, rather than a real world mortgage-backed security. So in the next section, we look at how much hedging real world TBA mortgages with swaps and agency debentures actually improves hedge effectiveness versus hedging with Treasuries.

METHODOLOGY

Our goal is to determine the hedge effectiveness of hedging mortgages with various alternative securities. Ergo — we hedge FNMA TBAs couponed from 6.5 to 8.5% with each of the following — the 10-year Treasury, the 10-year swap and the 10-year benchmark note. We used the following methodology:

1. Calculate the empirical hedge ratios for a given mortgage using 20 days of empirical data. This allows us to set up a position in which we are long $100 of mortgages and short ($100 times the empirical hedge ratio) of Treasuries, Agencies or swaps. The empirical hedge ratio will be different for each instrument.

2. Rebalance our hedge each successive 20-day period. We close out the prior position and tabulate long mortgage position performance versus our short of the hedging instrument. We assume all mortgage securities are rolled. Treasury shorts get funded at the 10-year Treasury repo rate, which is usually on special. 10-year Agency debentures are assumed to be funded at general collateral levels. The new position is derived from the then-current 20-day hedge ratios.

3. We then look at measures of hedging effectiveness. Our favorite measure is cumulative absolute performance (annualized). Under that view, absolute hedging errors are aggregated, then annualized, per the following equation:

$$CAPA = \frac{\sum_{i=1}^{n} |X_i|}{yrs}$$

where yrs is the number of years in the measurement period
$X_i = \Delta MtgPx_i - B \times \Delta HedgePx_i$

Example:
[\$1 of gains during one 20-day period] + [\$1 of losses the next]
= \$2 of hedging error.

We also show the annualized variance of performance, which uses the square of the absolute errors. Hence a series with a lot of small errors tracks better than one with several very large errors. This variance measure is calculated via:

$$AVP = \frac{\displaystyle\sum_{i=1}^{n} (X_i - \bar{X})^2}{n} \times \frac{260}{t}$$

where t = number of trade days in holding period

4. We also used shorter, (10- and 5-day) holding periods with the same methodology as in steps 1-3 above, (i.e. allowing for more frequent rebalancing). We continued to use 20-day empirical hedge ratios to set the size of the short position, as that length was needed to provided sufficient data to be meaningful.

The Results

Our analysis for 20-day holding periods is shown in Exhibit 3. The top part of the exhibit shows hedging with Treasuries; the middle part shows "what if" we hedged with swaps; and the bottom section depicts Agency hedges.

Focus on the first section, the top part of which includes cumulative absolute performance. During the 11/95-6/98 period, cumulative absolute performance was \$2.04/year for FNMA 7s. It more than doubled, to \$4.46/year, from mid-1998 to the present. The annualized variance of performance confirms this doubling. Performance variance in the earlier period was 0.46/year (annualized), versus 2.98/year during the later period. Thus, the intuitive conclusion that it is much more difficult to hedge mortgages with Treasury securities than it used to be.

The bottom section of Exhibit 3 hedges mortgages with 10-year Agency debentures. For FNMA 7s, the annualized sum of absolute performance was \$2.32 in the earlier period, and \$2.74 in the later period. The annualized variance of performance results confirms the fact that Agency debentures actually provided a better hedge in terms of hedging effectiveness in the earlier period (0.61 versus 1.26).

Now the punch line — in the earlier period, the 10-year Treasury actually provided a better hedge than did either Agency debentures or swaps. Note that for hedging FNMA 7s, the cumulative absolute performance (annualized) was \$2.04 for the 10-year Treasury versus \$2.33 for swaps and \$2.32 for 10-year Agency debentures. In the later period, Treasury securities had deteriorated so badly as a hedging instrument that both swaps and Agency debentures performed much better ($4.46 for Treasury securities versus $2.75 for swaps and $2.74 for Agencies). However, even the best hedge during that later period performed more poorly than did the poorest hedge in the earlier period.

These results had been foreshadowed by standard deviations in Exhibit 1 and the correlations in Exhibit 2. We showed that the standard deviations of mortgage-Agency and mortgage-swap spreads in the later period were comparable to or actually higher than those on mortgage-Treasury spreads in the earlier period. Moreover, yield correlations between mortgages-swaps and mortgages-Agencies were weaker than yield correlations between Treasuries and mortgages used to be.

Many investors will be surprised by the order of magnitude of the annualized sum of absolute performance. Recall from the discussion above that mortgages hedged with the 10-year have an annualized absolute error of $4.46 versus $2.74-2.75 for Agency debentures and swaps. That's 62% as much (or a 38% reduction in risk).

Exhibit 3: Hedging over 20-Day Holding Periods

Begin	End	6.5%	7.0%	7.5%	8.0%	8.5%
Mortgages Hedged with Treasuries						
Cumulative Absolute Performance Annualized						
11/1/95	6/30/98	1.85	2.04	2.04	2.18	2.44
7/1/98	3/14/00	5.19	4.46	4.02	3.43	3.17
11/1/95	3/14/00	3.15	2.98	2.81	2.66	2.72
Annualized Variance of Performance						
11/1/95	6/30/98	0.37	0.46	0.50	0.54	0.70
7/1/98	3/14/00	3.61	2.98	2.47	1.56	1.25
11/1/95	3/14/00	1.64	1.46	1.30	0.96	0.93
Mortgages Hedged with Swaps						
Cumulative Absolute Performance Annualized						
11/1/95	6/30/98	2.11	2.33	2.49	2.50	2.52
7/1/98	3/14/00	2.57	2.75	2.66	2.30	2.55
11/1/95	3/14/00	2.29	2.49	2.55	2.42	2.53
Annualized Variance of Performance						
11/1/95	6/30/98	0.47	0.52	0.62	0.63	0.74
7/1/98	3/14/00	0.89	1.06	1.05	0.67	0.75
11/1/95	3/14/00	0.63	0.74	0.81	0.67	0.76
Mortgages Hedged with Agency Debentures						
Cumulative Absolute Performance Annualized						
11/1/95	6/30/98	2.18	2.32	2.32	2.30	2.48
7/1/98	3/14/00	2.51	2.74	2.70	2.36	2.47
11/1/95	3/14/00	2.31	2.48	2.47	2.32	2.48
Annualized Variance of Performance						
11/1/95	6/30/98	0.58	0.61	0.62	0.60	0.70
7/1/98	3/14/00	1.11	1.26	1.12	0.72	0.74
11/1/95	3/14/00	0.79	0.88	0.84	0.67	0.74

Exhibit 4: Hedging over 10-Day Holding Periods

Begin	End	6.5%	7.0%	7.5%	8.0%	8.5%
Mortgages Hedged with Treasuries						
Cumulative Absolute Performance Annualized						
11/1/95	6/30/98	3.53	3.57	3.90	3.94	3.69
7/1/98	3/14/00	6.24	6.03	5.56	4.66	4.25
9/1/99	3/14/00	5.30	5.21	5.25	4.97	5.83
11/1/95	3/14/00	4.58	4.53	4.55	4.22	3.91
Annualized Variance of Performance						
11/1/95	6/30/98	0.86	0.79	0.88	0.88	0.84
7/1/98	3/14/00	3.07	2.82	2.48	1.62	1.29
9/1/99	3/14/00	2.33	2.36	2.34	1.66	2.02
11/1/95	3/14/00	1.74	1.60	1.52	1.18	1.02
Mortgages Hedged with Swaps						
Cumulative Absolute Performance Annualized						
11/1/95	6/30/98	3.49	3.46	3.93	3.97	3.82
7/1/98	3/14/00	4.35	4.15	3.60	3.00	3.17
9/1/99	3/14/00	3.83	3.59	2.88	2.28	3.78
11/1/95	3/14/00	3.82	3.73	3.80	3.59	3.57
Annualized Variance of Performance						
11/1/95	6/30/98	0.91	0.78	0.90	0.89	0.83
7/1/98	3/14/00	1.12	1.12	1.08	0.66	0.64
9/1/99	3/14/00	0.73	0.65	0.52	0.27	0.83
11/1/95	3/14/00	0.99	0.92	0.98	0.81	0.76
Mortgages Hedged with Agency Debentures						
Cumulative Absolute Performance Annualized						
11/1/95	6/30/98	3.73	3.67	3.98	4.03	3.80
7/1/98	3/14/00	4.34	4.15	3.77	3.08	3.11
9/1/99	3/14/00	2.98	2.74	2.69	2.27	3.74
11/1/95	3/14/00	3.96	3.85	3.89	3.66	3.53
Annualized Variance of Performance						
11/1/95	6/30/98	1.04	0.90	0.94	0.90	0.85
7/1/98	3/14/00	1.26	1.21	1.13	0.67	0.68
9/1/99	3/14/00	0.49	0.49	0.44	0.26	0.86
11/1/95	3/14/00	1.12	1.03	1.02	0.82	0.79

Exhibit 4 shows results for an analysis notched down to 10-day holding periods. Note that all numbers are larger than in Exhibit 3, because there is less scope for "natural" netting. If a hedged position loses $1.00 in one 10-day period, and makes $1.10 the next, Exhibit 3 (using the 20-day yardstick) would have only picked $0.10 net, whereas Exhibit 4 picks up an absolute error of $2.10. Note also that we have added one more six month period (from 9/1/99 to 3/14/00). This was again meant to capture the recent period in which market participants believe that the correlation between mortgages versus agencies and swaps has risen. We wanted to test the extent to which that has occurred. (This period could not have been included for 20-day holding periods, as there were too few observations.)

Exhibit 5: Mortgage Spreads

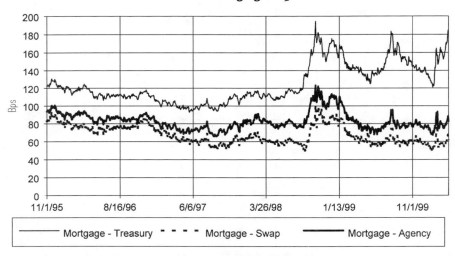

The 10-day holding period results are, by and large, very similar to those for 20-day periods in Exhibit 3. In the early period, swap and Agency hedges for 10-day holding periods were about as effective as Treasury hedges. In the later period they were more effective. However, the order to magnitude of risk reduction is less than many would have thought. As an example, look at hedging FNMA 7s. There is a $4.15 annualized cumulative error on swaps and Agency debentures versus $6.03 for Treasury securities (69% as much, for a 31% risk reduction).

Now let's look at the 9/1/99-3/14/00 period. Treasuries, swaps and Agency debentures were all more effective hedges during the latest six month period than for the entire 7/1/98-3/14/99 period. This is because (as shown in Exhibit 5) mortgages held up very poorly in the late 1998 period versus all alternatives — Treasuries, swaps and Agency debentures.

However, note that even over the 9/1/99-3/14/00 period, there was quite a bit of residual risk. The absolute cumulative error (annualized basis) for hedging FNMA 7s is $3.59 for swaps, $2.74 for Agencies and $5.21 for Treasuries. Moreover, over the last six months, Agency debentures were a better hedge for mortgages couponed 7.5% or below. For the FNMA 8 and 8.5% securities, swaps and Agency debentures performed equally well. Bottom line — clearly, hedging has gotten slightly easier over the past six months, during which time Agency debentures surpassed swaps for hedging effectiveness.

Exhibit 6 is very similar to Exhibit 4, except that we once more notch down our holding periods, this time to 5-day segments. Errors are larger, as there's simply less time for netting. Note that Agency debentures were again the best hedge for FNMA 7s over the past 6 months; the Agency debentures carry only 46% of the risk of hedging with Treasuries ($5.69/$12.34).

Exhibit 6: Hedging over 5-Day Holding Periods

Begin	End	6.5%	7.0%	7.5%	8.0%	8.5%
Mortgages Hedged with Treasuries						
Cumulative Absolute Performance Annualized						
11/1/95	6/30/98	4.63	4.63	5.01	5.07	5.06
7/1/98	3/14/00	11.58	10.48	9.82	8.17	6.56
9/1/99	3/14/00	12.46	12.34	12.31	11.52	9.79
11/1/95	3/14/00	7.34	6.90	6.88	6.27	5.64
Annualized Variance of Performance						
11/1/95	6/30/98	0.74	0.67	0.79	0.89	0.84
7/1/98	3/14/00	5.20	4.57	4.21	3.23	2.39
9/1/99	3/14/00	5.97	5.98	5.88	4.89	4.46
11/1/95	3/14/00	2.48	2.20	2.12	1.81	1.45
Mortgages Hedged with Swaps						
Cumulative Absolute Performance Annualized						
11/1/95	6/30/98	5.05	4.78	5.13	5.24	5.08
7/1/98	3/14/00	6.96	6.50	6.52	5.85	5.54
9/1/99	3/14/00	5.84	6.28	6.45	6.71	7.15
11/1/95	3/14/00	5.79	5.45	5.67	5.47	5.25
Annualized Variance of Performance						
11/1/95	6/30/98	0.85	0.74	0.86	0.95	0.86
7/1/98	3/14/00	1.93	1.57	1.63	1.41	1.33
9/1/99	3/14/00	1.12	1.24	1.31	1.22	1.87
11/1/95	3/14/00	1.27	1.07	1.16	1.13	1.04
Mortgages Hedged with Agency Debentures						
Cumulative Absolute Performance Annualized						
11/1/95	6/30/98	5.15	4.98	5.16	5.11	5.08
7/1/98	3/14/00	7.17	6.78	6.45	5.67	5.34
9/1/99	3/14/00	5.27	5.69	5.89	6.10	6.68
11/1/95	3/14/00	5.93	5.68	5.66	5.32	5.18
Annualized Variance of Performance						
11/1/95	6/30/98	0.89	0.78	0.84	0.92	0.84
7/1/98	3/14/00	1.81	1.62	1.63	1.33	1.29
9/1/99	3/14/00	0.88	0.99	1.06	1.01	1.81
11/1/95	3/14/00	1.25	1.11	1.15	1.08	1.02

Some market participants are very surprised by our results. They make the point that it appears that the OASs of collateral to the LIBOR curve have been very stable. Yes, that is certainly the case. We confirmed that using FNMA 7.5 collateral, as shown in Exhibit 7. Note that the Treasury curve has no bearing at all on the LIBOR OAS results. The Monte Carlo paths are centered on forward LIBOR rates, while the cash flows are discounted at current LIBOR. Moreover, PaineWebber (along with most other major mortgage dealers) have recast our OAS model to allow mortgage rates to be driven by the swap curve. Following that revamping, we have back-filled three years of LIBOR OAS data, the results of which are reflected for 30-year FNMA 7.5s in Exhibit 7.

Exhibit 7: OAS On FNMA 7.5% Collateral

Period	LIBOR OAS		Treasury OAS	
	Average	Std Dev	Average	Std Dev
1/1/97-6/30/98	8	6	30	5
7/1/98-Present	15	18	56	13
9/1/99-Present	2	3	54	9

Focus on the results for the last six month period. Since 9/1/99, average LIBOR OAS on FNMA 7.5 collateral had been 2 basis points, with a standard deviation of 3 basis points. Compare that to a standard deviation of 9 basis points on the Treasury OAS over the same time period. Note that the low standard deviation on the LIBOR OAS reflects the fact that LIBOR OAS takes into account changes in the shape of the curve and changes in volatility. It is important to realize that while many investors rely on OAS, few investors strive to completely hedge out the shape of the curve and changes in volatility.

Caveats are in order. First, note that only over the most recent period (9/1/99-3/14/00) has the LIBOR OAS had a lower standard deviation than the Treasury OAS. For both of the longer sub-periods (1/97-6/98, and 7/98-3/14/00), the LIBOR OAS was higher than the Treasury OAS. Second, during periods of low interest rates, mortgages tend to behave very differently from their OAS duration. They tend to widen in rallies and tighten in sell-offs, which increases volatility (clearly seen from the numbers). Thus, while LIBOR OAS performed well in measuring value in collateral during the most recent period (9/1/99-3/14/00), it has clearly not always had that exemplary role.

CONCLUSION

There is no question that 10-year swaps and 10-year Agency debentures now provide a better hedge for mortgages than do 10-year Treasuries. However, the hedge improvement is not nearly as dramatic as most market participants expect. There is a substantial amount of basis risk which does not get hedged out when using swaps or Agency debentures. In this environment there is also a substantial amount of curve risk and volatility risk. These risks are not being hedged in using a simple Agency or swap hedge.

Our bottom line is as follows. Don't be lulled into a false sense of security with a Roberto Benigni energy level approach (that life would be beautiful if you had only used Agency debentures or swaps to hedge mortgages). While reality may be simplified on the silver screen, in the very real world of mortgages, it is not.

Analysis of and Strategies with Callable Securities

Douglas Johnston
Senior Vice President
Fixed Income Research
Lehman Brothers

INTRODUCTION

In recent years, volatility has come to be viewed as an asset class in its own right. Next to duration, curve, and spreads, investors realize the importance of having a view on the likely range of yield movements and its impact on security prices. While many money managers do not trade options outright due to account restrictions, assets with embedded options are accessible, such as mortgage-backed and callable securities. In fact, in April 1999, both Fannie Mae and Freddie Mac, two large federal sponsored agencies, began to issue large, "benchmark" callable structures giving investors highly liquid vehicles to buy or sell volatility.

Callable securities offer opportunities for many fixed-income investors. With the callables' exposure to changes in the yield curve and volatility, these securities expand the investment universe and give investors an additional tool to outperform their benchmarks. However, with the anticipation of enhanced yield come commensurate risks. This article discusses the salient features of callable securities, discusses the risks due to changes in market variables, and highlights strategies that can be employed to manage those risks and improve portfolio performance.

WHY CALLABLES?

Callable securities have substantial diversity in structure with call lockouts ranging from a few months to longer than 10 years. Price diversity allows the investor to choose between discount, par-priced, or premium securities. For indexed investors, not including callables in their asset allocation is equivalent to being short an asset class of sizable market value.

Callable securities make up an asset class that investors can use to enhance returns under appropriate conditions. For example, in 1997 it paid to sell

I would like to thank Andy Sparks for his comments on earlier drafts of this article.

volatility. And similar to mortgage-backed securities, callables performed well with declines in both actual and implied volatility. Using Lehman Brothers' indices, the monthly excess returns of the agency callable sector over duration-matched Treasuries in 1997 was 53 basis points.[1]

Of course, returns are not always good. In particular, the rally and flattening of the Treasury and agency curves at the end of 1997 increased the probability that some callable securities would be redeemed. Callable securities are more sensitive to changes in the shape of the yield curve than nominal securities. In addition, the late 1997 spike in implied volatility caused investors to reevaluate the risk premium required to sell volatility. Both effects combined to widen nominal spreads on callable instruments, as reflected in their muted performance in late 1997.

There are risks associated with investing in callable securities. In addition to the usual vagaries of supply and demand, callables have embedded options that are sensitive to changes in the slope of the yield curve. The value of the options is partly a function of forward rates, which are dependent on the spot level of rates and spot yield spreads.

Another risk is volatility, which has two forms. The first is realized volatility. Owners of callable instruments are expressing the implicit view that yields will remain relatively stable, enabling the investor to capture the yield spread over duration-matched noncallable securities. Another way to express this is that callable securities have negative convexity leading to poor returns in a volatile market. Large swings in rates can necessitate rehedging, leading the investor to lock in lower returns. If these moves in rates are large enough, callable securities will underperform.

Many investors use callable securities within a total return strategy rather than a buy-and-hold strategy; therefore, the second volatility risk is to changes in implied volatility, which is the market forecast of future rate uncertainty. When a position is unwound, the value of the callable security will depend on the new level of implied volatility. If implied volatility were to increase, callable security prices would decline. Therefore, callable investors must have views on the likely range of rates over the investment period and the market's perception of future rate uncertainty at the horizon date.

How much additional return is required to compensate for these risks is the central question for investors. Nominal spreads, and therefore prices, reflect the market's perception of the value of these risks. This article discusses the risks and rewards and the tools needed to determine if an investment in callable securities is right for a particular portfolio.

DISSECTING THE CALLABLE

A callable security gives the issuer the right to redeem the security at predetermined prices at specified times. For example, the traditional 5-year security that

---

[1] This chapter was written in early 1998. Consequently, the data and illustrations are through 1997.

is noncallable for one year (denoted "5nc1") is redeemable at par at any time starting on the anniversary of its issue date. Different structures may have a schedule of prices for which the issue can be redeemed or specific dates on which the issue may be called.[2] The underlying theme, however, is the same: by purchasing a callable security, the investor gives the issuer the option to buy the security back. Therefore, investors who own callable securities have sold embedded interest rate options and need to be compensated appropriately.

Compensation for selling the embedded option comes in the form of a higher static yield. For example, on 12/5/97 a generic U.S. agency 10nc3 was offered at a yield spread of 94 bp to the 10-year on-the-run Treasury, the 6.125% of 8/15/07. In contrast, a generic 10-year U.S. agency bullet was offered at a nominal yield spread of 32 bp over the 10-year. The additional 62 bp in static yield on the callable was compensation for selling the embedded call options. Determining the fair value of the embedded options and understanding the risks and rewards in selling them is essential for the callable security investor.

A portfolio of a bullet security and an option to buy that security can mimic a callable security. For example, a 10nc3 with only one call date can be separated into a long position in a 10-year bullet and a short position in an option to buy that security starting three years from its issue date. The option is typically referred to as a "3×7 option," referring to the option's expiration in three years with an underlying term of seven years.[3]

Returning to our example, the 10nc3 was offered at $100 for a yield of 6.856%. A 10-year bullet with the same coupon and a yield of 6.236% would be priced at $104.57. Thus, the embedded option was sold for a price of $4.57, thereby lowering the cost of the callable security. The relationship between the callable security and the bullet to maturity can be represented as follows:

Callable security price = Bullet to maturity price − Value of embedded options

Types of Callables

One factor that differentiates callable securities is the type of embedded option. One example, that we define as an American callable, is the type that is continuously callable at the noncallable period. The issuer may redeem the bond at the specified price at any time during the call period. Another type is a Bermudan option, which gives the issuer the right to call the bond on specified dates that typically coincide with coupon dates. Finally, issuers have recently begun to structure callable securities with a European style option, a one-time call feature that is a Bermudan option with only one call date.

---

[2] In addition, many callable securities have "notice" periods—a set number of days notice the issuer must give the investor that the security will be called. For example, callable Treasuries are discreetly callable on coupon dates with 120 days notice from the issuer.

[3] A corresponding option in the over-the-counter derivatives market would be a 3×7 European style swaption.

The most flexible of the options is the American, which gives the issuer maximum flexibility in timing the call decision. Callables with this type of embedded option will be the least expensive. Bermudan options are slightly more restrictive with their schedule of call dates. The European option limits the issuer to only one call date, giving the investor increased call protection. European style callables can be easily synthesized using bullet securities and over-the-counter options.

Bermudan and American options embedded in callable securities actually represent a package of options that are conditional in nature. For example, with a Bermudan callable security, if the issuer calls the issue on the first call date, the remaining options on subsequent coupon dates naturally disappear. A Bermudan or American option cannot be exactly synthesized by selling a strip of options in the derivatives market because the package of individual options would be more expensive than the conditional option that is embedded in the callable security. The complex nature of the embedded option requires a more sophisticated valuation, such as option-adjusted spread (OAS) analysis.[4]

Another important feature of callable securities is the *lockout period*, the period during which the security cannot be called (time to call). Coupled with the time to maturity, the lockout period helps to determine the value of the embedded options. Time to call matters primarily due to the increasing dispersion of possible future rates the farther into the future one looks. For example, the embedded option in a 10-year noncall 6 month (10nc6M) European callable is a 6-month European option on a 9½-year security; the embedded option in a 10nc3 European callable is a 3-year European option on a 7-year security.

The uncertainty associated with 7-year rates three years hence is larger than the uncertainty associated with 9½-year rates six months from now. This rise in perceived volatility increases the expected payoff of the longer dated option, making the option more expensive. In addition, differences in the lockout period can alter the risk characteristics of the security. In particular, different lockout/maturity structures will expose the investor to different yield spreads and volatilities along the curve. This variation can prove useful for investors who are fine-tuning a curve view along with a view on volatility.

For Bermudan and American style options, the impact of the lockout period is more complicated. The 10nc6M European callable is exposed to the uncertainty in the 9½-year rate 6 months from now. The American and Bermudan style callables are exposed to the uncertainty in the path of forward rates. For example, the Bermudan 10nc6M callable would be exposed to the 9½-year rate 6 months forward, the 9-year rate 1 year forward, and so on including the 6-month rate 9½ years forward. In this case, the set of options embedded in the shorter dated lockout contains the options embedded in longer dated lockouts; the option value would be higher for the shorter dated lockout.

---

[4] Term structure models that use a lattice of interest rates are typically employed. Lattices are required to compute the expected value of the security's cash flows based on the evolution of the term structure. The necessary expectation is computed using a risk-neutral probability distribution and the method of iterated expectations called "backward diffusion."

Premiums versus Discounts

In addition to the maturity/lockout structure, investors must consider the relative strikes of the embedded options compared to where forward rates are trading. In other words, investors must consider whether the options are in the money (ITM), at the money (ATM), or out of the money (OTM). By comparing the coupon of the callable security to the par forward rate implied by the issuer's bullet curve, the option can be classified. Premium securities, which trade above par, have embedded options that are in the money and generally trade on a yield-to-call basis given the likelihood that the issue will be called. Discount callables, priced below par with a coupon below the going market rate, have embedded options that are out of the money.

Different options have exposure to different risks. Premium securities are exposed to extension risk. If rates rise, the option is worth less as the security becomes less likely to be called. In effect, this increases the duration of the security, extending the effective maturity beyond what the investor may have expected. Conversely, discount callables trade like bullets to maturity and are exposed to compression risk. If rates decline, the securities will shorten in duration as they become more likely to be called.

A security that is trading near par is usually associated with options that are at the money, which implies that the strike price is close to the forward price of comparable bullets. But this is not necessarily true. For example, new issue European callables are usually priced and callable at par. However, the amount the option is in the money depends on both the nominal spread and the slope of the bullet curve.[5] Flatter curves imply lower forward yields relative to spot yields, which implies that the option will move farther into the money holding nominal spreads constant. Investors should compare the coupon they are receiving to forward rates imputed from the issuer's credit curve.

Callable securities are exposed, in varying degrees, to extension and compression risk, which affect performance. As rates decline and the security is called early, the investor receives the principal back instead of continuing to receive the higher coupon. That is, the investor has to reinvest cash flows at a lower market yield than the original stated yield. If the market sells off and rates rise, the investor is holding a longer maturity note at below market rates. The decline in duration as rates rally (or increase as rates rise) is a characteristic of negative convexity (or convexity that is too low relative to duration.) Negative convexity, coupled with the dependence on volatility,[6] is an important reason for the additional spread investors earn on callable securities.

---

[5] As a rough approximation, $B = N - (Ym - Yc) \times Tc/(Tm - Tc)$, where B is the number of bp the option is in the money, N is the nominal spread, Tc is the time to call, Tm is the time to maturity, Yc is the bullet yield to the call date, and Ym is the bullet yield to the maturity date. If the nominal spread does not change but the curve flattens instantaneously (i.e., $Ym - Yc$ gets smaller), the option moves farther in the money. Nominal spreads for new issues tend to adjust as the shape of the curve changes.

Exhibit 1: Nominal Spread of FNMA 8.5 of 2/1/05-00 to Duration-Matched Bullets, and New Issue 10-Year Bullet Yield, January 31, 1995-November 30, 1997

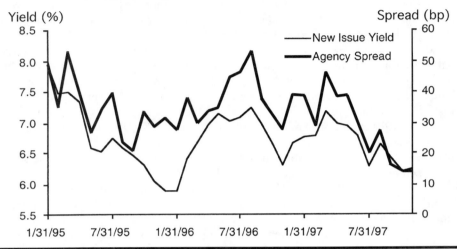

Whether the option is ITM, ATM, or OTM will influence the security's sensitivities to changes in market variables. For example, callable securities that are ATM have the most sensitivity to changes in market rates and implied volatility. This is because the risk characteristics of an option are highest when it is at the money. As the security moves deep into or out of the money, it trades more like a bullet with little optionality. Given the lower uncertainty and hedging costs the investor faces, nominal spreads will tend to tighten to equal duration bullets. Many times investors can find relative value in premium and discount callable securities in the secondary market.

Nominal Spreads

We next analyze how nominal spreads behave under different market conditions. Shown in Exhibit 1 is the nominal spread of the FNMA 8.5 of 2/1/05-00, which was an original $1 billion global 10nc5 issue. The spread is shown to the risk-weighted yield of a bullet portfolio consisting of FNMA 8.35 of 11/10/99 and FNMA 7.875 of 2/24/05. The callable, which was issued at par, quickly became a premium and its effective duration declined rapidly. Originally quoted at a spread over the 10-year Treasury, it began trading to call when yields rallied 100-150 bp.

---

[6] In particular, for a simple, one factor model of the short-term interest rate, it can be shown that two securities with equal duration will satisfy the following relation: $\sigma^2 (C_1 - C_2) = \theta_2 - \theta_1$ where σ is the volatility of the short rate, C_i is the convexity, and θ_i is the time value (theta) of the security. Thus, if $C_1 < C_2$ then $\theta_2 < \theta_1$. Securities with negative convexity should have positive carry versus positively convex securities of equal duration, and the spread is proportional to the amount of short-rate volatility.

Exhibit 2: General Behavior of Nominal Spreads* for Changes in Market Level

	OTM	ATM	ITM
Rally	↑	↓	↓
Backup	↓	↓	↑

*Callable - Duration-matched bullet yield.

Exhibit 3: Indicative Data and Risk Statistics for Selected New Issue Agency Callables, as of close 12/11/97

	2nc3m	2nc1	5nc6m	5nc2	10nc1	10nc3	10nc5
Yield	5.95	5.89	6.48	6.40	7.01	6.77	6.60
Fwd Yld	5.86	5.89	6.01	6.08	6.20	6.27	6.33
OADur	0.70	1.40	1.60	3.00	3.00	4.60	5.60
PV01 1Y	−0.21	−0.56	−0.29	−0.02	−0.46	−0.05	−0.04
PV01 2Y	−0.38	−0.79	−0.24	−0.81	−0.29	−0.04	−0.05
PV01 3Y	0.00	0.00	−0.26	−0.45	−0.28	−1.32	−0.11
PV01 5Y	0.00	0.00	−0.88	−1.65	−0.48	−0.87	−2.42
PV01 10Y	0.00	0.00	0.00	0.00	−1.46	−2.35	−3.09
Vega	−2.91	−2.30	−9.30	−8.96	−19.50	−19.62	−15.70

OADur = option-adjusted duration.   PV01 = price value of 1 bp change.
Vega = price value, in bp, of 1% change in implied volatility

A close correlation exists between the market level, for which we use the new issue 10-year bullet yield as a proxy, and the nominal spread of the callable. This is because as the option moves farther into the money, the risks associated with the option decline. That is, the option's delta goes to one and its gamma goes to zero, which reduces hedging costs. In addition, model misspecifications, such as uncertainty in volatility, are less egregious when the option is deep in or out of the money.

In 1997, premium callables performed well versus duration-matched bullets, due to both a decline in implied volatility and a rally-flattening of the yield curve, which caused the securities to trade more securely to call. The general behavior of nominal spreads for different callables and market yield changes is shown in Exhibit 2.

PERFORMANCE AND STRATEGIES

Sensitivities

One way to analyze the performance of callable securities is to look at their risk due to changes in the underlying variables, such as volatility or yield curve changes. Exhibit 3 highlights new issue callables ranging from 2-year (noncall 3 months) to 10-year (noncall 5-year) as of 12/11/97. A number of statistics are shown starting with the quoted yield to maturity (bid side) at the close of 12/11/97. The forward yields for agency bullets are shown corresponding to the first call date and the remaining maturity. For example, for the 10nc1 callable, the 9-year rate one year forward was 6.2%, which was 81 bp below the coupon of the new callable issue. Thus, the option embedded in the 10nc1 callable security is fairly deep in the money.

Even though the securities are priced at par, the amount that the options are in the money varies widely and depends on the shape of the issuer's bullet curve. The 2nc1 callable was at the money for the most part, and generally the short-dated lockouts had options that were deeper in the money. For simplicity, we ignored the later dated embedded options beyond the initial call date, which are slightly less in the money given the then upward sloping curve. Options that are trading far from the strike tend to trade at a higher implied volatility (producing what is called the *volatility smile*); therefore, it is important to consider the quoted yield and the reference forward yield.

The option-adjusted duration (OAD) for each security as well as partial durations with respect to key points of the yield curve are shown. Partial durations or key rate durations are computed by shifting a particular sector of the yield curve and examining the price change, holding all other inputs constant. This is a convenient method for determining the risk profile of the different securities and offers more information than the pure OAD, which assumes the curve moves in parallel. For example, the 10nc3 has a fair amount of risk in the 10-year but changes to the 3-year also have an impact on performance. This is due to the fact that forward rates partially drive the callable's performance and both the 3- and 10-year rates contribute to the 7-year rate three years forward.

To determine the overall price change due to a nonparallel shift in the curve, we multiply each of the partial durations by the amount that sector of the curve moved, in bp, and add the results. Since the partial durations are expressed in basis point price change per basis point yield change, dividing by 100 gives the price change per $100 notional. For example, if the 3-, 5-, and 10-year rallied by 5 bp, 10 bp, and 15 bp, respectively, the 10nc3 callable would gain about ½ point in price: $[(-5 \times -1.32) + (-10 \times -0.87) + (-15 \times -2.35)]/100 = 0.507$.

Exhibit 4 shows comparable statistics for bullet securities. With a modified duration of 4.3 years, the 5-year bullet has nearly the same parallel interest rate exposure as the 10nc3 callable security, which has an OAD of 4.6. However, examining the partial durations reveals that their exposures to different sectors of the yield curve are very different. In particular, going long the 10nc3 callable versus the 5-year bullet expresses a curve flattening view in the 3- to 10-year sector of the curve holding all else constant. Duration is useful for describing price changes for relatively small changes in yields over short periods; however, care should be used in extrapolating results.

Exhibit 5 shows partial durations for 10nc3 callable securities with different dollar prices, representing discount, par-priced, and premium securities.

The discount, with a coupon of 5%, has embedded options that are out of the money. It trades to maturity due to its lower likelihood of being called, and most of the interest rate risk is embedded in the 10-year sector of the curve. This highlights a recurring theme: as rates rise and the callable extends in duration, the investment is lengthening in a bear market compared to a comparable duration bullet. Callables offer an attractive yield over bullets chiefly to compensate investors for this risk. As rates move in either direction, callables underperform equal duration bullets.

The other component of risk highlighted in Exhibit 3 is the impact of volatility on callable securities. Vega refers to the change in price, in bp, for a 1% change in implied volatility. In general, callable securities with longer dated lockouts have more exposure to changes in volatility; however, as the lockouts get longer than about three years, the vega exposure of a callable security declines. This is due to mean reversion: interest rates tend to vary randomly but are "pulled" toward a central location, or mean. In other words, when rates are very high there is a better chance they will decline than rise further and vice versa. Mean reversion helps to explain why yields on longer maturity securities are typically less volatile.

Exhibit 4: Indicative Data and Risk Statistics for Selected New Issue Agency Bullets, as of close 12/11/97

Maturity:	0.25 yrs.	0.5 yrs.	1 yrs.	2 yrs.	3 yrs.	5 yrs.	10 yrs.
Yield	5.80	5.81	5.75	5.85	5.90	5.99	6.16
OADur	0.20	0.50	1.00	1.90	2.70	4.30	7.40
PV01 1Y	−0.06	−0.23	−0.90	−0.02	0.00	−0.01	−0.05
PV01 2Y	0.00	0.00	0.00	−1.78	−0.03	−0.01	−0.02
PV01 3Y	0.00	0.00	0.00	0.00	−2.67	−0.05	−0.07
PV01 5Y	0.00	0.00	0.00	0.00	0.00	−4.20	−0.08
PV01 10Y	0.00	0.00	0.00	0.00	0.00	0.00	−7.12

PV01 = price value of 1 bp change.

Exhibit 5: Partial Durations for 10nc3 Callables as a Function of Dollar Price

Price:	90.92	100.00	104.72
Coupon	5.00	6.77	8.00
PV01 1Y	−0.04	−0.05	−0.06
PV01 2Y	−0.04	−0.04	−0.07
PV01 3Y	−0.29	−1.32	−1.89
PV01 5Y	−0.65	−0.87	−0.62
PV01 10Y	−5.03	−2.35	−1.24

PV01 = price value of 1 bp change.

Exhibit 6: Total Return Performance for Callables versus Duration-matched Bullets, As of 12/22/97; 3-month annualized return

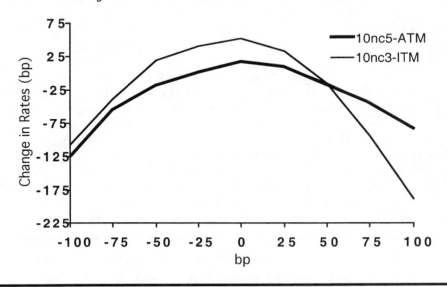

Total Returns and Strategies

Exhibit 6 shows the performance of two callable strategies compared to investing in duration-matched bullets. The performance curve for the 10nc5 security was for the FNMA 6.4 of 12/26/07-02 versus the FHLB 6.69 of 9/6/05, both of which have an effective duration of 5.88. Given the coupon of the callable security, the embedded options were close to being at the money. The 10nc3 performance curve illustrates a premium callable, the FNMA 7.49 of 2/7/07-00, versus the FNMA 6.59 of 5/24/01 with a duration of 3.05. The dollar price for the premium callable was 101-29+ (as of 12/22/97) highlighting the fact that the options were in the money by about 120 bp.

Total returns are shown as a 3-month annualized return as a function of yield changes, holding all other inputs constant. Although not apparent from the exhibit, the expected payoff from both strategies is near zero. For the 10nc5-ATM strategy, the performance curve is fairly symmetric and is similar to the performance of a buy-sell-buy butterfly trade or selling an option straddle. This is typical of a strategy that is short convexity. As discussed in the previous section, being long a callable security versus the duration-matched bullet has a risk profile similar to a barbell versus a bullet.

The 10nc5-ATM has an effective convexity of −48 versus 21 for the bullet, resulting in a net convexity of −69. As the market rallies the position becomes short the market, and the investor would need to purchase additional bullet securities to return to market neutral. This is an important aspect of hedging callable securities. As the market moves, the investor has to decide either to rehedge the position or to take on the market risk due to duration drift. Frequent rehedging can be costly and locks in any losses incurred.

The 10nc3-ITM strategy has an asymmetric performance profile, outperforming the 10nc5-ATM strategy in a bullish environment but faring worse if rates rise significantly. With embedded options that are in the money, the risk of ITM callables is that the option could move closer to being ATM. The duration of the callable changes the most as the option moves closer to being at the money. As yields increase, this exacerbates the duration mismatch that occurs as the callable is lengthening faster than the bullet security. When rates rally, however, the duration of the callable is more stable since its effective duration is already close to that of a bullet to call (1.91 years), which acts as a lower bound.

The underperformance of the 10nc3-ITM strategy in a bearish environment is the reason for the additional 34 bp of annualized return the investor receives over the next three months if the curve remains unchanged. This example shows that callable securities can offer an attractive way for investors to enhance returns according to their views on rates and volatility. Premium callables should be used when the bullish investor believes that rates are unlikely to rally very far. Discount or OTM callables are a better choice when the investor wants to sell volatility but prefers more protection in a bearish environment.

Time, or the expected investment period, also plays a critical role in the decision to buy callables or bullet securities. Exhibit 7 shows the performance of the 10nc3-ITM strategy versus the duration-matched bullet for two holding periods. In this example, the returns are not annualized for the 3-month holding period to facilitate comparison. As time passes and yields remain stable, the investor is rewarded with the additional spread that callables earn. However, for longer holding periods there is a higher probability of larger rate moves. It is this trade-off that investors must consider carefully. For example, if the investor has the view that rates may well be volatile in either direction over the near term but are likely to remain range bound over the next year, an investment in callable securities can substantially enhance returns.

The performance of callable securities in nonparallel yield shifts is shown in Exhibit 8. The flattening and steepening curves are chosen holding one extreme of the yield curve constant with the other end moving by 25 bp. For example, in the "BullFlat" scenario, the 30-year rallies 25 bp and the short end remains constant. The intermediate points of the curve are interpolated via duration. Although this picture is not entirely realistic, it shows how the callables will perform in nonparallel shifts to the yield curve.

In general, for any 25 bp twist in the curve, callables tend to outperform with the most improvement in a curve flattening environment. For larger curve twists, callables would underperform. The best environment for the 10nc3-ITM premium callable is a limited bullish flattener; bearish steepeners tend to hurt premium callables the most. This is indicated by net performance of −11.6 bp compared to a parallel 25 bp back-up in rates. Investors who have a limited bullish-flattening view should consider premium callables, whereas investors concerned about a significant steepening of the yield curve within a range-bound scenario should consider discount or at-the-money callables.

Exhibit 7: Impact of Time on Returns for 10nc3-ITM Callable versus Duration-Matched Bullet, as of 12/22/97

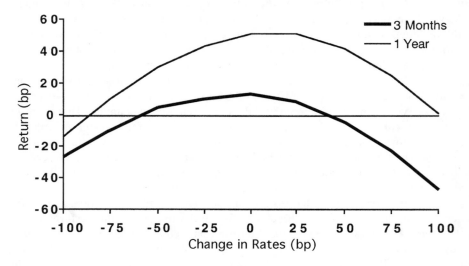

Exhibit 8: Callable Performance Versus Equal Duration Bullets for Nonparallel Curve Shifts, in bp as of 12/22/97

	0nc5-ATM	Net*	10nc3-ITM	Net*
Constant	17.6	—	52.0	—
Dwn 25 bp	1.6	—	39.2	—
Up 25 bp	8.4	—	31.6	—
BullFlat	14.0	12.4	64.4	25.2
BullSteep	6.4	4.8	34.8	−4.4
BearFlat	28.4	20.0	62.8	31.2
BearSteep	−1.2	−9.6	20.0	−11.6

*Net of parallel shift performance.

SUMMARY

Callable securities are an attractive way for investors to express their views on the likely range of rates, market direction, and changes in the slope of the yield curve. Available securities offer a diversity in price and structure that allows investors an opportunity to sculpt the payoff distribution that is most desirable. For example, premium callables, with embedded options deep in the money, are attractive for investors who wish to sell volatility but are concerned about a significant market rally.

This article discussed various aspects of callable securities, defined terminology, examined the behavior of nominal spreads, highlighted the risk factors, and looked at the return structure for various callable structures. But this article only begins the discussion of evaluating callable securities. Other aspects of investing in callable securities include the impact of changes in implied volatility and the choice of liquid volatility instruments for analyzing callables. Option-adjusted spread analysis is a key tool for analyzing embedded interest rate options and worthy of a discussion on its own. Finally, the pros and cons of different hedging strategies are of paramount importance and must also be explored.

Valuation of Floating-Rate Bonds

Michael Dorigan
Senior Associate
Andrew Kalotay Associates

Frank J. Fabozzi
Adjunct Professor of Finance
Yale University

Andrew Kalotay
President
Andrew Kalotay Associates

INTRODUCTION

Although several articles have addressed the valuation of risky floating-rate securities,[1] they fail to handle floaters with embedded or option-like features that have been introduced in recent years. In this article we demonstrate how to extend a valuation model described by Kalotay, Williams, and Fabozzi[2] (KWF hereafter) to value a variety of floaters. We begin with some background on valuation and the recursive valuation method. From there we move on to the valuation of the five floating-rate instruments: (1) a capped floater, (2) a range note, (3) a callable capped floater, (4) an indexed amortizing note (IAN), and (5) a ratchet bond.

---

[1] See, for example, Jess Yawitz, Howard Kaufold, Thomas Macirowski, and Michael Smirlock, "The Pricing and Duration of Floating-Rate Bonds," *Journal of Portfolio Management* (Summer 1987), pp. 49-56.

[2] Andrew J. Kalotay, George O. Williams, and Frank J. Fabozzi, "A Model for Valuing Bonds and Embedded Options," *Financial Analysts Journal* (May-June 1993), pp. 35-46. For an application to high-yield bond structures, see John D. Finnerty, "Adjusting the Binomial Model for Default Risk," *Journal of Portfolio Management* (Winter 1998), pp. 93-104.

---

* The authors wish to thank Douglas Howard of Baruch College, CUNY for providing the illustration and discussion on index amortizing notes.

Exhibit 1: Issuer Par Yield Curve

Maturity	Par Rate	Market Price
1 year	3.50%	100
2 years	4.20%	100
3 years	4.70%	100
4 years	5.20%	100

Exhibit 2: Issuer Spot and Forward Rates

Maturity	Spot Rate	One-Period Forward Rate
1 year	3.5000%	3.500%
2 years	4.2147%	4.935%
3 years	4.7345%	5.784%
4 years	5.2707%	6.893%

PRINCIPLES OF BOND VALUATION

Let's look at how an optionless bond is valued. The more a structure differs from an optionless fixed-coupon bond, the more detail that must be incorporated into the valuation process and, hence, the greater the complexity of the analysis. An optionless, fixed-coupon bond can be valued by methods found in any introductory finance text. Whether discounting the cash flows by spot or forward rates, the arithmetic is relatively simple. For example, assume the issuer par curve as it appears in Exhibit 1.

Using a standard bootstrap method, we can calculate the spot rates and, subsequently, generate the forward rates for each period extending out to the stated horizon. These forward rates are sometimes labeled with the qualification "unbiased" to reflect the fact that each was computed under no-arbitrage conditions. Exhibit 2 shows the spot and forward rates.

To value an optionless fixed-coupon bond, we discount each cash flow at the appropriate spot rate. Suppose a bond pays a 6.50% coupon.[3] Then the bond's value is

$$\frac{6.50}{(1.035)^1} + \frac{6.50}{(1.042)^2} + \frac{6.50}{(1.047)^3} + \frac{100 + 6.50}{(1.053)^4} = 104.64$$

Or, we can use forward rates for valuation as shown below:

$$\frac{6.50}{(1.035)} + \frac{6.50}{(1.035)(1.049)} + \frac{6.50}{(1.035)(1.049)(1.058)}$$

$$+ \frac{100 + 6.50}{(1.035)(1.049)1.058(1.069)} = 104.64$$

---

[3] To keep things simple, all the bonds in this article are assumed to be annual-pay.

Exhibit 3: 4-Year Binomial Tree

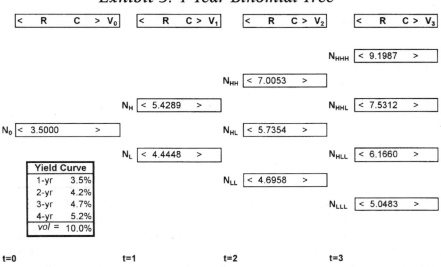

N_{HHH}	< 9.1987 >

The value is the same in both cases as it must be. Note that in the latter case with forward rates, the value of the cash flow is found by "rolling back" year-by-year at the one-period rates. This method is a prelude to the recursive valuation technique performed on a valuation lattice.

While the valuation method above works well for simple, optionless fixed-coupon bonds, it fails in cases where embedded options are incorporated into the structure, or where the interest rate paid by the bond floats on an index. For proper valuation, we require a valuation lattice.

To properly construct the lattice, an assumption must be made as to the volatility of the interest rates that make up the issuer yield curve. For the purposes of this article, a 10% volatility is assumed for the short-rate and we limit the lattice structure to that of a simple binary tree. Then we can assume that the probability of rates moving to the higher rate in the next period is 50%, leaving a probability of 50% that rates move to the lower rate. Exhibit 3 holds the binomial tree that satisfies our assumptions. It has been calibrated to assure that the rates at each node (N) satisfy the requirements for an arbitrage-free valuation tree. For now, we denote the higher "branch" of the tree with an "H" and the lower with an "L."

It is important to distinguish between the notation used to identify nodes and that used to describe a "path" to a certain node. For example, N_{HHL} can be reached by traversing the tree in an HHL pattern, i.e., move higher, then higher, then lower. But an HLH pattern would still place you at N_{HHL}. To capture path dependence, as it is known, requires the addition of at least one other variable, referred to as a state variable. We will see this in the sections on indexed amortizing notes (IANs) and ratchet bonds.

Exhibit 4: Valuation of a 6.5% 4-Year Option-Free Bond

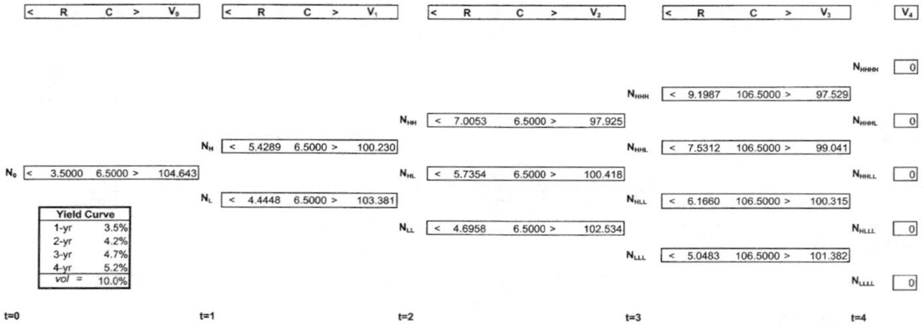

| < R | C > | V₀ | | < R | C > | V₁ | | < R | C > | V₂ | | < R | C > | V₃ | | V₄ |

For now, we can demonstrate the recursive valuation method using our optionless 6.5% bond. Take a look at Exhibit 4. At each node, 6.50 has been entered as the cash flow to be received at the *end* of the period. In addition to the coupon, the cash flows on the nodes at $t = 3$ reflect the repayment of principal (100) at maturity. Once the cash flows are in place, the valuation can begin.

Starting at $t = 4$, we compute the value of all future cash flows. Since there are no more, it's quite easy, so we enter a zero for V_4 at each node. Now we need to compute V_3 at each node. Start with N_{HHH} and recall that each branch has an equal probability of occurring. Then,

$$V_3[N_{HHH}] = \frac{0.5(0) + 0.5(0) + 106.50}{1.091987} = 97.529$$

The same steps are taken at each node for $t = 3$.

Moving recursively, we need to compute the values for each of the nodes at $t = 2$. Consider N_{HL}.

$$V_2[N_{HL}] = \frac{0.5(99.041) + 0.5(100.315) + 6.50}{1.057354} = 100.418$$

This same procedure is followed at each of the nodes at $t = 2$, and, subsequently, at $t = 1$. Now that you understand the method, let's compute the final value:

$$V_0 = \frac{0.5(100.23) + 0.5(103.381) + 6.50}{1.035000} = 104.643$$

The fact that the final value is equal to the values we computed using spot and forward rates is very important. It indicates that our tree is "fair," that is, even though it is computationally more complex, we have not created any spurious arbitrage opportunities within the structure. Also, note that the valuation of an optionless bond is independent of volatility assumptions. If the volatility were changed to 12%, say, the structure of the tree would change, but the value of the bond would remain constant.

Exhibit 5: Valuation of a Floating-Rate Bond with No Cap

<	R	C	>	Value		<	R	C	>	V_1		<	R	C	>	V_2		<	R	C	>	V_3

Index:	1-year Rate
Spread (bps):	25.00

N_{HHH} | < 9.1987 109.4487 > 100.229 |

N_{HH} | < 7.0053   7.2553 >   100.449 |

N_H | < 5.4289 5.6789 > 100.667 |

N_{HHL} | < 7.5312 107.7812 > 100.232 |

N_0 | < 3.5000 3.7500 >   100.893 |

N_{HL} | < 5.7354   5.9854 >   100.458 |

N_L | < 4.4448 4.6948 > 100.681 |

N_{HLL} | < 6.1660 106.4160 > 100.235 |

Yield Curve	
1-yr	3.5%
2-yr	4.2%
3-yr	4.7%
4-yr	5.2%
vol =	10.0%

N_{LL} | < 4.6958   4.9458 >   100.465 |

N_{LLL} | < 5.0483 105.2983 > 100.238 |

t=0   t=1   t=2   t=3

Now that we're comfortable with the recursive valuation method, let's move on to some floating- rate bonds.

Valuing Capped Floating-Rate Bonds

Consider a floating-rate bond with a coupon indexed to the one-year rate (the reference rate) plus a spread. For our purposes, assume a 25 bp spread to the reference rate. In Exhibit 5, we've taken the tree from Exhibit 3 and, as was the case with the optionless fixed-coupon bond, at each node we've entered the cash flow expected at the end of each period. Using the same valuation method as before, we can find the value at each node. Consider N_{HLL}.

$$V_3[N_{HLL}] = \frac{0.5(0) + 0.5(0) + 100 + 6.416}{1.06166} = 100.235$$

Stepping back one period

$$V_2[N_{LL}] = \frac{0.5(100.235) + 0.5(100.238) + 4.9458}{1.046958} = 100.465$$

Following this same procedure, we arrive at the price of 100.893. How would this change if the interest rate on the bond were capped?

Assume that the cap is 7.25%. Exhibit 6 provides a picture of the effects of the cap on the value of the bond. As rates move higher there is a possibility that the current reference rate exceeds the cap. Such is the case at N_{HHH} and N_{HHL}. The coupon is subject to the following constraint:

$$C_t = \max[R_t, 7.25\%]$$

Exhibit 6: Valuation of a Capped Floating-Rate Bond

< R	C >	Value		< R	C >	V_1		< R	C >	V_2		< R	C >	V_3

Index:	1-year Rate
Cap (%):	7.25
Spread (bps):	25.00

N_{HHH} < 9.1987 107.2500 >   98.215

N_{HH} < 7.0053   7.2500 >   99.273

N_H < 5.4289 5.6789 >   99.998

N_{HHL} < 7.5312 107.2500 >   99.738

N_0 < 3.5000 3.7500 >   100.516

N_{HL} < 5.7354   5.9854 >   100.224

N_L < 4.4448 4.6948 >   100.569

N_{HLL} < 6.1660 106.4160 >   100.235

N_{LL} < 4.6958   4.9458 >   100.465

Yield Curve	
1-yr	3.5%
2-yr	4.2%
3-yr	4.7%
4-yr	5.2%
vol =	10.0%

N_{LLL} < 5.0483 105.2983 >   100.238

t=0   t=1   t=2   t=3

As a result of the cap, the value of the bond in the upper nodes at $t = 3$ falls below par. Explicitly,

$$V_3[N_{HHH}] = \frac{0.5(0) + 0.5(0) + 100 + 7.25}{1.091987} = 98.215$$

Valuing recursively through the tree, we arrive at the current value of the capped floater, 100.516. This last calculation gives us a means for pricing the cap. Without a cap, the bond is priced at 100.893. The difference between these two prices is the value of the cap, 0.377. It is important to note that the price of the cap is *volatility dependent.* Any change in the volatility would result in a different valuation for the cap. The greater the volatility, the higher the price of the option, and *vice versa.*

What if an issuer wanted to offer this bond at par? In such a case, an adjustment has to be made to the coupon. To lower the price from 100.516 to par, a lower spread over the reference rate need only be offered to investors. Suppose the issuer decides that the coupon will be the 1-year rate plus 5 basis points. It turns out that this is not enough. Take a look at Exhibit 7. It shows the relationship between the spread over the 1-year reference rate and the bond price. At a spread of 8.70 bps over the 1-year reference rate the bond will be priced at par. The spread of 8.7 bps is also volatility dependent.

Now let's move on to another structure where the coupon floats with a reference rate, but is again restricted. In this next case, a range is set in which the bond pays the reference rate, but, outside of the range, no coupon is paid.

Valuing a Range Note

A range note is a security that pays the reference rate only if the rate falls within a band. If the reference rate falls outside the band, whether the lower or upper boundary, no coupon is paid. Typically, the band increases over time.

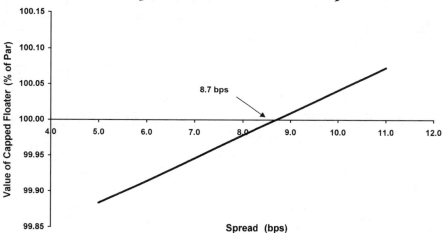

Exhibit 7: Spread to Index to Price Cap at Par

Exhibit 8: Coupon Schedule (Bands) for a Range Note

	Year 1	Year 2	Year 3
Lower Limit	3.00%	4.00%	5.00%
Upper Limit	5.00%	6.25%	8.00%

To illustrate, suppose that the reference rate is, again, the 1-year rate. Suppose further that the band (or coupon schedule) is defined as in Exhibit 8. Exhibit 9 holds our tree and the cash flows expected at each node. Either the 1-year reference rate is paid at each node, or nothing. In the case of this three-year note, there is only one state in which no coupon is paid. Using our recursive valuation method, we can work back through the tree to the current value, 98.963.

Callable Capped Floating-Rate Bonds

Now consider a call option on the capped floater. We must be careful to specify the appropriate rules for calling the bond on the valuation tree. For our purposes, any time the bond has a value above par, the bond will be called. (Here we assume a par call to simplify the illustration.)

Before we get into these details, it is important to motivate the need for a call on a floating-rate bond. The value of a cap to the issuer increases as market rates near the cap and there is the potential for rates to exceed the cap prior to maturity. As rates decline, so does the value of the cap, eventually approaching zero. The problem for the issuer in this case is the additional basis-point spread it is paying for a cap that now has no value. Thus, when rates decline, a call has value to the issuer because it can call and reissue at current rates without the spread.

Exhibit 9: Valuation of a Range Floater

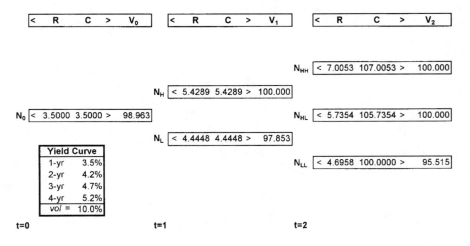

Exhibit 10: Valuation of a Callable Floating-Rate Bond with a 7.25% Cap

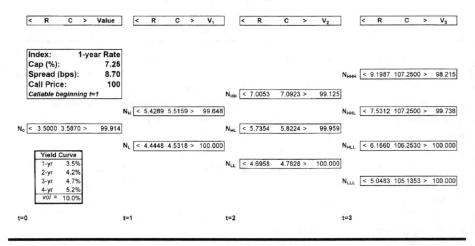

Suppose that the capped floater is callable at par anytime after the first year. Exhibit 10 provides detail on the effect of the call option on valuation of the capped floater. Again, for a callable bond, when the market price exceeds par in a recursive valuation model, the bond is called. In the case of our 4-year bond, you can see that the price of the bond at the previously mentioned nodes N_{LL}, N_{LLH}, and N_{LLL} is now 100 in Exhibit 10, the call price. The affect of the call option on price is also evident with today's price for the bond moving to 99.9140.

Exhibit 11: Spread to Index to Price Callable Cap at Par

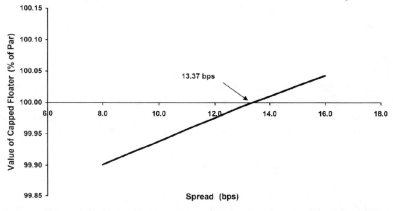

As with the case of a cap, the by-product of this analysis is the value of the call option on a capped floater. We now have the fair value of the capped floater versus the callable capped floater. So, the call option has a value of 100 – 99.9140 = 0.0860.

How would one structure the issue so that it is priced at par? Again, we have to offer the bondholder additional spread over the floating rate and the 8.7 bps the holder is already receiving for accepting the cap. In this case, an additional 4.67 bps is required, moving the total spread over the one-year floating rate to 13.37 bps. As before, we arrive at this 4.67 bp spread through an iterative process described above for the structuring of a cap. (Exhibit 11 shows the relationship between spread and value.)

To summarize, the callable capped floater offers benefits to the issuer, but there is a price. To avoid increasing payments as rates rise, the issuer can put a cap on the bond. However, investors will demand compensation in the form of higher coupon payments, i.e., a spread to the reference rate.

This spread is a burden that the bond issuer would like to avoid paying if rates decline and the cap has no value due to the low rates. A call option allows the issuer to retire the capped floater and reissue at lower rates. Again, the bondholder recognizes that the benefit to the issuer is a detriment to the holder and demands additional compensation, a higher spread.

Once the spread is determined, valuation of the callable capped floater is a simple application of the recursive valuation process which we have been using throughout this article. The coupon payments are defined at each node and the call option exercised at nodes where the market price exceeds the call price. All that is left is the discounting of the cash flow period-by-period back to the present to arrive at a price for the instrument, as we have just seen in Exhibits 6 and 10.

Now let's take a look at the indexed amortizing note for a couple of new valuation twists.

Indexed Amortizing Notes[4]

In this section we examine an indexed amortizing note (IAN), a bond whose principal payments are a prescribed function of the path of interest rates. Typically, principal payments are structured to accelerate in low rate environments. A typical IAN structure is described below.

Assume that the IAN has a four-year maturity and pays investors a 6% interest rate on the outstanding principal, P, in years 1, 2, 3, and 4. Regardless of what happens to interest rates, there is no principal payment the first year (the "lock-out" period). In years 2 and 3, the amount of principal paid depends on the level of the 1-year rate. If the 1-year rate is below 5%, 75% of the remaining balance is repaid; if the rate is between 5% and 6%, 50% of the balance is repaid; if the rate exceeds 6%, there is no principal payment. If a principal payment made in accordance with this formula brings the outstanding balance below 20% of the amount originally issued (which we take to be 100.0), the entire bond is retired immediately. (This is referred to as the "clean-up" provision.) At maturity in year 4 any remaining principal is amortized. The formula below summarizes the amortization schedule for the note:

$$
\text{time } t \text{ principal payment} =
\begin{cases}
0 & \text{if } t = 1 \\
0.75P & \text{if } t = 2 \text{ or } 3,\ R < 5\% \text{ and } 0.25P > 20 \\
0.50P & \text{if } t = 2 \text{ or } 3,\ 5\% < R < 6\% \text{ and } 0.50P > 20 \\
0 & \text{if } t = 2 \text{ or } 3, \text{ and } R > 6\% \\
P & \text{Otherwise.}
\end{cases}
$$

The IAN is a "path dependent" security. For a path dependent security knowledge of interest rates at any time, call it t^*, in the valuation process does not provide sufficient information to calculate the cash flow generated by the security at that time. Contrast this with the floating-rate notes we just completed reviewing in the previous section. In that case knowledge of the current interest rate was all that was needed to calculate the cash flow to noteholders each period

Path dependence arises because the outstanding amount of the IAN depends on prior interest rates. In the case of path dependence, the cash flow also depends in some manner on the level of the factor at all points in time t prior to the calculation date, i.e., $t < t^*$. In other words, for IANs, how interest rates got to their current level over time is relevant.

You are probably familiar with a number of securities that bear this characteristic. A CMO is another example of a path dependent security. One must know the amount of the underlying mortgage pool still outstanding at time t^* to calculate the time t^* cash flow of the CMO. This, however, depends on the prior prepayment experience which, in turn, is driven by the path of interest rates over the prior period.

---

[4] This section of the article is adapted from C. Douglas Howard, "Valuing Path-Dependent Securities: Some Numerical Examples" which appeared as Chapter 4 in *Advances in Fixed Income Valuation Modeling and Risk Management*, Frank J. Fabozzi (ed.), (New Hope, PA: Frank Fabozzi Associates, 1997).

Exhibit 12: Valuation Tree with Partitioned Interest Rate States and Cash Flows

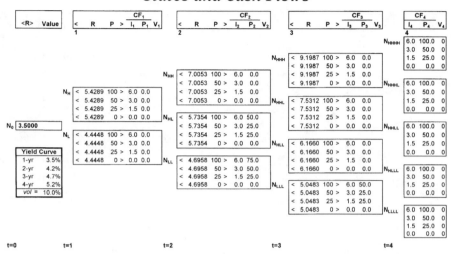

Monte Carlo simulation is the usual method of valuing of these path dependent securities. However, this technique offers a number disadvantages. It is computationally intensive. It does not comply with arbitrage-free principles. Finally, the path sampling that is part of every Monte Carlo analysis leads to inconsistent results. All of this can be avoided with an application of recursive valuation.

Recursive Valuation

Consider each node as an interest rate state which we label as $<R>$, where R is the rate in that state. Thus, $<7.0053>$ represents the interest rate state at N_{HH}. To value the IAN recursively, we partition the interest rate states as they exist at each node in the tree established in Exhibit 3 by further specifying how much of the IAN's principal, P, is outstanding *before* the principal payment of that year. The state $<7.0053>$, for example, is partitioned into $<7.0053, 100>$, $<7.0053, 50>$, $<7.0053, 25>$ and $<7.0053, 0>$. This additional variable, whose values partition the state as specified by the value of the stochastic interest rate variable, is referred to as a non-stochastic state variable and its range of attainable values is referred to as the *state space*.

Exhibit 12 displays the expanded tree in which these interest rate states are explicit. (There is additional information present in the exhibit that we can ignore for now.) Note that some states, such as $<5.0483, 100>$, cannot be reached. The bond will be entirely amortized by the time it reaches this state. If this is not apparent to you yet, it will be soon as we run through an example below. This phenomenon whereby certain states are not attainable will not make our forthcoming calculations incorrect, it just means that we will do some unnecessary calculations.

Exhibit 13: 6% Indexed Amortizing Bond
Valuation on Entire State Space

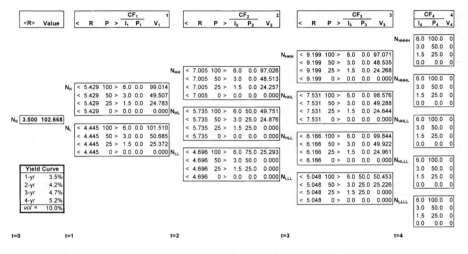

Once the time t 1-year rate and amount outstanding (prior to current-period principal payment) are *both* specified as, say, $<R, P>$, the time t cash flow can easily be calculated. The interest component is just 0.06P. The principal component of the cash flow is deduced from the value of P, the lockout period, the amortization table, and the clean-up provision, rules provided in the formula above. The state-dependent cash flow is the sum of interest and principal.

As before, we begin our recursive calculations at the right end of the lattice. Exhibit 13 shows, for periods 1 through 4, the cash flow $CF_t<R, P>$ just described broken out as principal, P_t, and interest, I_t.

Note, again, that $V_4<R, P> = 0$ for all R and P since there is no cash flow after year 4. Since the IAN matures in period 4, the cash flow is simply the sum of the amount outstanding and interest on that amount — a calculation that is independent of the 1-year rate at period 4.

The situation is more complicated in period 3. Here the amortization schedule and the amount outstanding interact to determine the cash flow. Consider, for example, the calculations corresponding to state $<5.0483, 50>$. The interest payment of 3 is calculated as 0.06×50.0. Also, since $5.0 < 5.0483 < 6.0$, 50% of the outstanding amount is prepaid in period 3. This principal payment of 25.0 leaves 25.0 still outstanding — an amount which exceeds the clean-up provision. The state $<5.0483, 50>$ cash flow is therefore $25.0 + 3.0 = 28.0$. Next we calculate $V3<5.0483, 50>$. Since 50.0 of principal was outstanding (before the period 3 payment) and 25.0 is paid off in period 3, the amount outstanding changes to 25.0. Thus, only the cash flows of the partitioned states with a principal value of 25 need to be discounted.

$$V_3 <5.0483, 50> = \frac{0.5(1.5 + 25 + 0) + 0.5(1.5 + 25 + 0)}{1.050483} = 25.2265$$

This number can be found in Exhibit 13, along with all of the other exhibits compiled via the recursive process.

Compare this with the analogous calculations for state $<5.0483, 25>$ in period 3. The interest cash flow is $0.06 \times 25.0 = 1.5$. The principal payment specified by the amortization schedule is again 50% of the amount outstanding which results in a payment of $\$12.5 = 25.0 \times 50\%$. This would leave only 12.5 remaining outstanding, however, so the clean-up provision requires that the entire amount of 25.0 be retired leaving nothing outstanding. Thus,

$$V_3 <5.0483, 25> = \frac{0.5(0 + 0 + 0) + 0.5(0 + 0 + 0)}{1.050483} = 0$$

The calculations in period 2 follow the same procedure. For example, in state $<5.7354, 100>$, the principal payment is 50.0, generating a cash flow of 6.0 + 50.0 = 56.0 and leaving 50.0 remaining outstanding. Hence, one moves from state $<5.7354, 100>$ in period 2 to either $<7.5312, 50>$ or $<6.1660, 50>$ in period 3, each with equal likelihood. Thus,

$$V_2 <5.7354,100> = \frac{0.5(6 + 0 + 49.2880) + 0.5(3 + 0 + 49.9218)}{1.057354} = 49.7515$$

Similarly, in period 1, one moves from state $<4.4448, 100>$ to either $<4.6958, 100>$ or $<5.7354, 100>$ in period 2, each with equal likelihood. Thus, $CF_1(<4.4448, 100>) = 0.06 \times 100.0 = 6$ (plus 0 principal) and

$$V_1 <4.4448,100> = \frac{0.5(6 + 50 + 49.7515) + 0.5(6 + 75 + 25.2928)}{1.04448}$$

$$= 101.5102$$

Finally, at time 0, there is only today's state $<3.5000, 100>$ to calculate. From this state we move to either $<4.4448, 100>$ or $<5.4289, 100>$, each with probability ½. The value of the IAN is

$$V_0 <3.5000,100> = \frac{0.5(6 + 0 + 99.0136) + 0.5(6 + 0 + 101.5102)}{1.03500}$$

$$= 102.6685$$

Selecting the Necessary State Space

As we previously observed, only the amounts in the list $<0, 25, 50, 100>$ can be outstanding at any point in time. This is because the IAN starts with 100.0 outstanding and this list is closed under the rules of principal amortization (including the clean-up provision). (For example, if we amortize 50% of 50.0 we get 25.0 outstanding, another number in the list.) In general, it may not be so easy to construct an exhaustive list of possible states or, commonly, the list of possible states may be very large. An effective numerical procedure is to partition the range of the state space (in this case, the range is from 0 to 100 outstanding) into a manageable number of "buckets", say 0, 20 - 30, 30 - 40, . . . , 90 - 100. Sometimes a surprisingly small number of buckets can lead to a very good approximation of the precise answer.

Notice also that not all the states can be reached. For example, in periods 1 and 2 only those states with 100.0 outstanding are reached. This is because the lockout provision prevents any amortization until year 2. Thus, even in year 2, the amount outstanding prior to that year's amortization must be 100.0.

From the standpoint of computational efficiency, it may be better to first pass *forward* through the lattice to determine which states are actually reachable. This is demonstrated in Exhibit 14 where we have highlighted the region of each period's state space that is actually reachable. Following this, during the recursive process described above, it is only necessary to calculate the CF_i and PV_i values for those states that are flagged as reachable in the forward pass. In our IAN example, this would result in substantial savings in computational time.

Consider Exhibit 15(a). The number of valuations necessary in period 3 has been reduced to 6. In Exhibit 15(b), the roll back passes into period 2 where, now, only three calculations are necessary. Exhibit 15(c) provides the full recursive analysis whereby we arrive at the same value for the IAN as in Exhibit 13, but in this case with fewer calculations.

Exhibit 14: 6% Indexed Amortizing Bond
Identification of Attainable States

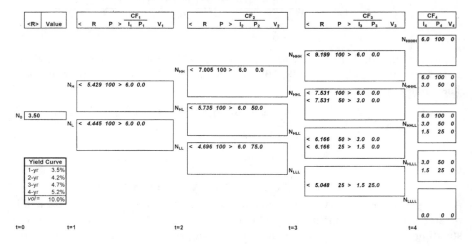

Exhibit 15: 6% Indexed Amortizing Bond
(a) Recursive Valuation: Step 1 on Attainable States

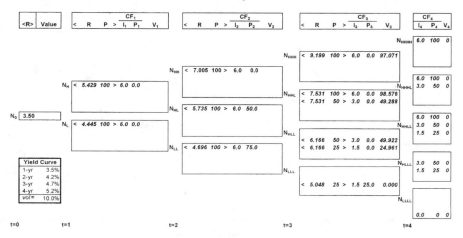

(b) Recursive Valuation: Step 2 on Attainable States

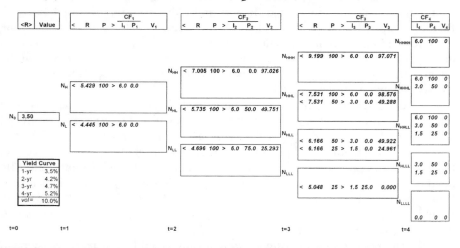

A *caveat* is necessary. In some situations, this forward pass may take more time than it saves. It may be better to compromise and avoid only some of the unused state space by (non-time-consuming) ad hoc reasoning. In the case of the IAN, for example, the unnecessary states in periods 1 and 2 could be avoided simply by recognizing the effects of the lockout provision. The best computational strategy will certainly depend on the application.

Exhibit 15 (Continued)
(c) Recursive Valuation: Step 3 on Attainable States

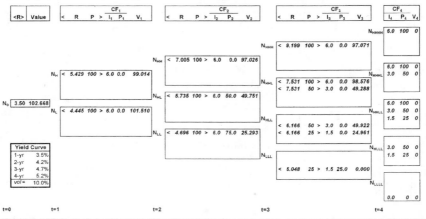

Ratchet Bonds

In this final, section, we introduce a structure that is relatively new to the capital markets. To value it, we will need to draw on all of the knowledge we've gained from our look at callable capped floaters and IANs. The ratchet bond carries a floating coupon that is capped and path dependent. It is designed to replace the callable bond in the capital structure of debt issuers. We've covered the valuation mechanics in the previous sections, so we can move quickly to the analysis of the ratchet structure. Since the ratchet is new, a few words are necessary to motivate its creation and usefulness to debt issuers.[5]

Consider an issuer that relies on callable bonds on an on-going basis to fund its activities. What cash flow pattern emerges from this financing strategy? The answer depends on the path of interest rates. If rates trend upward, the bond will remain outstanding and pay the stated coupon to maturity. If rates decline, the bond will eventually be called and refunded, presumably with another callable bond. As a result of the refunding, interest payments decline from previous levels. If rates continue to fall, the process repeats: the refunding issue is itself called and refunded. Thus, funding via callable bonds gives rise to interest payments that decline if rates decline and remain unchanged if rates rise.

The ratchet bond is designed to replicate the cash flow pattern generated by a series of conventional callable bonds. It is an adjustable (i.e., floating) rate structure on which the coupon rate is periodically reset at a fixed spread over an index, e.g., 10-year Constant Maturity Treasury (CMT). The coupon "ratchets" only downward; it cannot increase.

---

[5] A more detailed discussion of ratchet bonds can be found in Andrew Kalotay and Leslie Abreo, "Ratchet Bonds: Maximum Refunding Efficiency at Minimum Transaction Cost," *Journal of Applied Corporate Finance* (Spring 1999), pp. 40-47.

Exhibit 16: Binomial Tree for Ratchet Bond Valuation

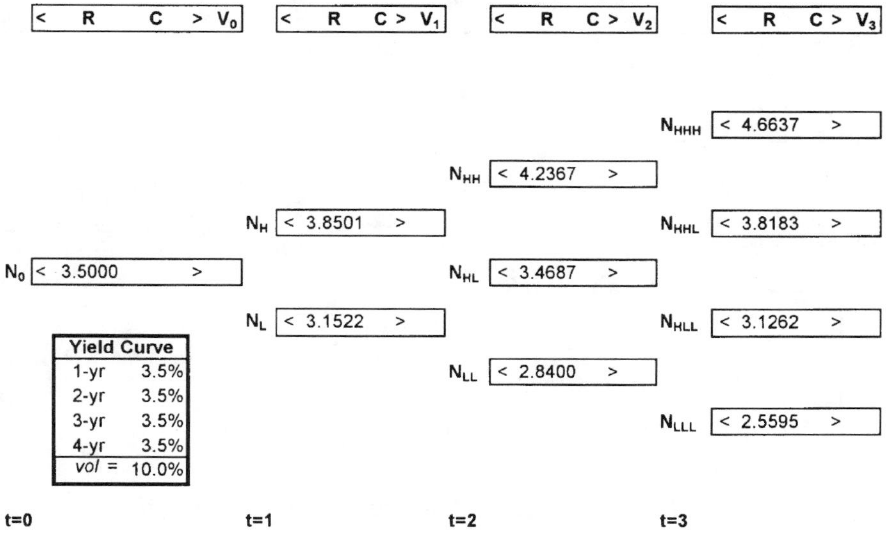

| < R C > V_0 | | < R C > V_1 | | < R C > V_2 | | < R C > V_3 |

N_{HHH} | < 4.6637 > |

N_{HH} | < 4.2367 > |

N_H | < 3.8501 > |

N_{HHL} | < 3.8183 > |

N_0 | < 3.5000 > |

N_{HL} | < 3.4687 > |

N_L | < 3.1522 > |

N_{HLL} | < 3.1262 > |

Yield Curve	
1-yr	3.5%
2-yr	3.5%
3-yr	3.5%
4-yr	3.5%
vol =	10.0%

N_{LL} | < 2.8400 > |

N_{LLL} | < 2.5595 > |

t=0   t=1   t=2   t=3

To illustrate the valuation process, we will make a change to our interest rate environment. For the ratchet bond analysis, the par yield curve is assumed to be flat at 3.5%. The short-rate volatility remains at 10%. Exhibit 16 holds the new binary tree on which valuation will proceed

Now, consider a ratchet bond that pays a coupon equal to the 1-year rate, set in advance, plus 24 bps (i.e., a spread to the index or reference rate). There is a two-year lockout period during which the coupon cannot reset. This last feature is equivalent to the call protection afforded by conventional callable bonds. Working with the rule that the coupon can only move (ratchet) down, we can pass forward through the tree and establish cash flows at each node. This forward pass is presented in Exhibit 17 where notation follows that from previous figures.

Path dependence is apparent as you move through the tree. Consider node N_{HHL}, which actually represents the current state for three different paths: HHL, HLH and LHH. Depending on the path taken, the coupon is either 3.7400 (in the case of HHL) or 3.7087 (for HLH and LHH). How is this the case? At node N_{HL} (or N_{LH} if you prefer) the lockout provision has expired and the current 1-year rate is 3.4687%. If the 24 bps spread is added to the rate, a coupon of 3.7087% is set for the bond for the next period. By this same procedure, the 3.08% coupon is set at N_{LL} (2.8400 + 0.2400 = 3.0800).

Once the cash flows are in place, the recursive valuation can begin. Exhibit 18 provides the full valuation, rolling back period-by-period to arrive at the 100.45 value of the ratchet bond.

Exhibit 17: Coupon Payments for 4-Year Ratchet Bond
Coupon is 24 bp spread to 1-year rate

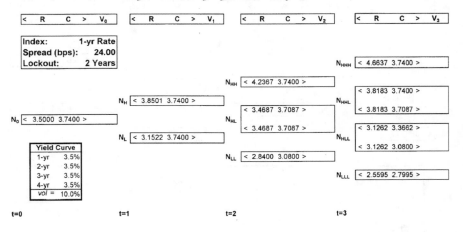

Exhibit 18: Value of 4-Year Ratchet Bond

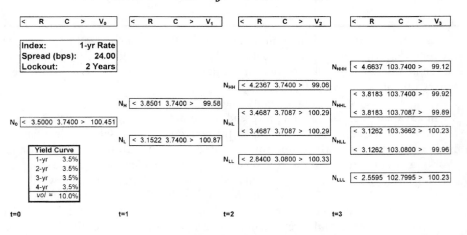

The structuring of the ratchet bond is analogous to that of a callable capped floater. If we want the ratchet bond priced at par, then we must adjust the spread to find a level that prices the bond at 100. Obviously, 24 bps is too large. We follow an iterative procedure to arrive at the appropriate figure.

Exhibit 19 provides the result of the iterations. The spread at which the bond is priced at par is 11.67 bps over the reference rate, leading to an at-issue coupon just below 3.62%.

Exhibit 19: Spread to Index to Price Ratchet Bond at Par

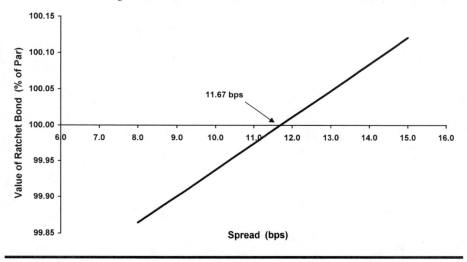

CONCLUSION

Floating-rate bonds are more difficult to value than their fixed-rate counterparts. However, the tools to perform the valuation are available to capital market participants. In this article we have demonstrated how lattice-based techniques can be extended to value a number of different structures. It proves itself to be a robust methodology, handling a range of issues from simple floaters to path dependent floating-rate structures.

Volatility in the Fixed-Income Market

Rich Gordon
Director
First Union Securities, Inc.

Lang Gibson
Vice President
First Union Securities, Inc.

INTRODUCTION

Generally, volatility is a statistical measure of the tendency of a market price or yield to vary over time. More technically speaking, historical volatility is the standard deviation of returns around a mean over a specified period (e.g., 90 days or one year). As volatility assumes a normal distribution of returns measured in standard deviations, it is possible to estimate probabilities of future price and yield movements. For example, when volatility of 15% is assumed on current interest rates, there is a 67% probability rates will move up or down by 15%. So, if interest rates are 5% and volatility is 15%, there is a two out of three probability that rates will range between 4.25% (5.0% − (5.0% × 0.15)) and 5.75% (5.0% + (5.0% × 0.15)).

Whereas stock price distributions are fairly normally distributed, the normal distribution assumption breaks down when we look at yield and option price volatility. As yields have some floor as to how much they will fall, the distribution of possible yields is skewed to the upside. Even more dramatic is the skewness of option prices: An option may only fall to zero but has unlimited upside, or downside in the case of an investor being short an option embedded in a bond.

Volatility is the most crucial element in evaluating an option as it is often the only variable not known with certainty in advance. Of the three major risks assumed by fixed-income investors — yield curve, credit, and option — option risk is the risk most often taken. In most cases, an option is embedded in the bond such that the borrower has an option to call the bond, or part thereof, at either discreet or continuous intervals, often after a lockout term. By selling the option to the borrower, the investor receives a premium in the form of a higher yield. To the extent the option is priced correctly by the market, the investor has a 50/50 chance that the realized income will break even with that of an option-free bond. Therefore, it is crucial the investor takes a view on the pricing of the embedded option. Although all other variables in the option formula are fairly certain, the future direction of volatility is the predominant unknown factor. To the extent the bond investor believes the embedded option's volatility is overstated by the market, the investor may take a view that the realized volatility will be lower than implied by the market by buying the bond and thus shorting the option. Everything else being equal, the bond price will appreciate if volatility does indeed decrease.

In this article, we will evaluate the following topics regarding volatility as it impacts fixed-income securities:

1. types of volatility
2. historical versus implied volatility
3. vega
4. fundamental factors linking MBS and agency valuations to volatility
5. how heavy issuance of callable debt affects the general level of volatility
6. the "right" volatility to use when valuing MBS and agencies

The article's objective is to clarify how volatility determines value in fixed-income securities to allow investors to make informed decisions.

TYPES OF VOLATILITY

In the fixed-income world, an investor should always be sure what volatility is being quoted — yield or price. Typically, volatilities for options on futures are based on the price of the underlying contract (e.g., 30-year Treasury future contracts). Likewise, volatilities on over-the-counter (OTC) options on mortgages are based on price. Conversely, option volatility for most other OTC fixed-income derivatives as well as embedded options in bonds is quoted based on yield. For instance, swaptions, caps, and floors are calculated using yield volatility. Below we define volatilities for various fixed-income instruments.

Treasury Volatility

Although OTC Treasury locks are traded and often used for hedging purposes, managers usually use the more liquid option on Treasury bond futures, for which volatility is quoted on price. As fixed-income managers usually strictly follow yield volatility, the price volatility needs to be converted into yield volatility using the following formula (all yields and prices are on a forward basis):

$$\text{Yield volatility} \times \text{Yield} = \frac{\text{Price volatility} \times \text{Price}}{\text{Dollar value of 1 bp}}$$

Exhibit 1: Matrix of U.S. Dollar Interest Rate Swaption Volatilities as of December 9, 1999

Expiration	Tenor						
	1 Year	2 Years	3 Years	4 Years	5 Years	7 Years	10 Years
1 Month	12.50	13.60	13.50	13.40	13.30	13.20	13.10
3 Months	12.30	14.10	14.00	13.90	13.80	13.70	13.60
6 Months	14.30	14.50	14.50	14.40	14.30	14.20	14.10
1 Year	15.90	15.80	15.60	15.40	15.20	15.00	14.50
2 Years	17.50	16.40	16.00	15.70	15.40	14.70	14.50
3 Years	17.40	16.30	15.90	15.50	15.20	14.50	14.20
4 Years	17.40	16.10	15.70	15.30	15.00	14.30	13.90
5 Years	17.20	15.90	15.40	15.00	14.60	13.90	13.40
7 Years	15.80	14.60	14.00	13.50	13.10	12.40	11.60
10 Years	13.60	12.40	11.80	11.30	10.90	10.40	9.60

Source: Bloomberg

Cap/Floor Volatility

Caps and floors on interest rates are options that pay any in-the-money difference between the index (e.g., LIBOR) and the strike rate on each reset date until maturity. For instance, a 3-year cap on 3-month LIBOR struck at 6.0% would pay the amount LIBOR exceeds 6.0% on each 3-month reset date over the 3-year term. Volatility for caps and floors is based on yield.

Swaption Volatility

A swaption is an option to enter into a swap at a future date. For instance, a 3-year × 7-year receiver swaption struck at 7.0% entitles the purchaser to an option three years in the future to enter into a 7-year swap to receive a 7.0% fixed rate and pay 3-month LIBOR. Volatility for swaptions is based on yield. Exhibit 1 shows volatilities for combinations of swaption tenors and expirations as of December 9, 1999.

HISTORICAL VERSUS IMPLIED VOLATILITY

A firm understanding of the relationship between historical and implied volatility is critical for assessing the value of options. Implied volatility is the consensus market expectation regarding the fluctuations of the underlying security for the remaining life of the option. It is forward looking. In the fixed-income market, for example, the value of options, and thus the level of implied volatility, can be inferred from the spread difference between callable and otherwise comparable noncallable bonds. In calculating historical volatility, the selection of the look-back period and the number of observations (e.g., daily, weekly, or monthly) can have a significant effect on the result. Exhibit 2 tracks the relationship of 90-day historical and implied volatility on the March 1999 Eurodollar contract over 1999. In fixed-income markets, historical volatility tends to have larger swings, especially in uncertain times. Furthermore, historical volatility tends to lag implied volatility.

VEGA

An option's value will change over time with movement in the underlying collateral, the passage of time, the risk-free interest rate, and volatility. The most commonly used term for measuring the sensitivity of an option's theoretical value to changes in volatility is *vega.* The vega of an option is the change in the theoretical value of an option under a 1% change in volatility. Vega is greatest for at-the-money options. The vega of all options declines as maturity approaches. Likewise, longer-dated options often have greater vega than short-term options.

Vega duration measures the change in a bond's value for a 100 bps change in volatility (e.g., if volatility changes from 15% to 14% or 16%, the bond price changes *x*%). We use the securities in Exhibit 3 to demonstrate vega duration as it affects pricing for option-embedded bonds as of December 9, 1999.

Exhibit 2: Implied and Historical Volatilities — Eurodollar Futures Call Options (March 99 Contract) Over 1999

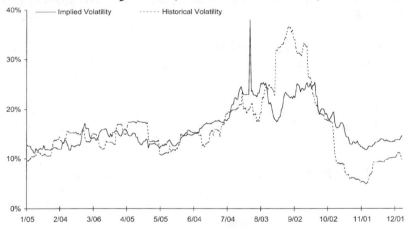

Exhibit 3: Comparison of Vega in Fixed Income Securities

Sector	Security	Average Life (years)	Vega Duration (years)
Home Equity ABS	EQHE9901, A3F	3.7	0.12
Agency CMO SEQ	FHL2134, H	5.8	0.22
Callable Agency	FHLMC 10 YR/NC3	6.8	0.21

ABS: Asset-backed securities; CMO: Collateralized mortgage obligation; SEQ: Sequential.
Source: Derivatives Solutions.

For instance, the home equity ABS price would change 0.12% if volatility changed 100 bps in either direction. Exhibit 3 demonstrates how the callable agency and the CMO have almost twice the vega duration of the home equity ABS for two reasons. First, prepayments in home equity ABS have less sensitivity to interest rates. Second, the average life of this security is shorter than the other two. Vega duration is a useful tool for determining how an investor's view on volatility will affect a bond's value.

FUNDAMENTAL FACTORS LINKING MBS AND AGENCY VALUATIONS TO VOLATILITY

Because MBS and callable agency debt contain embedded options, the valuations of these securities depend closely on volatility levels in the market. If an investor has a short position in an option, he or she will demand a higher yield for purchasing callable securities at high levels of volatility. Option valuation models that produce option-adjusted spread (OAS) calculations use volatility as one of the key input variables. Apart from the mathematical linkage, there are three fundamental factors in the market that link the valuations of MBS/callable agencies and levels of volatility. Each factor is discussed below.

Activities of the Agencies

Federal agencies buy MBS for their retained portfolios and hedge the negative convexity by either issuing callable agency debt or issuing bullet debt and buying swaptions in the OTC option markets to hedge the negative convexity. This link sets up the following dynamic: Agencies try to buy MBS at the widest spreads possible when derivative volatility, and therefore hedging costs, is as low as possible. The spread they achieve in this activity is the agency arbitrage spread (Exhibit 4). Heavy demand for MBS pressures spreads tighter, and heavy demand for volatility pressures volatility higher. This narrows out the spread the agency achieves through arbitrage and decreases its appetite for growth. When the achievable spread widens again, the agencies re-leverage, beginning the process all over again. Some agencies, such as some of the Federal Home Loan Banks (FHLBs), run almost a matched book where assets and liabilities are substantially swapped out to LIBOR, providing direct linkage between the OTC option markets and the fixed-income markets. Because of the size of the agencies in aggregate as a percentage of overall mortgage and MBS activity, the arbitrage and hedging employed by the agencies has created an inextricable tie between the mortgage and agency markets and volatility levels in the market.

Mortgage Originators

Large mortgage originators hedge their loan pipelines and servicing portfolios by buying volatility in the OTC option market, especially MBS options. Because there are few sizable natural sellers of volatility, MBS option volatility usually trades "rich" (i.e., volatility levels are high, and therefore it is expensive to buy it) to Treasury volatility. This is why the strategy of selling MBS calls and buying Treasury calls is a classic method for an investor to benefit from this supply/demand imbalance.

Arbitrage Accounts

Leveraged investors such as hedge funds are typically LIBOR-based. Many leveraged investors use caps and floors, swaps and swaptions or other OTC options to hedge the purchase of cheap MBS cash flows. By doing this, they create "hedged carry" over their cost of funds. Because of the leverage employed in their capital structure, these investors can create acceptable levels of return on equity for their shareholders. Some large banks essentially manage their portfolios on this type of basis. Similar to the agencies, large banks and leveraged investors create a strong link between MBS valuations and market levels of volatility through their opportunistic market activities.

HOW HEAVY ISSUANCE OF CALLABLE DEBT AFFECTS THE GENERAL LEVEL OF VOLATILITY

We again distinguish between historical and implied levels of volatility. Swaptions are typically priced using implied volatility. When callable debt is issued by the FHLBs, the agency enters into an agreement with a dealer. The agency, which has retained the call option in the debt issuance, turns around and sells the call option to a dealer, effectively creating a floating-rate liability at sub-LIBOR funding levels. When issuance of callables is heavy, the dealer community must buy large amounts of volatility from the agencies. The bid for volatility declines, and swaption volatility drops as a result.

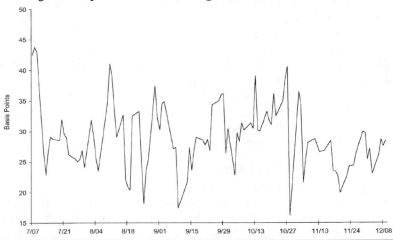

Exhibit 4: LIBOR Agency Arbitrage Spread
(January 7, 1999 through December 9, 1999)

Exhibit 5: Historical 3 x 7 Swaption Volatility
(January 1997 to December 1999)

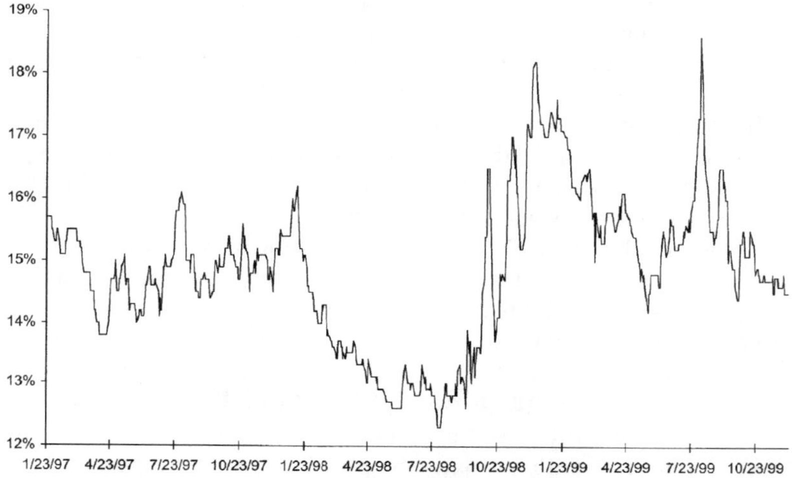

The putable/callable corporate structures that were heavily issued in 1998 have a similar effect on market volatility. In fact, issuance of these structures was so heavy during the first part of 1998 that it nearly doubled the amount of volatility dealer desks had to buy. The result was predictable, with longer-dated swaption volatility driven relentlessly to its lowest-ever historical levels (Exhibit 5).

THE "RIGHT" VOLATILITY TO USE WHEN VALUING MBS AND AGENCIES

Because the volatility input can have a large effect on the valuation of securities, the decision as to which volatility measure to use is an important one. Unfortunately, too often it is not clear-cut, and in some cases the answer is complex, reflecting the nuances of term structure modeling. Information in helping investors decide which volatility measures are most appropriate for different security types is presented below.

Callable Agencies

New issue callable agencies are priced using swaption volatility. This is because agencies that are typically LIBOR-based borrowers such as the FHLBs enter into swaption agreements with dealers to convert the fixed-rate option embedded debt to simple adjustable-rate funding to LIBOR. We believe secondary market agency callables are also properly valued using swaption volatility. In general, the best input for option pricing is the volatility of the first call. For example, in a 10 nc 3 structure, the first (and most valuable) option is priced using the 3×7 year swaption volatility (a 3-year option on a 7-year swap). This is used because three years forward, on the first call date, there are seven years left to maturity on the bond if it is not called. Using this methodology, any type of callable agency can be properly priced using the most current levels of market volatility implied from swaption prices.

Because market convention is to show the OAS of callable agencies at 14% volatility, the investor needs to be aware of how the structure would price at market swaption volatility to fully understand the risk/return attributes of the structure and to determine whether it is attractively priced. When market levels of implied swaption volatility are higher than 14%, structures shown at 14% volatility have the OAS overstated. The true hedging cost of the security, and therefore the hedged carry, is given by the swaption volatility. Swaption volatility levels can be found on Bloomberg by typing <TTKL> go <3> go <6> go.

Mortgage-Backed Securities

Fixed-rate MBS are usually priced in one of two ways. The first way is by using long-dated swaption volatility, usually the 3-year × 7-year swaption. This is our preferred measure for two reasons. First, it reflects the hedging cost for leveraged investors and ties valuations more closely to the swap market. As MBS valuations have become progressively more tied to the swap market, this measure should provide a sound framework. Second, it is easy to get the input value because it is easily available on Bloomberg.

The second possible input is to use the volatility of the futures contract on the 10-year Treasury or agency benchmark note. Some investors prefer this measure because the short expiry of the contract reflects the immediacy with which the prepayment option from the mortgagor can be exercised (mortgages are prepayable at any time). The biggest problem with this measure is that price volatility on the contract is available, but the user must use a formula to convert price volatility to yield volatility. Yield volatility is the appropriate input for option-pricing models.

Adjustable-rate mortgages (ARMs) and floating-rate CMOs present a problem in choosing a volatility measure because they contain different types of options. All have the same exposure to refinancing as in fixed-rate collateral. In addition, ARMs and floaters contain lifetime caps and, in the case of ARMs, periodic interest rate caps. The valuation of these caps is path dependent. Technically, the prepayment option in the ARM should be valued using the measures described above such as swaption volatility, and the caps should be valued separately using cap volatility (which is usually higher than swaption volatility). However, few analytical tools allow the user to split the analysis. We recommend ARMs and floaters be valued using both cap and then swaption volatility to show the investor the range of possible valuations and outcomes.

SUMMARY

An understanding of what drives volatility levels can help investors take a view of where volatility is headed in the future. If the investor can determine that an option-embedded fixed-income security is underpriced based on his understanding of "true" volatility and his own view on where volatility is headed, he can make an informed purchase decision, and vice versa. In this article we have provided an overview of volatility, explained the nuances of option-embedded fixed-income products, described the drivers of volatility levels, and suggested the "right" volatility to use in pricing fixed-income securities.

The Impact of Historical and Implied Volatilities on Valuing MBS

Stefan Szilagyi
Vice President
First Union Securities, Inc.

INTRODUCTION

In this chapter, we examine the relationship between realized and implied volatilities and the effect of using different volatility assumptions on the option values embedded in mortgage-backed securities (MBS). Computing the option-adjusted spread (OAS) to the swap curve and using historical and implied volatilities would show the leveraged investor an MBS's approximate true hedged return.

To accurately assess the value of options embedded in mortgage products, and thus OAS, it is critical to track reliable information on historical and implied volatilities and assess the statistical deterministic relationships between the two volatilities. These volatilities, as well as market interest rates, length of the options, strike price and risk-free interest rates, are important factors affecting the value of embedded options.

SPREADS AS MEASURES OF RELATIVE VALUE

Using spreads to various benchmarks as relative value indicators in the fixed-income market can be difficult but rewarding. The challenge consists not only in finding the right spread to the appropriate benchmark but also in determining whether a security maintains adequate returns under different interest rate scenarios. This challenge is exacerbated when implementing various strategies for maximizing risk-adjusted returns.

No single spread is universally accepted as the only indicator of relative value. To make better investment decisions, investors need to examine various spreads under different scenarios. When comparing several securities with similar durations and credit ratings, the one with the widest nominal spread seems to offer the best relative value. Nominal spreads are included in the calculation of a bond's internal rate of return (IRR). The drawback of using the IRR to discount a particular mortgage bond's cash flows is IRR's failure to take into consideration the timing and fluctuations of these cash flows. Another disadvantage of using nominal spreads as indicators of relative value is that the methodology works properly only in a flat interest rate environment. The Z-spread partially remedies the nominal spread's shortcomings. The Z-spread is added to the entire spot curve and the cash flows are present valued using this entire discount curve. However the Z-spread is not appropriate when quantifying the value of options embedded in spread products. OAS reflects the value and impact of embedded options, such as prepayments in MBS, and shows the strong deterministic relationship among interest rates, prepayments, and cash flows.

INTEREST RATE EXPECTATIONS AND THE IMPLIED FORWARD CURVE

Interest rates, implied forward rates, and historical and implied volatilities are important determinants of the value of embedded options in MBS. Expectations about interest rates are reflected in the implied forward market. If an investor's expectations regarding interest rates differ from those implied by forward rates and prove to be correct, the investor's valuation of embedded options and OASs will be accurate. Exhibit 1 shows the current (as of 10/19/99) and 1-year implied forward swap curves.

Exhibit 1: Implied Forward Swap Curve Analysis

Term	10/19/99 Swap Curve	10/23/00 Forward Curve
1 Week	5.3625	6.3628
1 Month	5.4071	6.3950
2 Months	5.5100	6.4363
3 Months	6.2006	6.4724
4 Months	6.1312	6.5124
5 Months	6.1200	6.5485
6 Months	6.1100	6.5885
9 Months	6.1600	6.7059
1 Year	6.2550	6.8240
2 Years	6.5200	6.8828
3 Years	6.6600	6.8695
4 Years	6.7000	6.9741
5 Years	6.8100	7.0203
7 Years	6.9200	7.0912
10 Years	6.9200	7.1120
15 Years	7.1800	7.3067
20 Years	7.2200	7.3309
30 Years	7.2100	NA

Source: Bloomberg

Exhibit 2: Historical Call Implied and Historical Underlying Volatility of Eurodollar Futures Options

Contract Expiration	Correlation Coefficient	R-squared	Daily Diffusion Index*		
			Implied Volatility	Historical Volatility	Difference
March 2000	0.77	0.59	2.665%	2.760%	0.095%
June 2000	0.46	0.21	2.191%	2.589%	0.398%
September 2000	0.34	0.12	1.493%	2.620%	1.127%

* Average of the absolute values of daily volatility changes.

Source: First Union Securities, Inc.

HISTORICAL AND IMPLIED VOLATILITIES

Implied volatility is the consensus market expectation of the price fluctuation of the underlying security for the remaining life of the option. Implied volatility can be used as an indicator of how different markets perceive the premiums of embedded options.

In the Treasury market, the level of implied volatility can be inferred from the spread difference between callable and noncallable bonds. By comparing historical to implied volatilities, an investor can also compare current to historical option values. Estimating the value of options embedded in mortgage products is complicated by the nature and determinants of prepayments (other than interest rates) and the existence of caps and floors (both interim and lifetime) in some floating-rate MBS.

Gaining insight into the interdependencies between historical and implied volatilities can be instrumental when assessing the value of embedded options. Moreover, because options embedded in MBS are short and long term, it is necessary to investigate the relationship between short- and long-term historical and historical implied volatilities.

My analysis on the interdependencies between historical volatilities of the underlying contract and historical call implied volatilities of Eurodollar futures options yielded the following four results. First, historical volatilities of the underlying contract and historical call implied volatilities are more correlated for short-term options than for long-term options. On average, implied volatilities are higher for short-term options than for long-term options, and the diffusion between historical and implied volatilities is greater the longer the term of the options (see Exhibit 2). Exhibit 3 depicts the relationship between historical and implied volatilities for Eurodollar futures options from March 1999 to November 1999.

Second, there is a moderate-to-weak deterministic relationship between historical and implied volatilities depending on the option's time to expiration. A better model would include other factors that seem to have a powerful role in influencing implied volatility. These factors are related to the uncertainty surrounding the federal government's reports on economic indicators or upcoming events that could have a strong impact on financial markets.

The third result is that historical volatility of the underlying contract and historical call implied volatility revert to their respective mean. When historical and implied volatilities are above or below their respective mean, the likelihood they will revert to their mean increases (see Exhibits 4 and 5).

Exhibit 3: Call Implied and Historical Volatilities of Eurodollar Futures Options (September 2000 Contract)

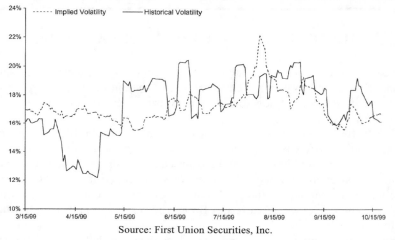

Source: First Union Securities, Inc.

Exhibit 4: Dispersion of Implied Volatility around the Mean Eurodollar Futures Options (September 2000 Contract)

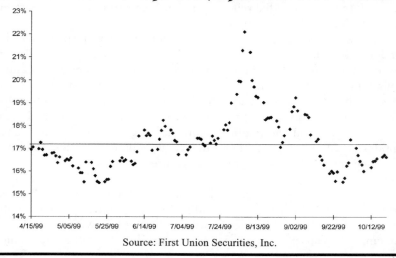

Source: First Union Securities, Inc.

Exhibit 5: Dispersion of Historical Volatility around the Mean Eurodollar Futures Options (September 2000 Contract)

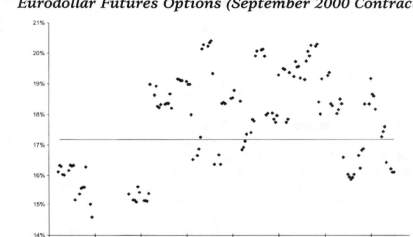

Source: First Union Securities, Inc.

Finally, when valuing embedded options it is important to differentiate between value and price. The value of the embedded option is determined by the volatility of the underlying contract over the life of the option. Although the implied volatility is important when obtaining the option's price, this volatility is overwhelmed by the volatility of the underlying contract near and at the option's expiration.

AN EMPIRICAL ANALYSIS OF IMPACT ON VALUE OF EMBEDDED OPTIONS

When effectively calculated, OAS can be a useful relative value measure of MBS. Past, present, and expected embedded option values can be estimated using historical and implied volatilities in OAS models. If the realized volatility of interest rates is lower than the implied volatility, option values will be lower and OASs will be higher than the market's expectations.

In my analysis, realized volatility is the 20-day historical yield volatility of the 10-year Treasury and implied volatility is the 3×7 swaption volatility. To quantify the impact of historical and implied volatilities on embedded option values, we selected three conventional generic mortgage-backed securities — one priced at a discount, the second priced near par, and the last priced at a premium. The valuation uses the swap curve as the benchmark and, as a result, has LIBOR OAS that is a more comprehensive measure of hedged return in MBS. Realized volatility is 1.54% lower than implied volatility, and the cost of embedded options is lower than suggested by the level of implied volatility. As a result, OASs are 8 bps wider for discounts and premiums and 10 bps wider for the security priced near par.

Exhibits 6 and 7 show OASs and the embedded options' costs when realized volatility is lower than implied volatility.

CONCLUSION

The challenge of determining the true hedged return of MBS can be seen as less complex through solving the enigma of historical and implied volatilities. Finding the right spread to the appropriate benchmark and using adequate historical and implied volatilities can make a tremendous difference in the valuation process. There is an inverse relationship between the length of the option and the correlation between historical and implied volatilities. The longer the option, the less correlation exists between the two volatilities. It is important to also examine whether a particular security maintains its return under different interest rate scenarios and changing implied and historical volatilities. LIBOR OAS calculated to the swap curve, using historical and implied volatilities, emerges as a comprehensive measure of relative value in mortgage products.

Exhibit 6: LIBOR Option-Adjusted Spreads Using Implied Volatility* as of November 15, 1999

Security	Coupon	Volatility	Price ($)	Z-Volatility OAS	OAS	Option Cost	Effective Duration	Effective Convexity
30-Year FNMA	7.00%	14.80%	98.3438	47	4	42	4.70	−1.0
30-Year FNMA	7.50%	14.80%	100.0313	65	8	57	3.90	−1.4
30-Year FNMA	8.00%	14.80%	101.9688	83	29	55	3.40	−1.3

OAS: Option-adjusted spread.
* 3×7 swaption volatility.

Source: Bloomberg

Exhibit 7: LIBOR Option-Adjusted Spreads Using Historical Volatility* as of November 15, 1999

Security	Coupon	Volatility	Price ($)	Z-Volatility OAS	OAS	Option Cost	Effective Duration	Effective Convexity
30-Year FNMA	7.00%	13.26%	98.3438	47	13	34	4.80	−1.0
30-Year FNMA	7.50%	13.26%	100.3438	65	18	47	4.00	−1.8
30-Year FNMA	8.00%	13.26%	101.9688	83	37	46	3.40	−1.4

OAS: Option-adjusted spread.
* 20-day historical yield volatility of the 10-year on-the-run Treasury.

Source: Bloomberg

Historical volatilities have a moderate-to-weak deterministic impact on implied volatilities. A sound modeling approach would be to include other factors as well, such as the uncertainty surrounding economic releases, and nonrecurring economic and political events that could have a powerful effect on implied volatilities. Such a study would include evidence for market efficiency, volatility persistence, volume, and speed of market adjustment to macroeconomic news, as well as the impact of market expectations regarding volatility.

Mortgage Spread Dynamics

Alexander Levin, Ph.D.
Treasury Research and Analytics Manager
The Dime Bancorp, Inc.

INTRODUCTION

Numerous attempts have been made lately at analyzing and modeling the mortgage spread dynamics. Interest in this subject is initiated by important risk management problems ranging from hedging a particular investment position (including mortgage servicing rights or the origination pipeline) to Value-at-Risk and Earnings-at-Risk measurement for the entire balance sheet of a financial institution. Given the profile of investment found in most banks, understanding the spread risk may be the missing link in a hedging strategy. Indeed, given the fact that the conventional interest-rate risk is usually kept under reasonable control, most of the mortgage spread risk is located in assets.

To illustrate the problem for this typical case, consider a balance sheet with total asset duration of 2, total liability duration of 2, and a 5% capital ratio. A resultant zero duration of equity creates an illusion that the interest rate exposure is perfectly hedged — provided that the rates on assets and rates on liabilities change in unison. The total exposure to rates on assets only is going to be 40. Thus, if all the assets are subject to mortgage spread risk and all liabilities are not, the significance of this factor seems to overwhelm everything else.[1]

Considerable spread widening that was caused by the sequence of financial crises of 1998 induced problems for the mortgage banking industry and mortgage investors, and resulted, among other things, in a sharp plunge in their positions. Thus, mortgage spread dynamics deserves more attention as it affects assets and equity significantly. An explanation of mortgage spread dynamics is the purpose of this article.

---

[1] The spread risk can be even higher than estimated above because the spread duration is usually greater than or equal to the effective duration. We discuss this subject later in this article.

This article benefits from collaboration with Jim Daras, Ken Schmidt, and Michael Purvis. The author is grateful to Robert Wyle, Diahann Rothstein, and Paul Barrett for providing some of the market and OAS data used in this article.

Exhibit 1: Swaption Volatility and Mortgage Spreads for FN TBAs

OAS VERSUS MORTGAGE INDEX SPREAD AND THE PROBLEM OF DIRECTIONALITY

Any analysis that is based on the behavior of any mortgage index indicator (MTGEFNCL, FNCL3030, etc.) versus some point of a benchmark can be misleading due to the following. First, the static spread ignores changing market volatility and therefore changing value of the embedded prepayment and other options. For example, the static spread should systematically widen when volatility increases (Exhibit 1). Second, spread to one point is inconclusive because the interest-rate curve changes shape.

Finally, spread measured to one point of the yield curve introduces artificial directionality (explicit dependence on the benchmark). Indeed, the rates of any term structure never perfectly correlate to each other. Let us assume that mortgages are priced to a curve that is equally weighted by the 2-year, the 5-year, and the 10-year points. Let us further assume that these three rates have the same volatility and 85% of cross-correlation. If the spread is measured with respect to, say, the 5-year point, it will exhibit a 100% − (85% + 85% + 100%)/3 = 10% systematic directionality. Therefore, if the 5-year point changes by 100 basis points, the mortgage index will systematically change only by 90 basis points simply because of the flawed reference method. Replacing the reference point by the 2-

year or the 10-year does not help — the resultant directionality will not disappear or even change.

Simply said, directionality is a systematic basis risk typically arising due to a flaw in the benchmark referencing method, or due to an improper selection of the benchmark itself. It is not easy to deal with mortgage spread directionality since this phenomenon affects both valuation and risk measurement and ultimately means that the mortgages are not actually priced off the chosen benchmark. That is why one should avoid introducing an artificial directionality when selecting the spread measure.

If mortgages are priced on an option-adjusted spread (OAS) basis, rather than a simple static spread basis, then all the points discussed above simply disappear. OAS is measured "beyond the option" and to the entire interest-rate curve. It represents the expected excess return over the benchmark (i.e., the relative attractiveness of the mortgage market to investors). We also restrict our attention here to the OAS for par-coupon fixed-rate agency mortgages. We will generally refer to this measure as "mortgage market OAS" or "mortgage spread," indicating that the entire fixed-rate agency MBS market is considered, not a particular bond.[2]

AUTOREGRESSIVE DIFFUSION MODEL

We start with a standard mean-reverting (therefore, stable) linear model:

$$\frac{d(\text{OAS})}{dt} = \varphi(\alpha + \beta r - \text{OAS}) + \sigma w \tag{1}$$

where r denotes some benchmark representative rate, α and β are parameters for the OAS equilibrium, φ is mean reversion, w is the white noise disturbing the process, and σ is OAS volatility. The value of $\alpha + \beta r$ determines the long-term equilibrium for the mortgage spread.

The case where $\beta = 0$ means the complete absence of any directionality. The choice of the benchmark rate (r) is not very important and will not strongly affect parameters of the model (except for the intercept, α). Although this statement seems to contradict what was stated in the previous section, one needs to remember that the OAS is already computed to the curve and not to a point. Rate r is just some benchmark indicator that "represents" the market. It can be the appropriate swap or Treasury rate (actual, averaged, or interpolated), or even the MBS index (MTGEFNCL) itself.

The model's parameters are fit using historical data such that the mean-square error (MSE) for $w(t)$ noise is minimized. As is known from statistics, this minimization would concurrently maximize the likelihood function — that is, the total probability that historical observations do, in fact, fit to the autoregressive (AR) model.

---

[2] Unfortunately, pricing of any particular MBS will exhibit directionality. As the market moves, premium and discount bonds migrate and demand changing excess compensation for prepayment risk.

The forward uncertainty in the mortgage spread grows according to the following theoretical rule applicable to equation (1):

$$\text{STD}_{\text{OAS}}(t) = \sigma \sqrt{\frac{1 - e^{-2\varphi t}}{2\varphi}}$$

If the mean reversion were zero, this formula would yield a familiar square-root-of-time rule for Brownian motion,

$$\text{STD}_{\text{OAS}}(t) = \sigma \sqrt{t}$$

Thus, in 1 month, the STD would be roughly 4.6 times daily volatility; in 1 quarter, −8 times daily volatility; in 1 year, −16 times daily volatility.

In the presence of a strong mean reversion such as $\varphi = 10\%$ per day,[3] the STD reaches the level of 1.75 times its daily volatility in a week, the level of 2.13 times its daily volatility in a month, and remains practically the same thereafter. If we recall that the underlying interest-rate process is close to Brownian motion, we conclude that the mortgage spread factor's relative importance declines over the time-horizon. It is most pronounced for short-term risk assessment and hedging.

PAR-COUPON OAS HISTORICAL ANALYSIS

In this section we will look at the pre-crisis history (February 1996-June 1998) and crisis and post-crisis history (August 1998-May 2000) of OAS to Treasury computed for the par-coupon 30-year agency MBS.

Pre-Crisis History, February 1996-June 1998

Exhibit 2 shows the pre-crisis history of OAS to Treasury computed for the par-coupon 30-year agency MBS. An analysis of Exhibit 2 indicates that the observed directionality is within 1%. That is, the Treasury market was then indeed a very good pricing benchmark for mortgages. The mortgage spread was quickly reverting to its equilibrium of about 56 basis points with $\varphi = 10.3\%$ and featured "high-frequency oscillations" with daily volatility of $\sigma = 2.31$ basis points. Roughly speaking, the uncertainty of OAS had been about 5 basis points for any time horizon exceeding one month.

Similar conclusions are valid using the LIBOR OAS as a pricing factor (Exhibit 2). With a relatively steady equilibrium of about −5.5 basis points, the LIBOR OAS dynamics was close to that of the Treasury OAS. Thus, for the pre-crisis period, both the Treasury curve and the LIBOR-swap curve could be successfully used as mortgage benchmarks.

---

[3] φ of 10% per day means that about 90% of the next-day spread is due to the previous-day spread, and 10% is due to the equilibrium. This is a very strong mean reversion. It is easy to compute that for a 1-month horizon, only 11% of the spread will be affected by the its current level.

Exhibit 2: Pre-Crisis History of Market Rates and Mortgage Spreads for FNCLs

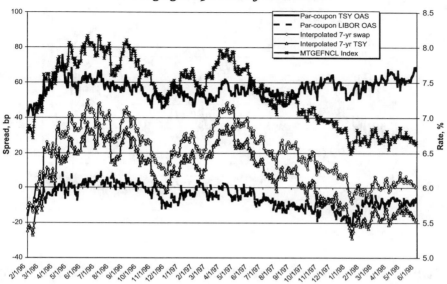

Crisis and Post-Crisis History: August 1998-May 2000

We ran historical par-coupon agency OAS using an advanced pricing system. Some changes were made in the way the OAS was assessed. First, for the purpose of prepayment modeling, the MTGEFNCL index was simulated off the swap term structure. This index served as an indicator of refinancing incentives. Second, the broker's median speeds were plugged into the prepayment model.

Neither of these changes strongly affects in itself results of our study, even the choice of the swap curve for the MTGEFNCL modeling. The time series is plotted on Exhibit 3 while the obtained parameters of the autoregressive model of LIBOR OAS for different (contracting) historical intervals are presented in the Exhibit 4.

One clear conclusion that can be derived from this presentation is the presence of a strong directionality during the crisis and the absence of it in a steady-state mode. The LIBOR OAS equilibrium, once boosted by the crisis, has stabilized to the level comparable to the one observed before the crisis. It is also clear that a reliable diffusion model of the mortgage spread for the crisis itself simply does not exist. The characteristics of the OAS process become discontinuous during the crisis, suggesting a "jump" model and not a continuous diffusion that could be modeled with process (1).

It is also seen without a thorough quantitative analysis that the mortgage market has not been trading off the Treasury after the series of 1998 crises (the equilibrium of the Treasury OAS has been unstable).

Exhibit 3: Post-Crisis History of Market Rates and Mortgage Spreads for FNCLs

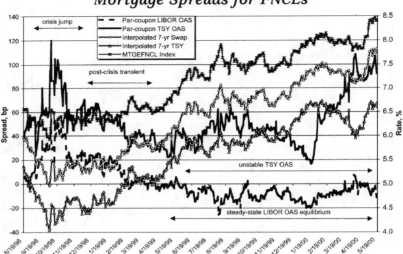

Exhibit 4: Parameters of the LIBOR OAS Autoregressive Model

History	LIBOR OAS average, bp	Independent variable: 7-yr swap			Independent variable: MTGEFNCL		
		Beta	Phi, daily	MSE, daily	Beta	Phi, daily	MSE, daily
Last 6 mos	−8.50	2.66%	11.00%	2.53	1.66%	11.0%	2.53
Last 9 mos	−8.77	−0.89%	14.10%	2.67	−2.85%	13.7%	2.65
Last 12 mos	−8.41	−2.43%	14.60%	2.81	−4.22%	15.0%	2.81
Last 15 mos	−6.71	−5.33%	14.60%	2.71	−6.38%	15.3%	2.7
last 18 mos	−2.65	−10.84%	9.40%	2.98	−12.47%	9.1%	2.98
last 21 mos	1.16	−15.44%	10.04%	3.93	−18.21%	9.52%	3.92

JUMP-DIFFUSION MODEL

In the presence of potential jumps,[4] a better model for mortgage OAS is as follows:

$$\frac{d(OAS)}{dt} = \varphi(\alpha + \beta r - OAS) + \sigma w + \sigma_{jump} w_{jump} \tag{2}$$

where $w_{jump}(t)$ denotes a random Poisson process of discrete jumps of random heights. The frequency (intensity) of this process q, (1/yrs) and the expected magnitude σ_{jump} need to be known to proceed further. Unfortunately, it is much harder to find reliable input for the jump statistics than for the statistics of process (1). Jumps are very infrequent and irregular. For the reported historical 4-year period

---

[4] Jump models have been used in mathematical finance since Robert C. Merton, "Option pricing when underlying stock return is discontinuous," *Journal of Financial Economics*, 3 (March 1976), pp. 125-144.

of LIBOR OAS, we observed one jump of about 45-50 basis points magnitude and a few months in duration.

Assuming that the required statistics for jumps are known, the product of $\sqrt{q}$ and σ_{jump} is mathematically proven to play the role of "equivalent volatility" and can be substituted in the assessment of OAS's standard deviation for any time horizon. However, the resultant probability distribution for the mortgage spread will not be normal as it mixes the normal diffusion and the Poisson process. Namely, it will have fatter-than-normal tails, signaling a greater-than-normal chance for a large spread move.

Computational Example

Consider a horizon exceeding one month. We know that the spread's steady-state daily volatility is about 2.5 bp. Let's assume $q = 0.2$ (1/yr), $\sigma_{jump} = 50$ basis points meaning that we expect to have one random jump in five years on average with an average magnitude of 50 basis points. Then, $\sqrt{q}\,\sigma_{jump} = 22.4$ basis points annually, or 1.4 basis points per day, and assuming that the disturbing forces $w(t)$ and $w_{jump}(t)$ are independent, we estimate the resultant daily volatility to be around

$$\sqrt{2.5^2 + 1.4^2} \approx 2.8 \text{ bp}$$

resulting in a 6.1 bp STD for any horizon exceeding one month. This number can be plugged into the risk management system.

One could argue that the mean reversion for the jump component might not be the same as the one for the diffusion. Indeed, market corrections caused by global economic events will generally be slower than the transients in the steady-state trading. One can check that the jump risk component becomes dominant once its mean reversion is less than 2% per day.

SPREAD DURATION: A MEASURE OF THE MORTGAGE SPREAD RISK

As we quantified the dynamics of mortgage spreads, we turn our attention to its impact on price volatility. The key notion in this assessment is mortgage market spread duration. This measure differs from other duration definitions as shown in Exhibit 5.

Except for modified duration, all other measures come from the OAS analysis. Since a changing par-coupon OAS means, in essence, changing mortgage market, the refinancing incentive and prepayment speed will change as well. Therefore, mortgage market spread duration will coincide with effective duration for fixed-rate mortgages only. For ARMs, these measures will differ significantly amid the coupon adjustment process. The "personal" spread duration measures exposure to the discount spread only, but within the framework of option-adjusted valuation; it is different from the modified duration. For a set of FNCL fixed-rate securities and CMT GN ARMs, we present all the duration measures in Exhibit 6 for market rates and volatility as of August 31, 2000.

Exhibit 5: Different Duration Measures

Duration Measure	Measures price sensitivity to	Comments
Modified Duration	Discount rate	Static measure that ignores cash flow variability
Mortgage Market Spread Duration	Par-coupon (mortgage market) OAS	Varies OAS and prepayment speeds, but not CMS or CMT indices
"Personal" Spread Duration	OAS for a particular MBS less par-coupon OAS	Varies OAS only, but not prepayment speeds, CMS or CMT indices
Effective Duration	Benchmark interest rates	Varies benchmark rates, prepayment speeds and all market indices, but not OAS

Exhibit 6: Duration Measures for Widely Traded Agency MBS

MBS	Modified Duration	Mortgage Market Spread Duration	"Personal" Spread Duration	Effective Duration
FNCL7.0	5.72	4.58	4.80	4.58
FNCL7.5	5.29	3.93	4.43	3.93
FNCL8.0	4.62	3.22	4.00	3.22
FNCL8.5	3.57	2.52	3.52	2.52
FNCL9.0	2.33	1.94	2.99	1.94
G2AR5.5	2.90	3.83	3.50	2.52
G2AR6.0	2.65	3.44	3.22	2.14
G2AR6.5	2.42	3.04	2.96	1.80
G2AR7.0	2.28	2.76	2.73	1.56
G2AR7.5	2.19	2.51	2.55	1.40

All sensitivities have been derived using the LIBOR OAS measurement and the 1-factor Hull-White term structure model with a constant volatility and a zero mean-reversion.[5] Since the forward evolution of the MTGEFNCL index (used to identify the refinancing incentive) was modeled off the relatively steep forward swap rates, the forward prepayment speeds were lower than if the slightly inverted Treasury curve had been employed. Therefore, the proposed switching of the mortgage market benchmark from Treasury to LIBOR results, among other things, in longer duration measures. In addition, the relative values of these measures also depend on the pricing benchmark. For example, the mortgage market spread duration would have been surely less than the "personal" spread duration for all the instruments — if the Treasury curve had been used as the benchmark. This holds true also for ARMs because they tended to get some value appreciation (arising from a high fully indexed coupon) if prepayments slow down.[6] This statement may not be valid if the benchmark (LIBOR) curve is steep enough to impair this appreciation effect. Correspondingly, prepayment variability may, in principle, extend OAS durations.

---

[5] A zero mean-reversion forces the term structure to change in a parallel fashion thus providing consistency between different risk measures.

[6] See Alexander Levin and D. James Daras, "Non-Traded Factors in MBS Portfolio Management," Chapter 5 in Frank J. Fabozzi (ed.) *Advances in Valuation and Management of Mortgage-Backed Securities* (New Hope, PA: Frank J. Fabozzi Associates, 1998).

CONCLUSIONS

Empirical observations confirm that the mortgage market has switched its benchmark from Treasury to LIBOR. In a steady-state pre-crisis mode, both the Treasury OAS and the LIBOR OAS computed for the par-coupon agency MBS had little or no directionality and exhibited notable stability of their equilibria. In a steady-state post-crisis mode, the LIBOR OAS has little or no directionality and a stable equilibrium, but the Treasury OAS has never been stabilized. The spread process is always strongly mean reverting. Thus, in a steady-state mode, the spread process can be viewed as high-frequency random oscillations around the stable equilibrium.

These observations can be backed by some economic arguments. Namely, in an economy dominated by LIBOR-based borrowings, stability of LIBOR OAS for mortgage banking means, in essence, stability of net interest margin adjusted for optionality and curve-risk-neutrality. As this margin retains relatively stable equilibrium, so does the spread. The jump occurs when underlying economic conditions change — including financial crises, prevailing interest-rate market, and dominating borrowing mechanism (i.e., mostly when the benchmark changes).

We have been able to quantify mortgage spread dynamics using a one-dimensional autoregressive model that has two independent components — continuous diffusion and irregular jumps. Parameters of the diffusion process can be fit to steady-state historical observations. Parameters for the jumps (intensity and magnitude) can only be assumed. In the presence of jumps, the probability distribution of the mortgage spread contains fatter-than-normal tails thus increasing the risk of a large price move.

Portfolio Yields and Durations

Jonathan Carmel
Vice President
Lehman Brothers

Lev Dynkin
Managing Director
Lehman Brothers

Jay Hyman
Senior Vice President
Lehman Brothers

Phil Weissman
Vice President
Lehman Brothers

Wei Wu
Vice President
Lehman Brothers

INTRODUCTION

This article explores the properties of various measures of portfolio yield and duration. In particular, we examine market weighted averages of security durations, market weighted averages of security yields, dollar duration weighted averages of security yields, and their relation to portfolio internal rate of return (IRR). We show the following. First, the market weighted average of security yields provides the expected return of a portfolio over the coming period under the assumption of no change in security yields. Second, the market weighted average of security durations is the sensitivity of portfolio return to changes in the dollar-duration weighted average of security yield changes. Third, the dollar duration weighted average of security yields provides a first order approximation of the portfolio IRR and this approximation holds with the greatest precision when intra-portfolio yield variations and security convexities are small.

Intra-portfolio yield variations are likely to be large whenever either: (1) the yield curve is steeply sloped, generating large yield variations across maturities, or (2) credit spreads are wide. We provide a second order approximation for the portfolio IRR based on the dollar duration weighted average of security yields, which is appropriate in these situations or for portfolios with extremely convex securities.

Most investors use IRR as a measure of "portfolio yield" if held to maturity. For this to be true, all interim cash flows need to be reinvested at the same IRR. This assumption is also required for the yield-to-maturity of a bond to measure its expected return. The greater the percentage of early cash flows and the greater the slope and volatility of the yield curve, the more troublesome this reinvestment assumption becomes.

The market weighted average of security yields will be closest to the portfolio's IRR in situations in which roll down returns are trivial. Generally, this occurs when the yield curve and term structure of spreads are flat and/or the portfolio's cash flow profile is heavily backloaded. The magnitude of credit spreads, however, does not affect the closeness of the market weighted average of security yields to the portfolio's IRR, provided the term structure of these spreads is flat.

PORTFOLIO YIELD TO MATURITY AND TIME RETURN

To maintain focus on the essential issues, this analysis will consider a zero volatility environment in which all changes in bond yields are perfectly predictable.[1] The current yield curve can have any shape and can change over time, but all such changes are completely deterministic.

Notation

V_{port} and V_i are the current market values of the portfolio and the portfolio's holdings of the ith bond respectively. Let $w_i = V_i/V_{port}$. w_i is bond i's portfolio weight. y_i is the continuously-compounded yield to maturity of bond i at time t. It is the IRR for bond i defined in the following equation:

$$V_i = \Sigma_j e^{-y_i[t_j - t]} c_{t_j}^i \tag{1}$$

where $c_{t_j}^i$ is the cash flow that arrives at time t_j from the portfolio's holdings in security i and $t_j - t$ is the number of years until date t_j. Similarly, y_{IRR} is the IRR of the portfolio's cash flows at time t defined from

$$V_{port} = \Sigma_j e^{-y_{IRR}[t_j - t]} c_{t_j}^{port} \tag{2}$$

where $c_{t_j}^{port}$ is the portfolio cash flow that arrives at time t_j. Additionally, define

---

[1] The appendix treats stochastic bond yields.

$$D_{IRR} = \frac{-1}{V_{port}} \frac{dV_{port}}{dy_{IRR}}$$

where D_{IRR} is the sensitivity of the portfolio's return to changes in its IRR.

Expected Returns and Yields

The yield to maturity of an individual security is often used as a gauge of the expected return from holding the security to maturity. For a risk-free zero coupon bullet bond, yield to maturity does indeed provide the exact return from holding the security to maturity. For coupon-paying bonds, the issue becomes more complicated. One approach is to view the coupon-paying bond as a portfolio of zero coupon bonds in which each coupon and principal payment is treated as a separate entity. In this case, the original bond's yield to maturity can be viewed as an amalgamation of the expected holding period returns of the zero coupon bonds in this equivalent portfolio. In general, a bond's yield to maturity will be a nonlinear combination of the yields of its component cash flows, which are the spot rates off the corresponding credit curve. However, continuing to view a bond as an equivalent portfolio of zero coupon bonds, we can interpret yield to maturity as being, to a first-order approximation, the dollar duration weighted average of the yields of the bond's component cash flows.

Alternatively, one can view yield to maturity as providing the expected return from holding the bond to maturity subject to the assumption that one will be able to reinvest interim coupons at the bond's current yield to maturity. However, this assumption is typically untenable, particularly when the yield curve exhibits substantial volatility or slope.

The interpretation of IRR becomes especially troublesome for portfolios. Portfolios generally contain bonds that mature at different times. By design, the cash flow stream generated by a bond portfolio (coupon and principal repayments) is often relatively smooth over time. Thus the typical time profile of a portfolio's cash flows will be very different from the time profile of a zero coupon bond's cash flow. These differences exacerbate the problems that the interim cash flows create for the interpretation of portfolio IRR as a measure of the expected return for holding a portfolio until its "maturity."

Additionally, a portfolio may contain bonds with a wide variety of credit qualities. Unless each bond is replaced at maturity with a bond that trades at a similar credit spread, the portfolio IRR may be dramatically affected by the maturity schedule of the bonds in the portfolio. The portfolio's IRR may be affected by any changes in the overall time profile of portfolio's cash flows. These changes could be caused by reinvestment decisions or the distribution of cash flows. All of this diminishes the usefulness of the portfolio IRR as a measure of the expected return for holding a portfolio's assets until maturity. Instead, the ability to approximate a portfolio's IRR by the dollar duration weighted average of the yields of its component bonds is particularly relevant for imparting meaning to yield to maturity in a portfolio context.

Expected Return Over Short Time Intervals

Portfolio IRR can be used to calculate expected returns over short horizons. The portfolio's expected return over the next instant in time is given by

$$\text{Portfolio instantaneous expected return per unit time} = y_{\text{IRR}} - D_{\text{IRR}}\, dy_{\text{IRR}} \quad (3)$$

Recall that D_{IRR} is the sensitivity of the portfolio's return to changes in its IRR and dy_{IRR} is the (expected) change in the portfolio's IRR.[2] The expected portfolio return is the sum of two components: the static portfolio yield (IRR) plus the return coming from the expected capital gain or loss in portfolio value due to the change in the portfolio's IRR yield.

Equation (3), however, is rarely used in practice. Generally, it is simpler to assess a portfolio's expected return over short horizons using a formula based on the market weighted average of the yields of the portfolio's component securities. Here the analysis starts from the following expression for the expected return of an individual bond (bond i) over the next instant in time:

$$\text{Security } i \text{ instantaneous expected return per unit time} = y_i - D_i\, dy_i \quad (4)$$

where D_i is bond i's duration, $(-1/V_i)(dV_i/dy_i)$. Since a portfolio's expected return is the market weighted average of the expected returns of its component securities, the portfolio's expected return over the next instant can also be expressed

Portfolio instantaneous expected return per unit time

$$= \sum_i w_i y_i - \sum_i w_i D_i dy_i \quad (5)$$

The portfolio's expected return is equal to the sum of the market-weighted averages of:

1. The individual security yields.
2. The expected capital gain or loss return of the individual securities.

At this point, we introduce the following notation:

Let $y_{mw} = \Sigma_i w_i y_i$

y_{mw} is the market weighted average of the individual security yields. Let

$$D_{mw} = \Sigma_i w_i D_i$$

D_{mw} is the market weighted average of the individual security durations. Let

---

[2] Since we are working in an environment in which all yield changes are known in advance, dy_{IRR} is also equal to the realized yield change. All yields are continuously compounded.

$$dy_{\$\text{dur}} = \frac{\Sigma_i w_i D_i dy_i}{D_{mw}}$$

$dy_{\$\text{dur}}$ is the dollar duration weighted average of the expected yield changes of the portfolio's component securities.

Equation (5) can be rewritten as follows: the portfolio's instantaneous expected return at time t is[3]

Portfolio instantaneous expected return per unit time
$$= y_{mw} - D_{mw} dy_{\$\text{dur}} \tag{6}$$

From equation (6), the portfolio's expected return can be expressed as the sum of:

- the market weighted average of the individual security yields and
- the (market weighted) portfolio duration times the dollar duration weighted average of the expected individual security yield changes.

If we make the simplifying assumption that the yields of all bonds in the portfolio will remain unchanged over the coming month, then equation (6) shows that the instantaneous return per unit time is given by the market weighted yield. This is not true for the IRR; even if we assume that all security yields remain unchanged, the portfolio IRR can change as portfolio composition changes due to coupon payments and maturities.

More surprisingly, equation (6) shows that D_{mw}, the market weighted average of security durations, is the sensitivity of portfolio return to changes in the dollar duration weighted average of individual bond yields.[4]

Note that D_{IRR} is the sensitivity of portfolio return to shifts in the portfolio's IRR. However, D_{mw} is the sensitivity of portfolio return to changes in the dollar duration weighted average of individual bond yields. In general, these two sensitivities will not be identical.

---

[3] If we consider discrete yield changes, rather than infinitesimal yield changes, then the second order approximation of the expected portfolio return is

$$y_{mw} - D_{mw} \Delta y_{\$\text{dur}} + (1/2) C_{mw} (\Delta y)^2_{\$\text{dur}}$$

where $\Delta y_{\$\text{dur}}$ is the expected change in the dollar duration weighted average of the yields of the portfolio's component securities;

$$(\Delta y)^2_{\$\text{dur}}$$

is the dollar duration weighted average of the squares of the expected yield changes of the portfolio's component securities; and C_{mw} is the market weighted average of the convexities of the portfolio's component securities.

[4] In this zero volatility environment, equation (6) provides the portfolio's realized instantaneous return, as well as its expected return, and $dy_{\$\text{dur}}$ is both the expected and realized change in the dollar duration weighted average of security yields.

PORTFOLIO IRR AND THE DOLLAR DURATION
WEIGHTED AVERAGE OF ASSET YIELDS

We have just seen that the market weighted average of security durations (D_{mw}) is the sensitivity of the portfolio return to changes in the dollar duration weighted average of the portfolio's security yields while D_{IRR} is the sensitivity of the portfolio return to changes in the portfolio's IRR. In this section, we show that the dollar duration weighted average of security yields is, to a first order approximation, the same as the portfolio's IRR. Thus, while D_{mw} and D_{IRR} will, in general, not be identical, to a first-order approximation, they are sensitivities to the same variable. In situations in which this first order approximation holds with greatest precision, D_{mw} and D_{IRR} will have very similar values.

Let $V_i(y)$ be the present value of the cash flows that the portfolio will receive from its investment in security i discounted at yield y. Recall that y_i is the observed yield to maturity of bond i. $V_i(y_i)$ is the current market value of the portfolio's holdings in security i.

$$\text{Let } y_{\$dur} = \frac{\Sigma_i w_i D_i y_i}{D_{mw}}$$

$y_{\$dur}$ is the dollar duration weighted average of the yields of the portfolio's component securities.

Consider a portfolio of n securities. By the definition of portfolio yield to maturity, the value y_{IRR} that solves the equation

$$V_{port}(y_{IRR}) = V_1(y_{IRR}) + V_2(y_{IRR}) + \ldots + V_n(y_{IRR}) \tag{7}$$

is the portfolio's IRR. Note that $V_i(y_{IRR})$ is not equal to the value of the portfolio's holdings of bond i. Instead, it is equal to the present value of the cash flows from the portfolio's investment in the ith bond discounted at yield y_{IRR}.

From the standard first-order duration approximation

$$\frac{V_i(y_{IRR}) - V_i(y_i)}{V_i(y_i)} \approx -D_i(y_{IRR} - y_i)$$

$$V_i(y_{IRR}) \approx V_i(y_i) - V_i(y_i)D_i(y_{IRR} - y_i) \tag{8}$$

$V_i(y_i)$ is simply V_i, the current market value of the portfolio's holding's in bond i. From equations (7) and (8),

$$V_{port}(y_{IRR}) = \sum_i [V_i - V_i D_i(y_{IRR} - y_i)]$$

$$V_{port}(y_{IRR}) = \sum_i V_i - \sum_i V_i D_i(y_{IRR} - y_i) \tag{9}$$

Note that $V_{port}(y_{IRR}) = [V_1 + V_2 + ... + V_n]$; the market value of a portfolio equals the sum of the market values of its component assets. Substituting this into equation (9) produces

$$\sum_i V_i D_i (y_{IRR} - y_i) \approx 0 \tag{10}$$

In equation (10), we assume that the analyst knows all the prices, durations, and yields for individual securities. The only unknown in equation (10) is the portfolio yield. Solving for y_{IRR},

$$y_{IRR} \approx \frac{V_1 D_1 y_1 + V_2 D_2 y_2 + ... + V_n D_n y_n}{V_1 D_1 + V_2 D_2 + ... + V_n D_n} = y_{\$dur} \tag{11}$$

From equation (11), the dollar duration weighted average of bond yields provides the first-order approximation of the portfolio's IRR. To the first order, D_{mw} and D_{IRR} provide return sensitivities to the same entity.

THE ACCURACY OF THE FIRST-ORDER APPROXIMATION OF PORTFOLIO IRR

Equation (11) is based on the first-order duration approximation of bond return. It holds with the greatest precision in situations in which the first-order duration approximation is most accurate. For the current application, these conditions are:

1. intra-portfolio variations in yield are small ($y_{IRR} - y_i$ is small for all i); and
2. security convexities are close to zero.

First, we consider the effect of intra-portfolio yield variations on the tightness of the match between the dollar duration weighted average of security yields and the portfolio IRR. Exhibit 1 considers two portfolios. The first portfolio consists of all bullet bonds in the Lehman Gov/Corp Index. The second portfolio has 50% of its holdings in the bullet bonds in the Lehman Gov/Corp Index and the remaining 50% of its holdings in the bullet bonds in the Lehman High Yield Index. The mixed Gov/Corp, High Yield portfolio can be expected to have significantly more intra-portfolio yield variation than the Gov/Corp only portfolio. The exhibit presents results for August 31, 1993, and September 30, 1998, dates in which intra-portfolio yield variation were likely to be especially high. The Treasury curve was especially steep in August 1993, generating substantial yield differentials between long and short maturity assets, and the spread sector crash in early Fall 1998 led to wide yield differentials across credit qualities in late September 1998.

Exhibit 1: Effect of Intra-Portfolio Yield Variation on Dollar Duration Yield and Portfolio IRR

Date	Portfolio	IRR	Dollar Dur. Yld.	Mkt. Wtd. Yield
8/31/93	Gov/Corp Bullets	5.73	5.70	5.07
	50% Gov/Corp, 50% HY (Bullets)	7.30	7.18	6.74
9/30/98	Gov/Corp Bullets	5.23	5.22	4.97
	50% Gov/Corp, 50% HY (Bullets)	6.69	6.54	6.46

The dollar duration weighted average and portfolio IRR match quite closely for the Gov/Corp index at each date. The match is substantially worse for the mixed Gov/Corp, High Yield portfolio. The market weighted average of portfolio yields provides a very poor indicator of portfolio IRR in all cases presented in the exhibit.

The second-order duration/convexity approximation:

$$V_i(y_{IRR}) \approx V_i(y_i) - V_i(y_i)D_i(y_{IRR} - y_i) + (1/2)V_i(y_i)C_i(y_{IRR} - y_i)^2$$

can be used to show that to a second-order approximation:[5]

$$y_{IRR} \approx y_{\$dur} + \frac{1}{2}\sum_i \frac{w_i C_i}{D_{mw}}(y_{IRR} - y_i)^2 \tag{12}$$

From equation (12), the ratio of the market weighted average of security convexities divided by the portfolio's market weighted duration (D_{mw}) provides a measure of the extent to which the dollar duration weighted average of the portfolio's security yields is likely to be appreciably different from the portfolio's IRR.

If all securities in the portfolio have non-negative durations and convexities, then the fraction on the right-hand side of equation (12) will be non-negative. For securities with non-negative durations and convexities, the dollar duration weighted average of individual security yields will never be greater than the portfolio IRR, provided terms beyond second order are of trivial significance.

Exhibit 2 separately considers a low convexity subset and a high convexity subset of the two portfolios considered in Exhibit 1. The low convexity subset consists of maturities of 5 years or less. The high convexity subset consists of maturities of 25 years or greater.

As predicted in equation (12), the dollar duration weighted yields are always less than or equal to the portfolio IRRs in Exhibits 1 and 2, and the dollar duration yields match the portfolio IRRs in Exhibit 2 more closely for the short maturity portfolios than the long maturity portfolios. The market weighted yields seem to do a bet-

---

[5] It can be shown that when one replaces equation (8) with a second-order duration/convexity approximation, equation (10) becomes

$$\sum_i V_i D_i(y_{IRR} - y_i) = \frac{1}{2}\sum_i V_i C_i(y_{IRR} - y_i)^2$$

Equation (12) immediately follows.

ter job approximating portfolio IRRs for high convexity portfolios. While convexity poses a particular problem for the use of dollar-duration weighted averages as approximations of portfolio IRR, they do not appear to be an important factor determining the accuracy of market weighted yields as an approximation of portfolio IRR.

SECOND ORDER APPROXIMATION OF PORTFOLIO IRR

While market weighted averages worked well for the high convexity portfolios considered in Exhibit 2, one cannot rely on them in general to be good approximations of portfolio IRR. For portfolios containing high convexity assets, the more prudent procedure is to solve explicitly for the portfolio's IRR directly from the portfolio's cash flows.

Failing this, equation (12) provides a mechanism for generating the second order approximation. Setting equation (12) to an equality creates a quadratic equation, which can be solved in closed form. The solution, y_{IRR}^{so}, is the second order approximation to portfolio IRR. Alternatively, one can approximate the solution by replacing y_{IRR} with $y_{\$dur}$ in the right-hand side of equation (12). Exhibit 3 uses this short cut to approximate portfolio IRR for the portfolios in Exhibits 1 and 2 in which dollar duration weighted yields differed noticeably from portfolio IRR. The second order approximations presented in Exhibit 3 match the portfolio IRR quite well.

Exhibit 2: Effect of Portfolio Convexity on Dollar Duration Yield and Portfolio IRR

Date	Quality	Maturity	Convexity/ Duration	IRR	$Dur Yield	MW Yield
8/31/93	Gov/Corp Bullets	Short (≤ 5 yr)	3.5	4.38	4.37	4.21
		Long (≥ 25 yr)	18.9	6.40	6.39	6.39
	50% Gov/Corp, 50% HY (Bullets)	Short (≤ 5 yr)	3.6	6.31	6.21	5.88
		Long (≥ 25 yr)	17.7	7.80	7.61	7.82
9/30/98	Gov/Corp Bullets	Short (≤ 5 yr)	3.6	4.66	4.66	4.65
		Long (≥ 25 yr)	20.3	5.72	5.65	5.70
	50% Gov/Corp, 50% HY (Bullets)	Short (≤ 5 yr)	3.4	6.38	6.29	6.23
		Long (≥ 25 yr)	19.1	7.23	6.97	7.19

Exhibit 3: Accuracy of Second Order Approximation of Portfolio IRR

Date	Quality	Maturity	IRR	Dollar Dur. Yield	y^{so}
8/31/93	Mix Gov/Corp HY	All	7.30	7.18	7.31
	Mix Gov/Corp HY	Short	6.31	6.21	6.31
	Mix Gov/Corp HY	Long	7.80	7.61	7.79
9/30/98	Mix Gov/Corp HY	All	6.69	6.54	6.69
	Mix Gov/Corp HY	Short	6.38	6.29	6.39
	Mix Gov/Corp HY	Long	7.23	6.97	7.22

Exhibit 4: Accuracy of Market Weighted Yield as an Approximation to Portfolio IRR

Date	Quality	Maturity	IRR	MW Yield	Diff. (bp)
8/31/93	Gov/Corp	All	5.73	5.07	66
		Short	4.38	4.21	17
	Mix Gov/Corp HY	All	7.30	6.74	56
		Short	6.31	5.88	43
9/30/98	Gov/Corp	All	5.23	4.97	26
		Short	4.66	4.65	1
	Mix Gov/Corp HY	All	6.69	6.46	23
		Short	6.38	6.23	15

PORTFOLIO IRR AND THE MARKET WEIGHTED AVERAGE OF SECURITY YIELDS

We can use equations (3) and (6) to understand the relationship between the market weighted average of the yields of the portfolio's constituent securities and the portfolio's IRR. Setting the right-hand sides of equations (3) and (6) equal to each other, we obtain

$$y_{mw} - y_{IRR} = D_{mw}dy_{\$dur} - D_{IRR}dy_{IRR} \tag{13}$$

Recall that $dy_{\$dur}$ and dy_{IRR} refer to the expected changes in portfolio yield per unit time. These changes will tend to be largest when the yield curve or term structure of credit spreads is highly positively or negatively sloped. Equation (13) suggests that the differential between portfolio IRRs and market weighted yields will be greater during periods such as August 1993, when the yield curve was steeply sloped, rather than September 1998, when the yield curve was relatively flat. This is confirmed in Exhibit 4. The September 1998 market weighted yields performed much better than those of August 1993 in matching their respective portfolio IRR, despite the erratic nature of credit spreads in early fall 1998.

The expected change in portfolio yield per unit time ($dy_{\$dur}$ or dy_{IRR}) will invariably be much lower for long maturity assets than for short maturity assets. For instance, the Lehman Treasury spline for 9/30/98 showed no difference in fitted yields between 20- and 25-years. The difference between the 5-year yield and the 1-month yield from the same 9/30/98 spline was 32 bp.[6] The difference in magnitude of $dy_{\$dur}$ or dy_{IRR} for long maturity portfolios versus short maturity portfolios is much greater than the magnitude of the differences in portfolio duration. Therefore, from equation (13), one would expect market weighted yields to much more closely

---

[6] For 8/31/93, the corresponding numbers for 25-year yield minus the 20-year yield was 13 bp, and the 5-year yield minus the 1-month yield was 139 bp.

approximate portfolio IRRs for very long maturity portfolios rather than for short (or mixed) maturity portfolios. Exhibit 2 confirms this. In all cases, the market weighted yield closely approximates portfolio IRR for the long maturity portfolio, but provides a very poor approximation of portfolio IRR for the short maturity portfolios.

PORTFOLIO DURATION

Portfolio duration

$$D_{IRR} = \frac{-1}{V_{port}} \frac{dV_{port}}{dy_{IRR}}$$

contains a derivative with respect to shifts in the portfolio's IRR, whereas individual security durations

$$\frac{-1}{V_i} \frac{dV_i}{dy_i}$$

contain derivatives with respect to the individual security yields. Since a portfolio IRR is not a linear function of the yields of the individual securities in the portfolio, it follows that D_{IRR} cannot equal D_{mw} in general.

Modified adjusted duration is Lehman's measure of the sensitivity of a bond's return to a parallel shift in the Treasury par curve, holding spreads and volatility parameters constant. Modified adjusted duration can be expressed as

$$\frac{-1}{V_{port}} \frac{\partial V_{port}}{\partial y_{par}}$$

for a portfolio and as

$$\frac{-1}{V_i} \frac{\partial V_i}{\partial y_{par}}$$

for an individual security where dy_{par} is a unit change in the Treasury par curve.[7] In both cases, the derivative is with respect to the same entity. Therefore, the modified adjusted duration of a portfolio is exactly equal to the market weighted average of the modified adjusted durations of the portfolio's constituent securities.

The sensitivity of security duration to shifts in security yield is always given by

$$D_i'(y_i) = D_i^2 - C_i$$

In order to discuss the sensitivity of portfolio duration to changes in portfolio yield, one must identify the specific form of portfolio duration and yield under

---

[7] Since the dy_{par} is multi-dimensional, dV_i/dy_{par} and dV_{port}/dy_{par} are gradients. However, linearity is maintained.

consideration. The derivative of D_{IRR} with respect to the portfolio's IRR is given by the analogous formula:

$$D_{\text{IRR}}^2 - C_{\text{IRR}}$$

where C_{IRR} is the convexity calculated directly from the portfolio's cash flows. However, there is no simple formula for the derivative of D_{mw} with respect to shifts in y_{mw} unless one restricts attention to parallel shifts in the yield curve. With parallel shifts in the yield curve, $dy_i = dy_{\text{IRR}} = dy_{mw}$. Here one can treat all of these yield differentials interchangeably, and the formula

$$D' = D^2 - C$$

will hold for all forms of portfolio duration.

CONCLUSION

When comparing portfolio and benchmark yields at the start of a given month, the traditional measure of yield employed is the market-value weighted yield. This provides a crude estimate of short-term expected returns under a simple "no change in yields" scenario. IRR is a measure of the long-term increase in portfolio wealth to be expected in a held-to-maturity context, but is problematic for portfolios with relatively smooth cash flow profiles over time. Portfolio IRR is most often used in applications such as dedication, in which a portfolio is purchased to match a set of liabilities. The highest IRR portfolio to match a given liability stream also has the property of matching the liabilities at the lowest present cost.

The closeness of fit of the dollar duration weighted average of security yields to portfolio IRR depends on security convexities and the cross-sectional variation in yield. This cross-sectional variation in yield is driven by credit spreads and the distribution of constituent securities across the yield curve. The closeness of fit of the market weighted average of security yields to portfolio IRR does not depend on the cross-sectional variation in yields. Instead, it is determined by the rate with which portfolio yields are expected to change as time passes. This effect is largely captured by the slope of the relevant parts of the yield curve and the time-structure of credit spreads. Of course, the fit also depends on the maturity distribution of the various bonds in the portfolio.

In addition, we demonstrated that (1) the market weighted average of security durations is the sensitivity of portfolio return to changes in the *dollar duration* weighted average of security yield changes, and (2) the dollar duration weighted average of security yields provides a first order approximation to portfolio IRR. We also provide a simple second order approximation of portfolio IRR based on the dollar duration weighted average of security yields.

APPENDIX: STOCHASTIC BOND YIELDS

In this appendix we derive the analog to equation (13) in the presence of stochastic bond yields. Actual interest rates processes are more complicated than those considered in the body of this article. Actual yields evolve stochastically over time. Let μ_i be the expected change in the yield of bond i at time t. Similarly, let σ_i be the volatility of the yield process for bond i at time t. The portfolio's expected return over the next instant in time is given by

Portfolio instantaneous expected return per unit time

$$= y_{\text{IRR}} - D_{\text{IRR}}\mu_{\text{IRR}} + \frac{1}{2}C_{\text{IRR}}\sigma_{\text{IRR}}^2 \tag{A1}$$

where μ_{IRR} is the instantaneous expected change in the portfolio's IRR (y_{IRR}). (This was denoted dy_{IRR} in the section that treated zero volatility interest rate environments.)

σ_{IRR}^2 is the instantaneous volatility of the portfolio's IRR, and C_{IRR} is

$$\frac{1}{V_{\text{port}}} \frac{d^2 V_{\text{port}}}{dy_{\text{IRR}}^2}$$

Equation (A1) replaces equation (3) under stochastic yields.

Similarly, the expected return on bond i over the next instant in time is[8]

Security i instantaneous expected return per unit time

$$= y_i - D_i\mu_i + \frac{1}{2}C_i\sigma_i^2 \tag{A2}$$

With stochastic yields, equation (5) is replaced by the following expression for the portfolio's expected return over the next instant in time:

---

[8] More formally, let the total change in the yield of security i, dy_i, come from the diffusion $dy_i = \mu_i dt + \sigma_i dz_i$ where μ_i and σ_i may be functions of time and current and past yields. The innovation driving the shock to the ith bond, dz_i, may have arbitrary correlation with the innovations driving the yield shocks of other bonds in the portfolio. Note that each bond yield is modeled directly, rather than the instantaneous risk-free rate and spread. However, since μ_i and σ_i are allowed to be arbitrary functions of time and yield history, this form is completely general (except for the exclusion of jump processes). Ito's lemma implies

$$\frac{dV_i}{dt} = \frac{\partial V_i}{\partial t} + \frac{\partial V_i}{\partial y_i}\frac{\partial y_i}{\partial t} + \frac{1}{2}\frac{\partial^2 V_i}{\partial y_i^2}\sigma_i^2$$

which results in

$$\frac{dV_i}{dt} = V_i y_i - V_i D_i\frac{\partial y_i}{\partial t} + \frac{1}{2}V_i C_i\sigma_i^2$$

Equation (A2) follows.

Portfolio instantaneous expected return per unit time

$$= \sum_i w_i y_i - \sum_i w_i D_i \mu_i + \sum_i w_i \frac{1}{2} C_i \sigma_i^2 \qquad \text{(A3)}$$

Let $C_{mw} = \Sigma_i w_i C_i$

C_{mw} is the market weighted average of the individual security convexities.

$$\text{Let } \sigma_{\$cvx}^2 = \frac{\sum_i w_i C_i \sigma_i^2}{C_{mw}}$$

$\sigma_{\$cvx}^2$ is the dollar convexity weighted average of the squared yield volatilities of the individual securities.

$$\text{Let } \mu_{\$dur} = \frac{\sum_i w_i D_i \mu_i}{D_{mw}}$$

$\mu_{\$dur}$ is the dollar duration weighted average of the expected yield changes of the portfolio's component securities.

Equation (A3) can be re-expressed as follows: the portfolio's expected return over the next instant in time is

Portfolio instantaneous expected return per unit time

$$= y_{mw} - D_{mw} \mu_{\$dur} + \frac{1}{2} C_{mw} \sigma_{\$cvx}^2 \qquad \text{(A4)}$$

Note that the market weighted average of security durations continues to provide the sensitivity of portfolio returns to changes in the dollar duration weighted average of the expected changes in the yields of the portfolio's component securities. Here the convexity correction involves multiplying the market weighted average of individual security convexities by the dollar convexity weighted average of the squared volatilities of the individual security yields.

By setting equations (A1) and (A4) equal to each other, we obtain

$$y_{mw} - y_{IRR} = (D_{mw} \mu_{\$dur} - D_{IRR} \sigma_{IRR}) + \frac{1}{2}(C_{IRR} \sigma_{IRR}^2 - C_{mw} \sigma_{\$cvx}^2) \quad \text{(A5)}$$

Equation (A5) replaces equation (13) in the presence of stochastic yields. Incorporating the effects of stochastic yields tends to increase the difference between the portfolio's IRR and the market weighted average yield. Due to diversification effects, unless all bonds in the portfolio have perfectly correlated yields, σ_{IRR}^2 will be less than the dollar duration weighted average value of σ_i^2. All else equal, the second term on the right hand side of equation (A5) will tend to be positive.

Challenges in the Credit Analysis of Emerging Market Corporate Bonds

Christopher Taylor
Director
Emerging Market Telecom/Media
Global High Yield Research
ING Barings

INTRODUCTION

Emerging market corporate bonds can be an attractive asset class. That is, they have the potential to provide investors with attractive risk-adjusted returns. However, the asset class also raises unique challenges which require a disciplined approach to manage.

APPROACHES TO INVESTING IN EMERGING MARKET CORPORATES

There traditionally have been two approaches to investing in emerging market corporate bonds: top-down and bottom-up. Neither approach is necessarily contradictory or mutually exclusive. However, in practice they are often treated as such. The top-down approach essentially treats investing in corporates as "sovereign-plus." The bottom-up approach can treat emerging market corporate bonds as "U.S. credits-plus." Investors have become more sophisticated in recent years — to a large extent due to the recurrent crises in Mexico, Asia, Russia, and Brazil, and the consequent massive sell-offs throughout Emerging Markets. But, there are still many inefficiencies. We believe that investing in emerging market corporate bonds can be most profitably done utilizing techniques practiced for high-yield bonds, but the macro-environment and micro-factors unique to individual countries must be taken into account. In other words, a matrix approach is needed.

Prior to the Mexican crisis in 1995, little attention was paid to corporate fundamentals. Most investment was "name lending" — the local blue chips would get loans at rates slightly above sovereign bonds. Hence the treatment of emerging market corporates as "sovereign-plus." Often this was justified since many of these blue-chips had credit ratios and characteristics which in the United States would have earned them investment-grade ranking. However, several times these investment decisions were made based on name and reputation, rather than sound credit decisions, and investors got stuck with low quality bonds.

Conversely, many investors bought these names based on their strong credit ratios and attractive yields relative to U.S. names with similar ratios. However, comparing ratios across borders obscures as much as it reveals. Investors should pay close attention to ratios and other credit statistics. Investors should also adjust for the fact that (1) emerging markets are inherently more volatile (thus ratios should be stronger), (2) inflation accounting distorts results (especially when inflation is increasing), (3) accounting standards are less rigid in many emerging markets, (4) the legal system is less developed and reliable in many of these countries, (5) recessions tend to be more severe, and (6) governments tend to intervene (and support their companies) more.

These factors should not deter investors from acquiring these bonds. We believe that investors are usually adequately compensated for these risks, considering the high yield on most emerging market corporates. However, it does mean that investors should be aware of these risks, and more to the point, on how to manage them.

Each subsequent crisis (Asia in 1997, Russia and Brazil a year thereafter) has brought more discipline to emerging market corporate bonds. As investors gain more experience, they have adjusted their approach to the asset class. Underwriting standards have improved significantly.[1]

EMERGING MARKET CREDITS VERSUS U.S. CREDITS WITH SAME RATING

In theory a BB rated emerging market bond should have the same default risk as a BB U.S. bond. In other words, the BB corporate rating should already incorporate sovereign risk. Many of the emerging market corporates that we look at have solid investment grade ratios for U.S. standards. But, of course, these issuers are not based in the United States, they are located in a region where the economic and political environments are more volatile. This is why these issuers are rated BB rather than investment grade. However, to argue that a BB company should carry a premium relative to U.S. BB credits is discounting twice, since the BB rating already incorporates a penalty for sovereign risk! The solid investment grade ratios are what enabled these companies to survive even a drastic downturn such as occurred in Mexico and Argentina in 1995, or in Brazil and Argentina during 1999.

---

[1] See, for example, Christopher Taylor, "Suggested Guidelines for New Issuance," *Global High Yield Research*, ING Barings, 2000.

Asian corporates are different, since prior to the Thailand collapse they were by-and-large not constrained by the sovereign ceiling. They also had more access to local and commercial bank credit than Latin corporates traditionally had. Consequently, Asian corporates as a general rule had higher leverage, higher levels of short-term debt (i.e., more potential for liquidity problems), and less transparent accounting. Thus, despite their higher ratings, they encountered more problems when their economies collapsed.

Most companies in Latin America have proven that they can survive even drastic macro-economic turbulence. With an economic decline and liquidity squeeze equivalent to what the U.S. experienced during the 1930s, a large majority of these companies managed to survive. We doubt that many U.S. single-B or even double-B companies would have been able to survive a downturn and liquidity squeeze so severe. To be sure, there were defaults in Latin America in the past several years. But, considering the extent of the regions economic volatility, the percentage is relatively low.

Of course, credit risk is not the only factor influencing bond pricing. Trading risk (e.g., volatility and liquidity) is another significant variable. Latin bonds are inherently more volatile and less liquid than U.S. high-yield bonds. Ironically, the latest market crisis comes out of the United States, not emerging markets. Since the 2000 NASDAQ crash, emerging market corporate bonds have taken a significant hit, along with U.S. high-yield bonds. Investors in emerging market corporate bonds should be aware that their asset class suffers whenever any other asset class sneezes. This is true even when their own fundamentals — corporate or sovereign — are relatively strong.

Investors should ensure that they are adequately compensated for this extra trading and liquidity risk, even when they believe default risk is already priced into the assets. A good approach might be to compare yields on a basket of similarly rated U.S. and emerging market corporates. Whenever spreads for the latter come too close to the former (say within 100 to 200 basis points), one might wish to reduce exposure. This does not always guarantee good results. For example, during 2000, single-B U.S. corporates underperformed similar Latin corporates, since the former had more speculative, venture capital-like characteristics. However, by and large Latin corporates outperform their U.S. counterparts in bull markets and underperform in bear markets. But, we emphasize that this is because of trading and liquidity risk, not default risk.

TIERING THE CREDIT

Often, trading in emerging market bonds — especially those whose ownership in concentrated with locally based investors — is based on a company's local reputation, as opposed to credit fundamentals. But, a blue chip reputation and credit strength may or may not be related. Instead, we recommend that investors rank credits in three categories based on standard credit risk measures (e.g., cash flow ratios, risk and volatility of industry, size of company, competence of management, etc.). Of course, many of the perceived blue chips will still be top tier credits if ranked by such a methodology — but not always. Short-term, companies which are perceived locally to be blue chips will probably trade better than those which have top-tier characteristics according to U.S.-style methodologies.

But in the end credit fundamentals are usually the determining factor in whether a bond is repaid. Especially now that many emerging markets are opening up to competition and slaying the inflation dragon, perception will sooner or later catch up with reality. In the past, many blue chips became big, or remained big, not because of strong management. Instead, it was because of their political connections or high import barriers, and/or their ability to export thanks to high inflation and weak currencies, and/or because competitors could not emerge due to limited access to capital or lack of political connections. However, in a more stable environment with a healthier currency and better access to capital and lower import barriers and privatization, new competitors are emerging and management competence becomes the key variable.

In countries where reform has been underway for some time now, many of the blue chips whose managements were incapable of dealing with the new environment have already been eliminated. In other countries, there is still a significant divergence between companies which are locally viewed as blue chips and those that are top-tier credits based on more relevant credit guidelines. We caution that short-term U.S. investors could get frustrated since a significant part of emerging market trading is still dominated by "name trading." However, most market participants have become more sophisticated and are more likely to do thorough credit analysis. Over time, we continue to believe that the divergence between perception and credit reality will continue to close, and thus investors who today do their credit homework should outperform those who buy based on name trading.

Tier one credits are those that are constrained by the sovereign ceiling, meaning those that would be solid investment grade if they were located in a more stable environment. Tier two credits are not necessarily constrained by the sovereign ceiling. If they were located in a typical OECD country they would probably be BB or possibly borderline investment grade. Tier two credits tend to have some significant credit issues which bear watching, but not significant enough to cause a serious risk of default. Tier three credits, in contrast, have significant default and/or rescheduling risk. These credits should have a sizable risk premium, since in emerging markets creditors usually have little recourse under local law in the event of default and local courts are somewhat inefficient.

JUDGING COMPANIES BY INFORMATION PROVIDED

Many investors are turned off from investing in emerging market corporate bonds by the historically pathetic levels of disclosure these companies provided. There are still some companies which treat investors shabbily. (Often, not coinciden-tally, these companies are perceived blue chips whose credit fundamentals do not measure up to market perception.) However, we believe that in general the level of disclosure continues to improve significantly. Many emerging market compa-nies — especially the better managed ones — have learned to treat investors as a key constituency, rather than a nuisance to be tolerated. On the other hand, there are still quite a few poorly managed companies that do not provide their investors with even minimum acceptable information flow.

We believe that investors should demand a healthy premium for the bonds of companies which do not service their investors' legitimate information require-ments properly. Lack of information flow and poor credit risk and weak manage-ment often go hand in hand. These companies are usually riskier, since foreign investors are usually the last to learn of any bad news. Also, the lack of information and bad news are usually correlated, since most companies would be more than happy to spread any good news. An unwillingness to open up to investors is often an indication of a traditional-type management which is incapable of changing with the times. And even if these uninformative issuers were good credits, we have learned that the bonds of companies which do provide good information to inves-tors usually hold up better in a bear market and rebound faster in any recovery.

We have developed several rules of thumb. First, avoid private compa-nies (i.e., ones that don't report to a stock exchange) unless their bonds are regis-tered with the SEC and they have a New York-based investor relations firm. With private companies it becomes very difficult to get hold of financial results once they take a turn for the worse. Private company bonds virtually always lag other-wise equivalent-risk bonds. Also, secondary trading tends to be very illiquid, especially in bear markets.

Second, demand a premium for issuers that do not have a New York-based investor relations agency. Usually those companies which are not prepared to incur the expenses of an investor relations agency also have an unconstructive view towards investors. Often there is a close correlation between managements which treat investors as an important constituency (and thus usually have better performing bonds), and those which have the skill set needed to compete in a liberalized and rapidly changing economic environment. We should emphasize that there are several emerging market issuers which have excellent investor relations programs without having a New York-based agency supporting them, but they are the exceptions.

Third, demand a premium for companies which do not file U.S. generally accepted accounting principles (GAAP), or at the least an annual U.S. GAAP rec-onciliation. In other words, demand a premium for 144A bonds over SEC-regis-tered bonds. We are not necessarily saying that other GAAP's are less conservative. Indeed, we can point to examples where U.S. GAAP is too liberal (e.g., depreciation allowances) or too cumbersome (e.g., deferred taxes). How-ever, at least U.S. GAAP is the devil the greatest number of investors know. Also, it seems to be the most comprehensive and the most thorough in disclosure.

We can think of several instances where a good cash flow company turned into a marginal one when statements were converted into U.S. GAAP — maybe because a "small" subsidiary or some parent company operations had to be consolidated or because a new policy on accounts receivable or inventory obsolescence or revenues accrual had to be recognized. Essentially what we're saying is that it is easier to have a higher degree of confidence in the companies which report under U.S. GAAP. Full U.S. GAAP numbers would be ideal, but an annual reconciliation is acceptable. Often companies once they have to show a reconciliation will change their local-GAAP policies so as to avoid too large a discrepancy between the two standards.

Nonetheless, we believe that investors should always check the reconciliation, just to understand the differences in what is reported quarterly (local GAAP) and what is filed at year-end with the SEC (U.S. GAAP). If the differences are only tax-related or (non-cash) depreciation and amortization, one can have a high degree of confidence in quarterly numbers. If the differences are more substantial, investors should question management more thoroughly and take quarterly results with a grain of salt.

Also, for a new issue the standards of due diligence and disclosure in the prospectus are higher in an SEC-registered issue than in a 144A. We find that in most instances disclosure in 144A prospectuses is relatively limited. On the other hand, SEC-registered deals require a legal opinion regarding adequate disclosure, which forces the underwriter (and issuer) to do a more thorough job in due diligence and disclosure. Therefore, we think investors should demand an adequate premium for 144A issues compared to SEC-registered deals. Of course, this premium should vary according to credit risk. If the issuer has high-quality credit ratios, it should be very small. On the other hand, for high-risk credits this premium should be substantial.

In Asia disclosure and transparency have improved since their crisis a few years ago. Nonetheless, by and large accounting standards remain significantly below par and much worse than Latin practices. Ironically, the more blue-chip-like a company is perceived to be, the worse its transparency is likely to be. We recommend that investors think twice before investing in non-U.S. GAAP Asian companies. If one decides to do so, pay close attention to discover whether any accounting tricks are being played. For example, many issuers are notorious for not consolidating heavily indebted subsidiaries, or disclosing significant guarantees or other contingent exposure to liability.

DEBT STRUCTURE MATTERS: COVENANTS

Historically many Eurobonds were poorly structured, although admittedly this has improved in recent years. In the past, if there were covenants at all, they were usually a maintenance ratio such as debt/capital. These ratios are not very meaningful even in the United States (after all, debt is repaid with cash, not with a capital ratio), but especially not in emerging markets where underdeveloped legal rules and/or inefficient local court systems make enforcement and/or recourse if these covenants are violated rather difficult. We can think of several instances where emerging market companies violated their debt/capital covenants and went right on paying dividends or making acquisitions. The whole idea of covenants is to give investors leverage if things don't go as planned. Also, capital-based maintenance covenants give companies an incentive to incur off-balance-sheet debt or inflate their asset values. Since such debt is often secured and/or effectively has first claim on cash flows, these covenants effectively work against the interest of bondholders rather than protecting them.

These issues do not matter so much for blue chips with strong financial ratios (but not perceived blue chips with poor credit ratios). For top-tier credits, good bond structuring is relatively unimportant (assuming the credit does not deteriorate while the bonds are outstanding!). However, for companies with weak ratios, emerging market investors should in our opinion pay more attention to structure, since this can have a significant impact in how a credit develops. Usually if an investor buys a second tier bond it is with the hope that the story will improve, or, if the yield is sufficiently attractive, that the story will stabilize. A well-structured bond should give investors comfort that management won't take actions to worsen the credit, and gives investors leverage to prevent management from doing so. Instead, we have seen perceived blue chips with negative cash flow and an acquisition track record issue bonds without any covenants at all. Investors have only themselves to blame if these deals blow up.

The key credit variables revolve around cash flow ratios. There is plenty of room for disagreement as to which particular ratio is best, but conceptually most analysts agree that some form of ratios which measure cash flow earnings relative to fixed cash payments (e.g., EBITDA/Interest or debt/EBITDA) provide the best measurement of credit risk. (In contrast, a capital-based ratio solely measures on-balance-sheet debt relative to historical investments — in other words, it is a backwards looking ratio). Thus, it follows that if one wants to create a covenant which best protects creditors, it should be a cash flow-based ratio. Also, although one can never create a forward-looking ratio, at least one can ensure that a ratio is as current as possible by requiring calculations on a pro forma basis. Most importantly, we believe that investors should require covenants that measure all fixed calls on cash flow, including off balance-sheet debt and mandatory preferred. Finally, any covenants should be self-enforcing, which is crucial in a region where legal recourse is difficult.

The high-yield market has over the years developed effective covenants. It has learned how to tie management's hands if it doesn't meet its projections, without this adversely affecting bondholders or requiring major legal expenses by creditors. This is done by means of comprehensive "incurrence" tests. Some form of cash flow based ratio is chosen to measure management's projections of cash flow relative to future fixed obligations, with some margin for error. Essentially, management can do whatever it wishes, but if it wants to borrow or pay dividends or buy back stock or upstream money to its parent it must meet this ratio (on a pro forma basis).

For example, a debt/EBITDA incurrence test in an issuer's covenant package is 4 times. On a historical basis the company has 3 times debt relative to EBITDA, but if management wanted to borrow more (e.g., to pay dividends) it would have to calculate the ratio based on the new debt level. It could incur as much debt as it wanted so long as the ratio remained below 4 times (usually known as "the ability to incur $1 of additional debt under the incurrence test"). This offers investors effective assurance that management's actions won't cause credit ratios to deteriorate beyond a certain point. If properly drawn, this clause makes it very difficult for management to borrow extra money for acquisitions or to pay dividends, etc.

Of course, general business risks could cause a credit deterioration, but no covenant can protect against such developments. Indeed, a maintenance covenant can worsen the situation by forcing management to focus on playing games (e.g., accounting tricks or off-balance-sheet liabilities) to avoid violating the covenant at the very time when they should be focusing on improving the business fundamentals.

Just as important for emerging market investors, where the legal system is not necessarily a reliable ally, incurrence covenants are to some extent self-enforcing. No bank will lend money or no board will declare dividends if that very act is a violation of the covenants. Under maintenance covenants, no such self-policing mechanism exists. The company is already in violation, so why shouldn't the board go ahead with other plans (e.g., pay dividends or pursue acquisitions), even if those cause further deterioration?

DEBT STRUCTURE MATTERS: CRITICAL ROLE OF MATURITY PROFILE

One lesson we should have learned from the recurring crises in emerging markets is that short-term debt is bad. Especially commercial paper proved itself to be a rather fickle source of finance for companies, while commercial bank debt could only be rolled over with difficulty — not to mention with significantly higher interest rates. We are encouraged that many emerging market firms have improved their debt profile and retired shorter term debt, even if it cost them a few hundred basis points extra. Even in the United States, commercial paper is usually not considered an appropriate and reliable source of capital for non-investment grade companies. Certainly in emerging markets, where capital availability is even more volatile, commercial paper must definitely be an inappropriate form of financing. It usually disappears just when it is needed most (i.e., during a major crisis).

We believe that those issuers which still use high-risk short-term debt (in particular, commercial paper) should probably be avoided, even if other credit fundamentals appear sound. A willingness to tolerate a risky level of short-term debt says something about management, and in emerging markets we prefer to invest in well-managed companies. Most emerging markets have underdeveloped lending systems, with only short-tenor debt available. This debt usually automatically rolls over, becoming effectively long-term debt ("evergreen"). Thus, we can understand how traditional management was comfortable with high levels of short-term debt. However, this automatic "evergreen" does not apply to foreign debt, where refinancing risk is significant. Companies which rely on significant amounts of short-term debt should be avoided.

Companies with bad ratios but no immediate refinancing requirements can usually muddle through for a while. In contrast, during crises companies with stronger financial ratios but steep refinancing requirements can be pushed under. After all, a default is not caused by unfavorable financial ratios (unless maintenance covenants trip them up), but rather by an inability to pay debt obligations. Thus, if there are no obligations coming due for a long time, the risk of default is reduced significantly, no matter how bad the ratios are in the interim. Debt structure (i.e., upcoming debt maturities) is the most important credit variable in emerging markets, even more so than cash flow ratios.

A closely related issue is debt arbitrage. Many emerging market companies borrow in U.S. dollars to avoid steep local interest rates. The flip side of these high local rates is good returns on cash deposits. Thus, many companies over-borrow hard currency and invest it in local instruments. During the good times this is a profitable strategy, but when a crisis hit the chickens can come home to roost. We simply do not like companies which engage in such arbitrage. Not only is it risky when there are devaluations, it also sends some negative signals about management. It says that management likes to gamble, and also to some extent that management does not see many profitable investment opportunities in its core business. If management's core businesses were strong, it wouldn't be wasting its energy on non-core activities such as financial arbitrage, trying to boost short-term profitability.

BREACHING THE SOVEREIGN CEILING

As a general rule, we believe that virtually all emerging market corporates should trade at a premium to their sovereign bonds. However, there can be a few exceptions. In Argentina several of the top tier credits trade tighter than Argentine sovereign bonds. This might be partly due to the strong fundamentals of Argentine corporates and in several instances their ownership by strong foreign parents. But, these conditions can also apply to other countries. The main reason we are comfortable with Argentine corporates trading through the sovereign is due to

Argentina's currency board. The currency board makes exchange controls and/or restrictions less likely; therefore the theory behind the sovereign ceiling argument becomes less relevant.

The sovereign ceiling argument is essentially one of structural subordination. Simplistically, it says that if the sovereign needs foreign exchange it will have first call on hard currency, to the detriment of other creditors with hard currency debt such as corporates. Therefore, corporates should always carry a risk premium relative to sovereigns. (This is another reason why we do not like corporates with significant amounts of hard currency short-term debt or commercial paper: the sovereign is more likely to restrict access to foreign currencies for short-term obligations than it is for repayment of long-term debt, especially bonds.) In most countries the structural subordination argument is valid. With a currency board, however, the government essentially removes its first call on hard currency and therefore corporates are no longer structurally subordinated. The central bank is not "lender of last resort" to the government, and therefore the government no longer has a superior status structurally.

Of course, one should always be cautious about government risk. Currency boards were created by politicians and thus can be abolished by them. Therefore, one should focus carefully on the longevity of the currency board and its popular support. If one contracts with an insurance company in Bermuda or buys a mutual fund in the Bahamas — both of which have currency boards — sovereign risk is hardly an issue. This analyst does not even know what the economic or political risk in either country is, but that proves our point. If one is confident that a currency board will remain in place, local political and economic risk become almost irrelevant to the credit story.

Of course, one is less secure in Argentina because the currency board has been in place for only a few years while in Bermuda and the Bahamas there has been at least half a century of confidence building. Nineteenth century Latin America has plenty of examples of currency boards being abolished and/or manipulated once the going got tough. Therefore, one should always be more skeptical about Argentina than one would be in small Caribbean islands with a different legal and political tradition. However, we believe that the 1995 and 1999 crises proved that the currency board has solid across-the-board popular support in Argentina. Because of this, we remain reasonably confident that for the foreseeable future — or at least until most of the corporate Eurobonds which we cover have been safely retired — the currency board will remain in place. Thus, for very strong local blue chips there is justification for their trading through the sovereign ceiling. We note that S&P also accepted this argument and rates several companies' credit ratings to higher than that of the sovereign. Having said that, even in Argentina sovereign risk remains a factor to be considered.

As a general rule, any time a corporate trades tight to a sovereign bond, the risk-reward equation goes against the corporate. At best, the corporate will slightly outperform the sovereign, assuming market sentiment remains bullish. At worst, if market sentiment sours, the corporate will significantly widen against the sovereign. Thus, a good rule of thumb remains to sell if spreads become too tight to the sovereign. Even for those selected corporates where investors are comfortable that trading very tight to — or even inside — the sovereign is justified (e.g., in Argentina or those with strongly committed multinational parents), we recommend that investors pay close attention to historical spread levels. Only if they are rich relative to historical levels are they likely to offer attractive risk-adjusted returns.

STABILITY OF A COUNTRY'S CURRENCY

All other things being equal, we look for countries with historically stable currencies. We usually disregard whether the currency is short-term overvalued or undervalued, since in the long run purchasing power parity usually holds. According to this theory, inflation usually catches up with a devaluation, thus in the longer-term arbitrage risk (borrowing in hard currency, revenues in local currency) is relatively modest. However, countries with volatile currencies usually have more risk of dysfunctional macro-economic policies. In the short term these policies may actually benefit certain corporates (e.g., economic stimulation benefits companies which sell to the domestic market, while weak currencies benefit exporters and producers — usually commodities — whose prices are dollarised). However, long term these policies increase cash flow volatility and cost of capital (or even reduce access to capital) and thus credit risk. Since by their very nature corporate bonds are long-term instruments, this is what matters.

For example, in Mexico inflation has already largely eroded the (alleged) short-term advantage of the December 1994 devaluation. In the interim, however, the government was forced to incur sharply higher interest rates and thus a severe recession in order to stem the resultant capital flight and inflation (which almost always follow devaluations). Thus, over a 2-year timeframe the currency arbitrage risk was minimal (inflation and thus unit prices caught up with the devaluation), but in the interim sales volumes collapsed and cost of capital skyrocketed. For some time this severely impacted some of the issuers' creditworthiness, even the exporters which were the alleged beneficiaries of the devaluation. Worse, capital markets were shut to new issuance, thus sharply increasing refinancing risk.

Our point is that for long-term bonds the currency mismatch (between local currency revenues and hard-currency borrowing) is not a major concern *per se*, since purchasing power parity usually holds (barring extreme exchange and price controls). However, countries with unstable currencies tend to have unstable macro-economic performances as well, and these are a major negative from a corporate credit perspective. One reason we are quite comfortable with Mexico at present is because since the devaluation debacle the government has learned its lesson and places a heavy emphasis on currency stability and avoids imbalances in the underlying macro economic fundamentals. In other words, the central bank has the upper hand over the economic growth advocates, and therefore economic growth — albeit slower at first — has become more stable and sustainable. Since stability and sustainability of cash flows (as opposed to short-term growth) are key credit variables for corporate bonds, conservative monetary policies are a significant positive.

We believe that one reason Argentine corporate bonds traditionally trade tight relative to sovereign bonds is because with the currency board, currency instability has been all but eliminated. Thus, the strength or weakness of the local currency is no longer a factor in corporate earnings, which makes them more predictable. Argentina has gone one step further and abolished inflation accounting (low inflation is fundamentally associated with a stable currency). This, of course, enhances the quality and reliability of earnings which should further reduce the risk premium required.

INFLATION ACCOUNTING

Inflation accounting makes it more difficult to truly understand what is going on in a company. Given that we all have time pressures, we prefer to invest in companies where we can easily and quickly understand what is going on. Also, given the complexities of inflation accounting, one is never quite certain whether one correctly understood what the numbers said. When we present an investment idea to investors, we prefer to be confident that we understand it ourselves; inflation accounting makes us somewhat less likely to stick out our necks. One rule of thumb we have developed is to disbelieve any numbers where inflation is above 50%, unless they have been translated into hard currency at the time of the transaction.

In some Eastern European and Middle Eastern countries, the income and cash flow statements are not restated, only the balance sheet. We find this methodology preferable to using comprehensive restatements as used in some Latin American countries. In our opinion the income statement is reasonably reliable so long inflation is modest; however, even with around 20% inflation the cash flow statement is distorted so as to make it almost meaningless.

In Argentina, inflation accounting was abolished in 1995. In our opinion, this justifies a lower premium for their corporate bonds since we can easily and better understand the numbers, and thus are less likely to get caught by surprise. In Brazil, inflation accounting was abolished in 1996, but unfortunately most companies continue to use it. Worse, most companies do not separately disclose the inflation and devaluation component of their interest expense, making it virtually impossible to calculate true interest expense. Since interest expense is a key variable in determining a company's credit risk, this is a negative for which investors should demand a significant premium.

In Mexico, inflation accounting still reigns with full force. Fortunately, however, inflation has come down significantly since the 1995 devaluation debacle. A big positive for Mexican corporates is their stock exchange's electronic database for reporting earnings. This database requires all Mexican companies to report relatively quickly (5 weeks after each quarter end, and 9 weeks after year end), and in relatively good detail. We believe this good level of disclosure helped many investors get comfortable with Mexican credits and helped in the relatively rapid rebound after the devaluation debacle. If Mexican reporting had been as slow as in Argentina or as uninformative and difficult to collect as in Brazil, we doubt many investors would have been willing to reenter the Mexican corporate sector after the devaluation — certainly not as rapidly as they did other countries.

For many emerging market credits, a key earnings variable is the strength of the local currency. Now that inflation in most countries is coming under control, the many companies which were able to compete based on their weak currency will have to start competing based on their core competencies. Many will not be able to not compete in this environment, and we believe investors should avoid these names altogether since their margins will only deteriorate. A good rule of thumb we have learned is to avoid companies which complain about the strength of the currency and loudly call for a devaluation, rather than proactively investing or restructuring so that they can compete regardless of the strength of their currency. Proactive companies will survive in the longer term (even if shorter term they have to borrow to finance these investments).

Also, with inflation coming down rapidly (which is directly related to a stable currency), cost control becomes a more important issue (e.g., as salaries rise to catch up with inflation), and operating margins no longer benefit from the inventory effect (i.e., inventory bought at lower prices results in lower cost of goods sold and better margins after the finished unit is sold at higher prices). This effects everyone's margins. Thus, investors should bet on companies which are focused on operating margins and results, not just top-line (sales) growth. We can think of several examples of companies which tried to grow (or acquire) their way out of uncompetitive cost structures. They almost always fail.

EXPORTERS VERSUS DOMESTICS

For most countries, the corporate sector (and the economies, for that matter) can essentially be broken into two sectors: the dollarized sector and the non-tradeable sector. Roughly, in most Latin countries, a third to a half of the companies (and of the economy) is dollarized. In export-oriented countries the percentage may be higher. In essence, producers in this sector base their prices on U.S. prices and/or international commodities. Thus, even though they may sell domestically and invoice in local currencies, they are reasonably hedged if they borrow in hard currencies. Products whose prices are dollarized include virtually all commodities such as mining products, chemicals, and paper, as well as internationally traded products such as autoparts, glass, electrical equipment, and transportation services (e.g., shipping, airlines).

Note that this definition of "dollarized" includes a broader sector than just exports. The key is whether a producer has the option to export. For example, a paper or packaging producer may sell virtually all of its output domestically. However, if domestic prices were too low relative to international prices it could always shift sales abroad. Thus it has pricing power domestically, and therefore can tie its prices to international rates. Unless the government imposes major price controls (always a risk after devaluations), these companies are relatively hedged against devaluations.

The dollarized sector is usually the biggest beneficiary from devaluations or weak currencies in general. In dollar terms there would not be much change in their revenues, but their local currency-based costs decline. (Of course, what they gain in better margins they usually lose in higher cost of capital and lower domestic volumes, but that's another story.) With stable currencies, as a general rule, one can expect dollarized producers to see tighter margins. In countries which have had a stable currency for a longer time, most vulnerable producers have already been eliminated.

In other countries, however, this weeding out process has only just begun. Once a currency strengthens, even the strongest producers will see a tightening of margins. Of course, on the positive side, the better run companies will be able to lower their cost of capital and extend their debt maturities. Countries with high inflation and volatile currencies, companies find it usually difficult to get financing beyond one year, and even then at high rates. To a large extent, the lower cost of and easier access to financing offsets the margin pressure.

However, the uncompetitive firms (and their unions) usually put heavy political pressure on the government to devalue (or adopt economic policies which in the end will cause a devaluation). Also, one harsh side effect of this necessary restructuring is unemployment, which puts political pressure on the government to reflate the economy (which almost inevitably causes devaluation). All these pressures increase the risks for all of the country's issuers, even the strong ones, until the transition process is several years old and these uncompetitive firms have been restructured or eliminated.

Assuming unchanged international commodity prices, revenues in dollar terms for these dollarized companies should be stable despite local currency instability. However, until inflation and interest rates decline to international levels, inflation and high real interest rates will continue to increase local currency-based borrowing costs. Thus, until the currency and inflation are totally stable, the strength (or weakness) of the currency and trends in inflation will remain key variables in companies' quarterly earnings and debt coverage ratios. Since this adds an extra element of instability and uncertainty — and thus risk — to companies' earnings, investors should ask for a risk premium for issuers in inflationary countries or those with volatile currencies.

Negative trends on margins due to strong currencies can to some extent be offset if these companies can sell more value-added products domestically. Companies tend to export very commoditized products, but locally sell more customized products. As a general rule, domestic sales tend to have more value added and thus better margins. For instance, a paper producer might export standardized paper rolls but for domestic customers it may cut and/or coat the paper, thus increasing proceeds per ton by several hundred dollars. With more stable currencies and lower inflation often comes more confidence and higher disposable income, and thus a stronger domestic economy and more sales opportunities.

In addition, exports have higher transportation costs and generally command a somewhat lower price in the international market than locally due to the absence of tariff protection. (Although tariffs in the third world are declining, they are often still sizable.) As a very general rule, however, we do not believe that the higher margin domestic sales fully offset the negative impact of the stronger currencies on margins for dollarized companies, although there are exceptions to prove our rule. The key is to do one's credit homework to thoroughly understand how each company is impacted by stronger currency and declining inflation on the one hand, yet benefits from stronger domestic spending and better access to capital markets on the other. Focus on long-term trends, not quarter-to-quarter changes.

REGULATORY RISK

A final word of caution when investing in bonds of companies dependent on the domestic sector, especially utilities: regulatory risk. Of course, this risk that concerns us is present in the United States and European utilities and telecommunication companies. Instead, it is the process. In the United States, no matter how antiquated and cumbersome utility regulations may be, at least there is a clearly defined process which enables all to know how to participate and ensures some level of fairness. In contrast, it seems at times that the process in several emerging market countries is somewhat opaque and may be arbitrary. Sometimes local companies' political clout can be a key variable in this process.

For example, a permitted price increase is "waived by consent" in order to help the government's inflation control program. Fortunately, most utilities with bonds outstanding in emerging markets have strong coverage ratios, so these events only have a modest credit impact. However, for the few marginal utilities investors should certainly demand a premium to offset this risk. Unless a utility has strong support from an investment grade parent (or is sovereign owned), investors should always demand a reasonable risk premium compared to sovereign bonds to offset regulatory risk. This is a risk factor investors should get comfortable with, for it is entirely possible that all of the sudden a significantly different regulatory regime has been imposed with little or no warning. To be fair many emerging markets seem to have learned that this scares off investors and are trying to amend their ways.

SUMMARY

We believe that investors who use the skills gained in analyzing U.S. credits (bottom-up) can make significant risk-adjusted returns in emerging markets, since they understand how to analyze cash flows. This has not traditionally been a common skill in emerging markets, where top-down analysis has been the traditional approach. However, we have raised the above issues in this chapter since there are also many factors unique to emerging markets, which sometimes we see U.S. investors not taking into account. Our point is that one should use high-yield style credit skills, but one should also be prepared for the unexpected. Do not assume that a Brazilian utility is just like a U.S. utility, but understand the differences as well. When all is said and then, however, use high-yield style disciplines. If you cannot get good information from management or get a good grip on cash flow, stay away from the bond altogether. On the other hand, if management is modern and informative, and helps you get comfortable with (which in our mind is usually synonymous with understanding) the risk, you can increase the probability of higher risk-adjusted returns.

Debt Covenants: Applications in Emerging Markets

Allen Vine
First Vice President
Merrill Lynch & Co.

David Sohnen
Assistant Vice President
Merrill Lynch & Co.

INTRODUCTION

The intense turmoil in global financial markets in the fall of 1998 forced a review of many long-standing investment concepts, changed trading practices of many investment houses, and commenced a search by the financial community for less volatile ways to make money. In hindsight, the events of 1998 are increasingly viewed as inevitable given the unknown risks of new sovereign and corporate issuers, the sharp increase in the speed of capital flows, and the profound changes in the investor base. At the same time, little in terms of new analytical tools has emerged to deal with the new challenges.

It is not clear whether new analytic techniques can be developed that could encompass the complexity of the modern financial markets. Sovereign risk, technical flows, and other key market drivers appear as inscrutable today as ever. Yet, the pressure to outperform has remained. The question now is what mechanisms can investors use to protect their capital while pursuing high yield opportunities?

One effective mechanism, standard in the U.S. high yield market but largely neglected in emerging markets, is the application of debt covenants. This article highlights how wider use of this tool can substantially enhance the safety of corporate investing, especially in the emerging markets, by forcing higher degrees of discipline on underwriters and transparency on issuers.

THE PURPOSE OF COVENANTS

Covenants are designed to protect creditors' access to cash flow and the underlying income-producing assets to service their loans by subjecting the issuer to certain restrictions. In the event of default, covenants delineate the seniority of asset claims. Covenants pertaining to a bond issue are generally included in the indenture — a formal contractual agreement between an issuer and bondholders (typically represented by a designated trustee) — where certain considerations, including protective provisions, redemption rights and call privileges, among others, are established.

By subjecting issuers to restrictive covenants, investors can achieve a higher degree of protection for their investment on the basis of the credit quality of issuers. Preventive measures, as opposed to reactive measures, can be particularly effective in markets where legal mechanisms make it difficult for creditors to enforce their rights. The issue of enforceability of claims is particularly relevant in emerging markets since, to date, there has been little precedent for bondholders being able to protect their rights through bankruptcy proceedings and liquidations.

Generally, covenants rely on tests to assure that an issuer maintains a certain level of credit quality. Incurrence covenants protect the interests of existing lenders by preventing a company from issuing additional debt if such issuance would violate certain predetermined covenants. For example, if a covenant allows maximum leverage of 5.0× and a new issuance of debt would cause leverage to rise above 5.0×, the issuer would not be allowed to sell additional debt.

Maintenance covenants require companies to remain within certain prescribed credit ratios. For example, if covenants require a minimum coverage ratio of 2.0×, and coverage slips to 1.8×, the company would typically be in default. If the debt were then accelerated, a bankruptcy court could assume control, provided that creditors do not accept consent offers by the company or a prepackaged bankruptcy-restructuring plan. In this manner, bondholders can demand repayment while the issuer is still generating positive cash flow, rather than wait for mounting operating losses to reduce the firm's value.

To be effective, covenants need to capture the essence of risks faced by debtholders. The risks include, but are not limited to, the following:

- Insufficient cash flow to cover interest.
- Insufficient liquidity to meet amortization requirements.
- Acquisition, merger, consolidation and asset transfer activities that adversely affect a company's cash generating ability.
- Adverse changes in the ownership structure.

Covenants need to warn creditors when these conditions may be arising and help protect investors when these conditions do occur. Some of the specific functions that covenants need to accomplish include:

- Deter aggressive use of leverage to the detriment of existing lenders.
- Trigger alarms while a company is still in a solid financial and/or operating position and allow bondholders greater recovery.
- Install further protection in the issues of weaker companies by securing sinking funds or prefunded interest payments.

Due to their relative safety, investment grade bonds generally include three basic covenants: (1) restrictions on debt, (2) restrictions on sale-leaseback transactions, and (3) consolidation, merger, and sales of assets.

High yield indentures usually include a majority of the main covenants and occasionally, other firm-specific covenants. This has been especially the case since the high yield market turmoil in the 1989-1991 period.

In emerging markets, corporate debt has been largely issued with limited sets of covenants, despite the repeated bouts of sharp market volatility and bondholder difficulties in enforcing claims. On a positive side, investors have made significant gains in securing greater transparency from emerging market issuers since 1995. The application of covenants can substantially enhance the usefulness of this hard-won transparency.

DEBT INDENTURES

The debt indenture is a legal document that imposes a number of restrictions, key among which involve an issuer's ability to raise additional debt and make distributions to shareholders. The indenture also details the execution, registration and delivery of the bonds, and the characteristics of the bond issue such as coupon rate, maturity, numbering and method of payment, among others.

Definitions of Covenants

Debt Incurrence and Limitation on Indebtedness
Debt incurrence and limitations on indebtedness provision limits a company's ability to incur additional debt unless there is sufficient cash flow to service all debt. Here, the interests of current bondholders are placed ahead of those of other potential creditors. As with other covenants, the limitation on indebtedness establishes an incurrence ratio. Usually, the covenant will specify a minimum coverage ratio, leverage and/or debt to total capitalization ratio (pro forma for the issuance of the new debt) before the company can incur additional indebtedness. In this instance, investors are concerned about coverage tests and the amount of cushion at the outset of the deal, the amount of subsidiary debt and preferred stock and subsidiary debt alternatives.

Limitations on Restricted Payments
Limitations on restricted payments covenant prevents the parent company and subsidiaries from distributing assets to junior creditors and equity holders before

senior creditors. Senior creditors have the first claim on a firm's assets in the event of a bankruptcy. Notably, senior creditors often try to avoid such proceedings, wherein their interests are renegotiated to reflect the interests of junior creditors and equity holders. As a result, the provision's principal purpose is to restrict stock repurchases, dividends, subordinated debt repurchases or early repayments, investments or guarantees of affiliate debt. The potential for default is monitored and limitations are established to mitigate the chance of such an event. If all the requirements are observed, the company will usually be able to make "restricted payments" of up to 50% of consolidated net income.

Restricted and Unrestricted Subsidiaries

By keeping subsidiaries "unrestricted," an issuer can grow its business outside the reach of covenants. In addition, a company can leverage such a subsidiary, but avoid consolidating its debt into debt totals used for incurrence or maintenance tests. Therefore, covenants restrict or limit payments to unrestricted subsidiaries. This covenant is often used to address joint ventures or foreign investments.

Limitations on Dividends and Other Payments

Limitations on dividends and other payments covenant prohibits or limits unannounced or unexpected dividends at both the parent and subsidiary levels. Without this protection, an issuer could decide to liquidate the company and divert cash flow to equity holders by paying out the entire proceeds as a special dividend to its stockholders. Also, the covenant may prevent the availability of subsidiary cash flow to pay parent company debt.

Net Worth Maintenance

Net worth maintenance provision requires the issuer to maintain a minimum level of net assets, or equity, as a cushion in the event of credit quality deterioration. Without a sufficient cushion, the company may be in default and will usually be required to repurchase outstanding debt at par plus accrued interest or at the applicable redemption price plus accrued interest. This maintenance covenant is generally tested at the end of each quarter on a rolling 6-month basis.

Limitations on Transactions with Affiliates

Limitations on transactions with affiliates indenture prevents self-dealing, and restricts the issuer from dealing with affiliates on a less than fair basis when it comes to the sale of assets, the terms of loans or the provision of products and services. The gauge is the "arm's length" measure which proposes a relatively equal bargaining position between contracting parties. The provision also restricts the issuer from engaging in business on a less than fair market value basis with stockholders who own more than 5% of the company's stock, unless the terms are approved by a majority of the "disinterested" members of the board of directors.

Limitations on Sale of Assets

Limitations on sale of assets provision prevents an issuer from selling assets, especially securitized assets, which would take away the security of current bondholders. In addition, the issuer promises not to sell assets outside the bondholders' claims for less than fair market value (the proceeds must be within 70% and 100% of fair market value) or for a certain percentage in cash (typically 75%). The key concern in this instance is that stripping of assets could leave the company as a shell, thereby leaving little if any value for creditors in a liquidation scenario.

Without this covenant, the issuer could sell the asset to an officer of the company or a newly created subsidiary that is not under the bondholders' jurisdiction, leaving subordinated bondholders with no security. Occasionally, a covenant on a senior debt issue will require that the company use a certain portion of proceeds from asset sales to retire senior debt, usually within one year.

Limitations on Sale-Leaseback Transactions

The company is limited in sale-leaseback transactions to leases with (1) a finite period, (2) renewable rights, and (3) unrestricted companies. A sale-leaseback to any wholly owned subsidiary is allowed as the assets of a subsidiary can be used to pay bondholders in the case of liquidation. If the subsidiary is wholly owned, bondholders need not share the proceeds with any other parties.

Limitations on Mergers, Consolidation or Transfer of Assets

A provision that restricts mergers, consolidations, and sales of all of an issuer's assets protects the bondholder against the impairment of the issuer's credit profile. Typically, mergers are forbidden unless (1) the company is the surviving entity, or the surviving entity is a U.S. or Canadian company that assumes the bond indenture, (2) the merger does not result in default, (3) the surviving entity's net worth is equal to or greater than the company's prior net worth, and (4) the company's pro forma interest coverage conforms to the covenant's minimum ratio.

Limitation on Liens

A limitation on liens covenant protects the relative seniority of income-producing assets. As a result, the company is forbidden to incur any liens (with specified exceptions), unless the notes are equally secured. This covenant typically applies to subordinated debt, but can apply to other types as well.

Negative Pledge

In a negative pledge the company promises not to pledge assets to secure a bond issue that have already been used to secure a currently outstanding issue.

Change of Control

Change of control provision protects creditors from a change in control (subject to a variety of definitions) by requiring the company to repurchase the bonds within 30 days from the change in control, usually at 101% of par plus accrued interest. The change in control is typically triggered following the purchase of control of the voting stock. If the company is unable to repurchase the entire bond issue within 30 days of a change in control, it would be in default.

Events of Default

Event of default provisions define the conditions under which the company would be in default. These include, among others: (1) delays of more than 30 days in paying interest on outstanding debt, (2) inability of the company to meet minimum ratios for more than 60 days, and (3) any legal action against the company that would disable it from repaying loans. If any one of these is violated, the trustee may declare the company in default and could accelerate the maturity of all notes to be paid immediately, so that all bondholders can receive equal payments.

Cross Default

A cross default clause states that if the company has defaulted on any material debt (usually defined as a dollar threshold level), all debt would be in default. In the event of a cross default, the trustee can accelerate the maturity of outstanding debt.

Other Issues Covered in Indentures

In addition to containing covenants, the indenture reviews the basic characteristics of the bond issue, including the items discussed below.

Optional Redemption

Optional redemption covenants related to optional redemption usually discuss the following:

- Length of the option's exercise period, usually four to five years.
- Call premium, often one-half the coupon or declining arithmetically to first par call.
- An irrevocable notice period of typically 30 days, only when the funds are readily available.

Puts Puts enable investors to demand repayment, usually three to five years after issuance. Brazilian issuers, for example, have widely sold putable bonds, as there are tax advantages in Brazil for bonds with maturities of at least eight years. Given limited investor demand for long-dated Brazilian corporate bonds, many investors were enticed with put options, which can shorten effective duration.

Equity Clawbacks Some indentures, particularly for technology or telecommunications issues, may offer equity clawbacks, usually at an issuer's discretion. This enables a company to purchase a part of the outstanding debt issue with proceeds of an equity offering. Key issues include the type of equity financing (initial public offering versus primary add-on or public versus private), the length of exercise period, the amount of principal that may be redeemed, and the call premium.

The theory behind this provision is that it enables the issuer to take advantage of equity proceeds to deleverage the credit, while at the same time benefiting bondholders by improving the capital structure of the issuer and presumably the trading levels of the outstanding bonds. Recently, provisions have become more standardized with the length of exercise period typically around three years, and the percentage to be retired in the 30% to 35% range. The provision is less common among deals smaller than $100 million as that level is often the minimum that assures secondary liquidity.

Sinking Fund, Excess Cash Flow Sweep In the 1980s, sinking funds were standard, although they have become less common lately, since bullet maturities afford issuers greater flexibility to direct cash flow to capital expenditures and working capital. An alternative to a sinking fund is an excess cash flow sweep, which is generally structured as an "offer to repurchase" and is used to reduce the average life to maturity. Excess cash flow sweeps and other mandatory redemptions enable investors to revisit their investment decisions.

BANKRUPTCY

In the event of default, bondholders typically attempt to quickly restructure the company's debt, even if it entails canceling large portions of existing debt, since full liquidation can take several years and involves substantial legal costs. Bondholders are usually forced to hold the bonds, unless specifically prevented from doing so by investment charters, as secondary markets demand at reasonable prices often disappears. If a company's business is viable and going concern value exceeds estimated liquidation value, investors can typically expect to receive a mix of new equity and new debt in a restructuring.

Forced Reorganization and Liquidation

If a company is in violation of covenants and shows unwillingness to address such violations, bondholders can take advantage of the remedies provided in their bond documentation. Most Eurobonds require between 25% and 51% of bondholders to act in concert to accelerate the maturity of the bonds.

When an out-of-court or prepackaged bankruptcy is not possible, the last alternative is to reorganize under local bankruptcy law. If a company defaults as a result of operations becoming permanently impaired as opposed to short-term liquidity problems, creditors can usually seek liquidation of the company. In emerging markets, bondholders can benefit by quickly approaching U.S. courts to limit issuers from giving local creditors priority treatment.

The seniority of claims can resemble the following:

- Workers receive up to one year's unpaid wages.
- The government collects payment of back taxes (in Mexico).
- Real estate mortgages, unless claims are unsecured.
- Senior secured creditors, usually banks.
- Senior bondholders.
- Junior bondholders.
- Equity holders (often receive nothing, as net worth is typically negative at this point).

Basics of Liquidation Analysis

Generally, the value of a firm's assets is the cash flow they generate and can be approximated by looking at appropriate cash flow multiples. This concept, however, implies that a company can exist as a going concern. If it can, then a firm's liquidation value can be separated into four parts, in order of percentage of value recovered:

- Cash and equivalents and accounts receivable.
- Concessions and/or brand names.
- Property, plant and equipment or subsidiaries.
- Equity value of future projects (backlog).

Not all of these items are appropriate for every case. Valuation of backlog is generally quite complicated — one must assume that the bankrupt company sells its backlog to a competitor or, as a junior partner, receives a fee from a joint venture — both difficult to estimate.

Bankruptcy Plays

Generally, investing in bankruptcies can offer substantial returns, given the high levels of risk. Occasionally, an issuer can emerge from bankruptcy in a stronger position or it can be acquired by a better-capitalized competitor. Sometimes, heavy selling can send bond prices below liquidation value or below the cash flow generating power of the company as a going concern, creating opportunities for bolder investors.

A company will generally be liquidated if the value of assets exceeds the cash flow they can generate. However, creditors seldom force companies into liquidation as bankruptcy costs are high and since the book value of assets is often overstated and proceeds of liquidations often fall short of total debt. Of the 1,096 bankruptcies in the U.S. between 1970 and 1990 that Professor Edward E. Altman studied,[1]

- 248 companies (22.6%) emerged as public companies.
- 199 companies (18.2%) emerged as private companies.
- 164 companies (15.0%) were liquidated.

---

[1] Edward I. Altman, *Corporate Financial Distress and Bankruptcy: Second Edition* (New York, NY: John Wiley & Sons, 1993), pp. 66-67.

- 72 companies (6.6%) were merged or acquired.
- 412 companies (37.6%) were in bankruptcy, but still in reorganization at the time of the study.

Even if all 412 companies that were still under reorganization were liquidated, 47.4% of the sample continued either on their own or as part of another corporation. However, applying the breakdown of the 684 companies that completed the bankruptcy process to those companies that were still in reorganization, 76.0% would have continued as public or private companies or were merged/acquired.

Complications in Emerging Markets

The degree of a country's integration in the world economy and local markets are among the key factors determining the extent to which creditors can recoup their money in case of the issuer's distress in emerging markets. Importantly, the defaults and reorganizations, which followed the Mexican Peso crisis in 1995, suggest that companies with assets in the U.S. and/or strong foreign owners have generated higher recovery values for investors compared to companies that had no such attributes.

Liquidation is seldom a feasible choice in emerging markets, where government and corporate contracts are often not fully enforceable and where local banks and creditors tend to get priority treatment. In addition, the difficulty in estimating recovery values and the risk that liquidation will be processed legally and fairly make bondholders lean towards reorganization and equitization of existing debt versus liquidation.

Also, a significant percentage of restructurings in emerging markets has followed sovereign crises, which have generally involved sharp currency devaluations and deep recessions. The flight of capital from the affected regions and the sharp increases in interest rates have often made the purchase of assets, even at distressed prices, tougher to make attractive or possible.

IMPORTANT COVENANTS

Prevention is generally the best defense, in our view, especially in markets where legal defense may be limited. For that reason, we believe that a certain set of covenants should be almost mandatory for all corporate debt issues from companies that are clearly not investment grade.

Limitation of Indebtedness

One of the key covenants that can preventively protect bondholders is *limitation of indebtedness*, which would limit a company from issuing additional debt except in small aggregate amounts. The less debt outstanding, the easier debt service should be and the fewer claimants could seek liquidation proceeds in the worst case scenario.

Negative Pledge

A *negative pledge* extends a limitation on indebtedness by restricting a company from using the same asset to secure more than one loan. The provision should also prohibit large amounts of new off-balance sheet debt.

Restricted Payments

The *restricted payments* provision is important because it prevents a company from transferring value to major stockholders, subsidiaries or other parties that could detract from the firm's value.

Change of Control

A *change of control* provision and limitations on mergers and acquisitions give bondholders the assurance that a merger would enhance firm value, or creditors can demand repayment. These provisions take on a special value in emerging markets for issuers with strong foreign ownership. The loss of this ownership can result in a significant deterioration of an issuer's overall credit attractiveness.

Maintenance Tests

Maintenance ratios, such as minimum coverage and maximum leverage (including off-balance sheet debt), ensure that there is sufficient cash flow to cover debt service, even if profitability declines. However, minimum debt to capitalization or net worth ratios are subject to ambiguity under certain accounting regimes and in highly inflationary environments. Thus, they generally can only be effective if done under U.S. GAAP standards and in a low inflation environment.

Cross Default

The *cross default* provision should protect creditors from a "selective" default by a company. The provision enables bondholders to demand 101% of par plus accrued interest if the issuer defaults on any other obligation, often above $10 million. If an issuer defaults on any material obligation, the company is likely experiencing limited liquidity and will have difficulty servicing remaining debt.

Prefunding and Performance Goals

For start-ups and companies without substantial short-term cash flow prospects, but attractive long-term fundamentals, prefunded interest payments can be attractive. Escrowed interest payments can make investors feel more secure and enable start-ups to focus on building their businesses. Covenants can require issuers to reach certain goals during the prefunded interest period, in lieu of maintenance ratios.

Limitations

It is important to recognize that even with these covenants, many limitations are likely to remain, including credit events caused by sovereign developments, privatization of quasi-sovereigns, dollar-constrained clauses, break-ups of conglomerates, complex holding structures, special purpose vehicles, start-up companies, and the loss of sovereign support for banks.

CASE STUDIES

Following are five case studies of Latin American companies that issued bonds in the early to mid-1990s, a period when covenant packages were very limited and did not include essential protective mechanisms for debtholders. In many cases, existence of simple incurrence tests could have prevented companies from over-leveraging. This, in turn, may have prevented some issuers from defaulting or at least preserved more value for creditors.

Buenos Aires Embotelladora (BAESA)

Buenos Aires Embotelladora (BAESA) was the largest bottler of Pepsi products outside the U.S., with operations in Argentina, Brazil, Chile and Uruguay. The company also distributes a proprietary brand of water, Budweiser beer, and other beverages. In 1994, BAESA invested approximately $400 million in the construction of soft drink production and distribution facilities in its franchise areas in southern Brazil and in 1995, the company announced plans to spend an additional $400 million in its Brazilian business.

Starting in 1995, weakening sales volumes in Argentina and Brazil led to a restructuring of operations, with layoffs in Argentina and a separation of Brazilian manufacturing and distribution operations. The company's operating performance was further negatively affected by start-up costs for expansion in Minas Gerais and Mato Grosso do Sul in March 1996.

In February 1996, BAESA sold $200 million in Eurobonds, mostly to refinance short-term debt. The issue was rated BB- by Standard & Poor's, which cited lower sales volumes, increased competition from Coca-Cola products, offset by high profit margins and the company's importance to Pepsi.

Restructuring Timeline

By July 1996, Pepsi took management control of BAESA. Despite cost cutting, operating performance in the first nine months of 1998 deteriorated further and BAESA was in violation of debt covenants that rendered $200 million in debt immediately due, in addition to $545 million in other short-term debt. Several months later, BAESA stopped making interest and principal payments altogether.

In October 1996, shareholders filed a class action lawsuit in the U.S. claiming that management misrepresented the financial condition of BAESA and artificially inflated the value of the company's debt and equity. Shortly thereafter, BAESA avoided liquidation by agreeing with the bondholders to defer interest and principal payments for six months. The company also received a $40 million commitment from Pepsi.

In April 1997, after the October standstill agreement expired, BAESA announced a restructuring plan whereby it would eliminate existing stock and give creditors a combination of cash, new equity, and additional debt. Following the plan's announcement, BAESA's bonds rose from a price of 65 to the low 70s. A month later, after a weak earnings report, BAESA's shares were delisted from the New York and Buenos Aires Stock Exchanges as net worth fell into negative territory, following the company's fifth money-losing quarter.

In an effort to raise cash, BAESA sold its Costa Rican unit for an undisclosed sum and the company' Brazilian unit as well as bottling plants to Companhia Cervejaria Brahma for $110 million in cash and the assumption of $45 million in debt. In addition, Brazilian creditors forgave $85 million in debt, leaving around $25 million in debt in Brazil.

In January 1998, creditors and shareholders accepted BAESA's July 1997 plan enabling the matter to be settled out of court. Under the new agreement, BAESA agreed to exchange $213 million in new debt and 98% of the equity for $700 million in already existing debt.

Recent Operating Performance
Total revenues fell 1% to $99.5 million in the first quarter of fiscal 1999 and EBITDA decreased 19% to $9.2 million as Argentine volumes rose 8%, offset by a 7.8% drop in the average sales price per case. Sales of third party products, such as beer, wine and other products, fell 50% to $2.3 million on lower prices.

Uruguay sales decreased 14.9% to $8.4 million in the quarter on a 13% decline in case sales volume and lower market share. BAESA's joint venture with CCU in Chile reported a profit in the first fiscal quarter of 1999 as a 5.8% decline in sales was offset by a 7.6% devaluation of the Chilean Peso.

In late 1998, BAESA's restructuring plan was updated, whereby the company would exchange $113 million in new debt and 98% of the company's equity for $727 million in existing debt. Pro forma for the restructuring, BAESA had shareholder equity of $80.6 million. In January 1999, the company's stock was delisted from the New York Stock Exchange, but it may continue to trade on the Argentine Bolsa.

Summary
Since BAESA's Eurobond issue did not contain covenants restricting large investments or minimum maintenance ratios, the company amassed over $700 million in debt while credit statistics deteriorated to the point where BAESA was unable to service debt. BAESA's restructuring plan resulted in a large loss for bondholders, as the company exchanged $113 million in new debt and 98% of BAESA's $80 million in equity for $700 million in existing debt, or resulting in a return of approximately 27 cents on the dollar.

Grupo Sidek
Through its subsidiary Grupo Situr, Grupo Sidek was engaged in the real estate and time-share market and was a leading Mexican hotel owner and operator.

Grupo Simec, Sidek's steel subsidiary, was a leading mini-mill steel producer and produces a broad range of non-flat structural steel products.

Restructuring Timeline

In February 1995, Sidek became the first Mexican company to default in the wake of the peso crisis, choosing to not repay a $19.5 million corporate note despite the company's $60 million cash position. Sidek virtually stopped communicating with investors and subsidiary Situr's bonds dropped to a price of 50 on the news, as most of the company's bonds would be in default due to a cross-default provision. The company later reversed its decision and made the payment.

In September 1995, creditors granted Sidek a 3-month extension to repay $170 million of the company's $1.5 billion in total debt. The company planned to sell golf courses and hotels in order to repay the $170 million credit line.

In February 1996, Sidek and subsidiaries agreed with creditors to defer principal payments during the restructuring process. However, the company announced that Simec was not a part of the restructuring and would continue to operate as an on-going business. In the meantime, Sidek agreed to monetize between $700 million and $1 billion worth of assets and split its debt into four categories:

- Debt incurred in the 1995 bailout package would become 4-year floating-rate secured notes.
- Debt secured by assets that were generating significant cash flow would be exchanged for 10-year secured 10% notes that became floating-rate notes after one year. Principal repayments are scheduled to begin in 2001.
- Debt secured by collateral and unsecured debt of subsidiaries with real estate properties worth more than their debts would become new 2.5-year convertible notes, which receive the cash flow generated by the previously secured assets, which could be forcibly converted into shares at expiration.
- Unsecured bondholders would receive 2.5-year convertible notes that could be forcibly converted at maturity.

Sidek completed the restructuring by March 31, 1998.

Recent Operating Performance

Sales fell 3.8% to $340 million in the first nine months of 1998 and operating income turned positive to $20.8 million. Grupo Situr's third quarter revenues rose 29%, including Simec's operations. In 1997, Sidek transferred its stake in Sidek to Situr, which increased Sidek's ownership of Situr from 60% to 92%. Real estate sale jumped 78%, while hotel and timeshare revenues fell 11% due to lower average occupancy rates.

Grupo Simec's sales in the first nine months of 1998 fell 1% to $175 million as a 1.0% rise in sales volumes to 478,411 metric tons was offset by a real

3% drop in average prices. A 7% cut in operating expenses resulted in a 23% rise in operating income to $25.5 million. Following the company's debt restructuring, most of Simec's $323 million of debt matures between 2007 and 2009, with some principal amortizations beginning in the year 2000.

Summary
Restrictions on payments and asset sales as well as maintenance ratio requirements could have limited Sidek's use of debt to finance real estate and hotel development. In order to finance the aggressive acquisition and development of hotels and resorts, Sidek borrowed heavily and monetized accounts receivables. Moreover, the company used the same account receivables to secure more than one borrowing under the fifth and seventh Mexican Acceptance Certificates, which would not be allowed under the "negative pledge" covenant.

Grupo Mexicano de Desarrollo
Grupo Mexicano de Desarollo (GMD) was engaged in the construction of a broad range of infrastructure projects throughout Mexico, including highways and toll roads, bridges, tunnels, water works, dams, airports, and port facilities. The company also participated in industrial, housing, and commercial construction projects, as well as real estate development. GMD conducted most of its construction operations through four subsidiaries, which were guarantors for the Eurobonds. The company was controlled by the Ballesteros family, which has been involved in the construction business for over 50 years.

Since 1990, GMD had played a major role in the Mexican government's program to develop a modern highway network, with the construction revenues of concessioned toll roads contributing about 76% of revenues during the five years ended December 31, 1995. In an attempt to accelerate the building process, the government had asked private contractors such as GMD to construct highways and collect tolls to recoup their investments. However, the companies encountered trouble when highway traffic fell below projections. Revenue generation was also negatively affected by the devaluation of the peso in 1994 and the slowdown in the Mexican economy.

GMD's credit profile deteriorated rapidly with the collapse of the toll-road concession market. The credit crunch was further toughened as a large percentage of the company's toll-road concession revenues were non-cash, in contrast to its costs and liabilities. (The company had $250 million of 8¼% notes and $120 million of floating debt outstanding.) GMD defaulted on its $250 million Eurobond interest payment in August 1997, soon after the Mexican government seized the construction and toll highway concessions.

Restructuring Timeline
In August 1997, GMD delayed a $10 million interest payment on its $250 million Eurobond issue as it waited for the results of the Mexican government's toll-road

restructuring plan. The government announced that it would repurchase GMD's concessioned toll roads for $309 million in cash, or roughly one-third of GMD's investments in those roads. GMD recognized a $600 million write-down on those investments and defaulted on the Eurobond interest payment.

GMD's largest "asset" — a $309 million cash payment from the Mexican government under a toll road rescue plan — would be the majority of the payout to creditors. The company also had sold 49.9% of its water works unit to Enron for $12.5 million in cash and the assumption of $25 million in debt.

U.S. bondholders feared that GMD would use most of the cash payment to repay local creditors. However, in April 1998 a U.S. federal court ruled that GMD would have to pay $82.4 million to international bondholders following its default. In May 1998, a lower federal court in the U.S. ordered the company to set aside assets to pay off the bondholders and barred GMD from pledging limited assets to other creditors. The ruling could set a precedent that may lead other courts to rule in favor of international creditors in foreign-based company bankruptcies.

In November 1998, the U.S. Supreme Court agreed to hear GMD's appeal to overturn the lower federal court's decision. This case could have a broad impact on the ability of American creditors to recover loans to companies with assets outside the U.S. A decision is expected by July 1999. GMD established an exchange offer whereby the $250 million 8¼% Guaranteed Notes due 2001 were swapped with newly issued certificates of the GMD Bondholder Trust estate established March 2000 in Bermuda. A Mexican master trust encompasses both the GMD Bondholder Trust and Mexican bank creditors. On May 15, 2000, GMD made its required deposit of $197.5 million into the Mexican master trust for the benefit of Mexican bank creditors and tendering note holders. The GMD Bondholder Trust estate makes up 48.44% of the Mexican master trust. The master trust is expected to distribute 51.56% of its assets to Mexican banks in cash in exchange for the release of its debt, and 48.44% to the GMD Bondholder Trust in exchange for the release of its debt. This breaks down to around 38.3% of par. For the benefit of its creditors, GMD has been permitted to continue operations, but on a much smaller scale.

Summary

GMD's covenants required it to maintain a net worth equal to 130% of the $250 million of Eurobonds outstanding, or $325 million. However, since the company wrote-up the value of its investments by 70% versus 10.5% inflation, it was forced to write-off $653.2 million following the announcement of the toll-road restructuring plan from existing equity of approximately $471.2 million, which resulted in negative net worth.

Had the company accounted for toll-road investments at more realistic values, GMD would likely have reached the minimum net worth of $325 million well before the announcement of the government's plan and could have been forced to restructure operations accordingly, in an effort to prevent future losses.

Covenants based on equity or capital are often ineffective, as these figures can be overstated, especially in countries with high rates of inflation. Moreover, GMD's covenants did not include effective incurrence or maintenance ratios such as minimum coverage or maximum leverage. GMD's coverage and leverage were rendered meaningless well before the default as the company generated negative EBITDA. More restrictive covenants could have led to an earlier restructuring, at which time the company had greater means to satisfy creditors.

Alpargatas

Alpargatas is an Argentine footwear and textile company that manufactures Nike Converse and Fila brand sneakers under license.

Cheap imports in the early 1990s and the 1995 recession in Argentina, which forced Alpargatas to abandon plans to spin off its shoemaking unit, hurt the company. In late 1997, the company was forced to suspend the sale of $175 million in debt after Asian market turmoil caused a worldwide market decline. The company reported losses of $77 million in fiscal 1997 compared to a loss of $16 million in 1996.

Restructuring Timeline

Alpargatas defaulted on $70 million of 9% convertible notes after delays in securing new financing left the company without adequate cash. Alpargatas tried to restructure debt through a $90 million stock sale, a $225 million new bond issuance, and a $200 million syndicated loan.

The stock sale needed approval of the shareholders, who saw the stock drop 61% in the nine months ended March 1998 after a previous debt restructuring was scuttled. Since the shares were trading at $0.23, less than the $1 minimum level at which the company could issue shares, Alpargatas received shareholder approval for a five-to-one reverse stock split to boost the share price. Newbridge Latin America, a buyout fund partly owned by the Texas Pacific Group, pledged to buy any unsold shares and had purchased $80 million of convertible bonds in 1997.

The funds from the stock sale and debt issuance were going to be used to refinance the $450 million of outstanding bonds and other debt as of March 1998; $265 million of which matures in 1999. The company had also planned to sell $50 million of non-core assets. In April 1998, the company asked creditors to wait for up to six months for repayment of debt while it worked out the details of the restructuring.

In July 1998, the Asian crisis dampened demand for risky emerging market debt and Alpargatas cancelled plans for the $225 million bond issuance. The company then offered to swap existing debt for a mix of shares and new debt and also sell new shares as planned.

In October 1998, a Brazilian unit of Alpargatas filed for court protection from creditors. The company then held talks in New York with creditors to restructure debt through the issuance of new 15-year bonds at a 6% coupon. The company's stock price more than doubled at the end of the month to $0.17 from prior week levels on expectations that talks with bondholders would enable Alpargatas to restructure more than $500 million in debt, install new management, and return to profitability.

In November 1998, Banco de la Provincia de Buenos Aires, one of the company's major creditors, said that it would analyze the restructuring proposal but could reject it outright instead of making a counteroffer. The shares jumped 47% from October 10 to November 10. Alpargatas called a 35-day work stoppage from January 1, 1999 at its textile plant in Tucuman due to financial problems brought on by the import of foreign products under conditions detrimental to the local industry.

A review of Alpargatas' credit statistics from 1993 through 1999 clearly shows how covenants would have protected bondholders. After generating 2.0× interest coverage and 6.0× leverage in 1993 and 1994, credit statistics deteriorated to nearly distressed levels in 1995 through 1997 and worsened in 1998 and 1999. Meanwhile, the company added a total of $300 million of debt in 1998 and 1999. Maintenance ratios would have sounded alarms in 1995, when coverage halved to 1.0× and incurrence tests would have prevented the company from adding so much debt while operating performance was declining. The company was unable to support the added debt, most of which was short-term bank debt, and bondholders ended up holding 7% of the equity of the company, which value fell precipitously when the company's shares were delisted.

Grupo Synkro

Grupo Synkro designs, manufactures, distributes and sells apparel, cosmetics and insecticides. The company makes socks, stockings, synthetics, sneakers, and cosmetics and had approximately a 50% share of the Mexican hosiery market.

In 1994, the company acquired Kayser-Roth, a U.S. hosiery company, for $170 million, funded with short-term debt. Following the Mexican peso crisis, the company's large short-term debt doubled in peso terms while operations slumped due to slowing economies in Argentina and Mexico. In addition, rocketing interest rates on the company's short-term floating-rate debt forced a restructuring and recapitalizing of the company.

Restructuring Timeline
In July 1996, Synkro completed the restructuring of $60 million of Kayser Roth's debt to GE Capital.

In August 1997, Synkro completed the restructuring of $494 million in debt. Holders of Synkro's $50 million Eurobond turned one-third of the bonds into equity, one-third into 5-year 12% bonds, and wrote off the rest. Holders of Synkro's remaining bonds swapped their debt into new equity. Synkro also repurchased $80 million of the new shares with a buyback fund that the company established before the crisis.

288 Debt Covenants: Applications in Emerging Markets

In 1998, Synkro sold the Camino Real hotel chain and its sneaker unit, Calzado Puma, among other subsidiaries. In late 1998, Synkro sold Kayser-Roth, which the company purchased three years prior for $170 million to Americal for $62 million.

Recent Operating Performance

Despite a 5.5% decline in revenue in the first nine months of 1998, Synkro posted a slight increase in operating profit to $6.8 million. As of September 30, 1998, Synkro had approximately $110 million in short-term debt and approximately $24 million in long-term debt.

Summary

Covenants restricting payments for acquisitions such as the company's $170 million purchase of Kayser-Roth (funded with short-term debt), could have helped Grupo Synkro avoid bankruptcy and the subsequent restructuring. Had bondholders blocked the acquisition, the company would have had much less short-term debt, which is what largely caused the default.